Nov

The Man
Who Lost
China

The Man Who Lost China

THE FIRST FULL

BIOGRAPHY OF

CHIANG KAI-SHEK

BY

BRIAN CROZIER

WITH THE

COLLABORATION OF

ERIC CHOU

CHARLES SCRIBNER'S SONS

NEW YORK

Library of Congress Cataloging in Publication Data

Crozier, Brian.
    The man who lost China.

    Bibliography: p.
    Includes index.
    1. Chiang, Kai-shek, 1887–1975.   I. Chou, Eric,
1915–   joint author. II. Title.
DS778.C55C7   951.04′2′0924   76–10246
ISBN 0–684–14686–X

1 3 5 7 9 11 13 15 17 19 C/C 20 18 16 14 12 10 8 6 4 2

PRINTED IN THE UNITED STATES OF AMERICA

Contents

AUTHOR'S NOTE   *vii*

A NOTE ON CHINESE NAMES   *xiii*

PART I: THE ENIGMA OF CHIANG KAI-SHEK

1. Conservative Revolutionary   *3*
2. "Ripe for Revolution"   *16*

PART II: CONQUEST AND INVASION (1887–1939)

3. Student in Japan   *31*
4. Chaos and Treachery   *47*
5. Enter the Comintern   *57*
6. Sun's Death, and After   *68*
7. The Northern Expedition   *82*
8. Shanghai Incident   *93*
9. Chiang's Re-marriage   *107*
10. Chiang "Unites" China   *121*
11. The Lost Revolution   *134*
12. Chiang Seals His Fate   *145*
13. Mao Marches Out   *157*
14. Japan and the Sian Incident   *173*
15. Japan Strikes   *191*

v

PART III: WORLD WAR AND CIVIL WAR (1939–1949)

16. Japan Bogs Down   215
17. Chiang and His Allies   229
18. One War Ends   251
19. The Marshall Mission Fails   275
20. Chiang Steps Aside   301
21. Chiang Loses the Mainland   327

PART IV: CHIANG'S ISLAND REDOUBT (1950–1975)

22. A Place of Refuge   349
23. The Last Twenty Years   363

PART V: AN ASSESSMENT

24. An Assessment   389

NOTES ON SOURCES   403
INDEX   419

ILLUSTRATIONS

MAPS
The Battle of the Yangtze and the Conquest
  of South China   160
The Long March: the Crossing of Szechwan, Kansu,
  and Shensi   162
Sino-Japanese Operations from July 1937
  to October 1938   203
The Communist Zones at the Time of the Japanese
  Capitulation (August 1945)   281
The Third Revolutionary Civil War: Operations
  during 1947   306

PHOTOGRAPHS BETWEEN PAGES 212 AND 213

Author's Note

Chiang Kai-shek was a hero of my boyhood and adolescence. I knew nothing about him except through the conversation of my elders and the headlines in the newspapers. My sympathies were naturally on China's side, for it was evident that the Chinese were peaceful folk who were being abused and whose territory was being invaded by the hateful and aggressive Japanese. Later, in my Left Book Club days, my hitherto uncritical admiration was shaken by allegations that Chiang had on occasion massacred many people. There were writers unkind enough to call him "fascist" and "a militarist". I didn't like people who were those things, and wondered whether after all the hero really was one.

Then came the Second World War, and suddenly Chiang Kai-shek was a hero again, even to those on the Left who had been denouncing him. For my part, in any case, I had lost the childish readiness to admire distant heroes. The eye-opening year for me was 1943, when I was working on the Central Desk of Reuters' news agency in London. I noticed almost simultaneously that two popular heroes of the early years of the war had ceased to be heroic, for reasons I didn't immediately grasp. One was Chiang Kai-shek; the other was Drazha Mihailovic, the leader of the legendary Yugoslav Chetniks. Mihailovic, as the senior men on the desk explained to me, was now "discredited", because he had stopped fighting the Nazis and instead was fighting his political rival, Josip Broz, better known as Tito. Indeed, Tito was now the new, generally approved "hero". Poor Mihailovic: the dustbin of history, as Khrushchev would have put it many years later, was about to claim him.

And what of Generalissimo Chiang Kai-shek? Now he was the head of a brutal and inefficient regime and had long since stopped fighting the Japanese. The men who were doing the fighting—those well-informed seniors of mine explained in all their patience to a junior foreign sub-editor—were Mao Tse-tung and his Communist guerrillas. I was not that ignorant, even then: the Left Book Club choice for a particular month had been Edgar Snow's *Red Star Over China*. From him I had learned that Mao and his men were really just "agrarian reformers", hardly Communists at all in the orthodox sense. I had even read as much (though to be accurate, this could have been later)—an identical assessment of the Chinese Communists—in the austere editorial columns of *The Times*.

Then came my years on the foreign desk of the London *News Chronicle* and the evidence—too strong by far to be ignored or dismissed—of the Kuomintang's corruption, brutality, and inefficiency. During the Chinese Civil War, the NC's China correspondent, Stuart Gelder, regaled his readers and ourselves with unbelievable tales (but true) of Nationalists transporting the same pile of captured Japanese equipment from place to place to impress foreign visitors to the "front". Was it he, or some other war correspondent (it does not matter) who claimed he had marked a Japanese helmet with a scratch and found it again in another pile in another place? What price then, my boyhood hero?

Even great men are flawed, of course, and the flaws may be in proportion to their greatness in other respects. Was Stalin a great man? He built "socialism in one country"—and sent millions to their deaths. And Hitler? He rescued a demoralised Germany from the slough of six million unemployed, and the consequences of a short-sighted and manifestly unjust peace treaty—and he exterminated millions of Jews. A Churchill, a Roosevelt, a de Gaulle—these men were not monsters as Stalin and Hitler were, but they had gigantic faults along with their extraordinary qualities. The case of Chiang Kai-shek was clearly no less complex than theirs, and the riddle of his fluctuating reputation was puzzling. Why was he a hero in some years, a scoundrel in others, again a hero, then forever a failure, a loser, and a reactionary fascist into the bargain?

The "McCarthy era" in the 1950s presented an unedifying spectacle of Americans in the grip of a witch-hunt, with its attendant fear and hysteria. But for all the distaste and indeed the revulsion at the Senator's demagogic antics, his investigations did throw a lurid light on some of the secret byways of the International Communist Movement, and in particular on the use made of writers and journalists—not necessarily Communists or even far to the Left—in the dissemination of falsehood, half-truths, calumnies, or subtle praise. In all conscience, there was enough to criticise in the Kuomintang regime and in Chiang Kai-shek's conduct of public affairs.

But the image-builders were not necessarily concerned with the facts as such. To give an extreme example, Hitler automatically and instantly ceased to be a blood-stained tyrant and murderer of the Jews and workers when Ribbentrop and Molotov signed their treaty in 1939; that is, he ceased to be so described in the columns of the Soviet press, on the bandwaves of the Soviet radio, and in the Communist press throughout the world. In Britain, the then leader of the Communist Party, the late Harry Pollitt, had his own moment of brief and public outrage, but he soon came to heel. It was too much for Stalin to expect of progressive and liberal writers in the West that they should suddenly find Hitler not to be such a bad chap after all. But they were far more responsive to the needs of Soviet-directed propaganda in the distant and less emotive case of Chiang Kai-shek.

I had thought about these problems from time to time over the years, before deciding that the time had come for a more searching inquiry into the life of the Generalissimo. This book is the outcome. As in the case of my previous biographies, *Franco* and *De Gaulle*, this is in no sense an approved, and still less an authorised, biography. I met and interviewed Chiang Kai-shek in January 1957, when on a tour of countries "in China's shadow" as special correspondent of *The Economist*. Since Chiang didn't speak English, the interview had to be interpreted from his language into mine and vice versa—which halved its material duration and diminished its interest. The physical description with which the book begins was, however, based on this meeting, and in other respects our conversathon threw an interesting light on the Generalissimo's thought processes. I discovered, somewhat to my surprise, that much progress was being made on Taiwan and that in particular a successful land-reform programme had been accomplished. On my return, I said as much in print and on the air, and was greeted with much scepticism, although specialists much better qualified than I to pronounce on the success or otherwise of a land-reform programme later confirmed my findings. The regime, then, was not as bad as it had been generally painted.

I returned to Taiwan in September 1974, to give some lectures by invitation of the Institute of International Relations in Taipei; but of course to take advantage of this opportunity to meet as many well-informed people as possible, not only in Taiwan itself but also in Hong Kong on my way, and probe their memories of Chiang at different times of his long career. For by then, I had begun my research for this biographical study. Among the personalities of the Kuomintang establishment who were kind enough to give me their very clear reminiscences were Ch'en Li-fu, who had been Chiang's private secretary at the time of the Nationalist entry into Shanghai in 1927, and Wang Shih-chieh, who as Foreign Minister had signed the Sino-Soviet treaty of 1945. There were many others besides, both in 1957 and in 1974; nor was my time spent exclusively with supporters of the regime, although I cannot reveal the names of opponents who gave me their views. I wish to record my grateful thanks to Dr. Han Lih-wu, then Director of the Institute of International Relations, and Dr. Ch'ien Fu, at that time Director-General of the Government Information Office, for the friendly efficiency with which they organised my appointments; Mr. G. M. ("Jimmy") Wei, Director of China Central News, for kindly making available to me most of the pictures that appear in this book; and others, too numerous to mention, who helped me with various kindnesses. In Hong Kong, too, I found people with long memories and a willingness to share them.

Among the informants who were not concerned to preserve their anonymity was a distinguished "old China hand", Mr. Kenneth Cantlie, who contributed some interesting anecdotes out of a store of ancient memories. I record my grateful thanks to him.

For the rest, as with my other biographical works, I have used the tools of the historian and academic researcher, as well as of the journalist. (By profession, I am the latter, not the former.) But by far my most important "live" source was Eric Chou, the well-known journalist and scholar, who lived through the years of war and civil war in China, in Chungking, Nanking, Peiping, and other places. Mr. Chou contributed liberally from his great fund of personal memories, retained by a remarkably photographic memory, and in addition translated copious extracts of Chinese books. Moreover, he read and commented on my text in detail, as a guarantee of its accuracy and "Chinese" authenticity. The writing, of course, is mine, as are the conclusions, and any undetected errors are my responsibility.

Since my own knowledge of the Chinese language is limited, and since I am not myself an academic, I lay no claims to having written a work of scholarship. What I do claim is that this was—at the time of writing—the first attempt of which I have knowledge to tell the story of Chiang Kai-shek's life from cradle to grave and to place it in the context of the history of his time. I can also say that the book includes a great deal of Chinese source material not previously published in English; and a considerable infusion of entirely new material, mainly from Eric Chou but also from my own conversations with qualified informants. It is perhaps relevant to add that for ten years—from 1954 to 1964—I was *The Economist*'s specialist on Chinese and Far Eastern affairs.

Apart from my own interest in the subject, the need for a serious study and reappraisal of Chiang has long been evident. When I finished this book in the late summer of 1975, only two biographies had appeared in English. Both were by Chinese writers: Hollington K. Tong (whose authorised biography first appeared in 1938, and was later brought up to date in a revised edition in 1953), and the other by S. I. Hsiung, better known in Western capitals for his successful play, *Lady Precious Stream*. In the first edition of Tong's biography, he was able to write without any sense of incongruity:

> Recent events in China have proved Generalissimo Chiang Kai-shek to be the greatest soldier-statesman of our time on the Continent of Asia. (Preface)

In a supplementary Preface some months later, he commented on "the disappearance of the Red menace". For when the Japanese had invaded China, the Communists had proved that they, too, were "Chinese". Few Western readers would have raised an eyebrow on reading these passages. Yet how distant and out of perspective these judgments seem today!

I have tried to take a more objective view of my erstwhile hero.

London, September 1975.

A Note on Chinese Names

It is customary to lament the supposed absence of a satisfactory system for the transliteration of Chinese into romanised "English". In fact, there is an ingenious and remarkably satisfactory system developed by Dr. George A. Kennedy, Director of the Yale Institute of Far Eastern Languages, and his associates, during the Second World War at a time when an urgent need arose to train Americans quickly to become proficient in spoken Mandarin (Peking dialect). The Yale system is simplicity itself, and any student whose native tongue is a variety of English will almost instantly pronounce Mandarin intelligibly by its intelligent use, although the tone-deaf may find it hard to get the four tones right. (But then, there are tone-deaf Chinese with the same problem!)

Why, then, it may be asked, have I not used the Yale system for the Chinese common and proper nouns that occur in this work? A good question. I have used, in most cases, the utterly absurd Wade system (in which the letters do not necessarily correspond with the sounds associated with them by English speakers and may be modified by cumbersome apostrophes), simply because it is, unfortunately, in almost universal use. An example or two will make the point clear.

Everybody knows who Mao Tse-tung, Chou En-lai, and Chiang Kai-shek are; and unless the reader speaks Mandarin, it will not bother him or her to be told that if these well-known names are pronounced as so written they will not sound the way they ought. That is Wade's contribution to popular confusion. In Yale, the first two would be transcribed *Mau Dze-dung* and *Jou En-lai*; which, even without the diacritical tonal accents, is a very fair approximation of the actual sounds made by a Mandarin speaker when referring to these Communist leaders. With Chiang Kai-shek, there are further complications. That is the way the world knows him, but his real name (in Mandarin) is Chiang Chung-cheng (Wade system), which the Yale system would transcribe *Jyang Jung-jen*. *Kai-shek* is a courtesy name, originally used only by friends and family; and to make matters still more complicated, it is a Wade attempt to cope with a *Cantonese,* not a Mandarin, name. Because Chiang's early revolutionary associations were with Sun Yat-sen and other Cantonese, he was given a Cantonese courtesy name. The Cantonese, I understand, pronounce it (in Yale) *Jyang Gai-she'*, the final apostrophe (not used in Yale, actually) being a Crozier attempt to represent a glottal stop. A Mandarin speaker reading out the characters that correspond to Chiang Kai-shek would pronounce them *Chiang Shieh-shih* (in Wade) and *Jyang Shye-shr* (in Yale).

I hope I have made my point. To be practical, what any reader bereft of Chinese needs to remember when silently pronouncing the names in this book is that the Wade system relies on the following conventions:

p is pronounced b (e.g. pa = ba as in Baa-Baa Black Sheep)
p' "   "   p (e.g. p'a = pa as in Padre)
t "   "   d (e.g. ta = da as Dartmoor is pronounced
                    by "educated Southern English", but not
                    by, say, Scots or Americans)
j "   "   r (e.g. jen = ren as in warren)
t' "   "   t (e.g. t'a = ta as in tarnished)
k "   "   g (e.g. ku = goo as in goose)
k' "   "   k (e.g. k'u = coo as in coon)
hs "   "   as h in hew (or the ch in the German *Ich*)
ts "   "   dz (e.g. tsai = ds as in loads of)
t's "   "   ts (e.g. t'sai = ts as in lots of)
ui "   "   way (e.g. sui = sway)
ü "   "   as in the German ü or the French u (this
                    sound occurs frequently in this book, for
                    instance every time the "Christian general",
                    Feng Yü-hsiang, is mentioned.)

A final note: I have followed the Wade transliteration with personal names and with some Chinese words, but *not* with place names. Here again, I have been guided by the desire to avoid confusing people with unfamiliar spellings. Everybody is familiar with Peking, and many are aware that it was once called Peiping. There is therefore no point in spelling the first Peiching (as a strict adherence to Wade would suggest) or Beijing (Yale); or the second Peip'ing (Wade) or Beiping (Yale).

The Man
Who Lost
China

I | The Enigma of Chiang Kai-shek

1. Conservative Revolutionary

The face, with its lively black eyes and white military moustache, and its shaven head, was inscrutable—not because of any "oriental" lack of expression, but because he wore a permanent smile of Chinese courtesy to a visitor. He spoke very rapidly in a light, high voice with much sibilance in the Chekiang dialect which isolated him from that great majority of his subordinates and followers who came from other parts of China. For he had never troubled to master Mandarin, the standard Chinese of Peking, nor indeed any foreign tongue. At the height of his power, he reported every month to the "Enlarged Memorial Meeting of Sun Yat-sen", and those present would be compelled to stand to attention while he orated in his high-pitched way in words incomprehensible to most of them. He was thus not only quintessentially Chinese, but also a provincial.

Impervious to foreign influences, he married the American-educated daughter of a Chinese Christian minister and in later years relied heavily upon her command of a language he had never been able to master. His official biographer, Hollington Tong, was engaged to tutor Chiang in English for several months in the late 1920s. "But Chiang soon gave up because of the pressure of official business," he disclosed many years later. Having failed himself, he was determined that his elder son, Chiang Ching-kuo, should succeed. Ching-kuo's book, *My Father*, quotes several letters from Chiang Kai-shek in 1922 and 1923 insisting on the need to master English. A further letter came in 1943, when Ching-kuo was thirty-five or thirty-six, telling him to spend six hours a week on English and concentrate on grammar and reading. "Since you have a good grounding in Russian, it will be very easy for you to learn English," wrote Chiang Senior optimistically.

Mme. Chiang—née Soong Mayling—became a world-famous figure in her own right. According to the official biographers, she was Chiang's second wife, but actually she was his third, or even his fourth, if a concubine he lived with in 1912 is counted. Together, the Generalissimo and his wife presented an impeccable public image as an exemplary married couple. The image was probably true, for by the time Chiang Kai-shek married Soong Mayling in 1927, the fires of his youth had largely spent themselves. But as a young man, he was a notable womaniser, on familiar terms with the brothels of Shanghai. Despite this well-documented dissoluteness, Chiang adhered to a particularly austere Confucian school, with a great insistence on self-denial and self-discipline.

He was indeed thoroughly a Confucian both by upbringing and by conviction, but he became a Christian in honour of his marriage and thereafter gave every sign of devoutness, including daily prayer. Such paradoxes are not rare in men who make their mark upon the history of their times. And there was another, which is central to any understanding of his life and character. As a very young man, he had played a part in the Revolution of 1911 which had overthrown the Manchu dynasty, and he was a disciple of Sun Yat-sen, the "Father of the Revolution". As such, he considered himself a revolutionary. But to him, revolution meant nationalism, the overthrow of a hated "foreign" line of emperors, xenophobia, and an end to China's national humiliations. In every other respect—in all that concerned the philosophy and organisation of the State, manners and behaviour, Chinese traditional society, and the rigid respect of hierarchy—he was profoundly conservative; some (including others besides enemies) would say reactionary.

Although he himself belonged to one of the forces that had overthrown imperial China, he failed to understand that the Revolution itself was an irresistible force, which once started had a momentum of its own. He tried in vain to stem the tide, and to impose his authority in the midst of chaos and of self-seeking rivalries. This failure was to cause his downfall and the loss of continental China, but there were other causes as well. His misfortunes were gigantic: the invasion of China by the highly-disciplined forces of Japan; the Communist rebellion, led by an abler man than he; a misplaced idealism on the part of his principal allies, the Americans; and all this against the background of accumulated problems so vast in scale that only a China at peace could hope to solve them. Victory would have given him peace, but victory against the Japanese invaders was followed by defeat at the hands of the Communist revolutionaries. At last, beaten and humiliated but never crushed, he found refuge on Formosa—the "beautiful island" of the Portuguese explorers—and in old age reigned over a microcosm of the great country he had left behind, industrious, affluent, and contented. Every year, the President of the Republic of China would preside over the Double Tenth—the tenth day of the tenth month—in celebration of the anniversary of the Nationalist revolution; and shortly afterwards, on the last day of October, his family and his followers would celebrate his own birthday. Every New Year's Day, he delivered a message to the nation promising, or threatening, to return to the mainland. During the last two years of his long life, having lost the use of his legs, and refusing to see all visitors, the messages were muted or delivered by proxy.

On Saturday 5 April 1975, aged eighty-seven, Generalissimo Chiang Kai-shek died of a heart attack, the mainland still unrecovered. Indeed, not only had the return to the mainland eluded him to the last, but the Chinese People's Republic whose legitimacy he challenged had been admitted to the United Nations and his own Republic expelled. Humiliation and failure went hand in hand.

In common with those other political generals, de Gaulle and Franco, and other autocrats, Chiang Kai-shek identified himself with his country. Not everybody could share his view—effortlessly sustained for a whole lifetime—that in fulfilling his ambitions he was serving China. To him, this truth was unquestionable. It followed that disobedience was treason. When Dr. Sun died in 1925, Chiang was not on the short list of claimants to the succession. He already had his power base, however, as Commandant of the new military academy at Whampoa, and had been fashioning its graduates into a kind of Praetorian guard. Within two years, his Nationalist army had swept from Canton to Peking, and on paper, at least, he had conquered and unified China. The warlords—those picturesque provincial governors who ran their fiefs more often than not for private gain—had been defeated or changed sides. But it was a make-believe victory. For ten years, he was to be the dominant figure in China, but never its unchallenged master.

Two episodes in his early life marked him indelibly. One was his visit to Moscow at the end of 1923, as Sun Yat-sen's emissary on a mission of information. He came back deeply distrustful of the Russians and with an ineradicable hatred of Communism. The Father of the Revolution saw things in a different light and spurned the young man's advice, turning instead to the Bolshevik envoy— Borodin—on whose counsel the Kuomintang was reorganised on Soviet Communist lines.

The other episode, still not fully documented, spanned the decade from 1912 to 1922, most of which Chiang Kai-shek spent in Shanghai, initially as a penniless jobber on the stock exchange. At that time, he was a nobody. But by the end of the decade, perhaps because of services rendered to the gangsters of the Green Society that ran the great city's extortion rackets (although he never joined them in a formal sense), he enjoyed the friendship and protection of leading bankers and merchants. This, it turned out, was his second power base.

He struck a bargain with his rich protectors: they would finance his revolution and in return he would keep the leftists out of his government. His marriage to Mayling Soong was consonant with this bargain. In 1927, Chiang broke the local power of the Chinese Communists, first in Shanghai and later in Canton. Seven years later, under Nationalist pressure, the young Mao Tse-tung led his peasant forces on the legendary Long March to the remote caves of Yenan. From there he was to defy, then challenge and defeat the Nationalist leader.

When the Japanese invaded Manchuria in 1931 and embarked

on their conquest of China in 1937, Chiang Kai-shek reacted to the challenge in a manner that was strange in a nationalist and a patriot. He always made it clear that in his order of military priorities, the Communists came first and the Japanese second. The Communists were rebels and had to be brought to heel so that a united China could face the invader. This issue of priorities lay behind the bizarre incident at Sian in 1936, when Chiang was kidnapped by the "Young Marshal" Chang Hsueh-liang—who was to pay for his temerity with house arrest for life. The Young Marshal wanted Chiang to stand up to the Japanese and leave the Communists alone. Some of the more enthusiastic Sian rebels wanted to shoot Chiang, and it is one of the ironies of this curious story that his release was secured by none other than Chou En-lai, who had escaped from an encounter with a Nationalist firing squad in Shanghai nine years earlier. To be fair to Chiang, he did have his own plans for opposing the Japanese aggressors, but in his mind first things—fighting the Communists—came first.

When the Japanese invasion came, Chiang Kai-shek was at the height of his power and prestige. For ten years he had dominated the Kuomintang, and although his writ did not run over the whole of the vast country, no rival power compared to his own. Tong's description of him (quoted in full in the Author's Note) as "the greatest soldier-statesman of our time on the Continent of Asia" seemed a fitting tribute to the great man when his official biography appeared in 1938.

No other statesman's reputation has suffered so catastrophic a decline in so short a time as Chiang's. Some thirteen years after Tong had published his book, Chiang's regime had been utterly defeated by Mao Tse-tung's People's Liberation Army. The Kuomintang and its army had been forced to take refuge on Taiwan—the Chinese name which superseded Formosa.

Certainly every allowance must be made for the enormity of his bad luck in having to cope with two ruthless enemies both simultaneously and consecutively. But that is not all. The enigma of Chiang Kai-shek is a dual one. How did he achieve greatness? And how did he fall from the heights? For that matter, having fallen, how did he regain power and keep it to the end in his circumscribed island territory?

The answers to the two main questions, and to the supplementary one, must surely be sought in his extraordinary character and in the startling paradoxes of his personality. In common with other soldier-statesmen of our time, he was quite fearless, both physically and morally. He sometimes hesitated before making a decision, but once he had reached it, he would act ruthlessly and with incredible speed. Time and again, those who had challenged him were dead, gaoled, or defeated before they realised what was happening. Although of a military turn of mind, fortified by intensive professional training and experience in battle, he was a master of tactics rather than of strategy; and his real genius lay in political intrigue. Throughout his political life, he played off one faction against another and kept his personal followers in doubt over their standing in his eyes. In the Confucian tradition, he was remote and disinclined to take people—except his third wife, and later his son, Chiang Ching-kuo—into his confidence. Such was the fear he inspired in nearly all his subordinates and associates that very few of them ever dared to tell him the truth.

Despite his normally smiling and inscrutable appearance, he seethed within from nervous turmoil, betraying himself with a rapid tapping of his foot and the iterated Chinese exclamation of "Hao, hao". As a young man, he was said to have beaten his first wife repeatedly, and at times in later life, his inner tension would burst out in monumental rages. A film he was watching at home offended him. Stalking out, he ordered the projectionist to be thrashed. When seized with such rages, he would pound the table, fling his teacup at the bearer of ill-tidings, and yell uncontrollably.

In the summer of 1944 [wrote White and Jacoby], Chiang was strolling along a country road when he saw an officer leading recruits roped together. Such signs were common in country places, but Chiang was infuriated and beat the officer until a bodyguard rescued the man. When the Generalissimo was reminded of the horror of Chinese conscription, he summoned the general in charge of conscription and beat him unmercifully; the general was executed the next spring.

His frugality and austerity were legendary, not mythical. From about 1936 on, he neither smoked nor drank. Foreign observers who saw him (as they thought) tossing back little cups of fiery Chinese spirit with appropriate abandon were taken in by a polite deceit: Chiang's own cup was always filled with boiled water so that he could appear to be holding his own with less temperate companions. His wartime breakfast was of powdered milk and weak green tea. Gambling was not among his sins, and his only known recreation was walking. He dressed nattily in a high-necked khaki tunic and trousers, without insignia of rank. At home, even at an early age when such garb would strike his elders as unseemly, he wore the long gown and skullcap of the traditional Chinese scholar. Himself utterly honest and incorruptible (although his asceticism was practised in opulent surroundings and without a care for the morrow's sustenance), he was curiously tolerant of the rampant corruption around him or if not tolerant, blind to it. This was particularly true of his wife's family and his immediate entourage. When it came to lesser officials, and then only sporadically when his attention was drawn to particular cases, Chiang would fly into one of his rages and prescribe the death penalty. In 1934, he had seven officials summarily shot for enriching themselves at the expense of the State. On another occasion, divisional commanders persuaded Chiang to spare another erring official. But when their backs were turned, Chiang had the man shot anyway.

What is one to say of the ten relatively peaceful years of Kuomintang rule from 1927 to 1937? Since the Kuomintang was essentially Chiang Kai-shek, these were the years of his own dictatorship. All good and all evil have been attributed to this period. The truth does not necessarily lie half-way between the accounts of excessively uncritical supporters and those of ill-disposed detractors. Probably both good and bad were present in prodigious doses. Although corruption and inefficiency prevailed and worsened as time went on, many officials were devoted and hard-working. Modernisation made giant strides. Telegraph poles were planted and long-distance telephone wires radiated out through the remoter regions, including Szechwan, which was brought into the national union in 1937. Radio, too, brought a sense of national unity. Airlines went into service, with American and German as well as Chinese participation. Some 75,000 miles of new motor roads were laid, and a uniform paper currency was stabilised in 1934 on a sound basis of silver bullion in large deposits. Three years later, under the Pitman Act, the United States Treasury agreed to exchange the silver for gold, thus enabling Nationalist China to purchase arms abroad. In 1932, the Finance Minister, T. V. Soong—Mme. Chiang's brother—balanced the budget and converted the domestic debt, abolishing the *likin* transit dues, much resented by the populace since the T'aip'ing Rebellion. Scholarship and archaeology flourished in what amounted to a veritable renaissance. Punctuation—absent from the Chinese classics—was introduced, to the greater intelligibility of current texts. It was in that period that Hu Shih's "plain speech" (or *pai hua*) won general acceptance. In 1912, the year after Sun Yat-sen's revolution, only 2,793,633 pupils attended elementary schools. By 1935, the number had increased to 11,667,888, and the figures for high-school students rose from 52,100 to about 500,000. In 1912, only 4 colleges existed in the great empire. By 1933, there were 40 universities, 40 colleges, and 29 technical schools. The shelves of libraries, by then, held 4,500,000 volumes, with 43,000 students to browse among them.

That was the good side. The bad was no less worthy of attention. Democracy was one of Sun Yat-sen's Three Principles of the People, along with Nationalism and Livelihood. But under the Organic Law for the Republic of China, promulgated by the Central Executive Committee of the Kuomintang on 4 October 1928, the party itself was to keep the people in "tutelage" until such time as, in the party's view, it should be ripe for democracy. In practice, tutelage meant dictatorship and a pervasive police state. Ch'en Li-fu, Chiang's private secretary from 1925 to 1929, had made a start by setting up the Central Bureau of Investigation and Statistics (CBIS) after the capture of Shanghai (as he told me when I met him in Taipei in 1974); and by the mid-1930s the public security organisations had proliferated. More powerful and better organised than the CBIS was the Military Bureau of Investigation and Statistics (MBIS), which was under the control of the Military Council. The man in charge, Tai Li, was known as "China's Himmler". Tai Li dealt in spying and selected terror on behalf of the State. His "ears and eyes" operated at all levels of society and did not shrink from secret arrest and assassination. With the police state went a blanket censorship. Some authors have commented with approval on the proliferation of periodicals in Kuomintang China. But it should be pointed out that some of them lasted only weeks or months before being banned. And new ones came along to take the place of those that had been suppressed.

After his early disillusionment with Communism and his flirtation with gangsterism in Shanghai, Chiang Kai-shek had developed an admiration for fascism and Nazism. Ardent Nazis, such as

Colonel Max Bauer and Lieutenant-Colonel Herman Kriebel, had served the Kuomintang as military advisers. When Hitler came to power, Chiang secretly sent two of his army officers to Germany to study Nazi methods. Before the outbreak of World War II, Chiang also sent his second son, Chiang Wei-kuo, to study at a military academy in Germany. Wei-kuo was twice received by Hitler; he is said to have marched with the German forces into Austria.

The outcome of this interest in Nazism was the formation of a fascist-type elite, numbering at most 10,000 members, known as the Blue Shirts. The whole country was to be militarised, from the kindergarten to the grave. The slogan "Nationalise, Militarise, Productivise" summarised the educational policy of the Blue Shirts. Violence was in order against the enemies of the State, and there was to be a "permanent purge" of corrupt bureaucrats. The great enemy was Western liberalism, and the Blue Shirts had very little time for Sun Yat-sen's Principle of Democracy. Their aim was unabashedly totalitarian, and although Chiang Kai-shek continued to the end, with apparent sincerity, to protest his devotion to democracy, there can be no doubt that he identified himself with the Blue Shirts, whose members included many of his Whampoa Academy cadets.

At the time, the existence of the Blue Shirts was known, both nationally and internationally, but they operated in silence and obscurity, and rumour rather than fact prevailed. They played a curious role in Chiang Kai-shek's New Life Movement, tinging with fascism the Generalissimo's attempt to resurrect Confucianism as a basis for China's unity. Indeed, the amalgam was even stranger than that, for Mayling Soong Chiang had insisted that the New Life Movement should have Christian aspects as well. The four Confucian principles of Courtesy, Service towards fellow men, Honesty and Respect for the rights of others, and High-mindedness and Honour were to provide the moral foundation of the Movement. Puritanism, in the anti-permissive sense, was Christianity's contribution, and the YMCA joined in enthusiastically. As for the Blue Shirts, they saw their role as forcing the people to be puritanical and Confucian whether they liked it or not. Cabarets were made to close at midnight, and dancing was banned. Activists would burst into dance halls and cinemas and pour acid over people in Western dress. By moral precept, exhortation, and personal example, the Generalissimo and his wife thought they would regenerate the flabby spirit of ancient China. His failure was not the least of his disappointments.

Chiang Kai-shek could hardly complain that he lacked the means to enforce his authority, but too many of his initiatives petered out in a slough of bureaucratic bungling. In Nanking, the Nationalist capital, each document went through thirty-seven staging points, each adding hours or days to the delay. It sometimes took six months to get a reply to a memorandum. There were two kinds of official: the underworked and the grossly overworked. Chiang himself, unable to delegate, belonged to the second category. During the war years, he is said to have held no fewer than eighty-two posts. An incomplete list, compiled by the Ministry of Information (and quoted by White and Jacoby) was: Chief Executive of the Kuomintang; President of the National Government; Chairman of the National Military Council; Commander-in-Chief of Land, Naval, and Air Forces; Supreme Commander, China Theatre; President of the State Council; Chairman of the Supreme National Defence Council; Director-General of the Central Planning Board; Chairman of the Party and Political Work Evaluation Committee; Director of the New Life Movement Association; Chairman of the Commission for Inauguration of Constitutional Government; President of the Central Training Corps; President of the School for Descendants of Revolutionary Martyrs; President of the National Glider Association. To many Chinese, no doubt, this accumulation of functions contributed to the image of a godlike man, remote from the failing of mere humans.

This system, with its successes and failures, was nevertheless lurching towards greater things when the Japanese attacked in 1937. With his Japanese experience behind him, Chiang was well aware that his own numerous but ill-equipped armies were no match for the Emperor's great and modern military machine. Having made up his mind to fight, he chose the only strategy that seemed feasible in the circumstances: as Tsar Alexander I had done in the face of Napoleon's invasion of Russia, he chose strategic retreat, hoping that if he drew the enemy ever farther inland, he could avoid a fateful confrontation, preserve his forces intact and, in the end, perhaps, weaken the invader beyond hope. Abandoning Nanking, he was forced finally to set up his wartime capital in the Far West of China, at Chungking, beyond the rugged Yangtze

Gorges. In military terms, this strategy made sense; in social and political terms, it was the cause of Chiang Kai-shek's downfall. Vast areas and enormous populations were abandoned to the advancing Japanese. For protection against a ruthless conqueror, they could not look to the retreating Nationalists, but instead had to turn to the Communist guerrillas.

Mao Tse-tung had learned much since the harsh excesses of the Soviet he had set up in Kiangsi ten years earlier. He was more, not less, totalitarian than Chiang, but he had found a way of mobilising the latent power of China's teeming peasantry, by persuasion and relentless indoctrination. Chiang and his Blue Shirts had treated the peasants as an inert mass to be dragooned into obedience. Mao had found a way of causing them to identify with his brand of agrarian communism. His People's Liberation Army were drilled to avoid the excesses of soldiery on the loose, to help with the harvest, and to pay for food and shelter. During this period of revolutionary struggle, there was no mention of collectivisation of the land: instead, land was promised and distributed, when seized from fleeing landlords. In contrast, the Nationalists were caught in the obvious contradiction between Sun Yat-sen's promise of "land to the tillers" (fulfilled indeed, but too late, in Taiwan in the 1950s) and the Blue Shirts' threatened nationalisation programme.

The Second World War brought Chiang Kai-shek allies, and with them new problems. His American experience and ordeal were about to begin. President Roosevelt's choice as Commander-in-Chief of both the Chinese and the American forces in China was a man who loved the Chinese and spoke their language, but whose character was introverted and whose speech was earthy and outspoken between bouts of taciturnity.

The nickname "Vinegar Joe" sat aptly on Joseph Stilwell, who arrived in Chungking in 1942 to become the Generalissimo's Chief of Staff. From the start, the two men were at loggerheads. A fighting man, Stilwell wanted his Chinese allies to fight, and had no time for the corrupt and self-seeking bureaucracy of the wartime capital. In his candour, he described the whole government apparatus as "a manure pile"; his disrespectful name for Chiang Kai-shek was "Peanut". The antipathy was mutual, and in 1944, at Chiang's request, the President relieved Stilwell of his command. A year earlier, Chiang had reached the pinnacle of his world prestige, attending the summit meeting in Cairo as one of the Big Four, along with Stalin, Churchill, and Roosevelt. The Americans showered his regime with money, arms, and supplies of all kinds, including medicines. Much of this largesse found its way into a gigantic black market, and the great Chinese inflation set in, with only one rival in contemporary history: the Weimar Republic in Germany.

At war's end, the country over which the Generalissimo presided was a demoralised and devastated shell. Most of Inner Mongolia and Manchuria were in Communist hands, and the Soviet Red Army, invading China in the last few days of the war, turned over to Mao Tse-tung enormous stocks of arms and ammunition seized from the Japanese.

At the end of 1945, President Truman sent General George C. Marshall to China on a mission of peace and reconciliation between Nationalists and Communists. The intransigeance of both sides doomed the mission to failure. Civil war loomed ahead, and actually broke out early in 1946. At first, the Nationalists won quick but deceptive victories. But in the spring of 1948, the PLA—under the command of Marshal Lin Piao (later to die in mystery and disgrace after plotting to overthrow Mao's People's Republic)—went over to the offensive. Demoralisation swiftly set in, and Washington tired at last of pouring its dollars into the bottomless receptacle of Chiang's regime. As the retreat of his armies turned into a rout, the Generalissimo made a Confucian gesture of humility. On 21 January 1949, he formally resigned the Presidency, handed over to Vice-President Li Tsung-jen, and went to his birthplace in Chekiang to pray and meditate. But it was only the latest in a very lengthy series of resignations and withdrawals that had punctuated his extraordinary career since early youth. Each time, he had returned to power strengthened by the demonstrated ineffectualness of those who had held it in his absence. And so it was this time. As the Communists closed on his remaining bastions—Nanking, Canton, and Chungking—Chiang Kai-shek left the mainland for Taiwan with two divisions of his best troops. He had lost China, and yet preserved it—if "China" meant the centuries of tradition and civilisation which the Communists set out to obliterate. But his China was a country in miniature. For all its success, outstanding by any standards, the "province of Taiwan" could hardly compensate Chiang for the cataclysm of his mainland failure.

Throughout his adult life, Chiang Kai-shek kept a diary. This man, so monumentally stubborn and arrogant in his public life, was humbly self-critical in the privacy of its pages. Each day, the Generalissimo and his wife knelt together in prayer. His Will, dated 29 March 1975, attempted to perpetuate his failing dream beyond his lifetime in the words:

> Just at the time when we are getting stronger, my colleagues and my countrymen, you should not forget our sorrow and our hope because of my death. My spirit will always be with my colleagues and my countrymen to fulfil the Three People's Principles, to recover the mainland, and to restore our national culture.

And with that curious blend of modesty and pride, he added:

I have always regarded myself as a disciple of Dr. Sun Yat-sen and also of Jesus Christ.

The Generalissimo had taken his enigma with him to the grave.

2. "Ripe for Revolution"

Early this century, China was "ripe for revolution". This was the phrase used by Chou En-lai, the very able Premier of the Chinese People's Republic, to describe the situation as he saw it in Africa in the 1960s. But it was far truer of his own country in the early 1900s. There was no consensus to support the ancient imperial order. The Manchu dynasty was hated and resented. Misery was widespread. It was a time of national humiliation and domestic upheavals. Such situations tend to throw up revolutionaries and demagogues. The first of these to achieve lasting fame was Dr. Sun Yat-sen, but two younger men disputed his legacy; their names were Chiang Kai-shek and Mao Tse-tung.

For many centuries, the Chinese imperial system had showed its viability and resilience, but under the Manchus things began to go wrong. For one thing, the population—already large by European standards—began to explode. A precise census in 1778 returned 242,956,618 persons. And for the first time, no new land was available for the new millions. Presciently, the Manchus feared rebellion fomented from afar, and had restricted emigration overseas. The Chinese stayed at home, and multiplied.

An industrial revolution might have taken care of this problem, but there was none. More important, still, the foreigner came with his trade and his manufactured goods, which flooded the hinterland of the great ports and ruined the traditional handicrafts which in slack seasons had given idle peasants their livelihood. There seemed no way out; the industrial nations protected their own markets by tariffs on imports, and the Chinese could not export their handcrafted wares.

And then the foreigners came. In our age of jet travel and instant communications, it is not easy to grasp the cultural and psychological impact of their coming on the Chinese and their rulers. More than any other civilisation, China's had developed in isolation. Desert, mountain, and ocean shielded the Chinese from outside influences. They saw their vast country as the "centre of the world", with barbarians and inferiors both beyond the natural borders and within them on the fringes of the areas where the Han Chinese lived. In this situation, the concept of international relations between equal and sovereign States simply did not apply. The Emperor condescended to receive tribute from the barbarians, and saw no need for further intercourse.

An important part of this Chinese uniqueness was an ideographic language distinct from all others. There were so many characters and many of them were so complex that mass illiteracy was inevitable and those who mastered the written language could expect to be recompensed in their careers. The key to the offices of the State was, in fact, scholarship. The poor and the lowly were not excluded, however: a promising boy, even if he was poor, could hope to be given an education, either through benevolent local associations, or a rich man's favour. In time, he could sit for the competitive examinations that yielded entry into the governing elite.

In this sense, Chinese society was not divided by rigid class barriers. Yet democracy, in the modern Western sense of the term, was fundamentally alien to it. Society was rigidly hierarchical, and the virtues prized above all others were loyalty and good manners. There was a Chinese saying: "There cannot be two suns in one sky." Inside China, this meant that the authority of the Emperor was absolute; in the world, as a whole, it meant that China was the only country of significance. In the imperial autocracy, opposition was simply an absurdity, since to oppose was treason. Another peculiarity of Chinese society was that the Law did not develop there as it did elsewhere. There was a penal code, for criminals had to be punished; but civil law, in the Western sense, did not exist.

The Chinese attitude to religion was also unusual. Revelation played no part in their philosophical tradition, and this made them tolerant. As far as they were concerned, one superstition was as good or as bad as another, and if it pleased people to be Buddhists or Taoists, then so be it. In the West, Confucianism is often spoken of as if it were a religion, but this is to misunderstand it: it was a code of manners and of ethics. It was also a State philosophy, and as such it ensured essential stability through countless upheavals and through many changes of dynasty. Unfortunately, there was another side to it. If things are so stable that they become immutable, the result is stagnation.

During the centuries when the Chinese were finding themselves and building their unique culture and civilisation, they had shown a great genius for innovation, an inventive ingenuity second to none. Technically, they were well ahead of Europe in their major occupation of agriculture. Under the Emperor's direction, the disastrous floods of the Yellow River and other streams were contained by gigantic earthworks, and the watered land was put to the fullest possible use by terraced fields. But in agriculture as in the structure of the State and in art and literature, the time came by imperceptible degrees when the Chinese reckoned that they had achieved perfection in some remote past, which they called their "golden age". It seemed to follow that change *of any kind* could only be for the worse, and any innovations were discouraged. Everything that was good had already been done, thought, or written. Nothing new could be of value.

In this rigid order, the ruler had a moral role to play. His authority was absolute, but not necessarily permanent. He was required to be just, but if he manifestly ceased to be just, it was up to someone to remove him. Throughout Chinese history, many rebels took on this burden. If they failed—as most of them naturally did—they went down in history as traitors. But every now and then, a rebel leader succeeded; he would set up a new dynasty in his turn, the deposed ruler being said to have lost the "Mandate of Heaven".

Since the Chinese, unlike most other peoples, were not burdened by irksome laws, nor for that matter by the Judaeo-Christian concept of sin, there was room in their lives for other kinds of loyalty—to the village, the family, the clan. This environment was human and familiar, and within it the elders dispensed their arbitration in any disputes brought to their notice. Should a scholar or a merchant achieve success, then all members of his family or clan would naturally become his hangers-on. But the failures, the sick, or the old knew that they could turn to those around them for help.

It was this closed Chinese world that felt the shock of the foreign intrusions. The Chinese assumption of superiority was dented, then shattered. They could see for themselves that the techniques of the foreigners were superior to their own. It would have been consoling to assume that foreign philosophies were inferior, but even this comforting assumption did not stand up to the test of experience. To make matters worse, the foreigners were evidently quite disinclined to behave with the humility that was expected of them, and to pay tribute to the Emperor.

Indeed, when the Chinese turned down a request from the British that they should be represented in Peking by an ambassador, who would deal with the government on a footing of equality, the British went to war about it. At any rate, this was the way the British looked at it. But the Chinese saw it as an imperialist attempt to force them to import Indian opium. For that reason, it was called the Opium War. Without trying very hard, the British were the winners, and dictated the Treaty of Nanking on 29 August 1842. Canton lost its monopoly of seaborne trade. The Chinese ceded Hong Kong to Britain, opened their ports to foreign trade, and paid an indemnity of £21,000,000. This was the end of the old tribute system from "barbarians" to the Emperor.

Things were never going to be the same again. Other "unequal" treaties followed in 1844, 1858, 1879, 1881, 1883, 1885, and 1895. There seemed no end in sight to the humiliations and concessions forced upon China by intruders. The Americans were the first to secure extra-territorial rights, with their own courts of law on Chinese territory; other foreigners soon gained the same advantages. Now, if a Frenchman or an Englishman killed a Chinese, the accused could not be tried by a Chinese court.

In 1860, the British and French occupied Peking and burned down the Summer Palace. It was almost as if they were trying to prove the Chinese right in labelling foreigners as barbarians. The Russians soon came in on the act, grabbing the north bank of the Amur River and the Maritime Province, in which they founded Vladivostok. Though tolerant of all religions, the Chinese had kept foreign missionaries out. Now Catholic and Protestant gospellers were allowed to proselytise. It was bad enough to have to submit to white-skinned barbarians, but presently the Japanese—the rising great power of Asia—forced China to cede Korea and Formosa. Towards the end of 1897, the Germans occupied Kiaochow, and a great scramble for leases and concessions followed. Sovereignty had become a thing of the past. While the foreign intruders grabbed what they wanted, home-grown rebels also challenged the Emperor's authority.

It is difficult to grasp the sheer scale of the greatest of these internal upheavals—the T'aip'ing Rebellion (1850–1864)—but a comparison with some familiar Western bloodbaths may help to put this one in perspective. The Spanish Civil War, for instance, lasted less than three years, and cost about 500,000 lives. The American Civil War went on for four years and also cost 500,000.

The T'aip'ing Rebellion was far longer and more destructive: more than 20,000,000 lives were lost in fourteen years. The Second World War was about as destructive in less than half that time, and with the advantage of great advances in death-dealing technology. In some important respects, the T'aip'ing rebels provided a dress rehearsal for Mao Tse-tung's peasant revolution nearly a century later. Their great leader, Hung Hsiu-ch'üan was unusual for a Chinese in that he was a Christian. He preached the equality of all men and the sharing of all property. A born leader, he built up a vast and disciplined army, which occupied Nanking and overran much of South and Central China. In 1853, he and his followers proclaimed their "Heavenly Kingdom of Great Peace"; and in Peking, the Manchu rulers trembled. Like Chiang Kai-shek in this century, Hung Hsiu-ch'üan was a better conqueror than administrator. The tide turned against him in 1855, and his movement gradually disintegrated. The death blows were dealt by the highly successful army of General ("Chinese") Gordon.

Disorder became endemic. Bandits, disaffected Muslims, Miao tribesmen, all revolted, more or less successfully. And then in 1900 came rebellion of a different kind, this time encouraged from above and directed not at the seat of power but at the "foreign devils" who had been trying to exploit its weaknesses. These rebels cultivated the ancient art of Chinese boxing (better known nowadays as Kung Fu) in self-defence, and were therefore known as the Boxers. Their movement swept across the villages of North China. Any missionary outposts in their path were looted, then set on fire. They murdered Chinese Christians in their thousands. On 13 July, their ragged bands burst into Peking and besieged the eleven foreign legations. Next day an international force seized Tientsin— the scene of a massacre of French citizens thirty years earlier—and marched on the capital. A month later, these foreign troops broke the Boxer siege and freed the scared and hungry people who lived or had taken refuge in the legations. The Empress Dowager thought it only prudent to flee, and made her way to Central China with all her retinue. While the allied troops were raping and plundering, her imperial government was forced to sign the Boxer Protocol of 7 September 1901. The terms were tough. The foreign powers were to get the enormous sum of $738,000,000 in gold (including interest) over forty years. Court officials were to be punished, and the legation quarter was to be fortified and enlarged. All Chinese forts would be razed, and the foreign powers were to be allowed to set up garrisons along the railway to Shanghai. Now China's humiliation was complete.

Two men dominated the history of the next two decades. They were not unalike physically, but in character they were strikingly contrasted. One of them was Yüan Shih-k'ai, general and statesman; the other was Sun Yat-sen, physician and revolutionary.

General Yüan had won his battles in Korea, where he had risen to be the Imperial Resident. This was acceptable as far as it went, but Yüan was consumed with ambition and disgruntled with his lot. He thought he could see a way out of his provincial backwater and to the center and to the top. Rebellion would be too costly and too risky. Treachery seemed likely to be more rewarding. The Empress Dowager, T'zu Hsi, was cruel, capricious, vindictive, and avaricious. Her programme was simple: no changes and no reforms. The Emperor, Kuang Hsu, had dangerously progressive ideas. He plotted to seize her and neutralise conservative opposition to an ambitious plan of his, to open a University of Peking, to build a railway from the capital to Hankow, and to modernise the armed forces. General Yüan got wind of this revolutionary scheme and told the Empress Dowager about it. Forewarned, she struck first, and on 22 September 1898, she had the Emperor arrested and gaoled. As General Yüan had calculated, rewards came his way. He pointed out to the Empress Dowager that if she wanted to protect the imperial household, she would need a model army, and he was the man to create it. All he needed was money and a free hand. He got both, and by 1905 he had produced six well-trained divisions.

Three years later, all his schemes collapsed about him after a second act of treachery misfired. The wicked old Empress Dowager fell ill, and on 14 November 1908, sensing the end was near, arranged for the Emperor to be put to death, for no better reason than her vindictive nature. She herself duly died on the 15th. On his deathbed, Kuang Hsu had pleaded with his brother Prince Ch'un— who had been named Regent—to see to it that General Yüan was executed for betraying his reform programme of ten years earlier.

Prince Ch'un, however, was not of a murderous disposition. In January 1909, he let it be known that Yüan Shih-k'ai was having trouble with his feet, and the General was allowed to take sick leave and was relieved of all his posts. The new Emperor, P'u Yi, was an infant, and the Regent was weak. The court's eunuchs and women were competing in intrigue, and the throne was tottering. Prince Ch'un was hardly the man to save it. Even a hand-picked Provisional National Assembly, convened in October 1910, insisted on the convocation of a Parliament, which the Regent—much against his will—agreed to in 1913. Revolution was near, however, and when it struck on 10 October 1911, Yüan Shih-k'ai was given his chance of further betrayal.

This was Sun Yat-sen's historic hour. The conventional image of Dr. Sun (1866–1925) is of a great revolutionary leader and an indifferent ideologist, but the reverse is closer to the truth. He had a noble character, but an inadequate supply of the ruthlessness that revolutionaries need if they are to be successful. He totally lacked the gift for treachery which his opponent of the next few years, General Yüan, used to further his own ends and frustrate the revolution.

Both men, in their different ways, were nationalists, but Sun was also a patriot and at crucial moments put the interests of his country before his own. Yüan simply identified his interests with those of

China (much as a celebrated head of General Motors later identified his company's interests with those of America).

Sadly, Sun Yat-sen was an almost total failure as a revolutionary; yet the ideological principles he bequeathed to his movement were relevant to China's problems. If his followers had applied them intelligently and honestly, they might well have defeated the alternative ideology of Chinese Communism.

Sun was a broad-faced man of small stature, with a large moustache. He led an adventurous and precarious life. He was first talked about in 1894 in Canton, where he organised the first of a number of revolutionary secret societies. Through it and its successors, he made altogether ten attempts to overthrow the Manchu dynasty. Then came the successful one of 1911—which he learned about after the event, for he was in America at the time and did not reach Shanghai until Christmas Day. His first failure had come in 1895, and the following year he was kidnapped in London and held for ten days in the Chinese Legation building. He would probably not have been seen alive again, had he not succeeded in smuggling out word of his plight to an English friend who interceded on his behalf.

He turns up in Macao, in Honolulu, in the United States, in Tokyo, always plotting, always organising overseas Chinese communities. The revolution that broke out on the Double Tenth had been scheduled for a week later, but a bomb exploded accidentally in the Russian concession at Hankow on 9 October, and events took over. The young Chiang Kai-shek, aged twenty-four, was among the revolutionaries. He led a band of one hundred men and two girls who set fire to the Governor's offices at Hangchow, capital of his home province of Chekiang.

The Prince Regent was bewildered and mortally afraid. How wise he had been not to listen to his brother, who wanted him to execute General Yüan Shih-k'ai. If anybody could save the throne, it was General Yüan. But when Prince Ch'un's message came, Yüan was diffident. His foot, he said, was still bothering him. A week of haggling followed, and on the eighth day, having got what he wanted, Yüan was back in the service of the Manchus.

His price for coming back was a job from which no Prince Regent was likely to be able to dismiss him. His new title—Imperial Commissioner in Command of the Armed Forces—was just what he needed. The new model army—which he himself had trained and equipped—went into action and smashed the revolutionaries.

Yüan Shih-k'ai had no very good reason to save the Manchus, who had humiliated him, and he shared the view of the republican plotters that the dynasty should go. To this end, he was even prepared to go through the motions of setting up a republican regime—but of course with himself as President. His real ambition he kept to himself at that time: it was no less than to restore the monarchy, with himself as Emperor.

A rival general who stood in his way was murdered, and now General Yüan was in a position to dictate terms to the Prince Regent. On 7 November 1911, he was appointed Prime Minister, responsible to a new Provisional Parliament. A week later he entered Peking in triumph.

Alas for him, there were complications. On 30 December, Sun Yat-sen was elected President of the United Provinces of China by a revolutionary provisional assembly in Nanking. Ten days earlier, Yüan's representatives and Sun's had reached a secret agreement to set up a republic. The first President was to be the man who should overthrow the Manchus. Yüan was in a position to make sure he was that man.

On 12 February 1912, the Empress Dowager Lung Yü, tears streaming down her face, accepted the Abdication Edict that had been drafted under Yüan's supervision. It gave him "full powers" to organise "a" provisional republican government. Ironically, then, the Imperial House itself had proclaimed the Republic. The Edict said nothing about Sun's republic in Nanking, and Yüan, having betrayed the Manchus, now got ready to betray Dr. Sun as well. He sent off a telegram to the Provisional President, reminding Sun Yat-sen of his agreement to step down in favour of the man who had overthrown the Manchu dynasty: "Never shall we allow monarchical government in our China."

It is easy to imagine what Lenin would have done if he had received a telegram like that. But Sun was no Lenin. He protested against the proclamation of a Republic by Imperial Decree, but a promise was a promise: he stepped down in Yüan Shih-k'ai's favour, stipulating only that Nanking should be the capital and that his own government should continue in office until the new Provisional President was elected by the Senate and sworn in. Poor Sun was no match for Yüan. When Sun Yat-sen sent a delegation to Peking to "welcome" Yüan to the south, the wily statesman staged army mutinies in the imperial capital and in three other cities. How could he travel south, he asked, when the north was in turmoil?

As usual, he got his way. On 10 March, in a ceremony in a hall of the Imperial Palaces, he was sworn in as the second Provisional President of the Republic of China.

Although Yüan Shih-k'ai had deprived the Manchus of their throne (which they would have lost anyway), he treated them generously in retirement. Not that he loved them, but with his eye on the throne, he wished to preserve its dignity. The boy Emperor P'u Yi was allowed to live in the Summer Palace, with courtiers in attendance and no shortage of cash to keep up an imperial style. He was later to become Japan's puppet "Emperor" of Manchukuo; and later still, to work as a gardener for the Chinese Communists.

Another job loomed ahead for Yüan Shih-k'ai. Having tolerated the Republic, the time had come to dispose of it. What this really meant was that he must rid himself of that troublesome lot of revolutionaries, the Kuomintang. In August 1912, Sun Yat-sen had dropped the name of his revolutionary Alliance Society (T'ung-menghui), and renamed it the Kuomintang, which is sometimes translated as "People's Party" but more usually as "Nationalist Party". The Republic seemed likely in any case to destroy itself by the spectacle it was offering of its own follies, incompetence, and corruption. The Provisional Senators spent more of their time squabbling than working, and the squabbles sometimes turned into fist-fights. The national elections at the end of 1912 and the beginning of 1913 were still more unedifying. Votes were offered for auction and many of the new deputies belonged to more than one party. When Parliament met, much of its time went in legislating for the financial benefit of the members.

As an assassin, Yüan Shih-k'ai continued to demonstrate his prowess. In August 1912 he wined and dined one of the Kuomintang generals who had taken part in the Wuchang uprising, then had him murdered. Dr. Sun rushed to Peking to ask for an explanation. To placate him, the President offered him the job of supervising the extension of China's railway system—a thankless task, since no funds were available.

Money was indeed what General Yüan desperately lacked. The Manchus had left the coffers bare; few taxes were being collected, and the warlords were grabbing what they could. Yüan turned to the foreign bankers and negotiated a "Reorganisation Loan" of £25,000,000 guaranteed by the Salt Tax. The agreement was not concluded until 27 April 1913, but a minor difficulty stood in the way: constitutionally, Parliament was supposed to give its endorsement. When the deputies made it clear they were going to withhold their consent, the President simply ignored them, and had the loan agreement signed by his Premier and two ministers. Only £21,000,000 was paid over, and he immediately used £250,000 of it to meet the Imperial court expenses and £60,000 for his own office and the cabinet.

But the Kuomintang was still a thorn in his side. The Nationalists had won absolute majorities in both the House and the Senate in the 1912–1913 elections. As soon as the trusting Dr. Sun had left Peking after his visit in September 1912, Yüan had banned local "secret organisations", meaning bodies under Kuomintang control. Dr. Sun would have been well advised to watch over the course of his revolution; instead, he went off to Japan that winter to study the Japanese railway system. The brilliant younger man he had left behind to become chairman of the Kuomintang's executive committee, Sung Chiao-jen, was shot in the stomach and killed as he was boarding the train from Shanghai to Peking on 21 March 1913. He was only thirty-one. Yüan's assassins had struck again.

Even Sun Yat-sen could not swallow this latest outrage. Not too soon, he denounced Yüan in a telegram: "You are betraying the country. I must oppose you in the same way as I did the Ch'ing dynasty." On 5 May 1913 the Kuomintang majority passed a resolution in Parliament declaring the loan agreement illegal, and in the provinces on 10 July the party's generals went into action, responding to Sun's call to arms. This "Second Revolution", as it is known, was no better conceived or organised than the first. Within two months Yüan Shih-k'ai's troops had smashed it.

On 6 October, Yüan had himself formally elected to the office he already held provisionally. On 4 November he expelled all Kuomintang members from Parliament, and on 10 January 1914 he dissolved it.

All was now ripe for Yüan Shih-k'ai's dynastic plans. The major powers had recognised his government in October 1913, and on 1 May the following year, a revised Provisional Constitution gave him extensive power to rule by decree. In August 1915, he organised a public campaign to proclaim him Emperor. The Dragon Throne seemed at last within reach. A hand-picked National Convention elected him to it, and on 9 December he formally accepted imperial office, to be assumed the following New Year's Day. He even adopted the reign title of Hung Hsien, and had coins struck with his likeness upon them. P. S. Reinsch, the American Minister, rather liked the look of him, seeing a resemblance to Clemenceau, with brightly alert eyes, full of interest yet never hostile.

But Heaven was not about to confer its Mandate upon this treacherous autocrat. His downfall, swift and utterly unexpected, was masterminded from Tokyo.

With the Kuomintang banned, Dr. Sun reverted to his old pastime of creating conspiratorial bodies. His newest was a Revolutionary Party (Komingtang), with temporary headquarters in Japan. The imperial government in Tokyo was not prepared to see Yüan Shih-k'ai succeed to the Dragon Throne. The chaotic Republic suited the Japanese very well, for it was weak and disorganised, incapable of standing up to imperial demands. A restored Chinese monarchy, under a man as strong and capable as General Yüan, might defend itself.

On 23 August 1914, the Japanese had declared war on Germany. Almost immediately, they violated China's neutrality. Then on 19 January 1915 they presented their notorious Twenty-one Demands, at first in secret. Playing for time, President Yüan delayed acceptance of the Japanese ultimatum until 8 May, when he gave in. The Japanese were to take over German rights in Shantung; their leases in Manchuria were extended to ninety-nine years; commercial and industrial interests were given to Japanese companies. It was yet another unequal treaty.

The Reorganisation Loan had long run out. Yüan's star was on the wane. Penurious and humiliated, he pushed ahead nevertheless with his imperial plans. But on Christmas Day 1915, the Yunnan generals, financed by Japan, proclaimed their province's independence and denounced the imperial pretender. One by one the other provincial commanders joined in the revolt. On 22 March Yüan dropped his imperial plans. Shensi, Szechwan, and Hunan proclaimed their independence. Back in Shanghai, Sun Yat-sen vowed punishment for the usurper. Ill with shame and anger, Yüan Shih-k'ai died on 6 June 1916. Only three weeks before his death, he had tried to stem the tide of revolt by yet another assassination—this time of one of Sun's staunchest supporters and Chiang Kai-shek's revolutionary mentor, Ch'en Ch'i-mei. This deed did not save him, but merely added to the weight of opprobrium in which his memory is held.

II Conquest and Invasion

(1887–1939)

3. | Student in Japan

Chiang Kai-shek's father was of farming stock, and his mother was a devout Buddhist. (He shared both these accidents of birth, incidentally, with his great rival for the leadership of the Chinese people—Mao Tse-tung.) But Chiang Su-an was a salt merchant in a modest way—the first of his line to change occupations after three generations of farming. In later years, Chiang Kai-shek came to believe that he was a descendant of the Duke of Chou of the Chou dynasty, and went to much trouble to prove his claim.

The villagers of Chi Kou went to Chiang Su-an for counsel, for he was a scholarly man and they credited him with wisdom. His mother was Su-an's third wife, but she seems to have treated the children of earlier marriages with motherly impartiality. She had been married two years when Chiang Kai-shek was born. He is said to have been sprightly and prankish of disposition, but sickly in body. From the first, he displayed a life-long characteristic—his capacity for getting into difficult situations, then emerging from them somehow or other. At three (writes his official biographer Hollington Tong) he thrust a pair of chopsticks down his throat to see how far they would go. He found out that it was easier to put them there than to get them out again. His elders were more successful. "Are the vocal cords damaged?" his grandfather inquired solicitously. "Grandson can speak, grandson not dumb," cried the little boy, jumping from his bed.

Two years later, in the winter of 1892, young Kai-shek jumped into one of those man-sized water jars which the Chinese kept under the eaves of their houses to capture the rain. What had attracted him was a piece of ice in which he could see his own image. This time there were no elders around to help. In time, drenched, frozen, and the worse for a large intake of icy water, he scrambled out.

A swift mountain stream passed in front of the house. He often bathed there, and sometimes got carried away. (Chi Kou, the name of his birthplace, means "brook mouth"; another name for it was Wu Ling, or Military Ridge. The district bore the poetical name of Ch'in Hsiao—"the filial piety of birds". Those interested in the symbolism of names have much to play with there.)

The traditional Chinese educational system neglects the body, but with the local streams to swim in and the tall hills to climb, the boy soon shed his sickly disposition and acquired a fitness of body that was to last for the rest of his long life. His favourite pastime was war games, and in common with General de Gaulle he invariably insisted on being the "commander-in-chief". Often, it is said, he would stand on a higher piece of ground and harangue his playmates or tell them historical stories. That way, he acquired the early habit of public speaking. His interminable orations of later years rested on this precocious foundation.

The talk of the village often centred upon China's troubles. When Kai-shek was seven, China was utterly defeated by Japan, and forced to cede Korea, Formosa, and the Pescadores under the 1895 Treaty of Shimonoseki. This new humiliation, attributable to the Manchus, was being discussed around Kai-shek; much as the disasters of the Spanish-American War were table talk in the household of the future General Franco at much the same age. Such talk may not of itself create nationalist leaders, but it does serve to shape their resolve.

Even the Manchu court briefly took cognisance of the need for change under the ill-fated Emperor Kuang Hsu, who outraged the officials and his terrifying mother, the Empress Dowager, by launching the "Hundred Days of Reform" (June–September 1898) under the guidance of the radical reformer K'ang Yu-wei. But before he could complete his work, his mother cast him into gaol. After the Sino-Japanese war, the enlightened Viceroy of Hupei and Hunan, Chang Chih-tung, wrote *Learn*, an explosive pamphlet of which the astonishing number of 1,000,000 copies were sold. His theme was: "Learn the shame of being like Turkey. Learn the need to become like Japan." At that time indeed China was to East Asia what Turkey was to the eastern end of Europe: the sick man. At Chi Kou (writes Tong), *Learn* was studied by the literate and read out to the illiterates. The depredations of the great powers followed almost immediately, however, and the Boxer Rebellion was China's desperate answer.

None of this could have meant much to Chiang Kai-shek, except as a store of unconscious memories that would come to the surface later. He was so naughty and so often in dangerous scrapes that his worried mother thought he needed a touch of outside discipline. With the approval of her husband and father-in-law, she therefore engaged a tutor for him when he was only four. Accounts of his academic prowess differ, but he seems to have made a slow start, with a good deal of truancy to get back to his war games. But then, four is not normally a studious age. Before he was nine, though, he had completed his statutory reading of the four Confucian Classics which aspiring young Chinese were required to decipher and learn by heart before they had much idea of the meaning of the characters: the Master's own *The Great Learning*, *The Middle Way*, and *The Analects*, and the *Sayings* of his pupil Mencius. Between nine and sixteen, Kai-shek studied the Confucian Canons: *The Book of Odes*, *The Book of Ancient History*, *The Book of Changes*, *The Spring and Autumn Chronicles*, and *The Book of Rites*.

In 1895, when Kai-shek was eight, his father died. Thereafter, he was brought up by his mother and his grandfather. To both in later years Chiang Kai-shek was to pay tribute. Since he seldom favoured the world with biographical statements, it is worth quoting the one to his mother which took the form of passages in a message to the Chinese people delivered on the occasion of his "fiftieth" birthday (by the Chinese reckoning that the newborn are already one year old) on 30 October 1936. He spoke of

> . . . the indelible memory of my mother who endured so much in educating and bringing up the fatherless boy. Now, while the trees by her grave have grown tall and thick, I cannot but realise how little I have accomplished and how I have failed to live up to the hopes she had placed in me. . . .

During that period, he disclosed, the family went through great hardships, and his mother imposed an iron discipline on him, never hesitating to beat him if she thought he fell short of her stern standards. She was convinced that menial tasks were good for his character, so plenty of washing dishes and mopping the floor came his way. Chiang explained:

> It will be remembered that the then Manchu regime was in its most corrupt state. The degenerated gentry and corrupt officials had made it a habit to abuse and maltreat the people. My family, solitary and without influence, became at once the target of such insults and maltreatment. From time to time usurious taxes and unjust public service were forced upon us and once we were publicly insulted before the court. To our regret and sorrow none of our relatives and kinsmen was stirred from his apathy.
>
> Indeed, the miserable condition of my family at that time is beyond description. It was entirely due to my mother and her kindness and perseverance that the family was saved from utter ruin.

S. I. Hsiung throws light on the bitter incident recalled by Chiang Kai-shek. A citizen of Chi Kou had vanished after failing to pay his rice tax. The Manchu authorities, seeing there was no male head of the house in the Chiang household, arrested the youthful Kai-shek, hauled him before the magistrate's court, and threatened him with gaol if he did not pay the missing man's fine. The fine must have been paid, since he was released, but both Mrs. Chiang and her son were deeply seared by the injustice and humiliation of the treatment meted out to them in the name of the Dragon Throne. In later years, Chiang Kai-shek often referred to this incident as "the first spark that kindled my revolutionary fire".

In 1901, when Chiang was only fourteen, his parents arranged a marriage for him with a girl three years older—Mao Fu-mei. Had Chiang taken over his father's business as a salt merchant, the marriage could conceivably have been a success, but it was soon to founder when news of his womanising in Tokyo reached his home town.

When Kai-shek was seventeen he was tutored by a man called Ku Ching-lien, who ran a quaintly-named Pavilion of Literature in the town of Fenghua. There were classics and more classics. One of them, however, was perhaps more important than the others: it was one of the earliest and most famous of the Chinese military treatises, Sun Tze's *The Art of War* (which later events showed that he had grasped less firmly than his mortal rival for power, Mao Tse-tung), and the works of General Tseng Kuo-fan, the man who quelled the great T'aip'ing Rebellion. Another famous figure from Chinese history who captured Chiang's admiration was Wang Yang-ming, a scholar-statesman of the Ming dynasty. Many years later, in his Taiwanese exile, Chiang renamed the Grass Mountain the Yang-ming Shan (Yang-ming Mountain) in nostalgic tribute.

Kai-shek owed much to Ku's teaching, which guided him towards one of the more austere forms of Confucianism—the School of Confucian Scholars of the Sung dynasty (960–1126 A.D.), headed by Chu Hsi. Moral endeavour, self-denial, and self-discipline were its tenets. In later years, he would hold important conferences and training courses at the mountain resort of Lu Shan (known to Westerners as Kuling), because that was where Chu Hsi used to deliver his lectures.

More to the point at the time of Kai-shek's young manhood, however, his tutor told Chiang all he knew about Sun Yat-sen and the coming revolution.

From the Pavilion of Literature, Chiang went on to another establishment in the same town: the Dragon River Middle School. But he stayed only three months; he suddenly decided to go to Tokyo to start studying for a military career.

An odd habit of his at this time of his life is recorded by his biographers. An early riser, he would stand bolt upright on the verandah in front of his bedroom for half an hour, his lips tight, his arms firmly folded across his chest. The biographers speculate about what went on in his mind—idly enough, since they do not agree. In any case, he was soon to make it clear that his mind was seething with revolutionary and patriotic ideas. He chose a military career because he wanted action, adventure, and the chance to serve his country. And he chose Tokyo for his initial studies because the Japanese capital was the recognised centre of the military art. There was a further attraction, in that it was in Tokyo that he was most likely to mix with Chinese revolutionaries in exile.

In this year of decision—1905—Japan was still locked in its formidable contest with Tsarist Russia. Friends and relatives crowded around him to try to talk him out of his mad idea. But the young man was not the kind to be easily deflected. Instead of arguing, he did something which he knew would be profoundly shocking to those around him: he took a pair of scissors and lopped off his Chinese pigtail—or queue, to use the more dignified name. This was more than shocking; it was illegal in Manchu times, and had the breath of sacrilege about it. As he had guessed, this did the trick. Any young man who cut off his queue thereby ceased to be welcome. The farther he went from his native village, the better for those left behind. Never one for mollycoddling or clinging to her own, his mother raised the money for the trip.

In May 1905, Chiang Kai-shek sailed for Japan, but this first trip was an anti-climax. The imperial military academies had no room for revolutionaries and to exclude them, they had an arrangement with the Chinese Board of War: only Chinese students recommended by their own government were allowed to register. As far as Chiang was concerned, however, the trip was far from wasted, for it was in Tokyo at that time that he met the man who was to be his revolutionary mentor, Ch'en Ch'i-mei, generally regarded as the most gifted of Sun Yat-sen's early followers. Certain he was going to be back fairly soon, Chiang took lessons in Japanese.

His inclination was to stay on, in fact, and to soak up revolutionary talk from his new companions. But his mother saw no very good reason why he should be in Tokyo at all if he was not getting the schooling he was seeking. So she summoned him home, ostensibly on an irresistible family pretext: his sister was about to be married. Ever the dutiful son, he came home that winter.

A still more important family event took place shortly afterwards in 1908: the birth of Chiang's elder son Ching-kuo. It was Mao Fu-mei's one great contribution to the Chiang family. From the first, her life with Chiang Kai-shek had been unhappy. Her mother-in-law was strict and demanding, and exacted obedient attention. The official biographers praise Mao Fu-mei's generous nature, but she herself confided in her friends that she lived in fear of her husband's brutal nature and his beatings.

Chiang's military education had already begun, but in China, not Japan. Although ill on the day, in 1906, he passed a highly competitive examination for entrance to the Paoting Military Academy. He was one of only sixty successful candidates of the thousand and more from Chekiang province, but two things were held against him: he was a Han Chinese and not a Manchu, and he wore his hair short. In pre-revolutionary China, this could only mean a disdain for imperial tradition. It was suspected, correctly, that he might be a rebel—someone harbouring dangerous thoughts.

Most of the instructors were Japanese. Fresh from their spectacular defeat of the Tsarist armies and earlier, of the Chinese, they didn't bother to hide their contempt for the latter. One day, during a lesson in hygiene, the instructor produced a lump of earth and compared it with China. Seeing the puzzled looks on the faces of his pupils, he explained that China had 400,000,000 inhabitants, while the clod in his hand could hold 400,000,000 germs.

Disregarding military discipline, Chiang Kai-shek felt a cold rage coming over him. He stepped forward and divided the clod into eight roughly equal parts. With an angry stare at the instructor, he remarked that Japan had 50,000,000 people. "Could they," he asked, "be compared with 50,000,000 germs that could live on one eighth of this lump of earth?"

Struck dumb, but not for long, the instructor pointed at Chiang's shorn head and shouted a threatening question: "Are you a member of the revolutionary society?" But Chiang, it is said, stayed calm. "I am asking you whether my comparison was right or not," he said quietly. "Please do not raise another issue."

This was not the way cadets were expected to behave at the military academy. For Chiang, the risk was great. He might well have been expelled from the academy; worse still, he could have been placed under close arrest and have had to face a court-martial. For a start, he was summoned to the Chancellor's office. His luck was in. The Chancellor saw the justice of the young man's stand and contented himself with a severe reprimand. The incident was closed.

Before the year was out, Chiang was told that he was one of a limited number of students selected to go to Japan to study military science. His knowledge of the language had stood him in good stead. In the spring of 1907, he enrolled in the Shinbo Gakyo, or Preparatory Military Academy, in Tokyo.

For some time now, his classmates had decided that he was aloof. He was courteous enough, but made no effort to cultivate friendships or to respond to mildly friendly overtures. This didn't make him popular. His fellow-students called it pride, but that wasn't quite the right word for his attitude. As with Charles de Gaulle at a similar stage, Chiang Kai-shek was already dedicated to a career and a precise aim in life. He had nothing against friendship, except that it was a waste of his precious time. The one exception to this rule was Chang Ch'ün, who was a fellow-student of his at that time and won Chiang's lifelong trust. Apart from Mme. Chiang and Ching-kuo, Chang Ch'ün became Chiang's closest confidant.

It was a hard life, harder than any he had known even in the days of his widowed mother's hardships. The diet was spartan: one or two small bowls of rice a day, with "tiny portions of fish and a small dish of *daikon*"—a kind of radish (writes Tong). Forcing himself to make do with what he was offered, he resisted the temptation to seek extra food elsewhere, and developed a frugal appetite which he kept for the rest of his days.

During the long summer holidays, Chiang Kai-shek would make the long journey home to see his mother (rather than his wife). But he always broke his journey in Shanghai to meet revolutionaries and help them with recruiting and fund-raising. He had not yet joined any revolutionary organisation, despite the dark suspicions of his tutor in hygiene.

In Tokyo, however, Ch'en Ch'i-mei initiated him into the Tungmenhui (Alliance Society), and introduced him to Sun Yat-sen after the leader had addressed the first meeting Chiang attended. This was in 1908. Sun and Kai-shek had a long talk about the coming revolution. There is no written or visual documentation of this meeting, later hailed as "historic". As the hagiographers have it, Sun was deeply impressed by the eager young man, and remarked to Ch'en Ch'i-mei: "That man will be the Hero of the Revolution:

we need just such a man in our revolutionary movement." In retrospect, the second half of the remark seems more likely than the first, unless Sun Yat-sen was a more than normally tactless man, since Ch'en Ch'i-mei had grounds at that time for supposing that if the revolution was indeed to have a hero, surely he himself was destined for the role.°

Whether or not Sun Yat-sen was deeply impressed with Chiang at this first meeting, the converse was true. Chiang Kai-shek was an ardent young man in search of a leader. Now he had found his leader, at the height of Sun's activity and revolutionary magnetism, and he was quite carried away.

In those happy days, neither passports nor visas were in general use, and Chinese citizens were admitted into Japan without any formalities, regardless of their ethnic origin or their politics. If the Manchu court authorities pointed out, however, that some politically undesirable person was travelling to Japan or already there, the Japanese government would oblige by keeping that person out or deporting him if he had already arrived. Just such a request arrived concerning Dr. Sun Yat-sen; this must have been shortly after Chiang's meeting with him. Undoubtedly Sun had already built up a large revolutionary following in Japan. He had already been excluded from Shanghai, and now Tokyo was out of bounds as well. He set up his headquarters in Hong Kong.

During Chiang's stay at the military academy—which lasted rather less than two years—Sun Yat-sen made no fewer than seven of his abortive attempts at revolution, in various parts of north China. Many of his followers were killed, yet the Manchus were still in power. Chiang kept on offering his services to the cause, but he was always turned down, and always for long-term reasons. The best service he could offer to the revolution, and to China—said Sun Yat-sen—was to complete his military education.

Graduation came at the end of November 1909. The next formal

° Hsiung dates the Sun-Chiang meeting as earlier than March 1907, pointing out that during that month Dr. Sun went to Annam to continue his anti-Manchu plotting, and assuming that Chiang would have wasted no time in travelling to Tokyo on having been accepted for the Shinbo Gakyo—although the academic term did not begin until the spring. One must assume that Hsiung was mistaken, nevertheless, for according to the official records, Chiang first met Sun Yat-sen in Tokyo in 1908, the year of Ching-kuo's birth. (See S. I. Hsiung, *The Life of Chiang Kai-shek* [London, 1948], p. 55.)

stage was the Military University, but before that a cadet was required to prove that he could survive the rigors of military life at the lowest level. One bitterly cold morning in January 1910, Chiang Kai-shek clicked his heels and saluted Colonel Himatsu, commander of the 19th Field Artillery Regiment at Takada. Above them both in the hierarchy stood the famous "Long Beard General" Nagaoka, commanding the 13th Division of the Japanese Army, to which Himatsu's regiment belonged.

Rising three hours or so before the winter dawn, Kai-shek's first job was to groom his horse. Then he went on early morning manoeuvres. He spent the whole of every day in the open; the evening was for the menial tasks of a Japanese private soldier. In later years Chiang never claimed that he had actually enjoyed his Japanese years. It was a case of being grimly determined to see the thing through. He had little time for communication with those sharing his military life, but when he did speak, it was usually to say such things as: "It'll be worse still on the battlefield. Nothing is unbearable: you just have to get used to it."

Curiously, Chiang Kai-shek appears to have made no impression at all on his Japanese superiors. It never occurred to them that he was destined for greater things. Years later—in 1929, when Chiang Kai-shek was already famous—General Nagaoka tried to puzzle out the secret of Chiang's successes. He wrote an article recalling that he had invited Chiang to tea in Tokyo in 1927, with Colonel Himatsu. As usual Chiang was immaculately dressed ("like a smart filmstar," said Nagaoka) and almost excessively courteous. Taking his leave, Chiang wrote four Chinese characters on a panel: "Never neglect Master's instructions." That was it, thought Nagaoka. Loyalty and gratitude were the secrets of Chiang's rise to fame. As analytical appraisals go, this one was unusually unperceptive.

When news of the Hankow explosion reached Chiang Kai-shek, he decided to join the revolution immediately, temporarily abandoning his military duties. From that time forward, and especially from the time of his involvement in the fighting at Hangchow, Chiang Kai-shek's personal story merges with the history of modern China, at first obscurely and later as a dominant figure.

The Kuomintang chroniclers dubbed Chiang Kai-shek's strike force the "dare-to-dies". Before leading them in his successful attack on the Governor's *yamen* (office), Kai-shek wrote to his mother. "Forgive me for neglecting my filial duties," he pleaded.

And he went on to say how he wished his affairs and effects to be disposed of, should he die in battle. "I have sworn to give my life for the revolution." Her reply was worthy of any Spartan mother: "Die or not, do as your duty commands. Don't worry about things at home."

And now it was all over. Everybody agreed that he had done pretty well, for a young man, although the action was on a limited scale in the context of much bigger things—and in the end success had been at best only partial. Some time later, one of the Nationalist commanders wrote a short work—*The Record of the Independence of Chekiang*—singling out Chiang Kai-shek as the hero of the day. As a mark of esteem, he sent Chiang a copy of the book with a covering letter. In a Confucian mode, Chiang replied that he coveted no honours. If the book went into further editions, he hoped the author would do justice to other members of the task force whom he had not mentioned.

Hsiung, who records this exchange, does not date it but leaves one to infer that it must have taken place in August 1912. That was the month the Kuomintang was created; and it was also that month that Yüan Shih-k'ai had a Kuomintang general murdered. These events sum up the revolutionary state of play. The Manchus had been swept away, but what was the use of this fundamental change if all it did was to bring power to a Manchurian official without the slightest interest in the Three Principles of the People that were to provide the programme of the Revolution as Sun Yat-sen had conceived it? Chiang was disillusioned and unwilling to serve under General Yüan. That same month—August 1912—he decided to return to Tokyo to resume his military studies.

His first military and political writings belong to this period of 1912 to 1913. While studying, he took on the editorship of *The Voice of the Army*, a review to which he himself made frequent contributions. In the first issue he looked forward to a World Republic in which all races should live in harmony, only police forces to maintain order. There would be no wars, so armies would become unnecessary. With his feet more firmly on the ground, he examined the situations in Tibet and Mongolia and singled out Russia and Japan as China's most likely enemies. He dismissed China's chances of standing up to a Russian attack, or indeed to almost any aggression, and called for a standing army of 600,000 as the minimum for national defence. In comparison with China's size and its already enormous population, this was really quite a small force to have in mind. But even this would call for an expenditure of something between two-thirds and half the national income. Clearly, China could not afford a navy as well as an army, so it should concentrate on land forces.

Turning to China's internal administrative needs and perhaps anticipating his later struggles with the warlords, Chiang Kai-shek strongly criticised the system that concentrated both civil and military powers in the hands of one man: the provincial governor. If this system persisted, he wrote, China would be reduced in time to a loose assemblage of independent States. All military power should be in the hands of the central government.

At the time of this pontification, Chiang Kai-shek was twenty-five or twenty-six. He was thus ten years or more younger than a certain Charles de Gaulle was when his articles and books on the state of France's defences were stirring controversy in the 1920s and 1930s. There was no record that Chiang's writings, though equally controversial in the climate of the times, aroused a comparable agitation. But then he was a very young man, still almost unknown and writing in a foreign capital. In those days, any young man embarking on a military career in the Far East thought first of Japan, then of that other military power, Germany. Chiang Kai-shek was planning to go to Germany to complete his military education when Sun Yat-sen launched his "second revolution" to overthrow Yüan Shih-k'ai. Kai-shek immediately went to Shanghai to join Ch'en Ch'i-mei as chief of staff. In the approved revolutionary style, Ch'en proclaimed the independence of Shanghai on 22 July 1913. This time yet again, the revolutionaries had spoken and struck too soon. The arsenal was well defended, and Chiang was captured by a sentinel but managed to escape.

Chiang had been defeated, but he was not in disgrace. Indeed he seems to have emerged strengthened in Sun Yat-sen's eyes. Successful was hardly the word to describe the revolutionary leader's record. Chiang admired him the more for his courage in adversity. The approved biographers date the close friendship between the two men from this point. Together they sought refuge in Japan, which had lifted its ban on Dr. Sun's presence.

Their party banned by the treacherous Yüan, the Kuomintang leaders watched their Republic crumble in agonised frustration. True, their agents were active throughout the country. But from most areas, their reports were discouraging. In the south the situation was particularly forbidding. In any case, thought Ch'en Ch'i-mei, the south had been getting too much revolutionary attention. The real target areas, he argued, should be Peking and the north. Taking him at his word, Dr. Sun sent him to Dairen, where he spent six months reconnoitring. But the results were meagre in terms of intelligence.

The truth was hard. In this contest between the Kuomintang and Yüan's Republic, the Nationalists were outclassed in all departments. Their organisation was weak, their intelligence unreliable, their security as porous as an unglazed potter's jar. Chiang Kai-shek was soon to find all this out for himself yet again in the spring of 1914. He was sent on a mission to Shanghai, where he hoped to organise an uprising. His plans were thorough enough, but his means were inadequate. All strategically important points around the great city and on the neighbouring coast were to be occupied. But the garrison commander was an able man, who had disposed of a similar challenge a year earlier. He had an efficient security service, and on 30 May his police raided Chiang's headquarters. Chiang himself was almost captured when troops and police surrounded a friend's house he was about to visit. Spotting them from a distance, Chiang made his getaway.

In June Dr. Sun sent him and a companion to the Manchurian province of Heilungkiang to look into a local Kuomintang agent's report that conditions were ripe for an uprising. With his halting Mandarin and lack of local experience, Chiang was hardly the man for the job. After covering a good deal of ground, he reported that the chances of success in any uprising were precisely nil. It turned out that the Kuomintang agent who had reported more optimistically had been hoping to raise funds for his private use. The history of the Kuomintang on the Chinese mainland is strewn with similar stories.

Once more a long wait seemed to lie ahead. Back in Tokyo, Chiang filled his days with studies of Chinese philosophy and military writings, and (says Hsiung) took to recording each evening in his diary the mistakes he had committed during the day. Since he wasn't doing much at the time, one supposes that he did not have much information to impart to his diary. But the diary habit had gripped him, and he kept it up for the rest of his life.

Yet action was never far away. It came to Chiang again with the so-called "third revolution" in the autumn of 1915, which was no more successful than the earlier ones. Borrowing from Yüan Shih-k'ai's arsenal of "dirty tricks", Chiang involved himself for the first time—but not the last—in an assassination. Twice the defender of Shanghai had thwarted his attempts to seize the city. This time he must be removed. Two Kuomintang assassins—one with bombs, the other a marksman—found their target on 10 November. But they then surrendered. A supporting naval operation was botched on 5 December and the French police overran the revolutionary headquarters, which were in their concession. Chiang escaped by climbing over to the next building.

This latest failure deeply affected Chiang, who took to his bed with what may have been nervous exhaustion or perhaps—the term was not yet in use—a psychosomatic illness. He was still in hiding in Shanghai, and when word reached his mother, she made the long journey to nurse him back to health.

There is no record of what she thought of the kind of life her son was leading at that time. Chiang Kai-shek's approved biographers are understandably parsimonious with details of the Shanghai period. His ill-wishers are more generous. Chiang's friend Ch'en Ch'i-mei was his mentor in other things besides revolution. Whenever he frequented the houses of prostitution, Chiang was with him. At a banquet one evening in 1912, Kai-shek exchanged glances with a girl who worked as a parlourmaid to a famous prostitute. Her name was Yao Yi-ching, and the glances were ardent on both sides. Soon she became his concubine, and Chiang Kai-shek brought her to his home. Yi-ching had no children of her own, but when Wei-kuo was brought back from Japan—a circumstantial confirmation of the story that he was born out of wedlock in Chiang's Tokyo days—she treated him as her own.

Chiang was probably adept at evading arrest by Yüan Shih-k'ai's police, though very much a wanted man, because he was "in" with the Shanghai underworld—at that time dominated by the ruthless and notorious Green Society. This Chinese version of the Mafia controlled the opium, prostitution, and extortion rackets. It "sank its roots into all the filth and misery of the great lawless city, disposed of its gunmen as it saw fit, protected its clients by violence, was an organised force perhaps more powerful than the police".

If Chiang Kai-shek was being protected by the Shanghai gangsters, what did he have to offer them? He was daring and indifferent to danger, but by all accounts he was penniless. Certainly there is no evidence that he shared, at any rate in this period, in the spoils of gangsterdom. True, the gangs and he shared a common enemy in Yüan's police. And it was true also that the gang helped him when he was in trouble. His lot in those days were hunger and danger, though for a time he earned a living of sorts as a jobbing clerk on the Shanghai stock exchange.

In assassination as well as in the other departments of security, terrorism and counter-terror, the fight continued unequally. As far as Yüan Shih-k'ai was concerned, Chiang Kai-shek and Ch'en Ch'i-mei had become major nuisances: they had to be removed. Chiang indeed had given him further trouble in the spring of 1916 by seizing Kiangyin fortress on the south bank of the Yangtse River between Shanghai and Nanking. His troops deserted him, leaving him literally holding the fort alone. Here was another defeat to be chalked up, and once again he escaped.

Ch'en Ch'i-mei had taken over as Chairman of the Kuomintang Executive Committee, with Chiang as his assistant, as part of a belated attempt by the visionary Dr. Sun to tighten up party organisation. As always, funds were miserably short. An offer of a deal that would yield a large sum to the revolutionaries came to Ch'en, and he was tempted. He should have known better. The offer had come from a Kuomintang agent working for Yüan. On 18 May 1916, on his way to a meeting where the deal was to be clinched, Ch'en Ch'i-mei was gunned down.

Grief-stricken, Chiang composed a funeral oration for the man who had become his only close friend. "Alas! From now on where can be found a man who knows me so well and loves me so deeply as you did?" he lamented. It was a revealing document, with practical as well as emotional overtones. Who, he asked, was going to carry on Ch'en's work? Would it be those who had slandered Chiang Kai-shek? "I do not mind that you believed their lies about me when you were living. All I want is that I should have a clear conscience now that you are dead."

With Ch'en Ch'i-mei gone, Chiang was promoted in the leadership and moved up a notch in Dr. Sun's trust. Within three weeks of Ch'en's murder, the hated Yüan Shih-k'ai himself died, a broken man. With his passing went the last hopes of a monarchist restoration. Despite his death, several attempts were made to assassinate Chiang Kai-shek.

At that time Chiang Kai-shek was twenty-nine and his character fully formed. It deserves a few words. The "naughty boy" of Chi Kou had grown into an impulsive and adventurous adult. Brave to the point of foolhardiness, he ran extraordinary physical risks and (like Franco, de Gaulle, and Churchill) appeared to have a charmed life. He was personally austere and incorruptible, and loyal to his few friends. Later indeed he was to carry loyalty to self-defeating ends with associates unworthy of his trust. By inclination as well as by education he was a Confucian, and the fact that he later became a Christian convert does not affect the point. Deeply patriotic and an avowed nationalist, he was a revolutionary only in his readiness to take up arms against regimes he hated. His political ideas were a blend of modernism and conservatism; there was no point in modernising unless the traditional Confucian virtues were either restored or conserved. All the paradoxes of his character were present. His modesty was deep and unfeigned: throughout his life he discouraged excessive praise and was diffident and reluctant to talk about himself, yet he did nothing to discourage the cult of personality which undoubtedly spread among his followers and contributed to his power. And with his modesty of behaviour went a kind of sublime complacency. It apparently did not occur to him that his deeds and aspirations might be mistaken or that they might even turn out to be contrary to China's best interests—until gigantic failure brought a bout of humility.

That he had a gift for leadership is undeniable, but it was not always served by sound judgment. His military and strategic analyses made sense in geopolitical terms, but his understanding of politics was still rudimentary. He saw power mainly in military terms, and when he came to practise it in the manipulation of loyalties, real and apparent. In the end, it was probably his incapacity to understand the social and political basis of lasting power that was his undoing.

4. Chaos and Treachery

Between them, Yüan Shih-k'ai and the Japanese had wrecked the Nationalist revolution. Yüan had had his moment of success, but he had failed to restore the monarchy or to impose his authority over the whole of China. The Kuomintang stood exposed as incompetent, and Sun Yat-sen—its founder—as an unpractical dreamer. There had been a brief experiment in parliamentary democracy, but it had gone badly awry, and indeed the notion of democracy itself seemed to be discredited in Chinese eyes. The Manchus were gone, but nothing had been put in their place: China was entering a prolonged period of anarchy, with continuing foreign intervention.

Several rival centres of authority sprang up. There was a Republican government in Peking, and another one in Canton under Sun Yat-sen. There was even a brief restoration of the Manchu dynasty, but that lasted only eleven days in July 1917. And the power of the rival governments was largely theoretical. In

47

nearly all the provinces, the military governors ruled as they pleased. The age of the warlords—those provincial military governors who set up their own feudal baronies, much as in England before the War of the Roses—had begun.

The areas under the control of individual warlords shifted this way or that according to defeat or victory in battle. During the whole period from 1920 to 1926, China was wracked by civil war, and indeed by several simultaneous civil wars. Chiang Kai-shek's northern expeditions in 1926 and 1928 subdued the warlords—at least on the surface—but they went on reasserting themselves whenever the chance occurred. Nearly all of them were in business for personal gain and nothing else. Their rule was oppressive, capricious, and enormously costly to the ordinary people of China. The taxes they levied were innumerable, and they included cuts from the profitable opium and prostitution rackets. They forced peasants to grow opium instead of food crops, and in widespread areas caused actual famine. Chambers of Commerce were forced to pay contributions under threat that their towns would be looted if they did not. Opium Suppression Bureaux were set up as a device not to control the drug but to extort taxes described as fines.

It was against this background of brutal anarchy that Chiang's actions during the decade from 1916 to 1926 need to be seen. In fact he re-enters the story in the autumn of 1917. The "government" in Peking had dissolved Parliament on 31 May—illegally of course, but then not much that happened in this troubled period had any constitutional sanction.

Accompanied by two of the Kuomintang ex-ministers, Dr. Sun sailed to Canton. About 130 ex-deputies also travelled, under the protection of the First Fleet, whose commander had decided to support the revolution. With this rump of a Parliament, on 10 September 1917, Sun Yat-sen claimed a National Military Government, with himself as Generalissimo. He solemnly declared that the rival "President" in Peking was a traitor. As usual, poor Dr. Sun was unaware of treachery closer to hand. One of his top associates in the new government was secretly in touch with Peking and had the commander of the First Fleet assassinated. This man, Lu Yung-ting, now emerged as the leader of the so-called "Kwangsi clique", which systematically ignored or by-passed Sun's orders. In desperation the founder of the Republic resigned as Generalissimo on 4 May 1918.

The next three years were militarily and politically confusing.

Chiang Kai-shek had been posted to a Cantonese army—supposedly loyal to Sun Yat-sen under a man known as the Hakka General, Ch'en Chiung-ming. Kai-shek was unpopular with the troops, both because he insisted on a discipline which they found distasteful, and because he was a non-Cantonese in a wholly Cantonese force. Eventually he resigned and warned Dr. Sun not to trust the Hakka General—advice later shown to be well-founded, but disregarded by the ever-trusting Dr. Sun.

In the great world beyond China, stirring or tragic events had been taking place since the death of Yüan Shih-k'ai. In November 1917, the Russian Bolsheviks had seized power, and Sun Yat-sen cabled his congratulations to Lenin—as one revolutionary to another. A year later German resistance collapsed in the Great War, and China's Nationalists waited anxiously to see whether the territories and concessions wrung from the impotent Manchus were to be restored. Three times, no less, President Wilson of the United States had publicly foreshadowed the peace settlement of justice for all. His famous Fourteen Points (8 January 1918) included a call for an impartial adjustment of colonial claims, taking account of the interests of the population. Admittedly, this was too imprecise for China's needs.

At issue was the sovereignty of the Shantung peninsula, leased to Germany under duress in 1898. The trouble was that the Japanese, who had fought the war on the Allied side, also claimed Shantung. Feeling against Japan reached a climax in May 1919, when student organisations in Peking met to plan a "National Humiliation Day" to commemorate the Japanese Twenty-one Demands of 1915. Violent clashes on the 4th between the students and the Chinese police guarding the Legation Quarter gave a name to what became known as the May 4th Movement. Further demonstrations forced the resignation of the Peking cabinet on 12 June. On 28 June the Chinese delegation to the Versailles conference, lacking instructions from a non-existent government, boycotted the signing ceremony. Instructions did arrive on 10 July, but they were negative as well as late. Suddenly the world woke up to an injustice in a far-off place. At home Woodrow Wilson was attacked on the China issue.

And now the Bolshevik regime entered the scene. In July 1919, its deputy People's Foreign Commissar, Leo Karakhan, issued a Manifesto to the Chinese people. Here was a new voice, expressing unfamiliar but welcome sentiments. All territory wrongfully taken from China by the Tsar's empire was to be returned by the Soviet government. Control of the Chinese Eastern Railway was to be restored to China. The Russian claim to a share in the Boxer Indemnity was to be waived. Extraterritorial rights for Russians living in China would go. There was a *quid* for this generous *quo*, but a modest one: all the Bolsheviks asked was that Peking should recognise their new revolutionary government.

There was the rub. The Peking regime was too weak to recognise any government unless the resident foreign legations approved. They tried to compromise by withdrawing recognition from Tsarist diplomats living on the Russian share of the Boxer Indemnity. Howls of anguish came from the diplomatic corps, and the Chinese politicians decided that there was much to be said for gradualness.

Meanwhile the May 4th Movement was gathering strength and spawning various more or less revolutionary groups of socialist inspiration. One was the New Youth Society, whose members included the Dean of the School of Letters, Ch'en Tu-hsiu, and the University Librarian, Li Ta-chao. These two are worth mentioning because they later became the founders of the Chinese Communist Party. The Librarian's assistant was a tall, vigorous youth who was to wrest control of China from Chiang Kai-shek: Mao Tse-tung. In December 1919 Mao joined a new body, the first of its kind in China—the Society for the Study of Socialism. The forces of the coming struggle were thus assembling that year in Peking while Chiang was otherwise engaged.

What was Chiang doing? ° He was still in command of the Second Detachment of the Cantonese Army, but he didn't like his job and liked it still less as time went on. During one idle spell early in 1919, he asked for home leave and spent most of the year away from his post. He did go to see his mother, but he also spent time in Shanghai and in Tokyo. His best friend at the time was Teng K'eng, the chief of staff of the Cantonese Army, and twice during the summer Chiang wrote to him to tell him what he thought of the

---

° The chronology of this period is unusually obscure, and the two approved biographers contradict each other. I have summarised my own reconstruction of events.

Cantonese. There was no hope of reforming the Second Detachment, he complained. The soldiers' pay was wasted, and he was
ashamed of himself. He wasn't even allowed to choose his own
officers, and any suggestions he made were blocked. Conditions
were deplorable, and he recommended that the Detachment should
be disbanded.

In a second letter, on 9 July, he complained that things were
going from bad to worse, and he was "both physically and mentally
tired". Bandits were rampant in several districts, but because
discipline was so bad and internal dissensions were rife, it had not
been possible to send troops to suppress them. If he, Kai-shek,
didn't leave, people would say that he wanted to hang on to his job
and accuse him of being an adventurer.

This was an early example of a technique Chiang Kai-shek was
to use throughout his career, whenever things were not working out
as he would have wished. In later life his resignations invariably
served the purpose of demonstrating that he was the indispensable
man, so that he always returned with his power enhanced. Even
then, in 1919, both his superior and his hero—the Hakka General
and Sun Yat-sen—pleaded with him to come back and reorganise
the Cantonese Army. But he played hard to get, and didn't yield
until September 1920. Even then, the deciding factor was not the
pleas from his elders, but the assassination of a friend, Chu Ta-fu, by
order of the Kwangsi clique. The coffin was sent to Hong Kong,
where Chiang went to pay homage. Armed with operational plans
he had drawn up for the Cantonese Army to deal with the Kwangsi
force, he returned to Kwangtung province.

But not for long. His rift with the Hakka General was becoming
unbridgeable. In a letter both affectionate and severe, written in
November 1920, Sun Yat-sen tried to persuade him to stay and try
to get on with General Ch'en. Addressing him as "my dear Elder
Brother Kai-shek", as was the Chinese custom regardless of the age
of the writer, Dr. Sun wrote:

> The sudden tragic death of Chu Ta-fu is a loss to me
> comparable to that of my right or left hand. When I look upon
> the members of our party I find very few who are experts in war
> and also loyal. Only you, my Elder Brother, are with us, you
> whose courage and sincerity are equal to those of Chu Ta-fu,
> and your knowledge of war is even better than his. But you have

a very fiery temper and your hatred of mediocrity is excessive. And so it often leads to quarrelling and difficulty in cooperating. As you are shouldering the great and terrible responsibility of our party, you should sacrifice your high ideals a little and try to compromise. This is merely for the sake of our party and has nothing to do with your personal principles. Would you, my Elder Brother, agree with this? Or wouldn't you?

At first, Chiang was inclined to listen to his leader. But he was furious with the Hakka General because he had ignored Chiang's advice and failed to finish off the remnants of the Kwangsi force. Dropping everything, he went to Shanghai and called on Dr. Sun to explain his actions. But Sun Yat-sen was in no mood to listen to the complaints of juniors. As far as he was concerned, Ch'en Chiung-ming had done all he had hoped and more. He had cleared Canton of the Kwangsi clique. What did it matter if some of its misguided troops survived? He, Sun, wanted to go back to Canton and take over again as head of the Military Government. It was Chiang's duty to come with him. Sulkily, Chiang went home to Chi Kou.

Trusting as ever, Dr. Sun had assumed continuing loyalty during his long absence. The situation he found on his return to Canton at the end of November 1920 was not to his liking. He was Director and Minister of the Interior in the restored Military Government, but Ch'en had been feathering his nest and his list of titles was more impressive than Dr. Sun's: Minister of War, Governor of Kwangtung, Commander in Chief of the Kwangtung Army, and High Inspecting Commissioner for Kwangtung and Kwangsi.

On 12 January 1921 Sun summoned all available parliamentarians to a meeting in Canton. There was no quorum, but they voted anyway. Several times already Sun Yat-sen had been cheated of his rightful power as Father of the Revolution. Now he was going to have another try and make it look as legal as possible. In April the rump Parliament duly elected him Provisional President of China— all China—and on 5 May he formally took office.

Although the hagiographers present a picture of close friendship and cooperation between Sun Yat-sen and Chiang Kai-shek, the evidence is clear that Sun was paying no attention to his advice, nor taking the younger man into his confidence. Chiang had strongly advised Sun not to have himself elected by a rump Parliament since the election would lack legal force and in any case would be meaningless at a time when the south was disunited and unresponsive to his authority. First, he argued (as usual) all dissidents must be brought to heel.

Chiang's latest sulk had lasted nearly three months. During that time he was being pressed on all sides to go to Canton and serve his old master. He lost his temper with a Kuomintang emissary and sent him on his way. On 5 January 1921, Chiang wrote apologising for his behaviour. "I have a bad temper and am usually lacking in good manners," wrote Chiang contritely. ". . . I feel most ashamed of myself after careful reflection. I know myself that I have been ridiculous."

Sun's answer expressed forgiveness, but added: "You, my elder brother, are extremely self-willed to an almost incorrigible extent. Whenever you are disappointed at some trifle, you let your anger go unchecked."

After reading his visitor's letter Chiang recorded that he was "on the verge of tears". Yes, he would go to Canton, but against his better judgment—and only when Sun Yat-sen had ordered the Cantonese Army to march on Kwangsi.

But the Hakka General was in no hurry to act; nor was he ready to listen to Sun Yat-sen, let alone Chiang Kai-shek. Having defeated his rivals, he now commanded a big army of several divisions and thought the time had come to settle in business as the warlord of South China.

This was where Peking came in. The rule of the warlords lacked permanence, since ambitious subordinates could always challenge it. There was thus a "law of military natural selection", the outcome of which was ritually respected both by Peking and by the victorious warlord. By and large, the northern warlords had been appointed by Peking in the first place (as provincial governors), with appropriate honours and titles. It suited both sides very well that the fiction of Peking's authority should be maintained. If ever a warlord found himself displaced, Peking would waste no time transferring his titles and honours to his successor, in accordance with the law of military natural selection. Now that Ch'en Chiung-ming had emerged as the strong man of the south, Peking had excellent reasons for recognising the fact in the usual way, even though he had not been appointed by the northern government. The best of these reasons was that Sun Yat-sen was trying to take advantage of Ch'en's military victories and seeking to establish—or re-establish—himself as the rightful President of all China, a claim which Peking could not be expected to concede. On this issue the interests of the Hakka General and of the Peking authorities happily coincided. He wanted the honours, Peking wished to confer them; both sides wanted him to be boss and to cut Dr. Sun down to size.

In Canton that February 1921, Chiang Kai-shek could see all this with blinding clarity, even if the trusting Sun could not. He had come, reluctantly, because the master had summoned him, and also because he was eager for a chance to wipe out the remaining pockets of defiance in Kwangsi. The Director of the Military Government was more worried about his money—that is, his Government's lack of it—than about challenges to his power, which in any case was non-existent. The easiest way he saw of raising money was through the customs duties. The trouble was that the legations and embassies in Peking did not recognise his authority and refused to cooperate. Behind Sun's back, Ch'en was saying that the diplomats were right. That was why Sun Yat-sen was determined to have himself proclaimed Provisional President with at least a semblance of legality, so that this would place him on a footing of equality with the latest holder of the same office in Peking.

Chiang Kai-shek was absolutely against this plan, and said so in a long letter to Dr. Sun on 5 March 1921. This was not the time to elect a President, he wrote. With the Kwangsi enemy still at large and the south-west unconquered, the Parliament lacked a legal basis and there was no quorum. He went on: "After the subduing of the Kwangsi rebels, we could perhaps go forward from the north-east to attack the capital of our enemy." And there followed a sentence full of that sublime self-confidence he was later to display: "The unification of the whole of China is not a difficult task." He ended with a warning not to expect loyalty from Ch'en Chiung-ming.

Sun Yat-sen ignored this letter from the tiresome younger man. As it happened, Chiang Kai-shek did not take part in the Kwangsi campaign. On 14 June his mother died, and he immediately returned to Chekiang. Apart from brief visits to Kwangtung province, he stayed at Chi Kou until her funeral the following November. Though Dr. Sun was not present, he wrote a moving elegy to Mrs. Chiang which was read out at the service.

As Chiang Kai-shek had foretold, Ch'en Chiung-ming was about to turn traitor. Chiang's friend Teng K'eng, chief of staff of the Cantonese Army, was assassinated at Canton station on 21 March 1922. The Hakka General was immediately suspected, and no evidence pointing elsewhere has come to light. Certainly he had reasons for getting rid of Teng K'eng. The murdered man had been loyal to Sun Yat-sen. But there was a stronger reason: by depriving Sun of the most senior military man around, after Ch'en himself, he would force Dr. Sun at least to postpone and possibly to abandon, his proposed northern expedition. Chiang Kai-shek angrily proposed that Sun's thirteen brigades should be diverted secretly to Canton to restore the Generalissimo's authority, then to Kwangsi to mop up, before heading north on the much-delayed expedition.

When the Sun brigades reached Canton in April, Ch'en Chiung-ming sent him a telegram resigning from several of his many posts—a very Chinese way of partially taking his distance. Most of these one-man resignations were accepted, but Sun ordered Ch'en to stay at his post as Minister of War. Ch'en declined: he had moved his forces to new headquarters at Waichow, east of Canton, and was waiting on events.

Chiang was all for attacking Waichow, then cleaning up Kwangsi, but once again Sun Yat-sen overruled him. Chagrined, he went back to Shanghai and wrote a long letter to Ch'en Chiung-ming on 22 April, calling on him to rally to Dr. Sun and join in the northern expedition. There was no reply.

It now turned out that Ch'en had been in secret touch with the powerful northern warlords, who had put their own presidential candidate in office in Peking. From the northern capital a telegram now went out to Sun Yat-sen, urging him to resign. Ch'en Chiung-ming's followers supported this injunction. And on 16 June, doubtless feeling that by now he had constitutional rectitude as well as political and military power behind him, General Ch'en sent his Second Division to attack Dr. Sun's Presidential headquarters, bombarding the adjoining residence in the evident hope of killing the master.

Chiang Kai-shek was in Shanghai at the time, but later recorded that Ch'en Chiung-ming had offered his troops $200,000 and three days' licence to loot if they succeeded in killing the President. Stubborn to the end, Dr. Sun wanted to stay at his post, but he finally yielded to pressure from his staff and escaped—at one point walking alongside a rebel detachment which did not recognise him.

Sun Yat-sen's first place of refuge was the gunboat *Yung Feng* ("Everlasting Prosperity"), anchored at Whampoa. Although Dr. Sun had ignored his advice, and landed himself in this mess partly as a result, Chiang Kai-shek was nothing if not loyal. Speeding down from Shanghai, he joined his leader. The gunboat was their abode for fifty-six days. The heat was tropical, the food scarce, the water supply low. At night Chiang would slip ashore in search of food. By day he took his turn to sweep and scrub the deck.

They might have escaped shortly after taking refuge in the gunboat, but both clung to the hope that Chiang's colleague, Hsu Ch'ung-chih, who had been appointed to command the expeditionary force, would subdue Ch'en Chiung-ming. But victory went to the Hakka General. The bad news reached Sun and Chiang on 6 August with further details on the 7th. Two days later their spies reported another plot to have Dr. Sun murdered. Finally the captain of a British warship agreed to escort Sun and his small band of followers to Hong Kong, whence they went on to Shanghai.

In this further period of adversity, in the company of one whose loyalty (though not his obedience) had never wavered, Sun seems finally to have decided that Chiang Kai-shek was the man most likely henceforth to advise him well and support him steadfastly.

Chiang Kai-shek's meteoric rise was soon to begin.

5. Enter the Comintern

Though defeated, Hsu Ch'ung-chih had escaped into Fukien with part of his force. On 13 October 1922 he captured Foochow, and Sun Yat-sen immediately rewarded him by appointing him Commander-in-Chief, with Chiang Kai-shek as his Chief of Staff. Joined by other forces, the loyal army reached Canton on 15 December, and Ch'en Chiung-ming went into hiding. Some weeks of pacification followed, and on 21 January 1923, conditions were calm enough for Sun to return. He immediately restored the military government.

The ever-volatile Chiang was always having to be called to order or summoned to return. Before the recapture of Canton he had found a reason to go to Shanghai, and Sun wrote him perhaps the severest of all his letters:

What rubbish you talk! Since I could not go to Fukien myself, I have entrusted you with the responsibility of punishing the traitors. How could you so hurriedly think of giving it up like that? Things do not happen as we wish eight or nine times out of ten. To ensure success, it always depends upon your fortitude and persistence, your disregard of jealousy and hard work. . . . Don't you, my Elder Brother, remember the days when we were in the gunboat? All day long we could only sleep and eat, hoping to hear good news. . . . Whatever difficulties you meet, whatever hardships you suffer, do stay in the Army as long as I am struggling here.

Chiang did come back, but as soon as Dr. Sun had restored the Military Government, Chiang asked for indefinite leave to have his eyes tested in Shanghai. From the correspondence of that period, it does seem that his eyes were giving him trouble, although just what was wrong was never spelt out. With its vice, its money, and its power, the great port never ceased to fascinate Chiang Kai-shek. His revolutionary mentor, General Ch'en Ch'i-mei, had introduced him to the "blue chamber" district, with its brothels for all purses. There, at about this time, he met a harlot who particularly captivated him, Ch'en Chieh-ju. Whenever Chiang stayed in Shanghai during this period of his poverty-stricken youth, he lived in a windowless cubicle and worked as a jobber on the Shanghai stock exchange. The blue chambers were his glamorous refuge from these sordid surroundings. Chiang and Ch'en were lawfully married, and they lived together, when his official duties permitted, until— for reasons of heart as well as of state—he wooed and won Soong Mayling. During the Northern Expedition a few years later, Ch'en Chieh-ju played a role in some respects analogous to that of Soong Mayling in Chiang's later career. Nature had gifted her with intelligence as well as beauty, and Chiang's friends, and later his subordinates, treated her with great respect.

In the autumn of 1927, with the powerful support of the notorious Tu Yueh-sheng, leader of the Green Society, who by then had become Chiang Kai-shek's protector, she went to live in the United States. It was clear to those who met her that she was not at all short of money. Having settled down, she enrolled at Columbia University in New York, where she obtained a doctorate. She then moved to the West Coast and bought a house near San Francisco. In 1967, having written her autobiography, she was planning to offer it to a New York publisher when the Taiwan authorities had wind of her intentions. A large sum was produced to buy the copyright from her and kill her publishing plans. Richer still as a result, Ch'en Chieh-ju moved to Hong Kong, where she died in 1971. Her remains were returned to California, where she was buried.

Chiang, then, had other things to keep him in Shanghai besides his eyesight. He did not return to Canton until 20 April, and immediately got involved in fighting off further military rebellions against Dr. Sun. In the welter of attack and counter-attack, of shifting loyalties and fortunes, of rivalries and conflicting ambitions, few things were certain. One was that Sun Yat-sen's hold on power was never more than precarious, and never uncontested. It was about this time that he sought to regenerate his unsatisfactory fortunes through new allies: the leaders of the Bolshevik regime in Moscow.

On 4 July 1918, when Lenin and his followers had been in power only a few months, his Foreign Commissar, Chicherin, announced that Soviet Russia unilaterally renounced all the Tsar's "unequal" treaties with China, and agreements with Japan and other countries at China's expense. In addition to Leo Karakhan's manifesto of 25 July 1919, yet another conciliatory declaration came on 27 September 1920, this time in a formal note to Peking.

These repeated declarations of friendly intent naturally pleased all Chinese. In those early days, the Russians were inclined to dismiss Sun Yat-sen and his Kuomintang as a southern clique of little importance. But all Soviet overtures in Peking were rebuffed by various governments of the day, under pressure from Western embassies and Japan. The Soviet leaders therefore decided to seek links with the KMT. In time, as Sun realised that his power base was insecure and that he could not look to the Western powers, he was ready to respond to Soviet overtures.

Soviet interests were not necessarily represented by Soviet citizens. Lenin had set up the Comintern in 1919 to carry the Revolution to the farthest corners of the world. Men and women of all nationalities could and did serve the revolution. Thus one of the first Comintern agents in China was H. Sneevliet, a Dutchman travelling under the alias of Maring. Sneevliet-Maring reached China in the spring of 1921 and went south to Kwangsi to meet Sun Yat-sen, who deeply impressed him, and convinced him that the

Kuomintang was the main conduit line of Chinese nationalism. He was still more impressed when seamen went on strike in Canton and Hong Kong in January 1922 and he discovered that the Kuomintang was already well ensconced in the new Chinese trade-union movement.

Back in Moscow, Maring recommended that the Chinese Communists should enter the Kuomintang and try to gain control of it from within. This was a reversal of the previous line, based on the reports of the very first Soviet agents to enter China after the Russian Revolution, who had advocated close links with the northern warlords. As Sun had been forced out of Canton, Maring had a further meeting with him in Shanghai in August 1922. His advice to the Chinese leader was the opposite of Chiang Kai-shek's. Chiang was always calling for military action; Maring recommended the Communist techniques of mass propaganda and organisation. It seemed to Maring that Sun Yat-sen was taking it all in.

What of the Chinese Communists? How Chinese was their party? Certainly not one of the founders of the Chinese Communist Party spoke Russian or had learnt his Marxism-Leninism in Russia, although some—including Chou En-lai and Chu Teh—were students in France. The others, among them Mao Tse-tung, Li Ta-chao, and Ch'en Tu-hsiu, knew no Western languages and had never travelled outside China. Still, Marxism and Marxism-Leninism were non-Chinese ideas imported into China, and Lenin's Comintern played a leading role in the creation of the party. In fact, it was Maring, the Dutch agitator, and another Comintern man, the Russian Gregor Voitinsky, who brought the scattered Marxist groups together to attend the inaugural First Congress of the Chinese Communist Party on 1 July 1921. Both the Comintern men were present, to put the Chinese delegates right when they strayed. Twelve Chinese were there, and one of them was Mao. But neither of the real founders of Chinese Communism—Ch'en Tu-hsiu and Li Ta-chao—was present. Ch'en went on to be the party's first Secretary-General, but in time left the party. Li Ta-chao was later strangled by the police in Peking. At least six of the original twelve later defected. For that matter, Maring himself was to drop out.

The party, tiny and fragile as it was, was originally simply an instrument at the disposal of Lenin's Comintern. This became clear in August 1922, when Maring, after his second meeting with Sun Yat-sen, formally proposed that each member of the Communist

Party should also join the Kuomintang. Despite violent opposition from the party, the proposal was carried. Although Sun ruled out any alliance or coalition between his KMT and the CP, he was ready to please the Russians by welcoming Communists who joined as individuals.

The match had been made, but the wedding had to take place and the marriage to be consummated. Moscow now sent one of its leading diplomats, Adolph Abramovitch Joffe, who had been ambassador in Berlin, to China in August 1922. He failed to establish diplomatic relations between Peking and Moscow, and went on to Shanghai for meetings with Sun Yat-sen. On 26 January 1923 the Sun-Joffe communiqué was published. It recorded mutual agreement that conditions did not exist in China either for communism or for a Soviet system. The most urgent and important problems were unification and national independence. The Russians renounced extraterritorial privileges but kept the Chinese Eastern Railway, which they had appropriated in 1917.

There was evidently an understanding between Sun and Joffe that the Soviet Communists should reorganise the KMT on Communist lines, and on 6 October 1923, the Soviet Politburo sent an able man, Borodin, to do just that. Like so many Russian revolutionaries at that time Borodin was using a *nom de guerre*: a Jew like Joffe, his real name was Michael Grusenberg. He was not a Russian, but a Lithuanian.

The reorganisation of the Kuomintang was ratified at its First Congress in Canton in January 1924. Henceforth the Kuomintang had a National Party Congress, which was supposed to meet every two years, a Central Executive Committee meeting every six months, and a small Standing Committee (of five to nine members) —the equivalent of the normal Communist Political Bureau. The Communists did well out of these changes. Their party was still very small. Now its members could burrow within the larger KMT.

This, then, is the background to the next phase of Chiang Kai-shek's career.

Sun Yat-sen had made his own decision about working with the Russians and the Chinese Communists, but he wanted his own man's report on the revolutionary government in the Soviet Union. The man he chose was Chiang.

In 1957, with the benefit of thirty-four years' hindsight, Chiang

Kai-shek published his own account of his stay in Moscow—*Soviet Russia in China: A Summing Up at Seventy.* Tersely written (not by himself, though he closely supervised the draft, leaving it to his wife to check the English translation), it fills in details left out by the approved biographers.

On 5 August 1923, Chiang discussed arrangements with Maring in Shanghai. He reached Moscow on 2 September, accompanied by three assistants. He stayed in Russia—mainly in the capital—until 29 November, when he and his companions started on the long journey home, reaching Shanghai on 15 December.

The terms of reference of the mission were to study the post-revolutionary party system and the political and military organisations. It is clear, even from the approved biographies, that Chiang was profoundly disillusioned with revolutionary Russia at first hand. His own account explains why. Addressing the executive committee of the Comintern, he expressed confidence that the Chinese national revolution, based on fulfillment of Sun Yat-sen's Three Principles of the People, would succeed in two or three years' time. He declared that the Comintern did not understand the nature of the revolutionary movement in China and invited it to send more men to find out for themselves. While still in Moscow, he read a resolution of the Comintern about the Kuomintang, and "I was profoundly disappointed". Hsiung has him exclaiming: "Pooh! Look at what it says! To be so ignorant of a friendly party. How could it be the centre of world revolution?"

In Petrograd, Chiang and his companions inspected the Naval Academy and other service schools as well as the Kronstadt naval base. Nothing was said about the Kronstadt mutiny two years earlier, but "judging by the attitude of the local population and naval personnel . . . [one] could see that the revolt had left deep scars".

They saw ministries and local soviets and attended a session of the Moscow Soviet Congress. "I easily perceived that fierce struggles, both open and secret, were going on among various sections of the Russian society and among the Russian Communists themselves. I became more convinced than ever that Soviet political institutions were instruments of tyranny and terror and basically incompatible with Kuomintang's political system which is based on the Three People's Principles. This was something that I had to go to Russia to find out; I could never have imagined it if I had remained in China." The euphemistic reference to the Kuomintang (before it had acquired its own power to oppress) does not invalidate his assessment of the Soviet system.

Chiang had another reason to be disillusioned. He had tried to pin the Russians down on territorial questions inherited from the Tsarist empire, especially Outer Mongolia. In the Sun-Joffe communiqué the previous January, the Soviet diplomat had declared that his country "has no intention of practising imperialist policies in Outer Mongolia or causing its separation from China". But whenever Chiang brought the subject up, his Russian hosts became evasive or adamant. In fact, the Soviet authorities had sponsored a Mongolian People's Revolutionary Government on 6 July 1919, and showed no signs of slackening their grip.

Chiang had hoped to meet Lenin, but the Bolshevik leader was already in the coma that would end in death. Instead, Chiang met Chicherin, Kamenev, Zinoviev, Radek, and Trotsky—especially Trotsky, with whom he had several long conversations. He was struck by the fact that so many of the Soviet leaders who expressed esteem for Dr. Sun and seemed most sincere in their desire for cooperation with the Kuomintang were Jews. Quoting Lenin, Trotsky said Russia would give the utmost moral and material help to colonies and subcolonies in their revolutionary wars against capitalist imperialism, but would never despatch Soviet troops. He added a message for Dr. Sun: "Except direct participation by Soviet troops, Soviet Russia will do her best to help China in her National Revolution by giving her positive assistance in the form of weapons and economic aid."

With Lenin gravely ill, Chiang observed the struggle for power between the "internationalist clique headed by Trotsky and the domestic organisational clique headed by Stalin" (whom he does not appear to have met). What worried him was the thought that Sino-Soviet cooperation was built on frail foundations, at the mercy of the struggle for the succession in Moscow. Moreover, he thought, once the Russian Revolution had consolidated itself, the regime would probably resume the imperial ambitions of the Tsars.

Chiang Kai-shek reported on all this in writing on his return to Shanghai. In his account, Chiang does not reproduce this report, but he quotes from an explanatory letter to a senior member of the Kuomintang, despatched from Fenghua on 14 March 1924. The Russian Communist Party was not to be trusted, he wrote. The Chi-

nese Communists he had met in Russia always spoke slanderously of
Dr. Sun. He went on:

> The Russian Communist Party, in its dealings with China,
> has only one aim, namely to make the Chinese Communist Party
> its chosen instrument. It does not believe that our Party can
> really cooperate with it for long for the sake of ensuring success
> for both parties. It is the policy of the Russian Communist Party
> to turn the lands inhabited by the Manchus, Mongols, Moslems
> and Tibetans into parts of the Soviet domain; it may harbour
> sinister designs even on China proper.

Copies of Chiang's letter were circulated among members of the
KMT's standing committee. Neither the letter nor his report to Sun
Yat-sen had the slightest effect in the prevailing atmosphere of
euphoria over cooperation with the Communists. Michael Borodin
had arrived in Canton while he was away, and it was on the advice
of the man to whom Chiang sent his letter some weeks later—Liao
Chung-k'ai—that Dr. Sun had appointed Borodin political adviser
to the Kuomintang.

Dr. Sun seems to have been completely captivated by Borodin's
charm and engaging personality. A typical cosmopolitan and
revolutionary adventurer, Grusenberg had been taken to America as
a child and educated there. Under the name of Berg, he ran a
business school in Chicago, reading himself into Marxism. Borodin
was his name as an agitator. As such, the Comintern had sent him to
Mexico, to Scotland (whence he was expelled), then to Turkey,
where he won his way into Mustapha Kemal's confidence. He had
arrived with a warm letter of introduction from Leo Karakhan, the
man who had publicly renounced Russia's extraterritorial rights.
Not only did Borodin have charm, but he exuded sincerity and quite
won over the Chinese leader by declaring his own belief in and full
support for the Three People's Principles.

Chiang had been expected to provide a factual and informative
report, to smooth the path of cooperation—not a denunciation of
China's new friends. He got back in mid-December, probably too
late to reverse the course of events. He might have done better if he
had gone to Canton to report in person to his leader. Instead, he
hurried off to Chi Kou to offer religious homage to his mother. (It
seems likely, though the point remains obscure, that he wrote his

report to Dr. Sun on the long train journey across the Siberian steppes.)

Once again Sun Yat-sen started showing impatience with Chiang's moody indiscipline, and on 24 December 1923 he shot off a cable:

> *To my Elder Brother Chiang Kai-shek:*
> You have on your shoulders an extremely heavy responsibility from this trip. Please come to Canton immediately to report all matters, and plan in detail the scheme for Sino-Russian cooperation. Your opinion, which we respect, about the political situation and your proposals we want to discuss with you in person.

Reluctantly and in his own good time, Kai-shek obeyed this summons. He explained that he too, before going to Russia, had believed the Russians were sincere in their offer to help the Kuomintang. But he had come back completely disillusioned. In the short run, alignment with Russia and the admission of Chinese Communists into the party might prove useful in the fight against Western colonialism. But in the long run, Soviet Russia's world revolutionary programme was even more dangerous to China's independence than the old colonialism.

As usual, Dr. Sun rejected Chiang's advice. Cooperation with the Communists was imperative because of current revolutionary realities. There was only one way to prevent the Chinese Communists from stirring up class conflicts and sabotaging the national revolution, and that was to place them under the control and leadership of the Kuomintang. That way the Northern Expedition could be launched, and once it had succeeded, the Three People's Principles could be implemented. By then it would be too late for the Chinese Communists to disrupt the national revolution, if that was their aim.

Chiang tried in vain to inject caution into the leader's mind, on the basis of what he had seen at first hand in Russia. In return came a flood of rhetorical questions. Hadn't Soviet Russia recognised the Kuomintang as the only party that could lead the national revolution? Hadn't the Russians urged the Chinese Communists to join the KMT and accept its leadership? Hadn't Joffe admitted that Communism wouldn't work in China?

According to the official archives of the Kuomintang, Sun Yat-sen's original policy formula was *lien ê jung kung* ("allying with Russia and tolerating the Communists"). Typically, the Chinese Communists interpreted this formula in their own way as "an alliance with both Russia and the Chinese Communist Party".

Heavy with misgivings, Chiang attended the first National Congress of the Kuomintang, held in Canton a few days after his arrival. He could see that non-Communist members of the Kuomintang had already come under the influence of the new Communist members, who used their special relationship with the Soviet Union to best advantage. He heard Li Ta-chao, the first Communist to join the KMT, praise his new colleagues. "We join this party," he said soothingly, "as individuals, not as a body. We may be said to have dual membership. But it may not be said of the Kuomintang that there is a party within a party. . . . Our joining this party and at the same time keeping our membership in the Communist Party is an open and honourable action, not a surreptitious move."

Li Ta-chao's words had the desired effect, Chiang recorded. Any remaining Kuomintang suspicions were disarmed, and no special precautions were taken. Working through secret cells, the Communists rapidly extended their control and plotted dissension and disruption from within.

The Congress duly adopted the Constitution drafted by Borodin. Li Ta-chao and Mao Tse-tung were among the eight Communists elected to the Central Executive or Supervisory committees. Towards the close, on 24 January, Chiang Kai-shek was appointed Chairman of the preparatory committee for a proposed Military Academy at Whampoa Island, about fourteen miles from Canton. He was named as Commandant-Designate. So sceptical had he become about collaborating with the Communists, however, that he went into one of his periodical sulks, declined the appointment, turned the preparatory work over to Liao Chung-k'ai, and went home to Chi Kou. Once more, Dr. Sun deluged him with letters and telegrams, reminding him in ever more peremptory tones of his revolutionary duty of obedience. The calendar had reached April before he decided to obey and returned to Canton.

In Dr. Sun's mind, the Military Academy was to be the indispensable instrument of national unification. He badly needed a well-trained national army if he was ever to overcome rival warlords. In this the Russians had encouraged him, with promises of arms and training. While in Russia, Chiang Kai-shek had discussed the technical details at length with the Red Army chiefs. On his way back to Vladivostok, he had met the Commander-in-Chief of the Siberian Army, General Vasili K. Bluecher. When he had finally made up his mind to accept the job of Commandant at Whampoa, he sought the services of Bluecher as his Chief of Staff. The Russians agreed, and Bluecher turned up, using the pseudonym of Galen. Liao Chung-k'ai was appointed Political Commissar, with an able young French-educated Communist as his deputy. Fame later awaited the deputy, whose name was Chou En-lai.

Chiang held Bluecher in high esteem. "In my opinion," he was to write, "he was an outstanding Russian general as well as a reasonable man and a good friend. What was most unusual about him was that he had none of the traits associated with Bolsheviks." In later years, Chiang asked Stalin several times to send Galen back. Most of these requests went unacknowledged, but in 1939 the Soviet dictator revealed to a Kuomintang emissary that the general had been executed for "succumbing to the charms of a Japanese woman spy".

On 16 June 1924, Dr. Sun declared the Whampoa Military Academy open, setting the seal on military and political cooperation between the Nationalists and the Communists and the partnership between Chinese and Russians.

6. Sun's Death, and After

Against the treachery and skulduggery of the times, Dr. Sun Yat-sen continued to offer an example of nobility and trusting simplicity. Nobody else seemed in a hurry to imitate him. Aged fifty-eight and in the wake of the Kuomintang's First Congress, he turned his mind again to fundamental ideas. Everyone knew that his revolution meant evicting the Manchus, ending the unequal treaties, and asserting China's identity and sovereignty. But these aspirations were vague. The Communists, tiny in numbers, had entered the KMT in full possession of an ideology, knowing what they wanted and well instructed in the techniques of getting it. But what of the Kuomintang itself? What exactly did it stand for?

Dr. Sun's Three Principles of the People—the *San Min Chu I*—had been stated but left unexplained. He now set out to remedy this deficiency, in a series of weekly lectures spread over several months.°

Sun Yat-sen has been much criticised—and even dismissed—as a poor ideologist, but the criticism is not entirely fair. To start with, the true meaning of the Three Principles is itself rather cloudy because of the paradoxical "concrete vagueness" of the Chinese language.† Thus the First Principle—usually translated as Nationalism—is expressed in two Chinese characters, *Min Tsu*, meaning literally People's Race, and more generally held to mean National Solidarity. The Second, usually listed as Democracy, has a similarly tortuous derivation from two characters pronounced *Min Ch'üan* and meaning People's Rights. As for the Third, it has sometimes been rendered as Social Welfare or Socialism, and Dr. Sun himself has been quoted as saying it was nothing short of Communism; but the literal meaning of People's Livelihood (*Min Sheng*) is certainly closer to the spirit of the original.

Dr. Sun was trying to draw on foreign political ideas, including those of Rousseau, Jefferson, and Marx, and adapt them to China's

---

° One should perhaps not be too severe with the unfortunate Sun Yat-sen. He had made a start about two years earlier on a book, *Reconstruction of the State*, of which Part I, "The Principle of Nationalism", had already gone to press, and he had written portions of the rest. Then on 16 June 1922, the Hakka General Ch'en Chiung-ming went into revolt, turning his guns on Dr. Sun's headquarters. "My notes and manuscripts which represented the mental labour of years and hundreds of foreign books which I had collected for reference were all destroyed by fire. It was a distressing loss." (From Sun's preface, dated Canton 30 March 1924, to the first volume of his then current series of lectures: *San Min Chu I*, [Taipei: China Publishing Company, undated].) In *Soviet Russia and China*, Chiang Kai-shek wrongly dates the first lecture 30 March (p. 28), but this was the date of publication of the first volume; the first lecture was in fact delivered on 27 January 1924.

Sun had intended to devote six lectures to each Principle. The first two had their full quota, but the third was given only four lectures. Years later, the Nationalist government on Taiwan published a revised edition of *San Min Chu I* with two supplementary chapters by Chiang Kai-shek covering the ground Chiang believed Sun had intended to cover in the missing lectures, together with further thoughts of his own.

† In principle, the written language is monosyllabic, but in practice the spoken language is polysyllabic, since two or more monosyllabic ideographs cohere to form a longer word. Most abstract concepts—such as *nationalism* or *democracy*—are thus formed by separate components brought together, but each of which, taken singly, suggests a concreteness which the whole lacks. For an excellent discussion of this peculiarity, see Robert Elegant, *The Centre of the World* (London, 1963), pp. 155–56.

historical experience and actual condition. Although the fourteen lectures on the Three Principles of the People are occasionally naïve and do not rank with the greatest works of the political philosopher's intellect, there is a good deal of solid Chinese common sense in them.

Sun's most ingenious synthesis of Western and Chinese institutions was a new form of governmental structure: the so-called five branches of government—Legislative, Judiciary, Executive, Civil Service Examinations, and Censorship (or Control). Each was to have its elected Council (*Yüan*), but the people were to retain ultimate sovereignty through the exercise of four "powers": to vote (suffrage), to remove officials (recall), to initiate proposals (initiative), and to vote on major issues (referendum). A serious weakness was that he did not work out in any detail just *how* the people were to exercise their four powers.

In the confusion and brutality of the times, Dr. Sun's ideas made little impact. In 1924, however, the main problem for him was not the distant Utopia of his Three Principles, but how to gain control over the Revolution he had inspired. In the short term, he spelled out a revolutionary method in the form of a *General Outline of National Reconstruction*, issued on 12 April 1924, which laid down the use of force to remove obstacles, and peaceful means to resolve social and economic problems and prevent class struggle and social unrest. Chiang called the General Outline "the Magna Carta of our National Revolution", and was to invoke it after Sun's death as his licence to kill Communists.

Although forced into deals of opportunity with the warlords and their mercenary armies, Dr. Sun put his faith in the Military Academy at Whampoa as the key to final victory. Having established a seemly disinterest by turning down the job, Chiang Kai-shek threw himself into it with great energy and dedication once he had made a start. It must have been obvious to him that the post was a stepping stone to great power. In KMT politics hitherto, his youth and junior status and his natural distaste for politics had kept him out of the higher councils. Whether his advice was sought or merely tendered, it was not followed, as a rule. But as the man named to train the national army of the future, his stature was bound to grow. Now at last he could start building an army to serve China's central authority, should it ever be established, and not the greed and rapacity of an individual warlord. It is doubtful at that time Chiang was thinking of supreme personal power except in the very long term. For Sun Yat-sen was still alive, and indeed by political norms, fairly young at fifty-eight.

In some ways, Chiang's tenure as Commandant irresistibly recalls Francisco Franco's, only four years later, as Commandant of the new General Military Academy at Saragossa, after initially turning the job down. Both men were stern but imaginative disciplinarians, both were concerned to destroy provincialism ("regionalism", it was called in Spain) and promote national unity, and both were to become dictators. In terms of enduring success, however, the parallel breaks down.

Opening the Academy on 16 June 1924, Dr. Sun spelled out its purpose in simple and striking words:

> The foundation for our Republic scarcely exists. The reason is a simple one: our Revolution has been carried on by the struggles of a revolutionary party but not by a revolutionary army. Because of the lack of a revolutionary army, the Republic has been mismanaged by warlords and bureaucrats. Our Revolution will never succeed if this continues. With the establishment of this school a new hope is born for us today. From now on a new era has begun for our Revolution. This school is the basis of the Revolutionary Army of which you students form the nucleus.

Rising daily at 5 A.M., Chiang would dust and tidy his bedroom and start on a round of inspection, severely admonishing those still in bed. The first 500 cadets, chosen from 3,000 applicants by open examination, had been enrolled on 5 May, five or six weeks before the formal opening. Funds were short and the instructors were of uneven quality. Chiang's Russian friend, General "Galen", headed the Soviet team, and with Borodin's advice concentrated on turning out an indoctrinated force on the model of Trotsky's Red Army, able to goose-step on formal drills but skilled in modern warfare—above all, with a political purpose.

The cadets must have been confused by rival doctrines. The Communists brought zeal and Soviet backing into their lectures. But the Kuomintang had the numbers, and its men, too, were busy propagating Dr. Sun's newly defined ideology. On the KMT side, however, there were already early signs of ideological disunity. The

Academy's Political Commissar, Liao Chung-k'ai, represented the Left faction, which favoured all-out collaboration with the Russians and the Chinese Communists. The head of the party's Propaganda Department, Wang Ching-wei, was the middle-of-the-road man who put the KMT first and supported the Russian connection only because Dr. Sun advocated it. Then there was Hu Han-min, on the conservative Right, who was frankly against it.

Chiang Kai-shek's own position was ambiguous and puzzled his associates. Before going to Moscow, he had been full of enthusiasm for collaboration with the Bolsheviks. The fact that he had returned disillusioned was not generally known. Sun Yat-sen had ignored his adverse report, and Liao Chung-k'ai had taken no notice of his letter (quoted in the last chapter). He had not yet decided to oppose the Communists openly, was working closely with the Russians—especially "Galen"—and was generally regarded as a leftist. The Academy was short of funds because the government itself was poor.

Two private armies from Yunnan and Kwangsi occupied Canton at that time. They were officially regarded as "friendly" because they had helped put down Ch'en Chiung-ming. Actually, the two commanders, Yang and Liu, were not particularly interested in the Revolution but in lining their own pockets. In common with bigger warlords and gangsters elsewhere, they levied illegal taxes (but was anything "legal" in Canton?), and extorted protection money from the prosperous local merchants. Sun's taxing and enforcement powers were limited, and Yang and Liu were ill-disposed towards an Academy which was turning out the kind of officer that seemed bound to make trouble for the warlords. So they kept whatever they grabbed for themselves.

Sun was also still being prevented from getting his share of Customs dues. The Peking government's right to keep any surplus from Customs after repayment of the Boxer Indemnity was recognised by the Powers who benefited. In the spring of 1923, Dr. Sun had requested permission to keep the Canton Customs surplus for his government. The Powers turned down his request, and in December he announced that he would seize the surplus by force. The Powers' answer, at Britain's instigation, was to send a powerful international naval flotilla off Canton. Outraged, Dr. Sun called a press conference to declare that if the Powers would not help him, he would turn to Soviet Russia. When a Labour government came to power in Britain in January 1924, his hopes were raised and he cabled the Kuomintang's congratulations to Ramsay MacDonald, but MacDonald did not acknowledge them. The First Congress of the KMT was in session at the time, and it was still sitting the following day when the news of Lenin's death reached Canton. Off went another cable—this time to Moscow—and this one brought a warm telegram of thanks from Chicherin. Psychologically, the atmosphere could not have been more favourable to collaboration with Moscow.

The merchants of Canton looked upon Sun's "Central Government" with particularly jaundiced eyes. Not only did this dubiously constituted authority, having failed to get a share of the Customs dues, propose to levy fresh taxes on them, but it was in league with foreign and home-grown Communists. Tax us, the merchants threatened in May 1924, and we'll strike. Their resolve was strengthened on 29 June, four weeks after the Canton City branch of the KMT had presented a petition proposing a vote of censure on the Communist members of the party. Chiang himself had praised the Russian Communists in a public speech.

A few weeks later, disquieting reports reached Sun's ears: the merchants were arming a private army of 9,000 for a rising against his government. A Norwegian ship carrying that number of rifles was about to steam into Canton harbour. This new challenge interrupted Dr. Sun's lectures. What to do? Most of the leader's trusted commanders were otherwise engaged: he turned to Chiang Kai-shek.

The crisis that followed had a comic-opera flavour to it. Ever intransigent, Chiang sent his armed students to board the Norwegian ship and transferred the rifles to the Military Academy. The merchants duly went on strike; Chiang countered by proclaiming martial law. In Peking, confused events drew Sun like a magnet. He was really going to have to launch that long-delayed Northern Expedition, but money was short and the merchants had it. Surely a bargain could be struck? The perfidious Yang, head of the "friendly" Yunnanese army, whispered his poisoned advice: give the merchants their rifles, he said, and I shall collect a fine of $1,000,000 (Chinese silver) from them.

This was not the kind of advice Chiang Kai-shek ever relished. Stand firm, he counter-counselled: don't trust the merchants. And now the British Consul-General in Canton intervened. Fire on the merchants, he warned, and the Royal Navy will bombard the

Chinese army. Distracted and near panic, Sun wrote to Chiang on 9 September: "Kwangtung is now a place of death." The British could reduce his headquarters to ashes, and the gunboat *Yung Feng* and the Military Academy, too, with a few broadsides. On the East River, Ch'en Chiung-ming had launched an attack. And the Yunnan and Kwangsi armies were disobedient and greedy.

"We must discard everything," Sun's letter went on, "to find a new way of life. Now the best way is the Northern Punitive Expedition. . . . We must resolve to fight forward on our long trail. To use battlefields as our training school will yield wonderful results. Comrades of our Party must not hesitate."

Flight—even in the form of a Northern Expedition—was not Chiang's inclination. While Sun Yat-sen moved his headquarters and a few faithful troops to Shiuchow, leaving Hu Han-min in nominal military command, Chiang settled down to defiance at Whampoa. It was his turn to bombard Sun with telegrams, this time urging reinforcements. On 9 October Sun replied in secret code, ordering Chiang to leave Whampoa and join in. "Act immediately," he urged. "I will never go back to relieve Canton. Decide instantly and hesitate no more."

Still, Chiang stood his ground. "I have determined to defend this isolated island until death," he replied, "and now await your early return with your army to relieve us." He proposed to hand the arms to Hsu Ch'ung-chih for safe keeping.

Meanwhile the merchants had been haggling with some success. Under Yang's persuasion, Sun agreed to reduce the fine by half, then to $200,000. Now, rightly sizing up the situation, they talked Hu Han-min into accepting the $200,000 not as a fine but a *loan*. Sun agreed and ordered Chiang to hand over the arms to the merchants. In great and bitter gloom, he complied.

Sun's cable, Chiang's reply, Sun's order, and Chiang's compliance had all been compressed into that 9th day of October. Next day was the Double Tenth—the day of the Revolution—and the merchants' soldiers turned their new rifles on the loyal troops, killing several. At last Sun decided Chiang might have been right after all. On the 13th, he appointed Chiang Head of the Training Department at Cantonese Army headquarters. Reinforcements came from Shiuchow, and Chiang led his men into battle, routing the Merchants' Corps in two days of street fighting. On 17 October, the strike had been broken and order restored.

What of the Northern Punitive Expedition? There must have been times when even those most eager for it were discouraged. The traditional wisdom said there could not be two suns in the sky; yet China in 1924 had two governments, each claiming legitimacy, and it was not the Canton government that attracted international recognition. For that matter, neither government could impose a more than ceremonial authority upon the lawless warlords, those *tuchün*, or military governors, who pillaged the country and lived by the sword.

All this time, the situation in northern China was quite as confused as in the south. Three major figures dominated the struggle for power in the north. They were called Wu, Chang, and Feng. Wu controlled Peking and the surrounding province. Chang was the Manchurian warlord, whose title was "Commander-in-Chief of the Eastern Provinces". Feng, at that time a subordinate of Wu's, was to become warlord of the north-west. They were a study in contrasts. Wu, the scholar-general, had been a regular army officer; his long, rather sensitive face was crowned by a crew cut, and in common with most of his peers, he wore a moustache. Chang, his squat rather cruel face sporting a drooping moustache, had been a brigand during the Russo-Japanese war and on a Japanese payroll. Later, as an officer in the Chinese regular army, he had risen to be military governor of one of the Manchurian provinces.

The most picturesque was Feng. A big fat jovial man with an immensely broad face and a frame of great power, he was known as "the Christian general". But many people, after the events about to be described, thought a better name for him would be "the treacherous general". One way he had of displaying his Christian credentials was by baptising his troops *en masse* with a hose. As the effective head of the Peking province clique, Wu had put his own man in office as President of the Republic through a vote in Parliament on 5 October 1923, when only 33 out of 513 members present had voted for Sun Yat-sen. But then, each of the 480 who had supported Wu's man had received a bribe of $5,000.

Wu was determined to keep Dr. Sun down, and Feng was at his command. Chang of Manchuria was primarily worried about the Chinese Eastern Railway, which ran through "his" territory. The Russians were playing the Kuomintang card for all it was worth, but they were courting Peking as well. Who could blame them in the prevailing anarchy? Diplomatic relations had been agreed on 31 May 1924, and as part of the deal the Eastern Railway was to be jointly administered pending a later settlement. When Chang objected, the Russians told him they would use force if necessary, so he signed a separate agreement with them on 20 September.

In Canton two days earlier, the ever-optimistic Dr. Sun had announced the launching of his Northern Expedition, but it was of course frustrated by the Canton merchants' rebellion. A confused struggle was going on in the North, with Wu and Feng in alliance against Chang.

Then came the betrayal. Suddenly in mid-October, Feng turned his men around and marched on Peking. On the 25th, he seized the city. Wu was banished to a minor and distant post. Chang of Manchuria collected a few more titles with Feng's blessing, and Feng put his own puppet in office as President.

Why had Feng done it? James E. Sheridan, who reconstructed Feng's career with great and scholarly skill, found him disgruntled both over pay and over his subordinate role under Wu. But, says Sheridan, there was more to it than that. Japanese gold seems in fact to have been the inducing factor, and the changes in Peking suited them well. In these events, Sun Yat-sen saw another opportunity to set up the nationalistic and democratic Republic of his dreams. The treacherous Feng invited him to Peking. Should Dr. Sun make the journey? On the face of it, circumstances were far from propitious. Dr. Sun's views were well-known and not at all acceptable to the northern warlords. One thing they took particular exception to was the notion that they should go, yielding to constitutional government. The pro-Japanese faction was strong. Surely danger as well as dissension awaited him. Dr. Sun summoned his followers to Canton and sought their advice. All tried to dissuade him, but ever trustful in his ultimate destiny, he decided to go and started off on 12 November 1924. The next day as his ship passed by Whampoa, he spent the night at the Military Academy. To Chiang Kai-shek he said, "I am going to Peking. Whether I can come back is not yet certain. Anyway, I am going there to carry on our struggle. Having seen the spirit of this Academy, I know it can carry on my revolutionary task. Even if I should die, my conscience will be at peace."

Before his departure, Borodin had invited him to visit Moscow. What did Chiang think of the idea? Not much, said Chiang.

Cooperation with the Russians was one thing: that was needed, as a step towards China's freedom and independence. But the Communists always twisted the significance of events. If he went to Moscow, the Russians were sure to spread harmful rumours about the trip. Sun listened but said nothing.

The Nationalist leader's health was failing fast. He took to his bed at Tientsin on his way north, but struggled to his feet on New Year's Eve. Frustration awaited him in Peking, where the pro-Japanese faction, far from rejecting the unequal treaties as Dr. Sun would have wished, had traded endorsement for diplomatic recognition by the Powers. Broken in heart and now in body with cancer invading his vital organs, Sun Yat-sen died in the northern capital on 12 March 1925. His death probably saved him further and more bitter disappointments. Instead, it brought him posthumous canonisation as the Father of the Nation, and recognised as such by both Communists and Nationalists.

The struggle for the succession now broke out. Chiang Kai-shek was not at first among those seriously in the running. For one thing, he was regarded as too young, as he was still in his late thirties; for another he was a soldier—not a party man (though of course a member of the party). The three serious contenders—all more or less equal in the degree of confidence Dr. Sun had in them—were Wang Ching-wei, Hu Han-min, and Liao Chung-k'ai. The three had a further advantage which Chiang Kai-shek could not hope to match: all were natives of Kwangtung province. Dr. Sun was known to be very partial to his Kwangtung comrades. Like most Cantonese, he seemed to think that his compatriots were both intelligent and more revolutionary than comrades from other provinces. Those less privileged in the circumstances of their birth whispered behind his back about his inability to rise above "provincialism".

Wang was later to acquire a villain's reputation in Chinese history by collaborating with the Japanese during the war of 1937 to 1945, and accepting the title of President from the invaders. This attracted epithets that have stuck to his name, such as "traitor" and "puppet". But in the 1920s he was rightly regarded as a dedicated revolutionary. Had he not attempted to assassinate the Manchu Prince Regent in 1910? Gaoled, then freed by the Revolution, he carried with him a certain aura. Alone of the trio, he had accompanied Dr. Sun to Peking on the last journey. When the

Master lay dying, Wang Ching-wei had drafted his political Will, then transcribed it after Sun had revised it on 20 February 1925. Because of his later treachery, some KMT members tried to discredit the document, but as the Will merely expressed the wish that Sun's followers should carry on his work, and as nobody was named as his heir, there is no reason for supposing that Wang had any incentive to doctor it.

In China, age carried prestige and youth did not. Wang was handicapped in that he was the youngest of the three. In public he had always strongly supported collaboration with the Russians. He was therefore regarded as a leftist, but it was never clear that he had any particular principles. Liao Chung-k'ai was a more dedicated leftist, and was suspected by the right-wing Kuomintang men—on no very strong evidence—of being a secret Communist. He had spent a month in Japan at Dr. Sun's request to discuss KMT-Soviet cooperation with the Soviet envoy, Joffe.

The third contender, Hu Han-min, was a conservative and deeply suspicious of the Russians. His own revolutionary credentials were good, for he had helped Sun Yat-sen in pre-revolutionary days, notably through a newspaper he edited in Hong Kong. Hu was a classical scholar and had been Dr. Sun's private secretary—a job which for that matter Wang Ching-wei had also filled on occasion. One big advantage Hu had over the others was that before leaving for Peking, Dr. Sun had appointed him acting Commander-in-Chief.°

That was the line-up, but Chiang Kai-shek was the dark horse who overtook the rest of the field.

Two bloody happenings fanned the flames of anti-foreign sentiment in China. The Kuomintang always did well when foreigners made themselves more than usually unpopular; the Russians also benefited, as they were considered exceptions to the rule of deplorable foreign behaviour. The British termed these events "incidents", and the Chinese called them "massacres". It was all a matter of who was at the receiving end of bullets. The first was the "May 30th incident" (or "massacre", to the Chinese historians). International Settlement police under British command fired on a crowd of demonstrators in Shanghai, with many deaths.

° Tong (p. 79) says Chiang was really in full military control, but this is probably a hagiographic gloss.

Borodin could not hide his delight: "We did not make May 30th. It was made for us."

The second event was the Shakee massacre (or "incident"), on 23 June, when a French gunboat near the British concession in Canton, bombarded demonstrators who were protesting the Shanghai incident. The British opened fire with machine guns. Less than a fortnight earlier, on the 12th, Chiang Kai-shek had recaptured the city from the Yunnan and Kwangsi forces who had taken advantage of Sun Yat-sen's death to seize the seat of power.

In Canton especially, there was an atmosphere of xenophobia and victory when the Kuomintang met to reorganise itself and extend the area of its authority. The Military Government decided to call itself the "National Government", which sounded more established.° All forces loyal to the Kuomintang were now styled the National Revolutionary Army. On 1 July 1925, a State Council of sixteen and a Military Council of eight were elected. Wang Ching-wei was the chairman of both, and to most people he now began to look like the heir apparent. At the first meeting of the Military Council, Chiang presented his refurbished plan for the Northern Punitive Expedition, which called for the creation of seven armies and the construction of arsenals and heavy industries. About half the available revenues of Kwangtung province—totalling $40,000,000 Chinese a year—would be earmarked for military needs.

Though Wang Ching-wei leaned to the Left, he was acceptable to the Right of the Kuomintang, and it was doubtless this acceptability that gave him the chairmanship although he was younger than his rivals—in preference to Hu Han-min, whom the leftists execrated, and Liao Chung-k'ai, whom the rightists distrusted. Both the others were members of the State Council, however, and all three were on the Military Council as well—as was Chiang Kai-shek.

Murder and treachery were never far away in this post-Manchu period. On 25 August 1925, Liao Chung-k'ai was assassinated. It was undoubtedly a right-wing plot, and the plotters included Hu Han-min's younger brother Hu Yi-sheng. This was embarrassing.

° The Chinese words for "National Government"—Kuo Min Cheng Fu—literally means "Government of All Nationals" (that is, "of the People"); it was thus named to stimulate popular support.

Borodin was convinced that Han-min was implicated, or at any rate he saw political advantage in saying so, and demanded that he should be punished, since Yi-sheng had escaped. But neither Chiang nor Wang could bring themselves to believe the charge. Indeed, Chiang Kai-shek sheltered Hu in his own house. Not long after, a curious half-punishment was in fact devised for him: he was sent to Russia, of all places, as Special Envoy. Outraged by this outcome which seriously weakened their position in the party, a group of disgruntled rightists left Canton, heading for Shanghai or other northern destinations.

This left Wang Ching-wei as the front-runner, with Chiang running second. But there was a complication. The War Minister, Hsu Ch'ung-chih, was Chiang's military superior. Though not himself a very active contender, he was an obstacle to any political ambitions Chiang may have had. The three men—Hsu, Wang, and Chiang—constituted a "Big Three" Special Committee set up to take civil and military decisions after Liao's assassination.

More skulduggery. Hsu, it turned out, had been secretly in touch with the defeated Hakka General, Ch'en Chiung-ming, and officers in his command were implicated in the Liao murder plot. On 20 September Chiang and his Whampoa cadets suddenly disarmed Hsu's forces, which were later incorporated into Chiang's First Army Corps. The next day, Hsu Ch'ung-chih was dismissed as War Minister and stripped of his command of the Cantonese Army. He was expelled from Canton and settled in Shanghai. Now Wang and Chiang were the only two rivals left in the race to the top.

Defeated but never completely, Ch'en Chiung-ming was still a real thorn in the side of the Kuomintang. He had been making trouble at the beginning of the year, and now he went into action again. He had to be stopped, once and for all. Under Chiang's command, five armies launched their East River offensive on 6 October 1925. Exactly a month later, Chiang sent off a circular telegram of victory: "Today we are in Swatow, having covered a distance of over 600 *li* from our starting-point. The common people from all four directions have come out in crowds to see us and welcome us with food and drink." Swatow had been Ch'en Chiung-ming's headquarters. Ch'en took refuge in Hong Kong and thereafter stayed out of the news.

There is a touch of irony in a letter Chiang Kai-shek wrote at that time to Chou En-lai, who had been appointed to a party role attached to the First Division of the First Army. Complaining of poor party work in all regiments and of excesses by officers ("the worst [case] was that of a sergeant putting filth into a soldier's mouth"), he wrote: "We are working for a Revolution. If we do not start it by improving the life of the soldiers, all slogans of reforming and improving society are but empty words." The future Communist Premier's reply is unfortunately unrecorded.

Victorious in the field, Chiang Kai-shek now faced an unexpected political challenge. With an engaging sense of drama, the disgruntled KMT rightists gathered together before the coffin of Sun Yat-sen in the Temple of the Azure Clouds in the Western Hills outside Peking. There were only ten of them, but this did not stop them from issuing a splendid resolution, calling for the expulsion of all Communists from the Kuomintang, the dismissal of Borodin and all other Russian advisers, sweeping changes in the party's organisation, and its transfer from Canton to Shanghai. Chiang was at Swatow when the news of the Western Hills meeting came. He flew into a rage and denounced the participants. This made him—still— a leader of the left faction of the KMT.

Yet another rebellious group, calling themselves the Sun Yat-sen Society, went into active opposition to the Communists in Canton at that time.

Despite all this factionalism, Chiang Kai-shek now felt ready, at least militarily, to start on the active planning for the Northern Expedition.

7. The Northern Expedition

If a united China was ever to emerge from possibly the messiest revolution in history, the Northern Expedition was going to be necessary. Chiang Kai-shek was supremely confident that he could lead the new Revolutionary Army to victory, whatever the odds. The Communists, however, and especially the Russians, did not share his optimism. On paper, the facts seemed to support their scepticism.

Five "big" warlords stood between Chiang and his objective. Three of them were mentioned in the last chapter: Wu, Chang, and Feng.

Wu P'ei-fu. Wu, defeated by Feng's treachery, was posted to a distant place. Early in 1926, he staged a comeback from a base in Hupeh and occupied Honan as well, with areas of control in Hunan, Szechwan, and Kweichow. His armies probably numbered 250,000.

Chang Tso-lin. At that time, Chang was by far the most

powerful of the northern warlords. He controlled Shantung, Manchuria, Jehol, Chahar, and Hopei.° Estimates of the forces at his orders range from 300,000 to 500,000.

Sun Ch'uan-fang. Sun held East China from the Shanghai region to Nanch'ang in Kiangsi with about 200,000 men. He thus straddled the lower Yangtze valley, including Kiangsu, Anhwei, Chekiang, and Kiangsi.

The other two were the gigantic and picturesque *Feng Yü-hsiang* and *Yen Hsi-shan.* After ousting Wu, Feng had built up his army to about 275,000 men, but had overextended himself with a Mongolian adventure and left a flank exposed to the forces of Yen, who looked as if he might be forming an alliance with Chang. At that time, Feng controlled the provinces of Shensi, Kansu, Suiyuan (now Inner Mongolia), and Chahar—and could therefore claim to be regarded as the "warlord of the north-west" (although Sheridan unaccountably calls him the "warlord of the north-east").

Suddenly, on 1 January 1926, Feng announced that he was retiring and set off on a long journey. His ultimate destination was Moscow, where he was hoping to get supplies for his forces, known collectively as the *Kuominchün,* or People's Army. While he was away—for some months—his subordinate commanders withdrew the exposed forces and dug themselves in at the Nankow Pass in the Great Wall, within 50 miles of Peking.

Yen was the great exception to the rule that warlords were rapacious, destructive, and selfish. Not for nothing was he known as the "model" or "social" warlord; he built schools, promoted public health, campaigned against opium, built roads and bridges, and introduced all manner of land reclamation, irrigation, and advanced cultivation schemes. "Flanked by his Oxford-educated Chinese secretary," writes Barbara Tuchman, "he presided at a dinner table set in a foreign style with damask, silver, garnet-coloured crystal wine glasses and napkins intricately folded in the shape of roses, birds and pagodas. After dinner, guests were escorted through moonlit gardens by serving men carrying lanterns of painted gauze suspended from tall poles."

Both Feng and Yen spared Chiang Kai-shek the trouble of removing them; they joined the Revolution.

° The old name for Hopei province, in which Peking is situated, was Chihli, which means literally "under direct control"—that is, of the Imperial court and later of the central government.

To take on the vast hordes of the warlords, numbering in all not less than 750,000 armed men, at the start of 1926 Chiang had no more than about 85,000 soldiers, organised in six divisions. On paper it was not enough, but there was no question of waiting until he could match his opponents numerically. Chiang gave himself six months. While planning and training, however, military problems must at times have seemed secondary to political ones.

The Second Congress of the Kuomintang met in Canton from 1 to 19 January, under the chairmanship of Wang Ching-wei. It was decided that Dr. Sun's Will should be the permanent foundation of the Kuomintang; and Sun Yat-sen himself was proclaimed perpetual President of the party, from beyond his Peking grave. On the practical side, the Congress showed that the Communists had made good use of the earlier decision to allow them to join the KMT as individuals. Of the 36 members of the new Central Executive Committee elected by the 258 delegates, 7 were Communists. They included Mao Tse-tung, who became directly responsible for Propaganda under Wang Ching-wei. In addition, Ch'en Tu-hsiu, one of the Communist Party's founders, was given charge of Kuomintang affairs in Canton—a position he soon turned to his own party's advantage. Chiang Kai-shek, too, was elected to the Executive. Chiang reported on his military plans—of his 85,000 men, only 60,000 had rifles. There were also 6,000 military students who could, if necessary, be mobilised. On 1 February 1926, he was appointed Inspector General of the Revolutionary Forces.

About this time, Chiang became aware of a Communist whispering campaign against him and against the Northern Expedition. At the Congress, the Communist members had not raised any objections to his military plans, and even Borodin had approved them. After the Congress, however, Borodin was suddenly called away.° In his absence, Kissanka, who had become the head of the Russian military advisory mission, started saying that the Northern Expedition was doomed to failure. Chiang confided to his diary: "I offer them sincerity. They return deceit. It is impossible to work

---

° Chiang Kai-shek says (*Soviet Russia in China*, p. 37) that he "was suddenly recalled to Moscow for consultation for unknown reasons". Hsiung (p. 240) writes that he "went North to see Feng Yü-hsiang, the Christian General, in order to bring him over to the side of the Kuomintang", but seems to be on shaky chronological ground; he did meet Feng, but not until April (Clubb, p. 132). Feng went on to Moscow after his talk with Borodin.

with them." About this time, handbills describing him as a new warlord and attacking the expedition appeared in Canton. He suspected the Russians were behind these, too.

In this situation, Chiang Kai-shek looked around for jobs to resign from without too much damage, and initially picked on the post he did not yet hold—announcing on 8 February that he would not take up his appointment as Inspector-General of the Revolutionary Forces. The next day he called on Wang Ching-wei and presented his resignation from the National Military Council and as Canton's defence commander. Wang listened impassively, neither accepting his resignation nor refusing it. Chiang Kai-shek sensed at this time that he would soon clash with the man who was now his only real rival as leader of the Kuomintang and of the Revolution.

The psychological sabotage of the expedition continued. What was he to do? Wang Ching-wei remained silent. The time, thought Chiang, had come for an ultimatum. "If you do not want to accept my resignation," he told Wang on 27 February, "then Kissanka must be asked to return to Russia." Still Wang did not react.

On 8 March Chiang was back in Wang's office, to say, "The actual power of directing the Revolution must not fall into Russian hands; even in the matter of liaison with the Third International, we must draw a line somewhere. In no circumstances should we forfeit the freedom of making our own decisions."

That was the way these conversations read, as recorded by Chiang Kai-shek some thirty years after the event. At the time, however, he was still inclined to blame the Soviet attitude on Kissanka and his colleagues as individuals, rather than on his superiors in Moscow.

The whole business was unnerving, and Chiang was suffering from insomnia. On 28 February his diary mentioned that he had a "slightly calmer day", and for the first time for many days, a restful night. Two attempts on his life were made about this time (though Tong, who mentions them, is vague about the first), the second in March at his office in Whampoa. But the murder of Liao Chung-k'ai had alerted Chiang. He had started compiling individual files on possible opponents and plotters in Canton, both for future and for present use; and had set up an efficient secret service to watch on conspirators of the Right or Left.

Wang still kept his own counsel about Chiang's resignation. But he had begun to utter dark warnings to the younger man to get out of Kwangtung while the going was good; to stay might expose his life to danger. That, thought Chiang, was all very well. If he stayed, he might be murdered; but if he left, he could be charged with desertion. Worse, he discovered that Kissanka had learnt of his exchanges with Wang Ching-wei, from which he inferred that Wang was in collusion with the Russians.

Then came the "March 20th incident". On the 18th, Chiang was in Canton in his capacity as Defence Commander. The telephone rang at his office and he lifted the receiver. The voice at the other end was that of a Communist in charge of the Naval Forces Bureau.

"The *Chungshan* is at Whampoa," said the man. "Do you want her back in Canton?"

Chiang was taken by surprise. The *Chungshan* was the gunboat (now renamed) in which Chiang and Dr. Sun had sheltered after the Hakka General's rebellion in 1922.

"I didn't know she was at Whampoa," exclaimed Chiang. "By whose order did she leave Canton in the first place?"

The answer was evasive. "Bring her back," Chiang ordered.

Chiang quickly found out that "the commandant" had ordered that the ship should be sent to Whampoa to stand by. She was now moored opposite the Academy. But he, Chiang, *was* the commandant, so the orders must have been forged. The gunboat had been loading enough coal for a long voyage. By the evening of the 19th, the ship was back in Canton harbour. Her lights were left on all night and the engine was kept running. Stringent security precautions were apparently being observed.

"I sensed a Communist plot," wrote Chiang thirty years later. "That night I felt that at a critical moment like this what might happen to me personally was inconsequential, but for the sake of the Party and our revolutionary cause, I could no longer put off a decision."

Trusting no one, Chiang, on his authority as Defence Commander of Canton—a post which he had been unable to shed—proclaimed martial law. By his orders, twenty-five Communists, among them Chou En-lai, were arrested or placed under close supervision. It was 3:00 A.M. on 20 March 1926. More arrests followed in Canton, and the armed pickets of the Communist-controlled Canton-Hong Kong strike committee—set up to enforce a general strike against Hong Kong following the Shameen incident of 22 June 1925—had their weapons confiscated. A guard was placed on trade-union headquarters, and troops boarded the gunboat. For good measure, the Soviet advisers were placed under house arrest.

Chiang's coup was the more shattering for being totally unexpected. Neither the Chinese Communists nor the Russians—still less the latter—had been given so much as a hint of the ideological hatred Chiang had developed for them and what they stood for. In Moscow two months later, Feng Yü-hsiang was told that Chiang Kai-shek, during his earlier visit there, had given his hosts the impression of being more left-wing and revolutionary than most of the other Chinese they had met. The "March 20th incident" took both the Russians and the Chinese in Moscow totally by surprise, wrote Feng. "They could not figure out what had happened."

Quite suddenly, and in a peculiarly Chinese fashion, Wang Ching-wei conceded defeat in this indirect struggle for power. A diabetic, he was finding the current tensions very tiring. On the 21st, Chiang tried to write a letter to him, but the words would not come. "As I do not want to be hypocritical to my friend, nor can I empty my sincere mind to him," he wrote in his diary, "I have thought hard and found it difficult to put it down with my pen." On the 22nd, the Political Council met, with Wang in the chair, and endorsed Chiang's actions with an enthusiasm he found strange. Next day, Wang vanished, ostensibly for medical treatment. Later, a letter to a friend came to light: "I have been suspected and disliked, so I will never bear political responsibility any more." In May, shortly after Hu Han-min had returned from Russia, Wang Ching-wei left for France, where he stayed some time. Chiang was to plead with him to return, but Wang—hurt, humiliated, and unforgiving—stayed silent and away.

The Russians, too, conceded defeat. On 22 March—the day of the Political Council meeting, but before it had met—a man from the Soviet consulate in Canton called on Chiang Kai-shek, to ask whether his actions had been directed against the persons concerned or against Russia. The former, said Chiang, and he added that he hoped Borodin would come back soon. The Political Council went on to its meeting of support for Chiang, and decided to request Kissanka's recall.

A faint air of mystery still hangs over the March 20th incident. Was Chiang right in suspecting a Communist plot? After the event, he claimed to have discovered a plan to invite him aboard the

Chungshan, then seize him and remove him to Russia via Vladivostok. With him out of the way, it would have been relatively easy to use the National Revolution as a step towards the dictatorship of the proletariat. However, Chiang kept to himself the documentary evidence which he claimed was in his possession.

At a stroke, the incident had made him the dominant figure in the Kuomintang. One of his rivals was dead, another was about to return from exile discredited, and a third was about to go into exile. Chiang did not like politics; he had written in his diary, "Politics makes man lead a dog's life. . . . Where is morality? Where is friendship?" But he soon showed that he was a fast learner in the art of politics. The hopes of the right wing had risen at the news of his blows to the Russian and Chinese Communists. But Chiang now dashed these hopes with a letter to his students: "Our Master thought that to accommodate the Communists was one of the principles of our Revolution. I also think that the revolutionary front will not be united if we do not accommodate the Communists." He warned the right-wingers that he still considered the Western Hills conference a mistake.

In his own account of these events, designed to show that he had been consistently anti-Communist since his visit to Russia, Chiang makes no mention of these cautionary words (recorded by the diligent S. I. Hsiung). This relieved him of the necessity to explain his ambivalent behaviour. There is perhaps less mystery about it than may appear. If Chiang was to be the leader of the National Revolution,° then he would still need Soviet help, since his northern rivals leaned on the other powers. The aim was to keep the Communists in their place, not to drop them; to show the Russians they could not order him around, not show them the door. Moreover, the right-wing leader, Hu Han-min, was about to return from Russia: if he pushed his anti-Communist measures to the breaking point, Chiang would make it look as if Hu had been right all along. He had seized the leadership from the Left; he was not going to lose it to the Right. In fact, when Hu Han-min reached Canton from Russia in May, he was not offered a job, and he went on to Shanghai after a few days.

Chiang's olive branch for the Communists, after his suppressive

---

° The Chinese words for the National Revolution are *Kuo Min Kê Ming,* meaning "Revolution of the Nationals" (that is, of the people).

actions, was deftly drawn. Borodin, back in Canton on 29 April, had several sessions with Chiang, who found him "extremely conciliatory". On 15 May, Chiang Kai-shek called an emergency meeting of the Central Executive Committee. He took the chair for the first time, and in a tense atmosphere, secured approval for drastic new rules on Communists in the party. Even Borodin, with objections here and there, had conceded the need for these new rules, eight in number:

1. The Communist Party must order its members to refrain from attacking Sun Yat-sen and his Three Principles.
2. A full list of Communist members of the KMT to be handed over to the Chairman of the Central Executive Committee.
3. Dual members not to be eligible as heads of department in the KMT.
4. Communists with KMT membership forbidden to organise groups except with party permission.
5. Communist members of the KMT not to promote political activities without orders from the party.
6. The Chinese Communist Party and the Third International to submit to a joint Communist-Kuomintang conference any instructions to Communists before sending them to Communists with KMT membership.
7. No "pure" KMT members to join the Communist Party without first obtaining permission to leave the party; those who left and became Communists could not be readmitted to the KMT.
8. Party members ignoring these rules would be expelled, and otherwise punished.

Chiang was tactful enough not to press his victory too far. He even made an important concession by dissolving the Sun Yat-sen Society, whose provocative attitude had become embarrassing. The Communists forfeited a number of important posts, however. Mao Tse-tung lost his hold on Propaganda (although he was allowed to remain head of the Peasant Movement Training Institute, where to Chiang's later discomfiture he continued to train peasant agitators); two other Communists were ousted from important posts.

Now the last obstacle to the Northern Expedition had been removed. Early in April, Chiang had presented the party with detailed plans. On 5 June, to nobody's surprise, he was appointed Commander-in-Chief of the Northern Punitive Expedition. In true Chinese fashion, his pre-eminence was then recognised by a proliferation of further titles. He was elected Chairman of the Central Executive Committee and of the Military Council. He was also head of the Organisation and Military People's Departments of the KMT.

On 1 July, the Military Council issued mobilisation orders, and on the 9th the Revolutionary Army took an oath of loyalty and approved a manifesto defining the aims of the military campaign as being "to build an independent nation on the basis of the Three People's Principles and to protect the interests of the nation and of the people".

After all this build-up there was an air of anti-climax when the expedition actually started. For Chiang was otherwise engaged. The general strike in Canton had got out of hand. Every day there were violent clashes between pickets and police. The police commissioner resigned. Chiang moved in, sending troops to reinforce police patrols and secret service men to keep an eye on the professional agitators. Then there was a more mundane job to attend to: the General Chamber of Commerce seemed in no hurry to meet the special levy to finance the expedition. Chiang made the businessmen understand that their own best interests would be served by paying up. The sum needed was $500,000 Chinese. The businessmen paid up. The strikers, too, were given something to think about: their contribution to the war effort was to be 4,000 coolies. And they too paid up.

Even without Chiang, the Revolutionary Army had made a good start with the capture of Changsha on 12 July 1926. Chiang finally left Canton on the 27th to direct his forces. By the time his new army moved into battle, it had grown from 85,000 to about 100,000 men, the Kwangsi and Hunan armies having joined Chiang's banner. In line with Soviet advice, political commissars were attached at various levels so that each soldier was indoctrinated with the Three Principles, and doubtless with a fair dose of Marxism-Leninism. The men felt they knew what they were fighting for, and this gave them one great advantage over the warlords' forces.

Chiang, however, was leaving nothing to chance. In case his army's fervour should falter, he had laid down draconian disciplinary measures. Any officer who yielded territory was to be summarily shot, whatever his rank. If the commander of an army corps stood his ground and was killed while all around him were retreating, *all* his divisional commanders were to be executed. The same principle applied to lower-ranking groups. Doubtless this severity (rigorously enforced, says Tong) encouraged revolutionary *élan*.

Initially, however, it was not calculated to make Chiang popular with his subordinates. At the private level, moreover, he was also generally unpopular at first, except with the troops directly under his command, who were regularly paid and better supplied than the rest; resenting this discrimination, the others were dissatisfied. But successes were so rapid that there was little need for disciplinary harshness, and conditions for the army as a whole improved.

It was a thoroughly politicised army. Each army corps had a Kuomintang office and the party men, all with military training, had ultimate authority over military commanders. Treasury accounts (says Tong) were open for all to see, to eliminate extortion.

Although the northern armies outnumbered the revolutionaries by anything up to ten to one (depending on the head count), and were better armed and more seasoned, they were disunited, provincial in outlook, and liable to shifts of personal loyalty.

The National Revolutionary Army was something new in China's long history. Blazingly self-confident, its morale was boosted by rapid and sensational successes. As it marched northward, its ranks swelled. At times the fighting was hard; at other times, especially as the campaign gained momentum, the revolutionaries benefited from the other side's traditional Chinese attitude to war, which was that it was best to avoid it. The idea was yield to superior force, and if necessary join the "enemy".

The hardest fighting—against Wu P'ei-fu's forces—was on the approaches to the triple town of Wuhan,* then for the walled town of Wuch'ang itself, which resisted desperately, finally falling on 7 October. Nanch'ang fell on 8 November.

Not long after, the Revolutionary Army had grown to 264,000 men. Tightly disciplined, they earned popularity and the fame of their behaviour preceded them. The contrast between them and the forces of the warlords was striking. On arrival in a town, the latter

---

* Hankow, Wuch'ang, and Hanyang.

would requisition local houses, force the local merchants to pay the troops for two or three months, and help themselves to local labour. Chiang's army slept in temples and public buildings, paid their way and the soldiers' wages, and did not conscript the locals.

On 16 September, the Christian General, Feng Yü-hsiang, back from his long Mongolian and Russian absence, joined the Revolution—to the discomfiture of Wu P'ei-fu and Chang Tso-lin. By the end of 1926, the Revolutionary Army controlled Hunan, Hupei, and Kiangsi. In the second wave, Hangchow, capital of Chiang's home province of Chekiang, was taken on 17 February 1927. Shanghai fell on 22 March and Nanking on the 24th. Now the revolutionaries gripped the Yangtze valley and controlled ten provinces of South and Central China. That spring, however, fighting stopped, and the lull was to last about a year. Its causes were political.

8. Shanghai Incident

The simmering quarrel between Chiang Kai-shek and the Chinese Communists exploded during the first half of 1927—a period as crowded and confused as any since the Revolution had begun sixteen years earlier. In two great cities—Shanghai and Canton—and at scattered places in the country, the Communists made determined attempts to spark off uprisings. They failed. Instead, the Communist Party was smashed and diplomatic relations between China and Russia were broken off. Although Chiang came out on top, at one stage he was ousted from all his positions by a Kuomintang "government" deeply penetrated by the Communists. The year also saw the most spectacular of his resignations to date, and his third marriage.

At the start of 1927 three main obstacles stood in the way of Chiang Kai-shek's ambition to unite China under his revolutionary banner. With Wu P'ei-fu and his allies defeated, the only powerful warlord not on Chiang's side was the northern ex-bandit, Chang

Tso-lin. This obstacle was purely military. The political obstacles were perhaps more serious. There were the Communists, who were far from united, and there was the left wing of the KMT, dominated by Wang Ching-wei, who had turned sharply to the left after his clash with Chiang. The warlords proved easier to dispose of than the leftists and the Communists.

Chiang could hardly have expected Wang to like him for his anti-Communist coup of 20 March 1926, which in the end had driven Wang out of his job and of the country. But at the end of September that year, a letter from Wang put Chiang in an amenable mood. There was no difference between them, Wang wrote, about what had happened in March. Chiang Kai-shek replied immediately in a conciliatory way, and on 3 October he sent Wang a long telegram:

> I, your younger brother, am not educated and have no manners, so have offended you. I have just received your instructions, which are full of self-suppression and sincerity, and when I read them, I perspired all the more with shame. . . .
>
> You, my Elder Brother, left everything behind without casting a look at me, your younger brother, and the result has been that I have gone through all these difficulties single-handed. You, my Elder Brother, could throw away honours and positions, but could you shrink from responsibility? And friendship? I have borne it all this time, and now you surely can see my foolish devotion to you and know that I have nothing but friendship for you. . . .

Chiang went on to say that he was sending two of their colleagues to France to bring him back to take charge of party affairs.

But the grudge Wang nursed went deeper than Chiang knew. Later he understood that Wang had written to him only to remove his suspicions and make sure Wang himself could come back safely and in his own time. In fact, he did not return until the beginning of April 1927, and as soon as he was back, he started denouncing Chiang.

Politically, much went on in the intervening months. Chiang was otherwise engaged at the front, and had little time to spare for politics. Although he controlled the armed forces as Commander-in-Chief, and the party and government through his other posts, he remained answerable to the Kuomintang's Central Executive Committee—where his friends tended to be passive and silent, and his enemies active and vociferous. The committee was not large—thirty-six members—but sixteen of them were opponents. Of these, only seven were Communists. The others were either leftists or "radicals" who objected to the dictatorial powers Chiang had managed to concentrate in his hands. The non-Communist opponents included Sun Yat-sen's widow, whose maiden name was Soong Ch'ing-ling. Her sister Mayling was later to marry Chiang Kai-shek, and she herself went on to become Vice-President of the Chinese People's Republic. With her in opposition was her brother Sung Tzu-wen, better known by his anglicised name of T. V. Soong, who was much under American influence. Then there was Mrs. Liao Chung-k'ai, widow of Sun's assassinated left-wing Finance Minister. With them too was her stepson Sun Fo, a young man of uncertain temper; and about half a dozen others. One of these was a man named Teng, who had once been one of Chiang's most trusted associates but had turned radical and disloyal. For a surprisingly long time Chiang continued to treat him indulgently, but in the end he had the man shot.

The Central Executive Committee met in Canton from 15 to 28 October 1926, and passed vaguely anti-Chiang resolutions—for instance denouncing personal power but without naming the man who was exercising it. The Committee also called for the return of Wang Ching-wei and endorsed collaboration between the Kuomintang and the Communist Party.

From Moscow the Soviet leadership watched Chinese developments with hope and satisfaction. Chiang Kai-shek was carrying the Revolution northwards by force of arms—which was what they wanted him to do—but they must have felt there was a good chance that it would take a Communist turn. Surely this was not too much to expect with all the weight and guile of the Russian advisers and the Chinese Communists within the KMT.

With the advance of the Northern Expedition, it was becoming increasingly inconvenient for the government to operate from Canton. Chiang Kai-shek wanted it to move to Nanch'ang, because his own troops were stationed in that area. But this in itself was a good reason why the majority of the Central Committee preferred Wuhan, where it was argued that the military would be less likely to interfere in either party or government affairs. Moreover, the

Communists and their leftist supporters knew that they were more likely to find proletarian backing in the great industrial complex of Wuhan than in Nanch'ang. Called upon to mediate, Li Tsung-jen sided with the leftists. Outnumbered, Chiang gave in and agreed that the National Government should be transferred to Wuch'ang— one of the three towns comprising the industrial complex of Wuhan. He was soon to have cause bitterly to regret this decision.°

Indeed, before the government itself could move northwards, the Communists and their allies moved to Wuch'ang, where they set up a combined committee of the State Council and the Central Executive Committee. The members included such non-Communist leftists as Sun Fo and T. V. Soong. But the man who really counted was the Russian Borodin, who stayed in the background but in effect decided policy. At its first meeting on 13 December, the new committee voted itself full authority on behalf of party and government. True, the authority was described as "temporary", but from that moment Wuch'ang was the centre of anti-Chiang activity.

Attacks against Chiang continued. He found himself being described as "warlord" or "dictator" and pictures of him appeared everywhere with the German Kaiser on one side and Mussolini on the other.

What was Chiang to do? Never a man to shirk a confrontation, he spent a week in Wuhan trying to talk the committee out of its hostile attitude. But he got nowhere. By that time the government itself was installed at Wuhan, where it had formally started in business on 1 January 1927.†

The Communists thought victory was within their grasp.

° The approved biographers, Tong and Hsiung, both attribute the initiative for the decision to move to Wuch'ang to Chiang Kai-shek himself (Tong p. 144; Hsiung p. 265). I have preferred to rely on the account of Yin Shih (pseud.), *Li Chiang kuan-hsi yü Chung-kuo* ("Relations between Chiang Kai-shek and Li Tsung-jen and China"), p. 24, which is a more likely version of events.

† The chronology of this period is sometimes obscure. Clubb (p. 135), and Guillermaz (p. 117) say the government was based in Wuhan from 1 January 1927; Hollington Tong (p. 144) states that the move took place before the end of 1926; but on p. 142 he records that "all the important members of the Nationalist government went to Wuch'ang by way of Nanch'ang", where Chiang had his headquarters, arriving on 31 December 1926, staying there throughout January and February, and not leaving for Wuch'ang until 1 March 1927. This appears to discount other reports that Chiang stayed in Wuch'ang from 11 to 18 January.

Throughout the year and in widely scattered places, they stepped up the pace of revolution. They were split on the tactics and strategy of revolution, however. The Chinese Communists had been trying to win over the workers, especially in the great industrial cities of Shanghai, Canton, and Hankow. That was what they were supposed to do, as good Marxist-Leninists. But there was no getting away from the fact that in China there were very few urban workers and many millions of peasants. At the start, dogma was simply too strong for either the Chinese or the Russian Communists to act on this obvious fact. But the Comintern acknowledged the importance of the peasants as early as 1926, and Mao Tse-tung said the same thing more specifically and emphatically in a report in March 1927.

Of course, Mao really had a profound understanding of the peasantry, and he was also an organising genius.° Only he could draw this vast but shapeless mass together and mould it into a revolutionary force. The Kuomintang had put him in charge of the National Peasant Movement Institute in Canton, which he directed in 1925 and 1926, and he had made intelligent use of his opportunities. From there he went on to be the head of the National Peasant Association at Wuhan. His March 1927 report was the outcome of an inquiry on the spot in five districts of Hunan province. Nobody could complain that it was written in officialese. Instead, it was packed with powerful and emotional passages about millions of peasants rising "like a mighty storm, like a hurricane", to sweep imperialists, warlords, local tyrants, and evil gentry into their graves.

The real question at that time, however, was whether the Communists were going to take matters into their own hands or continue to allow the Kuomintang to make the Revolution for them, while they consolidated their positions, emerging at the decisive moment to take over. Stalin and his envoys kept pressing them not to move too fast. (One man who didn't agree with this sage advice was Trotsky, who was always trying to incite his Chinese colleagues to drop their Kuomintang links and go it alone.)

° The assertion that it was Mao who first realised that the peasants held the key to revolution in China is probably a myth. His *Report on an Investigation of the Peasant Movement in Hunan*, published on 15 March 1927, was nevertheless a decisively important document. For a discussion of the opposing views of B. Schwartz and K. Wittfogel on the "originality" of Mao's views, see Jerome Ch'en, *Mao and the Chinese Revolution* (Oxford, 1965), pp. 113–15.

If the Chinese Communists had listened to all the foreign advice they were getting, they would have been quite confused. The American Earl Browder, the Frenchman Jacques Doriot, and the German Thomas Mann, had been sent by the Comintern to China, where they made inflammatory speeches in Canton and Wuhan at the beginning of 1927. One of their main themes was that foreign troops should mutiny. The "foreign devils" no longer felt safe in their concessions and were beginning to quake in their shoes. The Wuhan government was hardly less inflammatory than the foreign Communists. Strikes were spreading in waves and demonstrators carried placards proclaiming "Death to the Imperialists". There was a witch-hunt on, and a rather lucrative one at that. "Anti-revolutionaries" were forced to pay extortion money, and if they failed to pay up, they were executed. In Hankow twenty-seven native banks were forced to close, and a kind of terror reigned there and at Changsha.

Chiang was not involved in all this. He attributed China's ills unreservedly to foreign depredations, but he dissociated himself from extreme xenophobia. Indeed, on 20 August 1926, at the start of the Northern Expedition, he had issued a proclamation, saying: "I shall hold myself completely responsible for the protection of life and property of all aliens in China, irrespective of their nationalities, so long as they refrain from obstructing the movement and operations of our Revolutionary Forces". In general, this injunction had been obeyed when the Nationalists entered various cities, although a serious anti-British incident was to occur in Hankow on 3 January, some months after the city had fallen to Chiang's armies. He was incensed when troops of the Sixth Army entering Nanking on 24 March attacked and looted various foreign establishments. Among them were commercial companies, Roman Catholic missions, and the consulates of Britain, the United States, and Japan. About a dozen foreign lives were lost. Refugees cowered by the city wall, sheltering not only from the soldiers, but from foreign gunboats which opened fire to disperse the looters.

Arriving on the scene, Chiang took ruthless action. The Third Division of the Sixth Army was made to surrender its weapons and thirty or forty men were executed. It was later claimed that an investigation had shown the hand of the Communist commissars in the way the troops had behaved, "in the hope" (writes Chiang) "of provoking a direct clash between the foreign powers and the

revolutionary forces". As Guillermaz points out, it is hard to see
what benefit the looting of foreign concessions could have brought
to the Communists at that point in the game. It may have been a
simple case of military indiscipline. There is no doubt, however,
that the speeches of the foreign Communists at that time were
adding fuel to the flames.

Almost immediately Chiang ran into even more serious trouble
in Shanghai. The great city had fallen to the Nationalist forces on 22
March 1927, largely as a result of a revolutionary strike involving
800,000 workers, organised by Chou En-lai and others. The
Communists had armed the pickets, and fierce street fighting
followed, in which 200 workers were killed and 1,000 wounded.°
Immediately they started turning the situation to their advantage by
organising a temporary city council.

From his headquarters at Nanch'ang, Chiang watched these
events with cold fury. First the leftists had set up their committee at
Wuhan and defied his authority within the Kuomintang. Now the
Communists had grabbed Shanghai. It was intolerable. He made
speeches, but to little avail. Sometimes he was conciliatory and
sometimes provocative. In one speech on 10 March, he was both,
when he said:

> I have never intended not to cooperate with the Commu-
> nists. In fact, I can claim to have brought them into the
> Kuomintang. . . . The Communists have now reached the
> zenith of their power and arrogance; if their activities are not
> checked, they will bring disaster upon the Kuomintang. . . .
>
> I must say again that I am not opposed to the Communists. I
> appreciate their support and sympathy, but I advise them not to
> take advantage of their influence in the Party to oppress the
> moderate elements of the Kuomintang.

° In his oral autobiography, recorded by Edgar Snow, Mao Tse-tung declared:
"In April [1927] the counter-revolutionary movement had begun in Nanking
and Shanghai, and a general massacre of organised workers had taken place
under Chiang Kai-shek." (*Red Star Over China*, p. 159.) This was presumably
the origin of the myth that "organised workers" were massacred at Nanking,
for which I know of no convincing evidence, although in later Communist
accounts the numbers "massacred" rose to dizzy levels. What happened at
Shanghai was another matter.

But the Wuhan group was in no mood for Chiang's strictures. The Central Executive Committee stripped Chiang of his job as Chairman of the Political Council, and subordinated his authority as Commander-in-Chief to a new Military Council. All the important posts he had held in the KMT were transferred to his rival Wang Ching-wei, at that time on his way back to China from his French exile. As if demotion was not enough, the committee went on to humiliate him by issuing a circular describing him as a dictator and an autocrat, complaining that his rule protected "useless and corrupt elements in the Party" and attracted "bureaucrats, merchants and other opportunists". Several important posts were allocated to Communists.

According to Chiang, the Comintern had persuaded Wang Ching-wei to return via Moscow. Despite all that had happened between them, Chiang still apparently clung to the hope that the old partnership could be resumed on Wang's return. At all events, the two men met several times in Shanghai, on his arrival on 1 April 1927 and over the next few days.

What happened next was illuminating. The next day, at Chiang's suggestion, a KMT man named Wu who was loyal to him called like-minded members of the Control Committee to a meeting to discuss the idea of a purge. The point was to get rid of the Communists, but while they were about it some landlords and other affluent people who had held themselves aloof from the Revolution would also find they were dispensable. Reporting to the meeting, Wu declared:

> . . . Borodin uses particularly loathsome methods to provoke and divide. Outwardly, he is very friendly, but this façade is the one which their training gives to both Russian and Chinese Communists . . . in action, they are evil and harsh. Deceit is the first verse of their gospel.

Was Chiang crouching, ready to spring? If so, he was keeping his thoughts to himself, for in his first talks with Wang Ching-wei he readily agreed to hand over his party jobs, and on 3 April he went so far as to acknowledge the authority of the Wuhan government.

The next day, Wang came out with a bit of trickery of his own. He and the Communist leader, Ch'en Tu-hsiu, who had gone to Shanghai, issued a joint communiqué reaffirming the Communist

Party's acceptance of Sun Yat-sen's Three Principles. They sought to dispel unpleasant rumours that the Communists were about to attempt to destroy the Nationalist Army and attack the international settlements, and that the Kuomintang was about to disarm the Communist pickets and expel the Communists from the party.

On the 5th, Wu's group decided to push ahead with the purge and set up a committee to work out the best way of going about it. The 6th was an eventful day—in Peking as well as in Shanghai. All armed groups in Shanghai, whatever their banner, were told that henceforth they would come under military discipline. Any that objected would be treated as rebels.

In Peking Marshal Chang Tso-lin startled the legations by sending police to search the Soviet embassy. They found plenty—probably more than Chiang himself had hoped. The co-founder of the Chinese Communist Party, Li Ta-chao, and thirty-five other Communists had taken refuge there. In odd drawers and corners were files and documents apparently proving Soviet collusion in all the anti-foreign agitation. Chang Tso-lin's Foreign Minister at that time was the imperturbable Wellington Koo, who later became famous as a Nationalist diplomat. It was his job now to break relations with Russia and tell the Russians they were about to be expelled. Nobody was going to accuse the Manchurian warlord of softness towards the Communists—or for that matter towards the Kuomintang. Some months earlier indeed he had denounced Chiang Kai-shek and the Christian General Feng as "Bolsheviks". By that criterion, Li Ta-chao was beyond hope. And the point was made when Marshal Chang had him and nineteen others strangled on 28 April.

Humour was not Chiang Kai-shek's strong point, but he found wry pleasure in the thought that his Manchurian rival could describe *him* as a Bolshevik.

It remained for Chiang to scatter his Wuhan enemies. A mood of depression and discouragement had come over him at the news of the Central Executive Committee's decisions to strip him of various jobs. Li Tsung-jen was also disturbed by the news from Shanghai, and left the Anhwei front to see Chiang in the great city. He arrived as Chiang had received a telegram from General Ho Ying-ch'in—commanding the First Army, which used to be Chiang's own—resigning his command. Shaken and emotionally disturbed, Chiang said, "Even the First Army is unstable. I can hardly carry on!"

General Li replied, "It won't do any good if you quit. The present crisis comes from the Communist plot to annihilate the KMT." He suggested that Chiang immediately wire other military supporters to come to Shanghai and purge the party. His own Seventh Army could be summoned to Nanking and entrusted with the purge in that city. Chiang agreed and acted accordingly.

On 6 April—the day Marshal Chang's police were raiding the Soviet embassy—Wang Ching-wei slipped away to Wuhan. The next day, military leaders supporting Chiang Kai-shek arrived in Shanghai and immediately went into a huddle with Chiang, Li, and the garrison commander, Pai Ch'ung-hsi, to discuss plans for getting rid of the Communists. On the 8th, Chiang Kai-shek set up a Provisional Administrative Committee for Shanghai, to replace the temporary council set up by the Communists. On the 10th, Chiang and his supporters—calling themselves a purge committee—met in formal session and adopted various proposals by decree. All applications for membership of the Kuomintang were suspended, any memberships up for renewal were subjected to a three-month inquiry, and every party member was required to report on his political activities to his local branch every fortnight. It was resolved that the Wuhan government should be rejected, and that the KMT should transfer its central headquarters to Nanking, where the National Government should also have its seat.

With the purge decree to justify his actions (though its legal basis was contestable), Chiang was now almost ready to strike. On 11 April 1927 he issued a secret order to disarm the 2,700 Communist pickets. On the 12th, Chiang's supporters went into action and carried out the "purge" simultaneously in Kwangtung, Kwangsi, Fukien, Chekiang, Kiangsu, Anhwei, Nanking, and Shanghai. Chiang Kai-shek's debt to Li Tsung-jen and his Kwangsi associates was enormous: the purge would have been impossible without them.

What happened in Shanghai, however, is obscure and probably always will be. Accounts are wildly contradictory and charge has been piled on counter-charge. Each side, for instance, later accused the other of being in league with the local gangsters. Tong says the Communists hired local ruffians and "bandit-soldiers of the local warlord" and put them in the uniforms of the Labour Union Corps. On 12 April, led by the Communists and accompanied by their wives and children (Tong goes on), the rowdies surrounded and attacked the headquarters of the 26th Army Corps, provoking counter-fire from the troops.

That was one way of putting it. But there is an alternative version—that it was the Kuomintang who had put the local gangsters into labour uniforms.° At a given signal (the account goes), the false labour leaders attacked the working-class organisations throughout the city and shot all who resisted and many who did not. A more extreme version of the same story alleges that Chiang Kai-shek had reached a prior agreement with the "powerful Shanghai banker, opium tsar and secret society leader," Tu Yueh-sheng, before entering Shanghai. The Green Society gangsters, together with the fascist Blue Shirts, were said to have massacred "thousands" of labour leaders and militant workers. Thousands? Even the Chinese Communist Party is less sweeping in its claims. The official Communist figures are 300 killed and 5,000 "missing". Some of the most promising young Communist leaders lost their lives either in the fighting that day, or by execution in the purge that followed the abortive general strike called on 13 April. One of those arrested and sentenced to death was Chou En-lai, but he escaped with the complicity of the brother of the divisional commander, who had been Chou's student at Whampoa.†

The obscurities are worth looking at. Would the Communists have felt strong enough to attack the Nationalist forces? It might perhaps have been more sensible for them to lie low and wait for a better moment than the morrow of a victory. But then, they made other attacks during the year. Hsiung probably comes closest to the truth when he writes that Chiang started to disarm the Communists and their labour organisations: "They had been restive and it was

---

° Ch'en Po-ta, Mao Tse-tung's ghost-writer, writes: "On April 12, 1927, Chiang paid 50,000 dollars to the gangsters organised by Huang Chin-jung, Tu Yueh-sheng and Chang Hsiao-lin, directing them to attack the pickets of the workers." (*Jen-min kung-ti Chiang Kai-shek* [*Chiang Kai-shek—Enemy of the People*], pp. 34–35.) The notion that Chiang paid the gangsters is, however, absurd; it is they who were paying him.

† One of the less extreme of the hostile accounts is that of Harold Isaacs, *The Tragedy of the Chinese Revolution* (Stanford, 1962), pp. 175–85. The "massacre" version mentioned may be found in a footnote to Philip Jaffe's annotated edition of Chiang Kai-shek's book, *China's Destiny* (London: Dennis Dobson, 1947), pp. 119–20 fn. For the official Communist account, see Guillermaz, p. 125. Edgar Snow sharpens the official figure of 5,000 "missing" in these words: "The toll of the 'Shanghai massacre' is estimated at 5,000 lives." (*Red Star Over China*, p. 62.)

touch and go. The side which struck first would be open to criticism, but practical people preferred to be criticised rather than be stricken."

Chiang Kai-shek himself, alas, throws no light at all on these events. His account is a masterpiece of euphemistic understatement: "On April 12, to prevent Communist uprisings, the Revolutionary Forces in cooperation with local labour unions and chambers of commerce, disarmed the Red labour pickets and kept Communist saboteurs under surveillance. Only then was the situation in Shanghai brought under control."

Certainly the pickets were heavily armed and therefore dangerous not only to Chiang himself but to the Kuomintang Revolution. That is, if the Nationalist list of weapons captured even approximates to the truth: 3,000 rifles, 20 machine guns, 200 Mauser convertible pistols, 400 automatic pistols, 800,000 rounds of ammunition, seven handcart loads of axes, and 2,000 long-handled pikes. It seems unlikely that such weaponry was intended for ceremonial display.

What of Chiang's relations with the local gangs? The Red Society was the first in the field. It was formed with the aim of overthrowing the Manchus and restoring the Ming dynasty.° It was a secret religious and political organisation, which grew out of the T'aip'ing Rebellion and had links with the Boxers. It enforced respect for elders and other traditional Chinese values, and indulged in superstitious ceremonies. As time went on, the Red Society turned to gangsterism. The Green Society started as a splinter group of the Red Society, but soon established an autonomous power base south of the Yangtze River, with Shanghai as its command post. Operating along the river, it enrolled seamen and dockers and went in for extortion rackets and the buying of favours. The usual trio of vices swelled its coffers: drugs, loose women, and gambling.

° The formal name of the Red Society was *Hung Men*, which literally means the "School of the Great Ones". The founders chose the character "hung" because the reign title of Ming Tai Tsu (the first Ming Emperor) was *Hung Wu*, while "men" (gate) meant "school" in a broader sense. The Red and Green Societies cooperated with each other while maintaining their autonomous territories. They did not merge, as has frequently been assumed by outside observers. Although the Green Society was very strong in Shanghai, the Red Society was also active there, under its boss Huang Chih-jung.

Chiang Kai-shek himself never joined the Society, but he did have close links with it. His early protector, General Ch'en Ch'i-mei, was a member and may have found this useful when he was Shanghai's military governor. He enjoyed the favour of Sun Yat-sen, always in search of supporters and never very selective in his friendships. Indeed, Sun Yat-sen and his associates had earlier decided that both the gangs could be used to the advantage of the Revolution. The main boss of the Green Society was the banker Tu Yueh-sheng (mentioned earlier) and he, too, helped Chiang Kai-shek. Ch'en Ch'i-mei's nephew, Ch'en Li-fu, was Chiang's private secretary from 1925 to 1929. With his brother Ch'en Kuo-fu, he headed the right-wing KMT group known as the "CC Clique". In Chinese fashion, Chiang Kai-shek adopted the Ch'en brothers as his own "nephews". It was his way of repaying his debt to his mentor.

At the time of the Shanghai coup, Ch'en Li-fu was private secretary to Chiang Kai-shek. He was also running the Organisation Department of the KMT, to which he had been appointed on 20 March 1926. As he told me when I interviewed him in Taipei in 1974, he created and organised the Central Bureau of Investigation and Statistics (Tiu-ch'ia T'ung-chi). The CBIS was later taken over by Li-fu's brother Kuo-fu. As the secret internal security service of the National Government, the CBIS had its agents in the colleges, universities and newspapers, and other "cultural" organisations. The managing directors of all Kuomintang newspapers also worked for the CBIS. And in the colleges and universities, the Directors of Moral Code (Hsiun Tao Chang) likewise worked with the CBIS, which also appointed censors in various towns and provinces.

The parallel Military Bureau of Investigation and Statistics (MBIS), under Tai Li, was concerned with counter-espionage, and ran all the secret prisons. It was organised along lines similar to both the Nazi Gestapo and the Soviet KGB, with agents in every walk of life.

Ch'en Kuo-fu had come to the KMT's Organisation Department from a political secret society known as the "A. B. Corps".

The CC Clique and their secret organisations helped to extend and maintain Chiang Kai-shek's power—just as the Ch'en brothers' uncle and the gangsters were among the powerful friends who helped Chiang to rise from poverty in Shanghai in the early 1920s, when he lived in a windowless cubicle and worked as a jobber on the Shanghai stock exchange. Others who helped Chiang were the banker Ch'ien, and the shipping man Yü, who became Chairman of the Chamber of Commerce. The International Settlements thrived on the mainland's troubles (as indeed did Hong Kong), and there was always some legitimate business to supplement the sleazy income from the rackets.

When Chiang Kai-shek returned to Shanghai in 1927, he was a victorious general, no longer an indigent youth. The bankers and gangsters (the terms were sometimes interchangeable) financed him with substantial "loans". No doubt in return they expected freedom from harassment and closures, such as went on at that time in Wuhan, and relief from the Communist grip on the local trade unions. According to one account, Chiang received loans of $15,000,000 Chinese on smashing the power of the Communist pickets, and of $30,000,000 later. These sums were probably loans in name only, and the second seems to have been very reluctantly conceded. More precisely, the merchants are alleged to have received "military advice to subscribe, with intimations that arrests may follow failure to do so". One prominent industrialist jibed when asked for $500,000 and was thrown into gaol; coming to his senses, he secured his release for half that sum—on a non-returnable basis.

Willingly or under duress, the Shanghai compradores and bankers financed the right-wing government Chiang was about to set up. Moreover, they made Chiang's Kuomintang independent of Russian financial aid. This gave him much more freedom of manoeuvre.

The coup of 12 April 1927 marked the final break between Chiang Kai-shek and the Communists with their left-wing Kuomintang supporters. Henceforth, despite temporary appearances to the contrary, it would never be healed.

9. Chiang's Re-marriage

Outraged at the killings in Shanghai, the leftists and Communists of the Kuomintang now tried to discredit Chiang for good. At a meeting in Wuhan on 17 April 1927, the Central Executive Committee passed a resolution listing twelve "crimes" allegedly committed by Chiang—including "massacre of the people and oppression of the Party". Chiang was expelled from the party and dismissed from all his posts. A warrant was issued for his arrest "for punishment in accordance with the Law against counter-revolutionaries". Indeed a price was put on his head, or rather two prices: 250,000 taels of silver alive, and 100,000 taels dead.

Did the leftists think Chiang would now depart, drained of his support? If so, they underestimated him. Under his chairmanship, the right-wing leaders of the KMT had been meeting in Nanking since the 15th. That night, at Chiang's orders, police and army surrounded labour and Kuomintang offices in Canton. All the

Russian advisers were detained, and 2,000 arrests were made. Several Whampoa cadets and some girl students were executed. All Communists who had escaped were given ten days to report, or face a firing squad.

✕ When Chiang moved, he moved fast. On the 18th—the day after Wuhan had put a price on his head—he proclaimed his answer: the formation of a rival government in Nanking. At his side that day was Hu Han-min. In a lengthy declaration, Chiang Kai-shek reaffirmed Dr. Sun's Three Principles, denounced foreign interference, and called for a total break with the Communists. "If we allow their horrible politics to prevail," he said, "all will be brought to nought."

A week later—on the 25th—300,000 people gathered in Wuch'ang to denounce Chiang and his new government. Chaos of the worst kind had returned to China, much as it had come in 1911 after the overthrow of the Manchus. Two governments both claimed revolutionary legitimacy and the mantle of Sun Yat-sen. In the north, Chang Tso-lin was in control, going his own way.

The Communists too had reached crisis-point. Should they take advantage of the split within the Kuomintang to carry the leftists with them into violence? Or should they bide their time and continue to nurse the party alliance? They, too, were split. On 27 April 1927, 80 delegates, theoretically representing some 58,000 Communist Party members, met in their Fifth Party Congress at Wuhan. In a compromise agreement, it was decided that the big landlords and "counter-revolutionaries" in the Communist areas should be dispossessed. But any land belonging to Nationalist army officers was specifically exempt.

In Changsha, where a group of Communists had been active both in the city and the surrounding countryside, the local army commander rounded up about 100 agitators and had them shot. Some of the leaders got away just in time. Among them was Liu Shao-ch'i, later to be President of the Chinese People's Republic before his disgrace in the Cultural Revolution of the 1960s.

Further north fighting had started up again. On 24 April Chiang Kai-shek presided over a conference of the Army and Navy—which, such as it was, had decided for "his" revolution. It was decided to resume the Northern Expedition. Almost immediately, however, the Nanking forces found that the Wuhan forces had had the same idea, and the Expedition again ground to a halt. Facing powerful Northern opposition, the Wuhan forces started marching on Nanking, and the Nanking forces on Wuhan. Sensing his opportunity, the Christian General Feng Yü-hsiang seized the western section of Lunghai Railway. The Northerners were outflanked; the Southerners had checkmated each other. The deadlock was complete and only Feng could break it. Neither Wang Ching-wei nor Chiang Kai-shek could do without him; and both turned his way.

At this juncture, Chiang had a lucky break. Stalin's Comintern envoy—the Indian M. N. Roy—unwisely showed Wang Ching-wei a telegram from Moscow making it quite clear that the Communists intended to take over the Kuomintang. He had apparently hoped that Wang would be delighted at the prospect of a bright and rosy revolutionary future, arm in arm with the Communists. But the telegram worried Wang, who could now see that partnership with the Communists was going to mean absorption (as Chiang had said all along).

Wang shared his anxieties with his leftist colleagues. The hope was expressed that Feng Yü-hsiang could offer a way out. Feng obliged by inviting Wang and other top leftists to Chengchow for talks which began on 10 June 1927 and lasted three days. The Wuhan leaders made some territorial concessions to Feng, but were then sent away empty-handed.

Next Feng went east to meet Chiang Kai-shek at Hsuchow on the 19th, and the two men reached complete agreement a couple of days later. This meant that Feng had decided to back Chiang and put whatever pressure might be necessary on Wang Ching-wei. On the 21st he sent Wang a telegram urging that Borodin—who was still around—should be sent home, and that those members of the Wuhan leadership who so wished should join the Nanking National Government. Those who did not, he added, should take this chance to visit foreign countries.

Sensing danger, the Chinese Communists decided at last to offer sweeping concessions. In a declaration on 30 June, they offered to discipline armed pickets and place all workers' and peasants' organisations under government supervision.

It was too late. Wang was still hostile towards Chiang, but the balance of power had now been tipped against him, and on 15 July, the Wuhan Nationalists expelled the Chinese Communists from the

Kuomintang. Roy had already left on the 3rd; Borodin departed on the 27th. Before leaving, he said to a journalist that he was not going to abuse Chiang Kai-shek in any way:

> I am convinced that he is honest in his fight for the Nationalist cause, but he is not enough of a personality to carry his work through alone, to take upon himself the gigantic task of liberating and reconstructing China and the Chinese Constitution, and he is surrounded by men whose interests are quite different; all they want is to further their own personal plans.

The last point at any rate was, and remained, true.

General Bluecher (Galen) came to Shanghai to take his leave of Chiang. Although he had been attached to the Wuhan government as the chief Soviet military adviser, the two men still held each other in high regard. "This was one of the most moving partings in my life," wrote Chiang many years later.

The Chinese Communists sought desperately to retrieve by violence what they had failed to achieve by guile. Three times, between the beginning of August and the end of the year, they started armed insurrections—and three times they failed. The first of these, on 1 August, has a double historical significance. The Communists now celebrate that date as the anniversary of the birth of the People's Liberation Army (PLA); and Western historians regard it as the starting date of the first civil war between the Nationalists and Communists. (Communist historians agree that a civil war did start that day, but they call it the Second Revolutionary Civil War, counting the Northern Expedition as the first.)

Chou En-lai had gone to Nanch'ang, capital of Kiangsi province. He knew that a number of army units commanded by Communist officers were stationed in and around the town. He and his colleagues reckoned that if these men staged an uprising and brought their troops with them, the Communist Party would have the nucleus of an army of its own. Also in Nanch'ang was General Chu Teh—later to be Commander-in-Chief of the People's Liberation Army, but at that time head of the Public Security Bureau. Others present also later became famous. They included Lin Piao (who became Mao Tse-tung's designated heir but died in disgrace in a plane crash) and Ch'en Yi (later Foreign Minister).

The Communists seized the town, then lost it when one of the

Kuomintang generals turned out to be less sympathetic than they had supposed.

Although the Wuhan group had now started persecuting Communists, it still showed no signs of love for Chiang Kai-shek. The eastern warlord, Sun Ch'uan-fang, taking advantage of the mutual animosity between Wuhan and Nanking, launched a counter-offensive and drove Chiang's forces out of nearly all the land captured on the north bank of the Yangtze. It was a frustrating moment. The Wuhan forces were attacking the Nationalist Army farther south, and Chiang's men had to defend themselves: there were no troops to spare to ward off General Sun. The Christian General Feng Yü-hsiang, trying to be helpful—both to himself and to Chiang—proposed that representatives of the rival governments in Wuhan and Nanking should meet under his auspices on "neutral" ground at Anking.

According to Feng, he had a second meeting with Chiang Kai-shek in August, this time in Chengchow. As a preliminary, he had sent the Muslim General Ma Fu-hsiang with a friendly message: "Chiang would like to be sworn brothers with you." His reply was: "Very good." Feng Yü-hsiang continues the story:

> So Chiang and I exchanged our dates of birth and we became sworn brothers.
>
> Upon our meeting, we kowtowed to each other four times [to complete the ceremony]. Chiang asked me: "Now that we have become the best of friends, what are you going to do to enlighten me?" I told him: "The people are our masters. We do what the people want us to do; we do not do what they dislike."
>
> "Anything else, Big Brother?" Chiang asked again. I said: "If we can live up to what I have just said, we will be able to enforce Dr. Sun Yat-sen's Three Principles. Since you have asked me again, I shall tell you this: we must share the nice things and the hardships unequivocally with our soldiers; we must eat what they eat and wear what they wear. If you can do this, our revolution will be successful."
>
> Chiang replied: "Very good, we must do so."

Chiang Kai-shek could see only one way to break the deadlock: since he was the real point of contention, he would have to go. It was the most spectacular of his repeated resignations to that date. In a long statement on 13 August 1927, he lingered on the "outrageous deeds" of the Communists and alluded to the Wuhan-Nanking deadlock:

> The eyes and ears of the common people have begun to lose their clarity and sharpness. For three or four months the advance of the Northern Expedition has merely reached the border of Shantung. Why is it that we had pushed forward so quickly? And why is it that we now go forward so slowly? Think quietly and reflect carefully, the reason is easy to understand.

For his part, he had long thought of resigning, but the right time had not come. If he had done so too soon,

> our Party would have suffered in the following order. First, our soul would have been lost, merely our corpse would have been left behind. Then stars would have moved their positions and things would have been exchanged with each other. I am afraid that even the name Kuomintang would long have ceased to exist. Then there would have been no opportunity left for the people in Wuhan to rise at leisure to drive away the Communists. . . .

He hoped the comrades in Wuhan would join those in Nanking, that the Northern Expedition would be resumed, and that the Communists in Hunan, Hupei, and Kiangsi should "be thoroughly got rid of". As for himself, Chiang, although he had resigned all his posts, as a member of the Kuomintang and a citizen of China he would continue to do his duty, "as long as I have a single breath left".

This last pledge had an ominous ring. But few supposed they had heard the last of Kai-shek. In his mind, as always, his resignation would demonstrate that he was the one indispensable man, the only conceivable "saviour of China". The French say: *reculer pour mieux sauter*. The Chinese have an equivalent, which Hsiung paraphrases: "The longest way round is often the shortest way home."

But Chiang's departure relieved the tension. There was no point now in the Anking conference proposed by General Feng. On 14 August 1927, five leading Nanking politicians, headed by Hu

Han-min, jointly signed a letter to Feng, drafted in an ironical classical style. Was it not absurd, they asked, to meet and discuss (a play on words, the Chinese for "conference" being two characters meaning "to meet" and "to discuss") when the two sides were still fighting each other? "Jade and silk—offerings of peace—together with swords and spears—instruments of war—are to be used alternately and simultaneously. Isn't this to be a laughing-stock for the whole world?"

When Chiang's resignation was announced, he was already on his way to his home in Fenghua, having left Nanking the previous day, 12 August. With him went a bodyguard of 200 men. He stopped briefly in Shanghai, where not long after he was followed by Hu Han-min and others. The serenity of the mountains of his native province drew him on, and the refuge he had chosen was the Hsueh Tou temple, a Buddhist monastery on a mountain spur in Chekiang. His retinue were quartered at Chi Kou, his birthplace, about six miles away and 3,000 feet down.

To American visitors who sought him out, Chiang declared, possibly with momentary sincerity, that he planned to spend the next five years abroad, studying politics, economics, and military tactics. "His seclusion," wrote one newspaper correspondent, "is a myth." He had donned a long Chinese robe, which gave him a scholarly and traditional appearance at variance with the brisk image of the military statesman. A vast correspondence was reaching him.

He had not, then, entirely escaped affairs of state. The pressure nevertheless was reduced, and Kai-shek was able to turn his mind to his personal life. His first marriage had been a disaster, despite the birth of his son, Ching-kuo; and allowing for the minimal intimacy which this fact implied, he hardly knew his wife, Mao Fu-mei. His military training first, then the Revolution, had absorbed his energies and interests. On his rare visits home, she tried repeatedly to persuade him to give up his military career, but she might as well have suggested he should give up life. Such incomprehension may have had something to do with his brutal treatment of her. Her own interests were domestic, and politics left her puzzled and un-touched. In 1921, perhaps because he had met his second wife, Ch'en Chieh-ju, he decided on a divorce. Tong declares that the arrangement was amicable, and marked by generosity on her side.

But this gloss is inconsistent with the facts. In Chiang's own mind, it was a case of being determined to get rid of his first wife. In a letter to his brother-in-law Mao Mao-ching, he wrote at that time:

> . . . for the past ten years, I have not been able to bear hearing the sound of her footsteps or seeing her shadow. To this day, there has been no home worthy of the name. My decision to divorce her is the result of ten years' painful experience. It has not been made lightly. Enlightened and wise as you are, I think you may be able to plan for my happiness, freeing me from the life-long suffering.

At the home of Dr. Sun in Canton, about a year later, Chiang Kai-shek met a young American-educated woman with a rich father. She had an intelligent grasp of politics, she loved her country, and he could sense that her ambition matched his own: the perfect consort and companion for a political and military man of action. Her name was Mayling Soong. Her father, Charles Soong, had been a Christian since his youth and had all the ardour of a convert. One of the first Chinese to get his higher education in America, he had returned an ordained minister of religion. But he had not found the propagation of the gospel incompatible with making a large fortune as a manufacturer and by selling Bibles. His wife shared his devotion to Christianity. She had borne him a balanced family of three sons and three daughters, all of whom achieved success or fame. Ch'ingling Soong became Sun Yat-sen's second wife and sided with the Communists. The eldest girl, Eiling, married the banker H. H. K'ung, later Finance Minister. One of the brothers was T. V. Soong, who was one of the leftists in the Wuhan government, but who was to become Chiang's Finance Minister. The other brothers, T. L. and T. A. Soong, both rose to prominence in Shanghai banking and industry.

The three Soong girls were beautiful, intelligent, and strong-willed. Having made up his mind Chiang acted fast, as usual. Mayling listened politely as he outlined his matrimonial aspirations, but (he later said) she "was not interested". In fact, she was engaged at that time to Liu Chi-wen (who later became Mayor of Nanking). She did, however, consent to get letters from him, and during the next five hectic years of military and revolutionary action, he wrote frequently to press his suit.

Chiang formally proposed to Soong Mayling in May 1927, shortly after his Shanghai triumph. The Soongs held a family council. Soong Eiling was in favour, but T. V. Soong utterly disapproved of Chiang as a person. Although the Soong sisters were independent and aspired to emancipation, Mayling had already made it clear to Chiang that she did not feel she could marry without her mother's consent; and Mrs. Soong didn't think much of the match.

So much emerged from the family conclave. As a soldier, Chiang was traditionally low in the Chinese social scale. Besides, he was married—to one woman or another—until he could *prove* that there had been a divorce. (He had certainly divorced his first wife; but there seems to be no record of his divorcing the second. There may have been some doubts about the validity of the ceremony which sealed his second marriage.) Then, again, rumours of other women in his life had reached Mrs. Soong, not to speak of *tong* connections in Shanghai. Not least, he was not a Christian. (One is reminded of Franco's struggle to gain the acceptance of his future bride's family.)

Was it love or political ambition that led Chiang Kai-shek to press his suit so determinedly? Probably it was both. In conversation with Eric Chou in 1948, Hu Lin (co-founder of *Ta Kung Pao*, generally recognised as the only independent newspaper in China before 1949), said:

> Chiang's remarriage was a calculated political move. He hoped to win over Madame Sun Yat-sen (Soong Ch'ingling) and T. V. Soong by becoming their brother-in-law. At that point, Chiang also began to contemplate the need to seek support from the West. With Mayling as his wife, he would have the "mouth and ears" to deal with Westerners. Besides, he thought very highly of T.V. as a financial expert. But it would be unfair to say that Chiang did not fall for Mayling. Chiang obviously considered himself as a hero. And in Chinese history, heroes tended to fall for beauties. For political considerations, Chiang would have done anything. To have a new wife would seem a logical move for Chiang to make in those circumstances.

But "love" comes through in this love letter from Chiang to

Soong Mayling, which appeared in a Catholic paper of Tientsin on
19 October 1927:

> I am no longer interested in political activities. But thinking
> about the people I admire in this life, you, my lady, are the only
> one. While still in Canton, I asked someone to convey my wishes
> to your brother and your sister [presumably T. V. Soong and
> Mrs. Sun Yat-sen], but without getting anywhere. At that time,
> it could have been due to political relationships.
>
> Now that I have retreated to the mountain and wilderness, I
> find myself abandoned by the whole world, full of despair.
> Recalling the hundred battles fought on the front and my own
> type of heroism, I cannot but feel that the so-called achievement
> is just an illusion or a dream. And yet, my lady, your talent,
> beauty and virtue are not things I can ever forget. The only
> question is: What does my lady think of this retired soldier who
> has been abandoned by the whole world?

At the time of Chiang's "retirement" in the late summer of
1927, Mayling had at last let it be known that as far as she was
concerned he would make an acceptable husband; but it was up to
him to talk her mother into sharing this view. He descended from
his mountain monastery and reached Shanghai with a small
bodyguard on 23 September 1927. Did this mean his return to
public affairs? he was asked. Not at all, was the answer; he had
come to win and claim his bride. All being well, the wedding would
be in Shanghai and they would travel abroad for a year.

On the 28th, Chiang sailed for Japan. Ignoring some hard things
he had said about the Japanese role in hindering his Northern
Expedition in his resignation statement, the Tokyo press gave him
much adulatory publicity. On hearing of his arrival, Mrs. Soong
crossed the island to its eastern side to put as much distance
between them as possible. There, at Kamakura, Chiang found her,
nevertheless; and she, under pressure from Eiling K'ung, at last
granted him an interview. Chiang had brought documentary proof
of his divorce from his first wife (the second ceremony apparently
being regarded as invalid), and (in a pregnant but cryptic phrase)
had "settled the other complications of which the gossips had made
much". Yes, but was he ready to become a Christian? Smiling, as he
usually did in conversation, Chiang said he would do his best and

was prepared to study the Bible. He could not give an advance commitment, but he would certainly try. Mrs. Soong's resistance was crumbling. Soon she said yes.

There were two ceremonies, both on 1 December 1927. The first, a Christian one, was solemnised in the bride's home by Dr. David Z. T. Yui. The second one took place at the Majestic Hotel, then at the height of its fame, in the presence of many guests. That day, Chiang and his bride left on their honeymoon, which they spent first at Hangchow, then at Mokanshan, where the wooded hills of Chekiang meet its placid lakes.

In some ways, Mayling had a softening influence on her husband. He learned to call her "darling" in English.

But as his accent was so ghastly [said Ch'en Fan, who served Chiang Kai-shek in various capacities until 1949], nobody really understood what he was saying. Overhearing him all the time, his bodyguards thought that "darling" must be a fashionable way of saying *t'ai t'ai*, or Madame. One day one of them was asked by Soong Mayling to convey some message to Chiang. The poor chap stood at attention, respectfully saying: "Sir, Darling asked me to tell you . . .."

Chiang could not believe his ears. But soon he realised that the bodyguard did not really understand the meaning of the word, and waved him away.

In the summer of 1946, Eric Chou went to Kuling to cover the Marshall mission. On several occasions he stood a few feet away from Chiang Kai-shek and Soong Mayling, clearly hearing them addressing each other as "darling". This was perhaps the only English word he used frequently.

Another later opinion may be quoted here. In private conversation with Eric Chou in the summer of 1948, Hollington Tong made this comment: "Madame [Mayling] has done the President a lot of good. She makes him more aware of international affairs. But most important of all, he has become a devout Christian since they were married. He is now so familiar with chapters and verses of the Bible that he could qualify as a preacher."

On the morning of his marriage in 1927, Chiang issued a statement the full significance of which did not become apparent until the struggles ahead showed it to be valid. "After our wedding," he wrote, "the work of the Revolution will undoubtedly make greater progress, because I can henceforth bear the tremendous responsibility of the Revolution with peace at heart. . . . From now on, we two are determined to exert our utmost to the cause of the Chinese Revolution."

After Chiang had gone to Japan, the two Kwangsi generals, Li Tsung-jen and Pai Ch'ung-hsi, and Ho Ying-ch'in had defeated the troublesome Sun Ch'uan-fang's forces near Nanking. The Christian General, Feng, had been doing badly against the Manchurian warlord Chang Tso-lin, and another warlord also called Chang, who had been attacking Honan province from Shantung. In his hour of need, Feng's thoughts turned to his recently sworn brother, Chiang Kai-shek. He persuaded the Shansi warlord (the "model governor" Yen Hsi-shan) to join him in a telegram inviting Chiang to come back. But Chiang, his own thoughts intent on romance, took no notice.

As Chiang had calculated, the situation went rapidly from bad to worse after his departure from Nanking. In September, a new government—in name "united"—was set up in Nanking. In it were members of the right-wing Kuomintang and also names from the broken administration at Wuhan. In November, Wang Ching-wei, in the unlikely company of Hu Han-min (his former friend and colleague, when all was said) set up yet another rival "national" government, this time in Canton; with them was T. V. Soong. In Peking, Chang Tso-lin, who on 18 June had proclaimed himself Generalissimo of the Chinese Land and Sea Forces, still held sway. More than ever, China looked ungovernable.

To this confusion the Communists added their share of violence. Twice more, that year, they made a bid for power. On 7 August, a few days after the abortive Nanch'ang rising, the Comintern's new man in China, Besso Lominadze, summoned the Chinese Communist Party's Central Committee to an emergency meeting. On Moscow's orders the party agreed to resist the temptation—to which Mao would gladly have yielded—to set up rural Soviets, for fear (still) of offending the Kuomintang.

Mao Tse-tung's hour had not quite come, in fact. The new revolutionary team included Chou En-lai and Liu Shao-ch'i, but Mao was deep in Hunan, hoping for revolutionary marching orders. When his instructions came, they had at least the merit, in his eyes, of involving much violence. Selected landlords were to be murdered, for being landlords, and many others should also be killed, for being bullies or reactionaries. Government officials in the towns—all of them—were to be killed as well. All this blood was supposed to imbue the "people" with the revolutionary spirit.

The insurrection—since known as the Autumn Harvest Uprising—was launched on 9 September. One of the strategic targets was the city of Changsha. On the 15th, deeming the attack to be hopeless, Mao called it off; for which he was stripped of all his party posts—a misfortune of which he remained ignorant, because of poor communications, until the following spring. Far from being stirred to revolution, the peasants had remained indifferent. The Nationalist forces had reacted with energy. The Communists lost much face.

Undeterred, the Communists were at it again in December. Although Mao had been sacked, the party had now come round to his view that there was no time to waste in setting up Soviets. Indeed the new line was "permanent revolution"—a constant series of violent risings yielding, in the end, final victory. But this time they were going to try urban revolution, and the city they picked was Canton, traditionally the great revolutionary centre of China.

On 11 December carefully trained Red Guards fell on the police, disarmed them, and set up a local Soviet government—later known as the Canton Commune. The programme it announced was left-wing enough to please Trotsky, although the action was in fact ordered by Stalin, with callous disregard for the consequences to the Chinese revolutionaries. Land was to be confiscated, wealth redistributed, debts cancelled, and industry nationalised. Here indeed, while it lasted, was the "dictatorship of the proletariat".

The euphoria was short-lived. On the 12th, the Nationalists launched a powerful military counter-blow, supported by a naval bombardment. The ordinary inhabitants of Canton—who, in non-Marxist parlance, might merit the title of "the people", lifted not a finger to defend the Soviet. The retribution was ruthless. Many thousands were massacred (how many is not precisely known), among them ten Russian citizens.

When the Russian consulate and commercial establishments were overrun and searched, proof was found that they had been used as centres for espionage and subversion, thus setting a pattern that has not changed to this day. On 14 December 1927, the National government closed all Russian consular and commercial establishments and diplomatic relations were broken. All over China, Communism was in retreat. The Comintern had lost its subversive base.

Chiang Kai-shek had come back to active life in time to give the order to close all Russian offices. Wang Ching-wei had gone to Shanghai at the time of his wedding and a reconciliation had taken place. While Chiang was on his honeymoon, the Central Executive Committee of the Kuomintang met in Shanghai, from 3 to 10 December and on the last day, Chiang was restored to his former post as Commander-in-Chief. The marriage itself had helped to swell the popular clamour for his return. More than ever, Chiang dominated the National movement.

10. Chiang "Unites" China

In 1928, Chiang Kai-shek resumed the Northern Expedition, captured Peking, and was appointed Chairman of the State Council and Generalissimo. On paper, at least, he united China under his rule. All but one of the great warlords had come over to his banner; and the last one—Chang Tso-lin—died as Chiang entered the northern capital. As for the Communists, Chiang might well have supposed—during the first few months of the year—that they would never recover from their defeats of 1927. True, the summer brought further clashes between Nationalist and Communist troops, but the Nationalists easily came out on top.

It soon became clear, however, that the sweeping victories of 1928 were illusory. Chiang's successes rested on the attractive power of his armies and little else. His claim to be the heir of Sun Yat-sen and the national ideal was far from universally accepted, and many of those who claimed to support the Three Principles gave no more than lip service. Among them were those most formidable enemies of Chiang whom he had defeated and would go on defeating but never decisively, until in the end their power and numbers were just too great for him: the Communists. Nationalist China in 1928 was like an apparently healthy patient disinclined to recognise that he was suffering from cancer.

After the collapse of the Autumn Harvest Uprising, Mao's forces had dwindled to a few hundred men. He marched them to a forbidding range of mountains straddling the border between Hunan and Kiangsi provinces and known as the Ridge of Wells. They reached their new mountain base early in November 1927, and the following February they were joined by Chu Teh with a force of his own. The combined forces were given the title of "Fourth Red Army of the Chinese Workers' and Peasants' Army". By that time, they numbered between 8,000 and 10,000 men. It is hardly an exaggeration to say that in the small area—at its largest thirty miles by thirty—under Communist control, Mao Tse-tung created the political instrument for his future conquest of all China. For it was there under his guidance that the People's Liberation Army grew to political maturity. From the first it was a highly politicised army, with constant indoctrination along with purely military training. It was also an egalitarian army. Pay was very low, but everybody, from the commanders down, drew the same five cents a day. Funds (wrote Mao himself years later) were "obtained exclusively through expropriating local bullies".

The psychological secret of Mao's army was his taking endless pains to make the peasants and the troops identify with each other. In the initial phase, the poorer peasants were encouraged to take part in the round-up of the landlords and of richer peasants and to participate in or witness the ensuing massacres. Since it was true enough that they had suffered from centuries of oppression and exaction, there was some motive for this participatory brutality, and the peasants came to see the army as their liberators and indeed as an extension of themselves. Moreover, Mao enforced a strict code of behaviour for troops billeted in peasant households.

While Mao was settling into his rocky headquarters, Chiang Kai-shek was preparing to resume his dictatorship over the Kuomintang and all it controlled. Much against their will, but recognising that he was indispensable, his colleagues had in effect made him dictator "for the duration". The qualification was important.

Having closed the Russian offices in mid-December, Chiang had gone back to Shanghai, partly no doubt to be with his bride, but largely also to force his colleagues into pressing him to return to the job. On 2 January 1928 a telegram duly came, urging him to come immediately to Nanking, where the government was installed, and resume his leadership of the Northern Expedition. On the 4th, after several more telegrams had come, he boarded the train for the capital. On the journey, two separate attempts to derail the train were frustrated, but this reminder that he had determined enemies did not dampen his pleasure at the noisy popular and ceremonial welcome that awaited him.

On the 9th, he formally resumed his duties as Commander-in-Chief, pledging loyalty to the Central Executive Committee and undertaking to resign on completion of the Northern Expedition. By now his colleagues knew what value to attach to one of Chiang's pledges of resignation. They needed his military skills and leadership but did not want to give him political power. Accordingly, he was elected Chairman of the Military Council, but only to ordinary membership of the Party Presidium. These Kuomintang party elections were held in Nanking in February. Everybody agreed that the military drive could not be resumed until they had taken place.

His colleagues may have wished to limit his power, but Chiang inevitably dominated the meetings. Towards the end of January he had made a bid for the support of educated opinion with a new manifesto, much publicised at the time. China, said Chiang, should negotiate an end to the unequal treaties with all governments prepared to talk. He warned those that were not that China would declare its treaties with them null and void, if necessary. The new policy towards Soviet Russia should be affirmed and carefully explained. It should remain in force until such time as the Russians produced "conclusive proof" that their attitude towards the Chinese Revolution had changed. There was a curious proposal in the manifesto—that China should aid the "oppressed peoples" of colonies and dependencies to liberate themselves—an interesting precedent for the very similar policy followed decades later, and with infinitely greater means to back it, by the Chinese People's Republic.

Chiang's position on internal affairs needs some background. The second of Sun Yat-sen's Three Principles of the People was Democracy, and it had been clear from the start that this was not going to be something to be enjoyed by the people in the immediate future. Back in 1924, the First Congress of the Kuomintang, heavily influenced by Borodin, had called for a party dictatorship. Dr. Sun himself had explained that the Revolution would go through three phases: military supervision, political tutelage, and constitutional government. During the period of "tutelage", the party was to have the monopoly of political power. But this period was to be used to train the people for local government. Depending on how long the training took and how successful it was, they could go on from local government to constitutional government and in time to a form of democracy.

That, at any rate, was the theory. And now—in January 1928—Chiang Kai-shek was calling for a clear and immediate definition of the three successive periods, so that the people should know where they stood. In all districts of China officials should be trained for self-government; specialist examinations should be held to find the right experts for the right jobs.

When the Kuomintang committees met in plenary session a few days later, they adopted all Chiang's proposals. And yet, his demand for a stated limit to the period of political tutelage was to remain a dead letter. The whole issue looked unreal and remote in February 1928. Officially, the period of "tutelage" had not even begun, since the period of military supervision was still in force. The first priority was to carry the Northern Expedition to final victory. The Generalissimo was asked how long he would need and said he thought he could finish the job by August.

The meeting ended on 7 February, and a few days later Chiang got in touch with Feng Yü-hsiang. The two men drew up detailed plans for resuming the Northern Expedition, and picked men for the top military jobs. Since Feng had only lately rallied to the Kuomintang, he was not at this stage disposed to question Chiang's supreme authority. It was agreed that the Generalissimo, in addition to his overall command, should personally lead the First Route Army, which numbered about 100,000 men. Feng was to command the Second. The Third went to Yen Hsi-shan, who had been governor of Shansi in the north ever since the Revolution of 1911. Li Tsung-jen, a comrade of Chiang's since the troubled Kwangsi days, took command of the Fourth Army, which was to stay in reserve. In the dark days of the Nationalist collapse in 1949, it fell to

Li to be Acting President of the Republic. The active phase of preparations now began.

Even at this feverish and expectant time, Shanghai drew Chiang, and he went there at the beginning of March with Madame Chiang.° Hollington Tong unpersuasively remarks that "he had never had any great love for the cosmopolitan metropolis on the banks of the Whangpoo, and had spent time in the city only when duty made it necessary". If it was not "great love", then it was something equally potent that beckoned him—friends, money, influence, the fascination of evil?—for he could never stay away from Shanghai for very long. This time, at any rate, it was not to praise it that he went there, but to inspect his troops at Lunghua Garrison and caution them to stay out of trouble involving foreign troops in the International Settlements. There had already been such incidents recently. "Shanghai," he said, "is a meeting place for the people of all nations. If our men here become disorderly, our task will be doubly difficult. The environment of Shanghai is so bad that almost any army, stationed here for three months or at most for half a year, becomes demoralised and practically useless. Therefore we, the officers, must make up our minds to control the troops and guard them against temptations, curbing vicious habits and setting an example to our soldiers."

Back in Nanking a few days later, he made his point by one of those ruthless acts of his. He had about fifty soldiers summarily executed for their alleged part in the Communist-inspired anti-foreign riots of the previous year. Many others were placed under military arrest.

This was his way of reassuring the foreign powers, whom he wished to cut to size but not to alienate. He then formally reassured them that there would be no anti-foreign excesses during the Northern Expedition. In return he called on the Powers to stop providing arms and money to the warlords, which would only prolong the civil war.

At the end of the month Chiang moved his headquarters to Hsuchow, the northernmost point of the Nationalist advance in the first phase of the Expedition. He now deployed his armies some way

---

° It is of course absurd to designate Chinese married women as "Madame" instead of "Mrs.", since their language is no more French than English. But the form "Madame Chiang" is so well established that I have stuck to it.

north of the Yangtze on an east-west line. Some 700,000 men were under his command—about seven times as many as when the Northern Expedition first started. Facing him were Chang Tso-lin's 400,000 men, led by his son, Chang Hsueh-liang ("the Young Marshal"), and half a dozen other commanders.

On 7 April Chiang ordered the general offensive. His strategy was clear, and at first went strictly as planned. The main thrust was that of his own First Route Army, driving northward along the Tientsin-Pukow Railway. Meanwhile, Feng Yü-hsiang's Second Army, and Yen Hsi-shan's Third were attacking Chihli from the south and west respectively, to draw the Manchurian warlords' forces away from the main theatre. Twenty-one days after the start of the offensive, the Nationalist troops entered Tsinan, capital of Shantung.

There, however, they were delayed by a new, unexpected, and ruthless foe: Japan. The long string of Japanese atrocities began with the so-called "Tsinan incident". For a while, the Japanese had taken a kind of pride in Chiang as a successful product of their own stern military education. Now they were beginning to see him as a threat to their predatory plans for northern China. Chiang had to be checked, somehow; if not, he now looked as if he might drive their protégé, Chang Tso-lin, out of Peking.

Japan chose to make an example of Tsinan, where there were important Japanese commercial interests. Under the peace settlement of 1919, Japan had taken over Germany's special privileges in Shantung. The Chinese had not recognised this situation, but the Japanese decided to invoke it anyway as a device to halt the Nationalist armies as they drove northwards. They moved a large force into the city.

Chiang Kai-shek was anxious to avoid a clash. His troops did not need to pass through Tsinan, which the Northerners had already evacuated, so he instructed his commanders not to enter it. One of them, however, either misunderstood the order or chose to flout it. Others followed suit, and soon Nationalists and Japanese faced each other in an atmosphere of growing tension.

Then came the first atrocity. The Japanese surrounded the local office of the Nationalist Foreign Ministry, cut off the noses and ears of the man in charge and of his staff of sixteen, and then murdered all of them. When Chiang sent the Nationalist Foreign Minister to negotiate with the Japanese commander, he was arrested. Under duress he signed a statement blaming the *Chinese* for starting the incident.

Meanwhile, Tsinan was being shelled and machine-gunned by the Japanese. Two options faced the Generalissimo. He could stand up to the Japanese and risk a punishing confrontation and the failure of his campaign, or he could bow down and continue the drive northward. Choosing the second course, he quietly pulled his troops out of Tsinan and shifted the main thrust of his campaign to Honan, where he went to take command. This retreat was to bring criticism upon his head when the dust of battle had settled. But the alternative course would have been disastrous, and would not have saved him from still more severe censure.

The Tsinan incident had halted the Northern Expedition by about a week. By the end of May, Chiang had routed two of the three warlords who still stood in his path: Wu P'ei-fu and Sun Ch'uan-fang. The third, Chang Tso-lin, was about to concede the glittering prize of Peking—and to lose his life. On 3 June, the Old Marshal sent a circular telegram to announce that his forces would now withdraw from within the Great Wall. He and his staff had packed their belongings and that day they boarded the train to Mukden, his former Manchurian headquarters. They didn't know that the Japanese, who had financed some of his endeavours and supported him so long as he was useful, had decided that now he had failed, he had become expendable. As the train neared Mukden, the coach in which the Old Marshal was travelling was blown up by efficiently sited Japanese bombs. Tso-lin's wounds were mortal.

Chiang did not immediately learn of this final and decisive stroke of good fortune, for the Young Marshal, Chang Hsueh-liang, kept the event secret until he had decided on his own best course. Very sensibly, his decision was to join the Nationalists.

Early in June, Chiang Kai-shek and his forces made their triumphant entry into the northern capital. Chang Hsueh-liang had announced that all his troops were being withdrawn to Manchuria. He then sent emissaries to Peking to negotiate with Chiang. They were unsuccessful, and Chiang sent his own emissaries to Mukden. One of them—a journalist named Hsiao Tung-tzu—was chosen with some discernment for his prowess at golf, dancing, and drinking, for these were Chang Hsueh-liang's favourite recreations. For weeks, the two men were constantly seen together—though only in the ballroom and on the golf course. At last Hsiao reported to Chiang Kai-shek that the Young Marshal was really being very understanding: he was quite prepared to come over to the Revolutionary Army, so long as his troops could remain in Manchuria. He was pleased to accept Chiang's offer of the title of Deputy Commander-in-Chief of the Revolutionary Army—an honour which other warlords had been denied. This typically Chinese solution left him in effect the Manchurian warlord. Probably Chiang had no choice in the matter, since he was unwilling to spare the resources for a Manchurian campaign. But he had a good and positive reason for allowing the Young Marshal to continue to occupy Manchuria: in that position he was a counter-weight against the Shansi warlord, Yen Hsi-shan, whom Chiang Kai-shek (rightly) did not trust. This was the advice Chiang had had from the cleverest of his personal assistants, Yang Yung-t'ai, at that time the Generalissimo's speech writer; and Chiang listened to him. (Yang was later assassinated during the suppression campaigns against the Communists.)

In the heady days of the capture of Peking, the news of ominous clashes nearly 2,000 miles to the south passed almost unnoticed. In June 1928, and again in July, Nationalist forces attacked the increasingly troublesome Communist strongholds in and around the Ridge of Wells. The first time, the Nationalists lost about 1,000 men through desertion or capture. The next time, they seized several Communist towns and occupied them, withdrawing after twenty days. By this time, all Nationalist eyes were facing north, and Mao Tse-tung's zone was left in peace until winter set in. On 22 July, the Nationalists suffered a serious defection, the forerunner of many to come in the later years of the civil war. That day, a whole Nationalist regiment went over to the Communists. Its commander was P'eng Teh-huai—internationally famous later as a Marshal of the People's Liberation Army and as the Defence Minister of the Chinese People's Republic until in 1959 he was disgraced for defending the Soviet connection in the great Sino-Soviet split. The troops he took with him in July 1928 were joined by local peasant groups and called themselves the Fifth Army.

Mao was in some trouble at that time. The land reform had brought many of the poorest peasants to the Communist side, but alienated many of the middle peasants whose cooperation was needed. The Nationalist blockade and the summer operations had hurt. Mao's troops were rarely paid and were ill-fed. Some went into revolt.

Politically, Mao was still under a cloud because of his failures of the previous year. For obvious reasons he did not attend the Sixth Congress of the Chinese Communist Party, which met in Moscow from 17 July to 1 September. The changes and decisions that resulted need not concern us in detail here, but it is worth noting that the real power passed to Li Li-san, an intellectual who had been a student in France and who would soon be involved in a monumental controversy with Mao Tse-tung. Chou En-lai was elected to the new Politburo, but Mao Tse-tung was not. But Mao did get a seat on the Central Committee. Communications, however, were so poor that Mao had no inkling of his partial return to favour until the winter had set in.

Chiang Kai-shek, too, was of course unaware of these developments at the time, although he was to refer to them years later in his book, *Soviet Russia in China*. The entry into Peking was the grand climax of his Northern Expedition, but his first concern was not so much with glory as with ritual and symbolism. Flanked by his top military subordinates, he made a pious pilgrimage to the Temple of the Azure Cloud on the west hill just outside the capital.° There, before the coffin of Sun Yat-sen, Chiang and his colleagues stood with bared heads. Soon (writes Hsiung), Chiang was sobbing uncontrollably.

The emotion was short-lived, and so was the euphoria of victory. Now that the fighting was over, the Kuomintang immediately broke out into fresh factional fights between leftists and conservatives and between supporters and opponents of Chiang Kai-shek. In late July 1928, he had gone to Nanking for a meeting of the KMT's Central Executive Committee. To nobody's surprise—for his habits were well known—he presented his resignation. This time he had a good ostensible justification. It had always been clearly understood that he was to be the Commander-in-Chief only for the duration of the campaign, and the fighting was now over. Chiang's real reason for quitting at this time, however, was to block his subordinate

---

° Since Nanking was to remain the capital, Peking ("Northern Capital") was re-named Peiping ("Northern Peace"), and the province of Chihli (Metropolitan province) was given the new style of Hopei (North of the Yellow River).

commanders, who wanted him to ignore the Young Marshal's offer of allegiance and press on with the military conquest of Manchuria. After all, they reasoned, Chang Hsueh-liang's father had commanded the anti-southern armies from Peking, and they reckoned that his son should be taught to submit the hard way. But Chiang was anxious to consolidate his power and with it the Revolution as he conceived it. Conquering Manchuria would waste scarce resources, and for the time being he was quite content with a formal recognition of Nanking's authority.

Chiang's subordinates thought he was wrong, but they were less than ever prepared to go it alone. There was no reason, they argued, why Chiang Kai-shek should not be Generalissimo in peacetime. And indeed, it would be useful and an honour to them if he became the Chairman of the State Council. In terms of real power, all this fell short of full satisfaction. True, he could add new titles to those he had already held, and he had once again demonstrated that he was the indispensable man. But getting people to obey him and respect his authority was quite another thing. In that sense, Chiang's power was illusory.

Chiang's colleagues and subordinates noted a change in him after the Northern Expedition had been successfully completed. They now found him "arrogant and conceited, uninhibitedly practising dictatorship". For his part, the Generalissimo subordinated all else to nationalism and patriotism. He identified himself with China and never for a moment doubted his claim to be the rightful heir to Sun Yat-sen's Revolution. But he saw the unity of China in terms of personal obeisance to himself. His military colleagues were willing to kowtow—at least up to a point—but not to an extent that would interfere with any spoils of war that came their way. By and large, his political colleagues were equally self-serving.

The Executive Committee did, however, approve Chiang's proposal that five *Yüan* (or Councils) should be set up in accordance with Dr. Sun's Will: Legislative, Executive, Judiciary, Control, and Examination. On paper, at least, Dr. Sun's distinctively Chinese concept of a Five-fold Constitution was taking shape. No doubt weary after this constructive effort, the members resumed their squabbling, the rightists walked out, and Chiang—left without a quorum—declared the session closed. It was mid-August.

A political lull followed, and Chiang tried hard to use it to persuade the leading KMT figures of both Left and Right to cooperate with him. He had more success with the Right than with the Left. Telegrams to Wang Ching-wei and Mrs. Sun Yat-sen, who were in Europe, went unanswered. In October the Executive Committee met in Nanking to implement earlier decisions. On the 4th it promulgated an Organic Law of the Republic of China. The period of "political tutelage"—that is, of Kuomintang party dictatorship—was formally announced, although no terminal date was specified. Henceforth the new central authority for all China styled itself the National Government (Government of the Nationals, or People).

On the 10th (the "Double Tenth", since it was the anniversary of the 1911 Revolution), Chiang Kai-shek took office as Chairman of the new State Council. The eighteen members included several rightists but no leftists. As part of the "spoils diplomacy" marking the achievement of "unity", the Council also included the northern warlords, Feng Yü-hsiang (the Christian General), Yen Hsi-shan, and Chang Hsueh-liang. As Chairman of the State Council and Generalissimo, Chiang Kai-shek had overriding authority. Moreover, it was agreed that he alone should have the privilege of receiving representatives of foreign powers. This made him in effect, though not in name, President of the Republic.

Chiang had thus, after his military struggles and resignations, achieved the summit of political ambition. He was forty-one, and had no reason to doubt the brightness of his star. He had chosen Nanking as the National Capital for good and practical reasons (which the late Hsiao Tung-tzu, managing director of the Central News Agency for some forty years, enumerated for Eric Chou in 1947 in Nanking, in a discussion of the prospect that Chiang might move his capital to Peiping to face up to the Chinese Communist armies in Manchuria). They were:

1. It was in Nanking that Dr. Sun Yat-sen proclaimed himself Provisional President of the Republic.
2. Peiping was too far from Kiangsi, where the Communists had established a stronghold from which Chiang Kai-shek intended to dislodge them.
3. Nanking offered the advantage of being close to Shanghai, which was the financial centre for the whole country.

4. Chiang's own troops were mostly southerners who would find it difficult to settle down in the north.
5. Chiang hoped that the proximity of Nanking to Shanghai would improve his chances of international publicity.
6. Chiang felt that Peiping had been the Imperial Capital for too long to be acceptable as the headquarters of the Revolution.

Feng Yü-hsiang's descent on the capital brought colour and eccentricity into the quarrelsome political scene. With his battered straw hat of notorious antiquity, his faded grey battledress of a private soldier, and his handmade cloth sandals, he was the living embodiment of a reputation for parsimony. Driving himself around the city in an army lorry, he loved to drop in unannounced on high officials and rouse them from slumber at pre-breakfast hours. These visits were more enjoyable to him than to them. He was made Minister of War, apparently in the belief that he would cut expenditure to the bone.

Yen Hsi-shan came to Nanking reluctantly and late to take up an appointment as Minister of the Interior. But not liking what he saw, he soon returned to his stronghold at Taiyuan, thereafter turning unhelpful.

The new arrangements were makeshift and looked it. At this pinnacle of his apparent power, Chiang found a precarious and shifting support among the militarists, the conservatives, and the tycoons of Shanghai. The Kuomintang's reformers were virtually unrepresented. It is not necessary to be a Marxist to note that apart from nationalism, nothing was now left of Dr. Sun's revolutionary hopes.

Immediately, with that restless energy of his, Chiang demonstrated his peculiar style of government: by moral exhortation and tongue-lashings on the spur of sudden indignation. On a tour of inspection in November 1928, for instance, he ordered the gambling and opium dens and the brothels of Pengpu closed within three days. At Anking he summoned the bewildered district magistrates and told them to stamp out banditry, build new roads, and open new schools. This, he said, was a new era.

Back in the political strife of Nanking, he complained, "Since the death of Dr. Sun we have not had a single day of perfect accord and solidarity." Office-holders, he ranted, "do not know the meaning of work. . . . Our office hours are short—only six hours a day . . . yet I have seen staff members lounging at their desks, gazing blankly into space, or reading newspapers, or sleeping."

Whatever the fate of the Revolution, a soldierly briskness followed Chiang. The year ended well for him. His inclusion of the Young Marshal in the State Council had angered Li Tsung-jen, but Chang Hsueh-liang now did what Chiang had hoped he would do. On 29 December 1928, he ordered the Nationalist flag to be hoisted above his headquarters in Mukden and publicly announced his allegiance to the National Government. It is ironical to think that eight years later, he would kidnap and humiliate Chiang in the notorious Sian incident. But that was in the future. At the end of 1928, Chiang could claim to have united China under his leadership, and the claim looked solid.

11. The Lost Revolution

The "unity" of China, which Chiang and the outside world thought he had achieved by the end of 1928, was a cruel illusion. The gigantic façade, impressive from the front, was seen from unkinder angles to have no real structure behind it.

Chiang Kai-shek had led his armies northward on a great wave of popular enthusiasm, and he must be given credit for the gift of leadership that drew rival armies and their commanders to his banner. But there lay the problem: although there had been stiff fighting here and there as the rivals tested his strength, he had not, in any true sense, mastered his enemies or conquered their territories. They had merely, in the traditional Chinese way, decided that he was stronger than they, and switched sides. That is why his advance had been so rapid, and why the Nationalist army, which initially numbered only 100,000 men, nominally totalled nearly 2,000,000 at the end of 1928—twenty times the starting figure.

Although the situations are not strictly comparable, it is instructive to reflect on the disparity between Franco's conquest of Spain and Chiang's apparent conquest of China. It took Franco about thirty-two months of grinding and bloody battles to defeat the Spanish Republic and make himself master of the whole country. It took Chiang only twelve months—nine of them in 1926 and 1927, followed by a political lull, then three months from April to June 1928—to "conquer" China, which is more than seven times the size of Spain. Franco annihilated his enemies, defeating them in battle and either driving the remnants into exile or executing them. Chiang contented himself with a formal change of allegiance. The main difference between China in 1926 before the start of the Northern campaign and China at the end of 1928 was that the war-lords who had previously defied the Kuomintang now claimed membership of it. In most cases, the local reality of their power remained unchanged.

Impatient for quick successes, which brought him temporary glory and prestige, the Generalissimo had neglected the only sound principle of territorial conquest in a feudal entity, which would have been to remove those who had initially defied him and replace them with men of his own choice, owing allegiance to the new Republic and to him as its head. When Caesar conquered Gaul, he did not leave Vercingétorix in power. Li Tsung-jen had been right when he urged Chiang to snub the Young Marshal and subjugate Manchuria by force of arms.

Chiang's failure to acquire the reality of regional power, his readiness to content himself with a meaningless allegiance, stand out as his most fundamental errors of judgment. Time and again, in the ensuing years, his authority was to be challenged in local rebellions. He always won, in one fashion or another. But these successive local wars drained his strength and diverted his attention from China's real problems. Meanwhile, the strength of the Communist base kept growing; and from 1931 Chiang had, in addition, to contend with the formidable invading power of Japan.

The great demobilisation crisis of 1929, in the wake of Chiang's triumphs, brought home to him, as nothing else could, the limitations of his authority. As even Hollington Tong—the official biographer and panegyrist of Chiang Kai-shek—admits,

the area over which the National Government actually ruled comprised only a few provinces. Feng Yü-hsiang was the strong man of the North and the great North-West; he held sway over Shantung, Honan, Shensi, Kansu, Chinghai and Ninghsia; his rival for power was Yen Hsi-shan, who, from his rugged stronghold in the Shansi hills, ruled Hopei, Chahar and Suiyuan. In the South, Li Tsung-jen controlled Kwangtung, Kwangsi, Hunan and Hupei. China was still broken up into regional spheres of influence, almost feudal States. . . .

Chiang's undisputed power was confined to only five of the lower Yangtze provinces.

Demobilisation lay at the heart of Chiang's problem because the regional warlords depended on their armed manpower. Logically enough, Chiang argued that since unity had been achieved and the fighting was over, most of the men under arms could be demobilised and return to civilian life. But the warlords did not need to be told that to demobilise was to lose the source of their power. All they needed to do was to stand firm, and their individual wills prevailed over Chiang's.

The situation was both grotesque and tragic. After the fall of Peking, about 2,200,000 were under arms in China. If the armies were counted as one, this was the largest army in the world in this time of relative peace elsewhere. Of this gigantic force, nearly 2,000,000—by Chiang's own estimate—were nominally obedient to the National Government and therefore to the Commander-in-Chief. The rest were wandering bands or remnants of the most stubborn of the local satraps. If Tong's figures can be trusted (they can be no more than approximations), the 2,000,000-man armed services were absorbing no less than 75 percent of the annual revenue of some $400,000,000.

Chiang had very clear ideas on what to do with the men who were to be demobilised. They were to be turned into a labour corps and used to build roads, plant trees, and mine minerals. In mid-January 1929, he summoned all the top generals to a Disbandment Conference in Nanking. The Kwangsi generals had 230,000 men under arms; Feng Yü-hsiang had 220,000; and Yen Hsi-shan 200,000. As for the State Council—that is, Chiang himself—it commanded some 420,000. It did not take the generals long to realise that what Chiang was proposing was the drastic reduction of their forces and the strengthening of his own (which were notionally those of the Republic).

According to Feng's account, when the conference began, Chiang Kai-shek led all the participants to a portrait of Sun Yat-sen, and insisted that each of them should take an oath of allegiance. He then proposed that each Route Army should retain twelve divisions and disband the rest. One of the weaker warlords pointed out that those with few soldiers under arms would have to recruit six or seven divisions to keep up with the rest. Chiang himself had recently absorbed more than ten new divisions into his own army near Peking, and was disinclined to listen.

One thing was formally agreed: that the country should be divided into six disbandment areas. This looked uncomfortably like business, and the warlords grew restless.

One afternoon Chiang Kai-shek invited Feng Yü-hsiang to bathe in the hot spring outside Nanking. When they were drying themselves, Chiang said: "It is often said that whoever holds Peking, Canton, Shanghai, and Wuhan in his hands controls the whole of China." Feng took this as a hint that Chiang wanted him to move against the warlords holding those areas. He replied evasively: "As a national leader, you must be magnanimous. So long as you can win popular support as well as the army's, it doesn't matter what places they occupy. They are all your brothers working for you."

On 7 February, after three weeks of talks, Feng Yü-hsiang suddenly walked out and the conference broke up.

The return to war was almost indecently swift. The first move was by Li Tsung-jen and the other Kwangsi warlords, when they turned on one of Chiang's generals in Hunan and removed him. This was the signal for Li Tsung-jen and Feng Yü-hsiang to resign from the National Government.

These dramatic moves took place during the preparations for the Third Congress of the Kuomintang, which was to take place in Nanking in March. One of the Kwangsi generals left Canton under a KMT safe-conduct to attend the conference, and was arrested on Chiang's orders as soon as he arrived. There was proof that he had been plotting, Chiang explained, doubtless truthfully.

Now came a long denunciatory telegram from Chiang's leftist rival, Wang Ching-wei, who was in France. Chiang had thought to placate him, as well as Feng Yü-hsiang and Yen Hsi-shan, by having them elected to the Central Executive Committee, but Wang was beyond placating, Feng was back in Shantung, and Yen was not interested. Against this troubled background, the meetings were stormy—not least because those members who had remained more or less loyal to Chiang did not see why he should be offering favours to those who had not.

Weakened and confused by their dispersal, by the arrest of one of their generals, and the sudden removal of another supporter in a coup in the north, the Kwangsi forces soon collapsed. By the end of April, Chiang was victorious in central China.

The Christian General was his next problem. When Feng walked out of the Disbandment Conference in February, his first objective had been to reassert his hold on Shantung where the Japanese forces—after protracted negotiations—were about to evacuate the Tsinan-Tsingtao Railway. To the astonishment of Feng and of the Japanese, Chiang Kai-shek requested the Japanese to delay their departure, so that his own troops—instead of Feng's—could move in. Feng retaliated by concentrating his forces in Honan and cutting the province's rail communications. He was still potentially a formidable threat, but Chiang had outwitted him, then neutralised him by facing him with an act of betrayal recalling Feng's own treachery years earlier against Wu P'ei-fu. Feng's commander in Honan was General Han Fu-chü, who had his full trust. Han, however, had been bribed by Chiang Kai-shek, and towards the end of May he defected to the KMT, with three divisional commanders and about 100,000 of Feng's best troops. One commander who did rather well out of bribes became known as "Triple-crosser Shih". He was not on Chiang's side for long, but his part in the defections of May 1929 was possibly worth whatever he was paid.

By then, Chiang was dealing with an extension of the Kwangsi rebellion, this time in Kwangtung. After fairly severe fighting, the Kwangsi forces were routed with heavy losses at the end of June 1929. Throughout the south and centre, Chiang now held, while it lasted, the reality rather than the semblance of power.

As always, the real yardstick was the government's ability to collect taxes. After the defeat of the Kwangsi clique, it could now do so in twenty-two provinces. Flushed with triumph, but still seething with anger, the Generalissimo now issued a manifesto to the nation, deprecating all charges of dictatorship, warning recalcitrants and appealing for national unity. As soon as the situation was stabilised, he added, he would resign and embark on his long-delayed trip abroad. The Shanghai merchants and foreign traders were dismayed. But those who had kept a tally of his resignations must have felt reassured—or disquieted, as the case might be.

Now came more shadow play. On 1 August Chiang called a meeting to implement the demobilisation measures decided at the beginning of the year. This time, the leading generals were not present; they were otherwise engaged. It was decided that the standing army should be cut to sixty-five divisions, each one pared down to 11,000 men. The resignation habit was catching: declaring that he could not raise the money to disband the army, T. V. Soong stepped down as Finance Minister.

Shortly after this unnecessary meeting, Wang Ching-wei returned from Europe. He immediately drafted and circulated a telegram denouncing Chiang in stronger and more specific terms than before. Not only had Chiang placed his wicked relatives and personal friends in all the best jobs, but he acted as though the nation were his private property. Moreover, he had betrayed China's sovereign rights by bowing to the Japanese in the Tsinan incident. It was time to "raise arms to wipe away this rebel".

Wang Ching-wei's return was a worry to Chiang. The leftist leader and his followers were dubbed the "Reorganisationists" because of their clear aim of reorganising the KMT and giving it a leftward slant. Feng Yü-hsiang and his friend Yen Hsi-shan, who had sided with him in the new clash with Chiang, held secret talks with the Reorganisationists. These followed a quintessentially Chinese episode in which Chiang and Feng exchanged flowery telegrams on the need, as the Generalissimo saw it, to experience the joys of foreign travel. At one stage, it looked as though both Feng and Yen would be going abroad, a prospect made more palatable to Feng by promises that his Kuominchün would be kept intact and paid from central funds, while Feng himself was to draw $200,000 for travelling expenses.

Feng thought he could do a deal with Wang Ching-wei, and Wang thought Feng might be useful to him for the strictly limited purpose of getting rid of Chiang. In the longer term, he had no more use for the Christian General than for the Generalissimo. Still, Feng was sufficiently encouraged to challenge Chiang again. This time he used the well-trained technique, popularised by Yüan Shih-k'ai, of getting his subordinate officers—twenty-seven of them—to denounce Chiang and call on Feng and Yen to lead a punitive campaign against the Generalissimo. By now it was 10 October 1929.

In the war that followed, Yen unaccountably stayed neutral, and Feng, crippled by the defection of 100,000 of his best troops, could not hold his own. By the end of November, the Kuominchün had been driven out of Honan. A clash between Russian and Chinese forces in Manchuria saved Feng, but only temporarily. (Soviet forces invaded Manchuria on 17 November 1929 and smashed the Chinese forces that had seized the Eastern railway some months earlier. Ironically, they were commanded by General Bluecher, who as "Galen" had been Chiang's adviser some years earlier.)

Another war of words now began. "Yen Hsi-shan," said a Peiping wall poster, "is off the fence and is now astride the tiger." It was he, indeed, who had fired the opening salvo on 10 February 1930, with a telegram to Chiang advising him to drop the idea of reunifying China by force and resign forthwith. For several weeks thereafter, an extraordinary flurry of lengthy and costly telegrams hummed back and forth between Chiang and Yen. As Hsiung puts it, the literary secretaries "must have had the time of their lives".

On the 21st, Wang joined in with a telegram denouncing the Nanking government for bribery, corruption, and dictatorship. Tiring of these exchanges, Yen Hsi-shan abruptly seized all the Nanking government's assets in his provinces and disarmed its troops. A fortnight later—at the beginning of April 1930—he took over as commander-in-chief of the anti-Chiang forces. As befitted the change in their military fortunes, Feng was his deputy. Six months of exceedingly bloody fighting followed in which, if the official Kuomintang figures are to be believed, the Yen-Feng forces lost about 150,000 men killed or wounded, for 30,000 killed and 60,000 wounded on the Nanking side. Feng Yü-hsiang was forced out of all offices of power; he outlived his downfall by 18 years, wrote much poetry and prose, occasionally tried a political comeback, and died mysteriously in a fire aboard a Soviet ship on 1 September 1948.

As for Yen Hsi-shan, Chiang allowed him in time to return and run Shansi province as "one of his stable of tamed warlords" (in Sheridan's phrase).

In the end, Chiang owed his victory over the Yen-Feng coalition and over the Reorganisationists largely to the Young Marshal,

Chang Hsueh-liang. In the summer of 1930, Wang Ching-wei had organised an "enlarged plenary session" of the Kuomintang in Peiping, with Generals Yen and Feng, and with the disgruntled Li Tsung-jen. Yen had agreed to head a State Council, in rivalry with Chiang's own, and formally inaugurated on 9 September. The omens, it seemed, had been carefully studied, for the announcement of this new government was made at 9:00 A.M. on the ninth day of the ninth month, in a year (1930) that was the nineteenth of the Chinese Republic; and, as Hsiung points out, the word "nine" in Chinese also means "long-lasting". Undeterred by this symbolism, the Young Marshal announced on 18 September that his support, which had been much sought by both sides, would go to Nanking. His forces quietly took over in Peiping, and the "government" died its death. The effect of this intervention was to make Chang Hsueh-liang the undisputed master of the north. He was just thirty. He had now added Hopei to the Manchurian provinces under his control, and Chiang rewarded him by appointing him Vice-Commander-in-Chief of the Chinese Army, Navy, and Air Force. Warlordism still flourished, for some.

The political initiative was now Chiang's once more, and on 10 October 1930, he announced a programme of five tasks: the eradication of Communism and banditry, financial rehabilitation, clean and efficient administration, economic development, and autonomy for the districts. The dejected leaders of the northern rebellion, including Wang as well as Generals Yen and Feng, formally accepted this programme and offered to retire, for what that was worth.

In mid-November, Chiang convened a Plenary Session of the Central Executive Committee. In stinging terms, he rebuked unnamed members of the party for corruption, abuse of privileges, and breaches of the law, all of which had been driving recruits into the ranks of the Communist Party. He himself confessed to (unspecified) blunders and admitted asserting his own views to the detriment of the public. The time had come, he said, to call a People's Convention and revise the Organic Law to produce a permanent constitution.

If Chiang thought his power was now unchallenged, he was very soon disabused. Hu Han-min, the leading Kuomintang right-winger, had listened sourly to Chiang's latest tirade. Chiang wanted—or said he wanted—to broaden the popular base of the government, but this was not to Hu's liking. Hu thought the party should have absolute control, and there was less than no point in denouncing abuses within it, as Chiang had done. Late in February 1931, the two men clashed angrily at a meeting on the Constitution. Hu Han-min threatened to resign as President of the Legislative Yüan. The offer was declined at the time but accepted a few days later by the Central Executive Committee. Chiang promptly placed him under house arrest.

Despite Hu's fears, there was not much that was "popular" in the People's Convention, which duly opened on 5 May 1931, at Nanking's Central University. All the 447 delegates were party men, or appointed by the party. They included nearly 50 members of the Central Executive Committee, government councillors, ministers, and dignitaries of one kind or another, among them the Panchen Lama, temporal leader of Tibet. The Young Marshal was there, too. The delegates listened to another harangue from the Generalissimo, declared their acceptance of Sun Yat-sen's programme, and formally launched the period of political tutelage of the Chinese people. The Provisional Constitution was adopted on 12 May and promulgated on 1 June.

Although Chiang's hold on power now sounded more legal than it had, it was again immediately challenged. Rebellions broke out in Canton and on the Peiping-Hankow axis, and in Canton Wang Ching-wei proclaimed yet another separatist government. To Chiang's dismay, Sun Fo was in it, with Eugene Ch'en.

On 31 July, three men concealed by the roadside, fired on Chiang Kai-shek's car at Nanch'ang. Their aim was wide. On being captured, they admitted that the Cantonese faction had sent them on an assassination mission.

It was at this time of apparently irredeemable national disunity that the Japanese Imperial Army invaded Manchuria on 18 September 1931.

The Chinese Communists, too, had been having dissensions of their own during this troubled period. The communist movement in China had thrown up two outstanding personalities: Mao Tse-tung and Li Li-san. (Chou En-lai had already displayed that intelligence and flexibility which were to ensure his political longevity, but he was not a leader in the way the other two were.) At that time, Mao's full stature had not become apparent to the party as a whole or its

Russian mentors, whereas Li Li-san had emerged from the Sixth Congress in Moscow as the party's secretary-general. Like Mao, Li Li-san was a Hunanese; he was seven years younger than Mao. The two men had attended the same teachers' training college, but had not taken to each other. Li had lived in France as a worker-student, and, already a Communist, had been expelled from Lyon University, where he had enrolled in 1919. He had gone on to Moscow, and this background gave him a distinct advantage over Mao in the Comintern phase of the world communist movement. Paradoxically, however, he was at least as Sinocentric as Mao, and his deep conviction that China was more important than Russia as a centre for world revolution was to be his undoing.

In the period that followed the Sixth Congress, the great issue was whether the revolution in China was to be based on the urban workers (as Marxist-Leninist theory and the Soviet leaders insisted) or on the peasants, in whom Mao saw the true revolutionary power of his overwhelmingly rural homeland. Despite his nationalism, Li Li-san did not question the wisdom of Leninism or of Stalin and his Politburo. On returning from Moscow in the spring of 1928, Li Li-san began to prepare for the city-based insurrections which, according to the textbooks, were to bring power to the Chinese Communist Party.

Under great pressure from KMT forces in late 1928 and early 1929, Mao and his followers evacuated their base in the Ridge of Wells and settled in a much larger area straddling the borders of Kiangsi and Fukien. Mao and his colleagues were content to sovietise the area under their control, but Li Li-san instructed Mao's Red Army to seize Wuhan and other big cities. Although Mao thought his instructions were futile, he was not in a position to defy them openly. Changsha was seized easily enough on 27 July 1930, the town being virtually undefended. After ten days of occupation in an atmosphere of sullen hostility, the Reds were driven out again by the Nationalist forces.

One or two further half-hearted efforts followed. The approaches to Wuhan were so well guarded that the Red Army could do no more than gaze at the triple city from afar. In all the target towns, the local Communist organisations were savagely purged.

Accused of Trotskyism, Li Li-san was removed from the Politburo and brought to Moscow in disgrace. There he spent many years, surviving the great Stalinist purges. He returned to China after the Communist victory, abjectly recanted his youthful errors, and was allowed to resume political work, eventually (1958) becoming Minister of Labour. He was, however, goaded to suicide by Mao's Red Guards during the Great Proletarian Cultural Revolution.

The main effect of the revolutionary failures of 1930 was that Mao Tse-tung had been proved right, although it was difficult to argue that he had been guilty of disobedience to party orders. Freed now from the harassment of misguided resolutions, he set about creating local soviets. The climax came on 7 November 1931 (chosen because this was the anniversary of the Bolshevik Revolution), when the Chinese Soviet Republic was proclaimed. On the 27th, Mao Tse-tung was elected its President, with Chu Teh as Chairman of the Military Committee and Chou En-lai as Vice-Chairman.

This was not, of course, a situation Chiang Kai-shek could tolerate. Indeed, by the time the Soviet Republic was proclaimed, he had already launched three attempts to dislodge the Communists from their Kiangsi base. The first was in October 1930, after the defeat of the Kwangsi rebellion; a second campaign came in May 1931; and a third, commanded by Chiang himself at the head of 300,000 men, was launched in July 1931. Despite local successes and heavy Communist losses, all three of these "campaigns of extermination", as Chiang called them, ended in Communist victories. Two more campaigns lay ahead before the Communists were driven out in 1934, to start on their epic Long March.

In the autumn of 1931, however, the daunting situation that faced Chiang Kai-shek was that the Communists remained unbeaten, that his authority remained contested on his own side, and that the Japanese were invading his country.

12. Chiang Seals His Fate

The greatest of Chiang Kai-shek's many errors of judgment can be dated precisely. It took place on 11 September 1931, when he instructed the Young Marshal, Chang Hsueh-liang, to take all possible care in avoiding clashes with the Japanese forces. Exactly a week later, as generally expected, the Japanese army attacked in Manchuria in the so-called "Mukden incident". "What shall I do?" asked Chang.

Chiang's reply was explicit: "In order to avoid any enlargement of the incident, it is necessary resolutely to maintain the principle of non-resistance." ° Beset by continuing domestic challenges to his authority, Chiang had taken a firm decision on his order of military priorities: bandits and other rebels first, foreign invaders second. It was a decision which in the end sealed his own fate.

° Kuomintang sources deny that Chiang Kai-shek used the words "principle of non-resistance". But they do not deny that he ordered the Young Marshal to avoid clashes with the Japanese forces.

As a Nationalist leader and the self-appointed heir to Sun Yat-sen's Revolution and champion of China against imperial depredations, it was expected that Chiang Kai-shek lead the nation in its resistance against the Japanese aggressor. Indeed, to be fair to him, he did intend to resist—but later. First, China had to be truly united under his leadership. What he failed to grasp was that by disappointing the people's hopes—and the people included the intellectuals and peasants as well as the soldiers—he was fatally undermining his own claim to be the unquestioned national leader. At a time of national emergency, it was generally felt to be unnatural for Chinese to be fighting Chinese. Had Chiang decided otherwise, the warlords would have forgotten their differences and rallied to his banner. Instead, general distrust further weakened his authority; and in time, the Communists would be able to claim that they were the true defenders of China's soil against the Japanese transgressors.

In that late summer, and in the long years of war that followed, Chiang Kai-shek was incapable or unwilling to grasp this truth. All he could see was that because China was disunited and weak, it was incapable of resisting a highly trained Japanese army. What he could not see was that China's disunity, which was one of the primary causes of its national weakness, could have been cured under his leadership by a patriotic appeal in the face of the enemy.

According to Wu Ting-ch'ang, who was the Generalissimo's Secretary-General between 1944 and 1948, Chiang Kai-shek misjudged the Japanese army's intentions in September 1931. It was because he was under the mistaken impression that Japan did not really intend to occupy China's territory that he ordered Chang Hsueh-liang to take evasive action. Two or three years later, the Generalissimo became convinced that the Japanese did indeed intend to invade, and possibly conquer, China. But this did not cause him to modify his order of priorities, in which he was guided by the traditional policy of past rulers: *jang wai pi hsien an nei* ("To expel foreign aggression, one must first pacify internal insubordination"). In context, it is clearly understood (from the Chinese character *an*) that the pacification is by force. Chiang had lasting admiration for General Tseng Kuo-fan, the man who quelled the great T'aip'ing Rebellion. Many Chinese thought General Tseng ought to have given priority to the contemporary incursions of the Western powers, but Chiang's hero thought otherwise—and Chiang followed his example. Years later, the Chinese Communists were to make much of this adulation: "What is the way out for Chiang Kai-shek?" asked Ch'en Po-ta (Mao Tse-tung's ghost-writer) in his book *Chiang Kai-shek–The People's Enemy.* "In fact, his grand master Tseng Kuo-fan made the arrangement for him long ago. That is: make peace with the foreigners and fight the people."

For their part, the Japanese knew exactly what they wanted and how they intended to get it. The famous "Tanaka Memorial" had spelt it all out beyond misunderstanding on 25 July 1927. The point is hardly altered by the fact that most scholars consider the Tanaka Memorial to be a forgery—for it is generally agreed that whether or not Baron Tanaka, the then Japanese Prime Minister, actually wrote the words attributed to him, or whether the Chinese forged them for him, is irrelevant. The Baron was said to have presented it to the Japanese Emperor as his plan for the control of Manchuria and Mongolia, and they disseminated it throughout the country as proof that the Japanese had aggressive intentions. Certainly the bulk of readers believed it to be authentic, and as time went on it became clear that the Japanese were doing just what the Tanaka Memorial said they were going to do. It outlined the economic resources of Manchuria and called for a policy of "Blood and Iron". Prophetically, the Memorial added:

> The way to gain actual rights in Manchuria and Mongolia is to use this region as a base and under the pretence of trade and commerce penetrate the rest of China. Armed by the rights already secured we shall seize the resources all over the country. Having China's entire resources at our disposal we shall proceed to conquer India, the Archipelago, Asia Minor, Central Asia, and even Europe.

The Japanese had been looking for a pretext to put their strategic plan into operation. The Chinese gave them one in June 1931 when they arrested four Japanese intelligence agents in a restricted military zone of Manchuria. They executed all four on 1 July. The invasion of 18 September, however, had long been planned. It found the Young Marshal engaged in one of his civil wars, but by no means without resources. Indeed, with his 400,000 men, he heavily outnumbered the invaders. But Chiang Kai-shek's orders were discouraging to any martial spirit. Having decided not to resist, Chiang announced on 23 September—five days after the invasion—that China was appealing to the League of Nations. Hsiung credits him with a belief that the League would do something, and adds with delicate irony: "Little did he realise that the League of Nations was about as good as Westminster Abbey— merely a resting-place for great statesmen." In a patriotic message that would have carried more weight if it had been accompanied by greater determination, Chiang urged every man and woman in China to rally to the Central Government.

But unity under a non-resistant Chiang Kai-shek held little appeal. Chiang sent envoys to Canton, saying he was willing to come to terms with the southerners in the interests of national solidarity. The southerners responded to the extent of agreeing to a "peace conference" in Shanghai. There in October, Wang Ching-wei, Sun Fo, and other leftists met Chiang Kai-shek, Hu Han-min, and other rightists. But the Canton group were in no mood for concessions. The simplest way to make peace, they argued, was for the Nanking government to move over and let the Canton government take over with authority over the whole of China. Hu Han-min, though representing Nanking, sided with the leftists on this issue and suggested that Chiang should be banished from China. With his well-established habit of resigning, Chiang was ready to step down, but not to leave the country. The usual futile bickerings followed, but in the end it was decided that a fourth Kuomintang Congress should be held in two separate places— Nanking and Shanghai. As soon as a new regime had been set up, Chiang promised, he would retire. The two meetings duly took place in November, but when it became clear that nothing was likely to be achieved, Chiang Kai-shek resigned all his posts. It was 15 December 1931.

About this time some 70,000 schoolboys and students invaded Nanking. They came from all parts of the country, and the "invasion" was the climax of disturbances that had begun with the Japanese drive into Manchuria in September. With every sign of spontaneity, the boys—aged from twelve to sixteen—had started rioting in various cities, calling for an immediate declaration of war against Japan. The invaders must be ousted, they shouted in a hundred different ways. Foreign Minister, Dr. C. T. Wang, was seriously injured in one of the student riots. At the end of November, some 12,000 students marched into Nanking and camped outside the government buildings. They demanded to see Chiang Kai-shek: nobody else would do. It was bitterly cold, and Chiang thought exposure to the weather for twenty-four hours would allow them to cool down. He then appeared on a balcony and harangued them. Their demands upon the government were insulting as well as unreasonable, he said. Their place was at school; the government would deal with the Japanese as they saw fit. Cold and disheartened, the young people went home.

But the lull was short-lived. After clashing with the police in the capital, many students were arrested. Shortly afterwards, many more from Hankow marched into Nanking. They, too, received a tirade from Chiang Kai-shek, who told them that they were allowing themselves to be used by the nation's enemies. The December incident was on a larger scale, and the ringleaders were still more determined. A group of youths from Peiping attacked the Kuomintang party headquarters and the Foreign Ministry. Another group stormed the building of the *Central Daily News*, destroying both the plant and the offices. The situation had got out of hand. Chiang Kai-shek called out the local garrison, which rounded up the students, who were occupying the Central University. Under military escort, the young rebels were driven out of the capital in small batches.

It was at this point that the Generalissimo resigned. Accompanied by Mme. Chiang, he left Nanking by air for an unstated destination, which turned out to be his native village in the Chekiang hills. As usual, Chiang's absent charisma worked its magic. On 2 January 1932, the government solemnly appealed to Chiang Kai-shek to come back at once. Even the students called for his return. Serene in his mountain home, Chiang Kai-shek played harder to get than ever. Alarmed, the politicians began to bombard him with telegrams. The other absent Kuomintang leaders—Wang Ching-wei and Hu Han-min—were also getting telegrams, and a common theme ran through all these messages: the urgent need for a "new policy towards Japan".

The war, which Japan insisted on calling an "incident", was rapidly giving the Imperial Army full control over the three eastern provinces. In one place after another, the Japanese were creating further incidents, which seemed to foreshadow a more generalised conflict. One such was alleged to have taken place near Lunghwa airfield in a suburb of Shanghai, where a group of Chinese—conveniently not identified—were said to have killed a Japanese sailor. Immediately, the Japanese consul presented the Chinese authorities with a pre-drafted list of demands. Japanese warships were ordered to proceed to the great city. It was clear that Shanghai was about to be invaded.

At last, both Wang and Chiang were simultaneously alarmed. Wang had been convalescing in a Shanghai hospital; he now journeyed to Hangchow (West Lake City), where Chiang Kai-shek, who had descended from his mountains, came to meet him. Reconciled at last, the old rivals spent a few days talking in Hangchow, then announced that they would go to the capital together. On 25 January, Sun Fo resigned as Prime Minister (President of the Executive Yüan), and Wang Ching-wei took his place. Chiang let it be known that for the time being he did not intend to take up any appointment. But his presence in the capital undoubtedly had a calming effect. Moreover, there was an advantage in the fact that he was not in office, for his previous orders not to resist the Japanese could now be disregarded. On the 28th, the Japanese army struck at the Chinese garrison in Shanghai. The Nineteenth Route Army fought back with desperate bravery in the face of discouragement from Nanking, with dwindling supplies and no material support. Their stand lasted thirty-three days, and only the arrival of heavy Japanese reinforcements forced them to retreat. Their commanders were Ch'en Ming-shu, T'sai T'ing-k'ai, and the relatively junior Chiang Kuang-nai. Soon their names were hailed throughout China as heroes of the anti-Japanese resistance. Their names were linked with those of Washington and Nelson as among the greatest national heroes of all history. T'sai T'ing-k'ai became a brand of cigarettes and was stamped on other articles for sale. Throughout China and from Chinese communities overseas, money had poured in—in total about $40,000,000 Chinese—to support the heroic Nineteenth Route Army.

On 4 March, a truce was signed in the Shanghai region. It was so unpopular that the Chinese who signed it was badly beaten up by students.

From Nanking, Chiang Kai-shek watched these events with a mixture of pain and sourness: pain for the new humiliations Japan was inflicting on his country; sourness for the rise of competing heroes in a fight in which he had played no part. Two days after the truce, Chiang was reappointed Chairman of the National Military

Council and *ex officio* Commander-in-Chief of the National Armies. Losing no time, he transferred the Nineteenth Route Army to Fukien—perhaps with the unformulated hope that they would destroy themselves against the Communist rebels.

One thing at least the Nanking government had done. Fearing armed resistance, it had at least proclaimed a Chinese boycott of Japanese imports. So widely was the boycott obeyed by the merchants and the ordinary purchasing public that Japanese exports to China in November and December 1931 reached only one-sixth of the usual figure. But economic boycotts, however loyally observed, do not deter or halt aggressors. More helpful to the Japanese were the devastating floods of 1931, which hampered any efforts that might have been made by local military commanders to help the defenders of Manchuria in the face of Chiang Kai-shek's dissuasive orders and which displayed the impotence of the central authorities in alleviating the people's hardships. The common people, known traditionally as Old Hundred Names, had never suffered more than in this year of floods and devastation. The Yangtze burst its banks where it met the Han River after torrential rains, and a vast area was flooded. At one time, the streets of Hankow itself were under water, and in two months perhaps 2,000,000 people were drowned. Whole villages were swept away in this "rainy day", against which so many tens of thousands of families had saved. And, as the flood waters retreated, dysentery, famine, and cholera took their place.

In this disaster, many wondered what had happened to the People's Livelihood—that Principle of Sun Yat-sen which the Kuomintang had pledged itself to honour. While the people were dying in the thousands, the KMT politicians were bickering over precedence and authority. The budding intellectuals had turned against Chiang Kai-shek and his colleagues because the Generalissimo was seen to be refusing to defend China against the Japanese aggressors. And the peasants, ignorant of political subtleties but aware only of official indifference, would turn readily to the man who seemed to offer a way out—Mao Tse-tung.

With their own special brand of imperial arrogance, the Japanese were adding to China's hardships. On 18 February 1932, they proclaimed the independence of Manchukuo, which was to consist of the former three eastern provinces of Manchuria, together with Jehol. To lend legitimacy to their conquest, they installed

Henry P'u Yi as regent. The young man, last of the Manchu Emperors, had been thrown out of his palace by Feng Yü-hsiang in 1924. He had no special reason to love the Chinese, and on 10 November 1931, yielding to Japanese entreaties, he boarded a Japanese steamer which took him from his residence in Japan's concession at Tientsin to his dynastic home. Two years later, he was to accept the throne that was in Japan's gift.

About the time P'u Yi was returning to Manchuria, the Chinese Communists were convening a "Soviet Congress" in southern Kiangsi. On 7 November 1931, they adopted a Provisional Constitution and announced a Provisional Soviet Government. The Kiangsi Soviet was not the only one of its kind: about five others had sprung up in different parts of China. It was dominated by Mao Tse-tung, with Chou En-lai and Chu Teh as his chief assistants. As usual, Chiang Kai-shek was more worried about the Communist experiment than the Japanese invasion. He decided to take personal command of the anti-Communist drive, which as on past and future occasions was called the "bandit-suppression campaign". This derogatory term was intended to confuse, but there was an element of truth in it. Banditry had indeed become endemic, and a typical example of it was the Red Spears group—one of a number of peasant secret societies calling themselves by such picturesque names as Heavenly Gate, Long Hair, Yellow Sand, and Big Sword. In their time, the Communists had absorbed some of the bandits, and so had individual warlords.

Chiang's only idea was to annihilate them. At a military conference on 9 June, he gave his troops their marching orders. In Hupei, Honan, and Anhwei, the Communists were routed. But Mao's Soviet in Kiangsi waxed undisturbed.

Years later, and with the benefit of hindsight, a well-informed Chinese (Hu Lin, one of the founders of *Ta Kung Pao* newspaper) gave Eric Chou his views about Chiang Kai-shek's failure to cope with the Communist challenge:

In a way, it was of his own making. In the early 1930s, he equated the Communists with bandits, hoping to impress ordinary people that Mao Tse-tung and Chu Teh were mere criminals. He banned Communist propaganda and literature, but it would have been better if he had let them circulate openly so that the people could see for themselves that the

Communists meant to overthrow the whole society, and were far more dangerous than ordinary bandits.

The Chinese people have been the victims of banditry for many generations. They tended to underestimate the menace of the Communists because they knew that bandits can always be bought or vanquished. Fighting bandits has never been taken very seriously by Chinese soldiers. When they were told to fight Communist bandits, they were psychologically unprepared to face a far tougher job.

Among the politicians the bickering continued. An unbridgeable difference separated Wang Ching-wei and Chang Hsueh-liang, and on 6 August Wang denounced the Young Marshal as wholly responsible for the Manchurian debacle. Perhaps gratuitously, he resigned, as did all his ministers. Not to be outdone, Chiang Kai-shek threatened three days later to return to private life himself unless Wang withdrew his resignation. Chang now resigned in turn, and in a telegram to Wang on 14 August, Chiang assured him that he would get his own way in northern China. With his diabetes and other problems, Wang Ching-wei was a sick man. In lieu of resignation, he was offered leave of absence for medical treatment, and the Generalissimo himself took over Chang Hsueh-liang's job as Commissioner for North China. With T. V. Soong as acting Premier, Wang sailed from Shanghai to Europe for treatment on 22 October.

Once again, the Generalissimo was unchallenged among the politicians—but only in Nanking, and not for long. Apart from the Communists, whom he would never subdue completely, another group of men were beginning to defy him in Canton. They were those "heroes" of the resistance to Japan in Manchuria, the Nineteenth Route Army. The three heroes—T'sai T'ing-k'ai, Ch'en Ming-shu, and Chiang Kuang-nai—dominated the Branch Political Council in Canton, which functioned quite independently of Nanking. Their fame had preceded them, and when the Nineteenth Route Army units arrived in Fukien in July 1932, the population "welcomed them madly, and respected them as gods". With its pine-capped mountains, the province was beautiful and had inspired generations of poets and painters; but its population was desperately poor. The ecstatic crowds that greeted the returning troops looked to them to alleviate their hardships, fill their bellies, and remove the injustices that weighed upon them. For a while at least, the army took these objectives seriously. Soon they were pasting up slogans: "Abolish all exploitative taxes, disband bandit-like provincial defence forces". Revolutionaries were plentiful in the Nineteenth Route Army. There were Trotskyists and Communists among them, and Ch'en (one of the three "heroes") was a leader of the so-called "Third Party"—formerly organised at the end of 1927 in a wave of indignation against Chiang Kai-shek's "white terror" after the capture of Shanghai earlier that year. In their first flush of revolutionary enthusiasm, they executed bandits (luring one to his death by treachery), improved roads, abolished many tax anomalies, and in general protected the peasants from the kind of harassment they had come to expect during the years of anarchy and misrule.

But the most spectacular of the Fukien reforms was a land reform programme under which all land was to be nationalised and distributed fairly to those who had been tilling it. This sounded much the same as Sun Yat-sen's "land to the tiller" slogan, but there was an important difference: Dr. Sun wanted individual farmers to own their plots, but the Fukien reformers kept the land deeds in government hands. Nor was the Fukien land reform in any way borrowed from the Communists, for the Third Party made no distinction between poor, middle, and rich peasants.

Soon enough the Fukien revolutionaries would openly challenge Chiang Kai-shek. But meanwhile, events in the north claimed his attention. Early in 1933, the Japanese forces, no longer content with Manchukuo alone, crossed the Great Wall into Jehol. With little Chinese resistance to delay them, they rapidly conquered the whole province, and their success was marked on 31 May 1933 with the signing of the Tangku Truce. For the Young Marshal, the fall of Jehol seemed to spell the end of the political road. Handing over his remaining troops to Chiang Kai-shek, he did what was expected of defeated warlords and started on a long foreign journey. On his way abroad, he signed on in a Shanghai hospital and cured himself of addiction to opium. In these dismal events, Feng Yü-hsiang saw a chance for a return to glory. On 1 May, he emerged from retirement and proclaimed his creation of a People's Federated Anti-Japanese Army. In July, glory did indeed come his way when the army cleared the Japanese out of Chahar province. From Nanking, Chiang Kai-shek watched this progression with a jaundiced eye. He was still not ready to fight the Japanese: bandits and Communists came first. And all Feng was doing with his Anti-Japanese Army was complicating life for the Generalissimo.

Chiang need not have worried too much. Feng was a volatile as well as a picturesque character, and in August he dissolved his Anti-Japanese Army and went back to retirement on the sacred mountain of Tai Shan. The Japanese moved back into Chahar.

About the time of the Tangku Truce, rumours of a forthcoming rebellion in Fukien were reaching Chiang Kai-shek.° The ringleader was clearly going to be Ch'en Ming-shu, who had been moving around in conspicuous secrecy from Shanghai to Hong Kong to Europe and back to Nanking. He returned to Fukien at the end of May—to a giant reception and banners hailing him as a "national hero".

Improbably, Sun Yat-sen's conservative disciple, Hu Han-min, supported the Fukien rebels, but only out of a shared hatred for Chiang Kai-shek. At the other end of the spectrum, Mao Tse-tung was to tell Edgar Snow that the Communist failure to unite with the Fukien rebels was one of the important errors of that period. Indeed, had they stuck together, the joint challenge to Nanking would have been more formidable than either taken separately. Chiang's approved biographer, Hollington Tong, dismissed the events of later 1933 as "the so-called Fukien rebellion, precipitated by a number of jobless politicians". Its real motive, he claimed, was a "pressing need for money by politicians who had lost their jobs". But there was more to it than this. On 20 November 1933, after a mass meeting, the rebels proclaimed a People's Revolutionary Government. A day or so earlier, Ch'en Ming-shu sent a personal telegram to Chiang Kai-shek, packed with scathing criticisms and calling on him to resign. In another telegram, the rebels appealed to the authorities in Kwangtung and Kwangsi to join them in overthrowing the Generalissimo. "Chiang Kai-shek's dictatorship and destruction of the nation," they declared, "have lasted for six years, and the people of the whole world hate his perverse and unrighteous actions."

In a further proclamation on 22 November, the rebels castigated Chiang Kai-shek for "disregarding the will of the nation and betraying the race"—so that "the Chinese people will become the slaves of Japan".

° For a detailed account of the Fukien Rebellion, see Lloyd E. Eastman, *The Abortive Revolution*, pp. 85–139.

These resounding words were followed by one of the great anti-climaxes of the decade. Once the rebellion had been proclaimed, Chiang lost no time in ordering a general campaign. His forces moved into Fukien in three columns, and the Generalissimo flew to western Fukien to take over personal command. Foochow was abandoned and Nanking marines—landed from gunboats—occupied the city. From temporary airstrips at Wenchow and Chuchow, the government's air force harassed the rebels with high explosives. In no more than two weeks, the Nineteenth Route Army was scattered and broken. The political leaders of the rebellion got away with cash from the Foochow banks and with their lives. Chiang's forces gathered scattered remnants and reorganised them as the Seventh Route Army: the heroic Nineteenth passed into history, its myth shattered.

Imperfect though his control remained, after a difficult year, Chiang Kai-shek towered over his rivals, and his spirits stood high.

13. Mao Marches Out

During 1934, Chiang Kai-shek drove the Communists out of their southern strongholds and launched a movement of national regeneration. He thought he had defeated the Communists—utterly and forever; and he hoped his New Life Movement would enable him to "win the peace" as he had won the war. But he had not won the war; he had merely driven the Communists away. And his policy of national regeneration was to peter out in the sands of popular indifference.

In mid-1933, Chiang Kai-shek had been fighting China's Communists for six years. As a military man, his frustration knew no bounds. Four times already, he had launched "extermination campaigns" against Mao Tse-tung's Chinese Soviet areas—and each time he had achieved no more than local successes. His mounting determination can be measured quantitatively. In the First Extermination Campaign, from December 1930 to January 1931, he had used 100,000 men; in the Second, from May to June 1931, twice

157

that number had gone into battle; the Third, from July to October 1931, employed 300,000; and although the Fourth, from April to October 1933, absorbed about 50,000 fewer soldiers, for the Fifth, which began in October 1933—almost immediately after the end of the Fourth—the Generalissimo mobilised more than 900,000 troops, 400,000 of whom went into immediate action. Against them, the Red forces were less heavily outnumbered than might be supposed, but were incomparably weaker in fire power. The Red Army in Kiangsi—which bore the brunt of the campaign—mobilised about 180,000 men, and could also count on about 200,000 partisans and Red Guards. But among them, the 380,000 men had no more than 100,000 rifles, and a limited supply of grenades and ammunition, and no heavy artillery. Chiang's 400,000 fighting troops had heavy guns and a modern air force of nearly 400 aircraft. The Reds had managed to capture a few of Chiang's planes, and had even trained three or four pilots, but they had no petrol supplies or maintenance staff; for that matter, they had no bombs.

The size of the force Chiang Kai-shek had assembled was a measure of his need and desire for victory. It was not simply impatience after six frustrating years: there was a new urgency about the Fifth Extermination Campaign. For by now, the Generalissimo was convinced that an all-out war between Japan and China was inevitable. "To get ready to fight the Japanese, he was determined to wipe out the Communists once and for all," according to Wu Ting-ch'ang, who was Chiang's Secretary-General between 1944 and 1948.

For some years, Chiang Kai-shek had relied on German military advisers. When Hitler came to power in 1933, Chiang invited one of the best-known German strategists, General Hans von Seeckt. It was von Seeckt who planned the strategy for the Fifth Extermination Campaign. To assist him, he had the services of the resident German adviser, Lieutenant-General Georg Wetzell. Hitler evidently thought that von Seeckt was usefully employed in China, for in early 1934, shortly after von Seeckt had gone back to Germany, the Fuehrer sent him back as head of the military advisory group, in succession to Wetzell. It is intriguing to reflect that even in these early days—about seven years before the extension of the Berlin-Rome Axis to Tokyo—the Nazis apparently approved of Chiang Kai-shek's policy of fighting his domestic Communists first, while leaving the Japanese invaders unchallenged.

Von Seeckt's strategy was sound, but very expensive. Under his guidance, the Generalissimo had hundreds of miles of military roads built. Here and there, in a great ring of concrete around the Soviet areas, thousands of small fortifications sprang up. As Edgar Snow put it, it was "a kind of Great Wall . . . , which gradually moved inward". In their tanks and armoured cars, and under cover of heavy air and artillery bombardment, the National forces moved forward a few hundred yards at a time in and around the provinces of Kiangsi, Fukien, Hunan, Kwangtung, and Kwangsi. They would then build new forts. The concrete vice gradually tightened.

At first the fighting was hard and bloody. Two victories on the Fukien-Kiangsi border broke the initial Red resistance. Under heavy bombardment, the Communists scattered into the mountains, leaving between 7,000 and 10,000 dead on the battlefield.° Then came a respite of a few weeks, when the Nineteenth Route Army went into rebellion in Fukien. Missing their chance of joint action with the Fukien rebels, Mao led his men to a new temporary headquarters in south Kiangsi. As the Nationalists advanced, they summarily executed any Red leaders they caught and made short shrift of stragglers. A ruthless economic blockade prevented all trade between the Soviet areas and the surrounding provinces. How many people died of starvation will never be known. Edgar Snow quotes "the Kuomintang itself" as admitting that about 1,000,000 were killed or starved to death in the battle for Soviet Kiangsi. The Red Army suffered more than 60,000 casualties, says the same author, this time quoting Chou En-lai.

By May 1934, the campaign had been in progress for seven months and Chiang was getting desperate. At that time, he was much influenced by China's foremost strategist, Chiang Po-li, former Commandant of Paoting Military Academy, who had convinced him that the outbreak of a Sino-Japanese war was close at hand. When it came, the two men agreed, it was bound to be a protracted one. On the Generalissimo's instructions, Chiang Po-li drafted a national defence plan, with the mountainous province of

---

° It is impossible to write with any confidence about the numbers involved on either side in the Fifth Extermination Campaign. The figures I have given are Edgar Snow's. Tong says Chiang Kai-shek had 300,000 men plus 20,000 cadets; his air force is given as 150 planes of various types. (Tong, 1953, p. 180) Clubb's figures are 700,000 on the Nationalist side and 150,000 Communist troops. Other competing estimates are available.

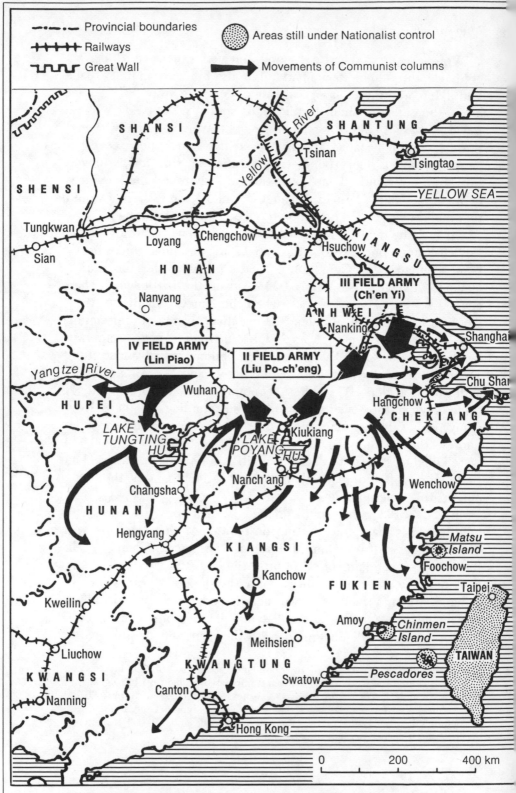

Legend

- ─·─··─ Provincial boundaries
- ┼┼┼┼┼ Railways
- ⅃⅃⅃⅃ Great Wall
- Areas still under Nationalist control
- ➤ Movements of Communist columns

SHANSI

SHENSI

SHANTUNG

Yellow River

Tsinan

Tsingtao

YELLOW SEA

Tungkwan

Sian

Loyang

Chengchow

Hsuchow

KIANGSU

HONAN

Nanyang

III FIELD ARMY (Ch'en Yi)

ANHWEI

Nanking

Shanghai

IV FIELD ARMY (Lin Piao)

II FIELD ARMY (Liu Po-ch'eng)

Yangtze River

Wuhan

HUPEI

LAKE TUNGTING HU

Kiukiang

LAKE POYANG HU

Hangchow

CHEKIANG

Chu Shan

Changsha

Nanch'ang

Wenchow

HUNAN

Hengyang

KIANGSI

Kanchow

Matsu Island

Foochow

FUKIEN

Taipei

Kweilin

Amoy

Chinmen Island

Liuchow

Meihsien

TAIWAN

KWANGSI

KWANGTUNG

Pescadores

Nanning

Canton

Swatow

Hong Kong

0   200   400 km

The Battle of the Yangtze and the Conquest of South China

Hunan as the centre of the war effort. Protected by the mountains, the Chinese high command should operate from Chihkiang and Hungkiang; the main air base was to be in Kunming, the provincial capital of Yunnan. Was Chiang Kai-shek going to be able to finish off the Reds before the Japanese struck again? Relentlessly, he kept up the pressure.

But in the end, he was cheated of full victory. Early in October 1934, when the campaign had lasted nearly a year, the Communist leaders held an emergency meeting at Juichin, deep in the Kiangsi Soviet. Mao Tse-tung, who had been down with malaria and a high fever, recovered in time for the meeting, which was held on 2 October. Chou En-lai, Chu Teh, and P'eng Teh-huai were there. The decision they took was drastic and momentous. The Kiangsi Soviet was to be abandoned to the Nationalists. Having decided, the Communists acted with incredible swiftness. On 16 October 1934, with less than a fortnight for preparation, the Long March began.

About 100,000 people took part. They included men, women, children, and old people. The Red arms factories had been dismantled, and the machinery was piled on the backs of mules and donkeys. There were pieces of silver, rifles, and machine guns and ammunition. Among the women on the march were Mao's wife, who was pregnant, and Chu Teh's. The Nationalists had no inkling of what was happening. The vanguard of the Red Army, under P'eng Teh-huai, captured the Nationalist forts in Hunan and Kwangtung by assault. With the local Nationalist forces in flight, the roads to the south and west were wide open.

There was an epic quality about the Long March, which neither time nor ideology can dim. True, it was not the only "long march" in history, or even in Chinese history; and Guillermaz, the French historian of the Chinese Communist Party, lists other comparable treks in modern China. But this one was no less impressive for not being unique. Moreover, its end result was the recovery of the Communist forces after their catastrophic defeat, enabling Mao to turn the tables on Chiang many years later. Nor did the Long March of 1934 lack its inspired publicists. The late Edgar Snow, who did more than anybody else to build up the image of agrarian reformism and heroism of Mao and his men, put it in these words:

Adventure, exploration, discovery, human courage and cowardice, ecstasy and triumph, suffering, sacrifice, and loyalty, and

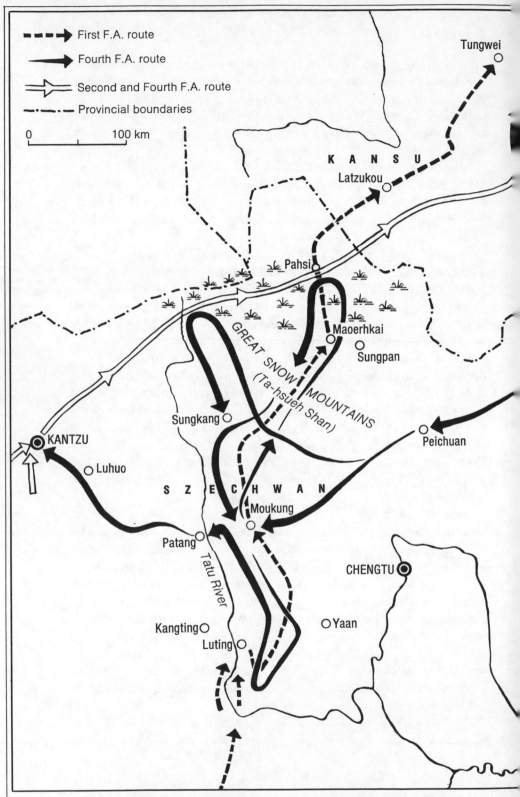

Legend:
- First F.A. route
- Fourth F.A. route
- Second and Fourth F.A. route
- Provincial boundaries

0 ——— 100 km

Tungwei

K A N S U

Latzukou

Pahsi

GREAT SNOW MOUNTAINS
(Ta-hsueh Shan)

Maoerhkai

Sungpan

Sungkang

Peichuan

KANTZU

Luhuo

S Z E C H W A N

Moukung

Patang

Tatu River

CHENGTU

Kangting

Luting

Yaan

The Long March: The Crossing of Szechwan, Kansu, and Shensi

then through it all, like a flame, this undimmed ardour and undying hope and amazing revolutionary optimism of those thousands of youths who would not admit defeat either by man or nature or God or death—all this and more are wrapped up in the history of an Odyssey unequalled in modern times.

Mao Tse-tung himself recorded the feat in poetry:

The Red Army fears not the trials of a distant march;
To them a thousand mountains, ten thousand rivers are nothing;
To them the Five Ridges ripple like little waves,
And the mountain peaks of Wumeng roll by like mud balls.
Warm are the cloud-topped cliffs washed by the River of
    Golden Sand,
Cold are the iron chains that span the Tatu River.
The myriad snows of Minshan only make them happier,
And when the Army has crossed, each face is smiling.

Much depleted by battles on the way, the marching Reds buried arms, ammunition, and silver here and there on the route. Some of the widest rivers and tallest mountains in Asia barred their way, but they pressed on regardless. One year later, Mao Tse-tung led about 20,000 armed men and their dependants into China's north-western province of Shensi.° There, they joined forces with 10,000 Communist guerrillas, who had set up their own independent Soviet. The Kiangsi trekkers had covered 6,000 miles.

Although Mao and his survivors lived to fight another day, the Fifth Extermination Campaign was nevertheless a victory for Chiang Kai-shek—although not a final one. It eliminated the Chinese Communists as a serious fighting force for several years. Patiently and efficiently, Chiang had carried out the strategic plan elaborated by his German advisers. Until the unexpected escape in October 1934, the blockade had been effectively maintained: not only had the Communists been denied access to arms and ammunition, they were hurt even more by the economic blockade,

---

° Here again, wildly varying figures are available for the survivors of the Long March. According to Tibor Mende, in *The Chinese Revolution* (1961), pp. 109–12, fewer than 30,000 reached Shensi. Tong says that only 25,000 armed survivors reached their destination; and Chiang Kai-shek himself says there were only 5,000 armed Communists left (*Soviet Russia in China*, p. 65).

not least the complete denial of salt supplies. On the Nationalist side, security measures had been greatly improved, and the Communists had been kept in the dark about Nationalist troop movements. For the first time, Chiang's status as a national leader had been more or less established. As a result, the regional military leaders found themselves obliged to make greater efforts than in the past to fight the Communists. Moreover, two of the most important of them—Li Tsung-jen and Pai Ch'ung-hsi—were busy with a reconstruction programme in Kwangsi after the recent troubles there. This meant that the Generalissimo did not have to look over his shoulder during the campaign. He thought he had made provision for everything, but he could not foresee the Communists' sudden decision to break loose and flee. On their side, when the Communists came to write—or rather, to re-write—the history of the Long March, they chose to ignore the fact that the decision had been taken to avoid the major defeat that would otherwise have been inevitable, and claimed that the real reason was that the Communists wanted to go north to fight Japan.

For nearly seven years, until early in 1934, Chiang Kai-shek had tried to deal with the Communist challenge entirely by military means. His recipes were suppression and extermination. It does not seem to have occurred to him that organisation and terror were not in themselves sufficient to explain Mao Tse-tung's appeal to the population. Nor indeed would Chiang ever admit that for all the brutalities of the Kiangsi period, Mao Tse-tung also offered the Chinese peasants the thing they wanted most—land—and with it, a chance for revenge on those who had oppressed them for so long—the landlords. Indeed, when Chiang launched the New Life Movement in 1934, he did not do so, at least consciously, as an alternative pole of attraction in competition with the Communists. His idea was both more simple and more fundamental: to regenerate the people as whole by a return to the Confucian principles, but with Christianity and fascism thrown in for good measure. The approved biographers attribute the Generalissimo's idea to a relatively trivial incident. Motoring back to his headquarters in Nanch'ang during the Fukien campaign, he saw a boy less than ten years old smoking a cigarette on the street. The sight shocked him, and he got out of his car, asked to see the boy's parents, and chided them for permitting such behaviour. Soon, said Tong, "there was a

conspicuous decline in smoking among juveniles". Such unwhole-
some personal habits, thought Chiang, were prolonging the back-
wardness of the Chinese people. What they needed was a new code
of behaviour.

Whether or not the smoking boy unwillingly provided the spark
that lit the New Life Movement, at about the time of the
incident—late in 1933 or early in 1934—Chiang Kai-shek addressed
a meeting of the Blue Shirt leaders. The Chinese people were weak,
Chiang said. They were selfish, undisciplined, and dissolute. "It is
necessary," he told the Blue Shirts, "to spread our revolutionary
spirit to the masses of the entire nation, and to cause them to have
faith in our group."

On 19 February 1934, Chiang formally launched the New Life
Movement at a mass meeting of about 50,000 people at Nanch'ang.
It was on this occasion that he told the story of the smoking boy. He
invited the crowd to look at Germany. Though defeated in the
Great War, the Germans had rapidly recovered. They had ceased to
pay the war indemnities forced upon them by the victorious Allies,
and were now well on the way to abrogating the unequal treaties
forced upon their country. Yet what of China? In contrast to
the Germans, the Chinese were still in humiliating bondage to the
unequal treaties. Nor was Germany the only example for the
Chinese people: with their Spartan discipline, the Japanese, too, set
an example which the Chinese might well copy.

Warming to his moral theme, the Generalissimo pointed to the
principles of behaviour enunciated many centuries before by
Confucius and the other great Chinese sages. Four of them in
particular he commended to their attention: *li*, a regulated attitude
of the mind and the heart; *yi*, right conduct in all things; *lien*, a
clear sense of discrimination, particularly regarding honesty in
personal and official life; and *ch'ih*, integrity and honour.

The slogan of the New Life Movement in fact joined these
Confucian principles of virtue into an amalgam: *li-yi-lien-ch'ih*—
generally translated loosely into English as "propriety, justice,
honesty, and sense of self-respect".

With his typical despatch and energy, and although he had a
military campaign on his hands, Chiang caused 200 groups of
students to be trained and sent out to lecture in public on the New
Life. In Nanch'ang alone, thirteen lecture stations were opened,
where New Life leaders gave daily lectures to mass audiences.

Pamphlets were printed, and civil and religious bodies were asked to distribute them as widely as possible.

To supplement the four virtues, eight principles were drawn up for the guidance of the people:

1. Regard yesterday as a period of death, today as a period of life. Let us rid ourselves of old abuses and build up a new nation.
2. Let us accept the heavy responsibilities of reviving the nation.
3. We must observe rules and have faith, honesty and shame.
4. Our clothing, eating, living, and travelling must be simple, orderly, plain, and clean.
5. We must willingly face hardships. We must strive for frugality.
6. We must have adequate knowledge and moral integrity as citizens.
7. Our actions must be courageous and rapid.
8. We must act on our promises, or even act without promising.

Not content with four virtues and eight principles, Chiang now announced ninety-five rules of daily behaviour. Be prompt, the Chinese were told, button up your clothes, stand straight, and do not eat noisily. "If we are to have a New Life that accords with *li-yi-lien-ch'ih*," Chiang declared, "then we must start by not spitting heedlessly." And again: "If we are to restore the nation and gain revenge for our humiliations, then we need not talk about guns and cannon, but must first talk about washing our faces in cold water."

It is instructive to contrast the approved Kuomintang version of the New Life Movement and what is now known to have happened. Neither Tong nor Hsiung, for instance, makes any mention of the Blue Shirts, since any admission of the existence of this fascist-type organisation would damage the carefully cultivated image of Chiang Kai-shek as a defender of "democracy" and a worthy recipient of American aid. Overtly, the work of propagating the New Life credo was given to the Young Men's Christian Association (YMCA)—a mildly incongruous choice since it meant that a Christian organisation was being asked to spread Confucian doctrines. It is true that there was nothing in *li-yi-lien-ch'ih* that was incompatible with

Christianity; for that matter, Chiang himself was a Confucian traditionalist who had adopted Christianity. There is nothing philosophically un-Chinese in this combination.

That the Blue Shirts did indeed play an important part in the movement now seems incontrovertible, on the evidence gathered by Lloyd E. Eastman. The Generalissimo's emphasis on the ancient virtues, on the "eight principles" and the "ninety-five rules" was one thing; quite another was the ultimate objective in his mind. At one point, he asked a rhetorical question, then gave his own answer:

> What is the New Life Movement that I now propose? Stated simply, it is thoroughly to militarise the lives of the citizens of the entire nation so that they can cultivate courage and swiftness, the endurance of suffering and a tolerance for hard work, and especially the habit and ability of unified action, so that they will at any time sacrifice for the nation.

In September 1933, five months before launching the New Life Movement, he had explained that the militarisation of society was one of three basic elements in fascism (the others being a sense of national superiority and faith in the leader). It is unlikely that he was unconscious of the parallel. (Some of the zealous excesses of the Blue Shirts in the New Life period were described in Chapter 1.)

For Western consumption, however, the picture presented was more aseptic. The movement was formally launched at Nanch'ang on 11 March 1934, at a mass meeting where the rough head count was said to have reached 100,000; 142 organisations were represented. Flanked by the governor of Kiangsi and the Commissioner of Education, Chiang Kai-shek—immaculately turned out, as usual —stood on the rostrum and was about to speak when he noticed an unkempt young man taking photographs of the gathering from various angles. Pointing a moralising finger at the unfortunate photographer, Chiang exclaimed: "That man! Now there's an example of the kind of person for whom the mottoes of our new movement—orderliness, cleanliness, and the rest—have little or no meaning." Exit the photographer.

Nanch'ang itself was the first to benefit from the new-old principles. A week after the mass meeting, thousands of people marched in procession through the streets bearing aloft multi-coloured dragons and shining pagodas from which fluttered elevating slogans, such as: "Don't spit. Cleanliness prevents sickness. Kill flies and rats: they breed disease. Avoid wine, women, and gambling." It is ironical to reflect that it was left to the Communists, many years later, to impose a dirt-free, rat-free, fly-free, and vice-free society on the Chinese people by the new techniques of relentless persuasion, wielded by ubiquitous and dedicated "cadres"

In Nanking, the capital, Premier Wang Ching-wei presided over a launching ceremony on 17 March, and there were similar meetings in Peiping, Canton, and other cities. It was Wang again who designated 27 August—the birthday of Confucius—as a national holiday, with impressive ceremonies to mark the occasion. Then on 30 November, Wang and Chiang—still as one in this phase of their public lives—issued a joint message to the nation appealing for the preservation of China's antiquities and historical landmarks, and announcing the creation of a new Central Historical Relics Preservation Committee. This, too, was the "New Life".

A curious but little-known fact about the New Life Movement is that its first General Secretary was an underground Communist. At one time, Yen Pao-han had worked for the Young Marshal as an English-language secretary. Ostensibly, Yen was a very devout Christian. But when the Chinese People's Republic was created in 1949, he became the Director of the Foreign Minister's Office.

During the World War II period, when the National government was in Chungking, Yen Pao-han was often taunted about the part he had played in the New Life Movement. He would always enumerate the following reasons for its failure:

1. The Chinese people hate to be told what is right and what is wrong.
2. The branch associations of the Movement were never supported by the local governments.
3. With policemen acting as supervisors of the people's conduct, there was widespread resentment.
4. The message was never put over convincingly to ordinary people, who simply could not understand what it was all about.
5. Most high officials were very cynical about the usefulness of the movement, and merely paid lip service to Chiang Kai-shek.

Eric Chou has vivid recollections of how ordinary people managed to get round the restrictions of the New Life Movement. When, for instance, eight people gathered round a table in a restaurant, they were not supposed to order more than four dishes and a soup among them. But the restaurants used bigger plates so that two dishes could be served simultaneously on one plate. Drinks were prohibited in the restaurants, so wines and spirits were served in teapots to fool the inspectors—most of whom were Boy Scouts.

A certain General Han Fu-chü (who had made a name of a sort for himself by betraying Feng Yü-hsiang) contributed one of the most popular anecdotes of the period. In a speech at a public meeting in Tsinan, he said: "I agree with the Generalissimo about the New Life Movement, wholeheartedly and obediently. But one thing puzzles me. If everybody walks on the left of the road, who will walk on the right? Besides, the left-hand side is bound to become overcrowded!"

Stirred by his own propaganda, the Generalissimo now harnessed the New Life Movement to the anti-opium campaign, which had been launched in 1928 but had got bogged down in bureaucratic sloth. As Chairman of the National Military Council, he took over the work of opium suppression in Kiangsi and other areas where the Communist "bandits" were being exterminated. Imposing the death penalty for making, selling, or trafficking in the drug, he ordered the execution of a Peiping police officer to show he meant business. KMT and government officials who smoked the stuff were given three years to cure themselves, and curative institutions were opened. A spate of deterrent laws followed. Those still involved in the drug traffic by 1937, even as accomplices, would be shot and their property confiscated. After the three-year period, convicted addicts would be taken to clinics by force and gaoled for five years after treatment. Officials ignoring the period of voluntary treatment would be sentenced to death.

On 29 May 1935, the civilian government decided to hand over the whole machinery for the suppression of narcotics to the Generalissimo, who took on the new title of Inspector-General for Opium Suppression. This, at any rate, was a field in which his ruthless energy paid off, and on 24 September 1935 the relevant committee of the League of Nations at Geneva noted marked results in the anti-drug campaign in China. That day, in Chengtu,

Chiang Kai-shek set 1 January 1936 as the new deadline for the voluntary registration of addicts, with the drastic penalties previously announced in store for evaders. When the New Year came, he banned the cultivation of the poppy in the six provinces of Kiangsu, Anhwei, Szechwan, Kiangsi, Hupei, and Hunan. He summoned an anti-opium conference, which met in Nanking from 1 to 3 February. All opium-smoking and drug-trafficking, said the Generalissimo, was to be eradicated within six years. But the six years were not available, the Japanese having decided long before the deadline to conquer China.

In general, however, it is fair to say that the opium-suppression campaign was more successful than the New Life Movement of which it was a by-product. At a time when Mao Tse-tung was pledging himself to emancipate the peasants and sweep away millennia of traditional oppression, and when the young intellectuals were stirred by the lure of revolution, the Generalissimo's appeal for Confucian virtue and Protestant primness fell on deaf ears. In the popular mind, and in the eyes of the intellectuals, this was a message from the past on behalf of the landed gentry and the commercial middle class. It skimmed over the surface of those living lives of hardship, disturbing nothing.

Yet, paradoxically, these were years when Chiang Kai-shek himself became, for the first time, a truly national figure, achieving a personal popularity that did not appear to rest upon successful propaganda alone. In the autumn of 1934, about the time when the Communists were breaking out of the concrete ring in Kiangsi and starting on their Long March, the Generalissimo and his wife embarked on a series of plane trips that took them all over China. The advent of air travel had made this "meet the people" programme possible for the first time. No previous ruler or public figure in China's long history could overcome the obstacles of time and space that ruled out any thought of visiting every province of the empire.

In the beginning, however, it was less a programme than a spur-of-the-moment plane-hopping jaunt. With Marshal Chang Hsueh-liang, back from his European trip, the Chiang couple flew to Loyang to visit a new military academy. Why not take a look at Sian (in Shensi, farther west)? suggested the Young Marshal. So the Generalissimo found himself, unwittingly, on the scene of his own kidnapping two years later. More spontaneous travelling urges followed, and by the time they had finished, they had covered 5,000 miles and visited ten provinces in the north and north-west.

To the people in remoter areas, the arrival of a leader—especially by air, in those days—was a break in monotonous lives, encouraging an effusive welcome. Other leaders in modern times—above all, perhaps, General de Gaulle—have basked in the adulation of crowds, drawing strength from the visual evidence of popularity. This was true of Chiang and his wife. Having tasted "popularity", they wanted more. Now the trips lost their spontaneity, turning into a systematic programme. The next flights took them to the provinces of the west and south.

Of these wanderings, the western trip was the most important politically. For this was, still, warlord country. In Kweichow and Szechwan, in Yunnan and elsewhere in the south-west, the feudal military men ruled undisturbed, for all the talk of China's "unity". To complicate the problem, the Kiangsi Communists were moving into these areas. In Kweichow, for example, they spent four months, destroying five of the local warlord's divisions, occupying his palace in Tsunyi, and recruiting 20,000 men. Evading Chiang's blockade, they suddenly turned southward in May 1935 and entered the southern frontier province of Yunnan. At that precise moment, Chiang and his wife were staying in Kunming, the provincial capital. Communist troops were reported ten miles away, and the warlord Lung Yun ("Dragon Cloud") hastily brought up reinforcements while the Chiangs moved out on the French-built railway. But it was soon found to be a diversionary move by a small Red force.

A forced march of eighty-five miles in one night and day (says Snow) brought the bulk of the Communist forces to Fort Chou P'ing on the Yangtze, which they took with ease, dressed in Nationalist uniforms. Then they ferried their entire army across the provincial border in Szechwan, and destroyed the boats they had captured from the Nanking troops.

This trip had ceased to be a public relations exercise. Furious, the Generalissimo and Mme. Chiang flew to Szechwan, hoping to stop the Communists on the Tatu River. The decisive moment came at a place where the river flowed swiftly through a narrow gorge with sheer walls rising thousands of feet. There an engineer named

Liu had built a famous iron-chain suspension bridge, known as the Lu Ting Chiao—"the bridge becalming the Lu River".° When the Reds arrived, they found that about half the wooded floor lashed to the great chains had been removed. Swinging hand over hand, and hurling hand grenades at the Nanking troops on the other side, the barefoot guerrillas nevertheless made it over the bridge, gaining access to western Szechwan. It was Chiang's last chance to cut them off. Thenceforth, the Reds were more troubled by altitude and other natural obstacles than the Generalissimo's exterminating forces.

For all these setbacks, Chiang's western trip had brought useful dividends, for it had enabled him to purge and discipline the provincial administrations in Szechwan and elsewhere. He was not to know that some years later he would be forced to move his national capital from Nanking to the Szechwanese town of Chung-king—a move which (as Tong rightly remarks) would probably have been impossible if the planted Communist agents and the officials they had subverted had not been removed.

° Not, as Edgar Snow has it, "the Bridge Fixed by Liu" (*Red Star Over China*, p. 197).

14. Japan and the Sian Incident

C hiang Kai-shek's troubles never came singly, and they crowded in on him in the second half of 1935. Although he had established himself as a kind of national warlord, his provincial rivals could never bring themselves to abandon the hope that they might in time supplant him. His curious reluctance to stand up to the Japanese was a convenient issue and a rallying cry. The Kwangsi generals—so often in rebellion and so often frustrated—launched an organisation which they called the "Anti-Japanese National Salvation Forces" in June. The two Kwangsi generals involved were Li Tsung-jen and Pai Ch'ung-hsi, and they now joined forces with Ch'en Chi-t'ang, who at that time was Commander-in-Chief of the Kwangtung Army. Similarly inspired, that familiar figure the "Christian General", Feng Yü-hsiang, went into action in the north, proclaiming himself "Commander-in-Chief of the People's Anti-Japanese Army". As usual, Feng's histrionics were short-lived. He didn't quite manage a confrontation with the

Japanese; instead, faced by a superior force loyal to Chiang Kai-shek, he announced yet another "strategic withdrawal".

Down south, the problem looked more serious; not that the Generalissimo could take the anti-Japanese pretensions of the three generals at all seriously. Before going into rebellion, they had sent telegrams to him calling on him to declare war against Japan. Not to be diverted from his preordained order of priorities, Chiang replied: "You cannot gamble with the existence of a nation on a momentary impulse." In fact, if the Kuomintang historians are to be believed, Ch'en Chi-t'ang had bought arms and ammunition from the Japanese themselves for their proposed anti-Japanese expedition. Tong quotes Major-General Seiichi Kita, the Japanese Military Attaché in China, as confirming this allegation on 12 June 1935.

At all events, on receipt of Chiang's negative reply, the "Salvationists" moved their troops fifteen miles into Hunan province, which has a common border with Kwangsi. Still conciliatory at this stage, the Generalissimo ordered his Hunan troops to move back and avoid a clash that might lead to a further dose of civil war. Money, it now turned out, was a more important issue to the rebel generals than the national resistance to Japan. Kwangtung was badly in need of it, and Kwangsi's income had dropped disastrously as a result of Chiang's campaign to suppress the opium traffic. Within six weeks, defections and dissensions broke the rebel movement. Ch'en Chi-t'ang fled to Hong Kong, and the Kwangsi generals benefited from Chiang Kai-shek's lenient mood. In return for a formal acceptance of his authority, Li Tsung-jen was appointed "Pacification Commissioner for Kwangsi", and Pai Ch'ung-hsi was made a member of the Standing Committee of the National Military Council. Chinese honour was saved.

Phony though their anti-Japanese stand undoubtedly was, those Chinese who resented Japanese encroachments and wanted to stand up to the interlopers had serious grounds for concern in 1935. At the beginning of the year there had been a brief hope that relations between China and Japan might be placed on a new, stable, and relatively friendly footing. Chiang Kai-shek had offered to conclude a treaty of friendship with Tokyo, on a basis of absolute equality. The relatively undemanding Japanese Foreign Ministry was inclined to accept, having chosen to interpret Chiang's offer as implying that he was ready to exclude the Western powers and turn to the Japanese for help and advice. But domestic developments in Japan decided otherwise. The military wanted brutal solutions and were moving consciously towards war. Ever faster, the soldiers were overruling the civilians. In January, the Japanese forces occupied territory in eastern Chahar on the ground that it properly belonged to Manchukuo. Further incidents came in May, and on 6 July the so-called Ho-Umetsu agreement called for the removal of all Kuomintang armies and organisations from Hopei province and the suppression of Blue Shirt activities there. There was more: Nanking was forced to promulgate a "Goodwill Mandate", promising to punish hostile acts or speeches against "friendly nations"—a euphemism for Japan. Further humiliation came in September when the Japanese merged the five provinces of Hopei, Shantung, Shansi, Chahar, and Suiyuan into an "autonomous" Chinese area which, in fact, the Japanese would totally control.

From Chiang Kai-shek came further appeasement. In a speech to the Fifth Congress of the Kuomintang on 12 November 1935, the Generalissimo declared: "We shall not lightly talk about sacrifice until we are driven to the last extremity which makes sacrifice inevitable." True, he added a mild warning that there were limits to China's readiness to compromise.

Not long before, Mao Tse-tung and Chou En-lai had arrived in Shensi at the end of the Long March. With another figure of later fame, Liu Shao-ch'i—who was to become President of the Chinese People's Republic, only to be disgraced and shorn of office during the Cultural Revolution of the 1960s—Mao went to work to organise the student movement in Peiping and Tientsin. Also with him was P'eng Chen (later to become Mayor of Peking under the People's Republic). For the students, as well as for the rebellious warlords, Japan's depredations were the perfect rallying cry. But an even better one was the heroism of the Red Army in retreat.

At Peiping Normal University at that time, Eric Chou's leftist schoolmates spread the word of heroic deeds on the Long March. That autumn he came to know Huang Chin, who had come to the northern capital from Tsingtao, where he had been having an affair with the actress Chiang Ch'ing (later to become Mao Tse-tung's fourth wife). Huang Chin (who also used the alias Yü Ch'i-wei) was himself to become Minister of Heavy Industry in 1949.

In those earlier days, Huang Chin was an occasional student at Peking University, but much of his time was spent at Yenching and Tsing Hua universities, to agitate and propagandise among the

students. He was one of the prime movers in organising the
Vanguard of National Liberation—which served as the prototype of
the Chinese Communist Party's youth corps. The "agitprop" was
highly successful. When Chiang's general Ho Ying-ch'in came to
Peiping at the beginning of December, Huang decided to make
things hot for him. It was he who had signed the humiliating
agreement with Umetsu five months earlier. On 9 December,
10,000 students demonstrated in Peiping against the Japanese. To
older men, it recalled the May 4th Movement of 1919, but on an
even larger scale. In Hangchow and Shanghai, in Wuhan, Changsha, and Wuchow, other students demonstrated or rioted. Everywhere, Associations for National Salvation sprang up. The "December 9th Movement" was born, and stayed much alive. For Chiang
Kai-shek, it was a major embarrassment; in the eyes of the Chinese
Communist Party, which had done the organising, it was an integral
part of the "people's revolution". Years later—in an article on the
December 9th Movement (Peking, 1961)—Liu Shao-ch'i was said to
have hailed the student movement as "marking the division of the
Reactionary Period and Revolutionary Period in China's history",
and attributed its success to "the guidance of the CCP and the
Thought of Mao Tse-tung".

Another act of rebellion came from within the Generalissimo's
own family. In 1935, his elder son Ching-kuo wrote to his mother
(whom Chiang Kai-shek of course had long divorced) to condemn
his father's politics. He delivered himself of this illuminating
passage: "The Soviet Union is our mother country. I feel glory and
delight to see my mother country, the Soviet Union, continue to
break records in various fields." The letter was postmarked
Leningrad, for Chiang Ching-kuo had been living in the Soviet
Union for ten years.

It was a curious case. Ching-kuo was only seventeen when he
went to Russia. Although Chiang Kai-shek had already turned
against the Communists, the fact was still not widely known, and he
was often described as the "Trotsky" of China. In 1925, Chiang had
lately taken over as Commandant of the Military Academy at
Whampoa. His son had arrived at Canton, then known as the
"revolutionary Mecca", and when the two met, his father was at a
loss to know what to do about his son's further education. At that
precise moment, the Sun Yat-sen University in Moscow requested
the revolutionary government to send a large group of students to

Russia. With Ching-kuo's eager assent, Chiang Kai-shek included his son in this group. There seemed good reasons for this decision: it demonstrated that he was friendly towards the Soviet Union, it gave his son a chance to learn revolutionary techniques for possible future use, and it solved the boy's educational problem. It was for similar reasons that he later sent his other son, Wei-kuo, to Nazi Germany.

Two years later, however, the experiment turned sour, when Chiang Kai-shek pounced on the Chinese Communists in Shanghai and elsewhere. But by then, there was no easy way for him to bring his son back to China. In fact, he did order the young man home, but Ching-kuo was not his own master. He sent a defiant message, refusing to obey and condemning his father. According to KMT sources (which must be trusted on this occasion), the message was dictated to Ching-kuo by Wang Ming (alias Ch'en Shao-yü), a Chinese Communist leader who was at that time in Russia. The years went by, and by 1936—the year of his second refusal—Ching-kuo had acquired a Russian wife and looked like settling down in the U.S.S.R.

Without defending the Generalissimo's order of priorities— "bandits" first, Japan second—Chiang Kai-shek must be given credit for self-discipline and single-mindedness in his determination to avoid conflict with the Japanese as long as possible. He had already instructed his strategic adviser, Chiang Po-li, to draft a national defence plan. In the winter of 1935, he had sent Chiang to Europe to study the legal provisions for general mobilisation in various countries. His first visit was to Italy, where he paid particular attention to the expansion of the air force. In his report to the Generalissimo, Chiang laid special emphasis on the significance of "air defence geography", arguing that in a country as vast as China it was most important that the air force should have speed and stamina. For a prolonged war, he pointed out, economic mobilisation was essential; propaganda should go hand in hand with military operations.

One of the main reasons for Chiang's reluctance to take on the Japanese was the precarious basis of his own hold on power. The warlords were egging him on, for if he stood up to the Japanese and was defeated, they could share the spoils of his own kingdom among them—or the nearest and strongest could grab everything for himself. Well aware of this danger, Chiang waited.

Nor is it fair to accuse him—as the Communist version of events has it—of ruling out all reconciliation with Mao Tse-tung in the national interest until forced into this course when kidnapped at the end of 1936. In fact, a full year earlier—at the end of 1935—he had sent a close associate to Vienna as his personal envoy to discuss joint Communist-Nationalist action against Japanese aggression with the Russian representatives in that city. But, for reasons that are still obscure, nothing came of it.

In principle, both the Russian and the Chinese Communists should have been ready to greet any initiative from Chiang Kai-shek, although they had little reason to trust him. The Seventh Congress of the Comintern in July and August 1935 had decided to encourage the formation of popular fronts wherever possible. In China, the Communists were told to seek collaboration with the Kuomintang. Rather unrealistically, given the desperately weakened condition of the Chinese Red Army after the Long March, the new line laid down that "the Soviets must become the centre around which the whole Chinese people is united in its struggle for liberation".

These instructions were naturally unwelcome to Mao Tse-tung, whose only immediate concession to the Comintern line was to stop his party propagandists from describing Chiang as a reactionary, and concentrate on calling him a "traitor to the nation". A more promising approach, thought Mao, was to the Young Marshal, Chang Hsueh-liang, and in the spring of 1936, the Communists secretly contacted him. They were welcomed by the Young Marshal, and he invited the Communists to send representatives to his headquarters in Sian.

Chiang Kai-shek was not altogether displeased at the warm relations that had developed between the Young Marshal and the Communists. When the time came to resume his bandit-suppression campaigns, he would now have a chance of eliminating both the Communists and Chang's forces simultaneously. This would remove the Young Marshal as a major factor in Chinese politics. More worrying to him were reports of the rapid recovery and growth of Mao Tse-tung's forces during 1936. In October, two Nationalist Army Corps had defected to the Communists in their new base area. On completing the Long March, Mao had only 20,000 guerrilla remnants; now he commanded about 80,000. Admittedly, many of them lacked rifles, but this group was once again looming ahead as a major force.

Relations between the Generalissimo and Chang Hsueh-liang were by now very cool. It had become fashionable to refer to the Young Marshal as "the non-resistant general". The rival warlords encouraged this habit. Chang himself thought it monstrously unfair, for had he not had precise orders from Chiang Kai-shek not to resist the Japanese when they first attacked at Mukden in 1931? Shortly after the Mukden incident, the two men had met on a train at Paoting, in Hopei province. According to an account which cannot be exonerated from bias, Chiang said: "The present condition is like a small boat tossed up and down by the frightening waves. Only one of us can cross over. If both of us try to cross, either we both sink or one of us jumps down. The problem is: you or me?" Quoting these words, Lu Pi (probably a pseudonym for a friend of the Young Marshal) added: "What he meant was: the whole country was now attacking non-resistance and the situation was critical. One of them, he suggested, must take the blame for non-resistance. Mr. Chang generously said: 'I will jump down!' "

Cured of his drug habit, Chang Hsueh-liang had toured European countries for about a year, and was a different man when he returned to China in the spring of 1934. With his taste for dancing, drinking, and golf went a sense of humour. A friend asked the Young Marshal on his return what he thought of Italy. "Oh, it was all right," he said, "macaroni on every table, Mussolini on every wall."

Why had he come back? For one thing, the Fukien rebellion had unsettled the whole country. He thought his return might help to stabilise the situation. Another consideration was that the North-Eastern Army had been calling for his return. Both officers and men were restless, and anti-Japanese sentiment consumed them. Fearing yet another rebellion, Chiang Kai-shek wanted the Young Marshal back at his post. As soon as he returned, the Generalissimo appointed him Deputy Commander of Bandit-Suppressing Forces in Honan, Hupei, and Anhwei, and as such directly under the orders of the Commander-in-Chief—Chiang himself.

The Young Marshal had strong reasons for being anti-Japanese. The Japanese had assassinated his father, and he himself felt deeply responsible for the loss of large areas of China to Japan. His friends and advisers shared his views. These included W. H. Donald, an Australian journalist whom he had been employing as his chief adviser since the end of 1928. "Donald of China", as he was to be known, was strongly in favour of Chinese national unity in resistance to Japan. What the Young Marshal's Chinese advisers found hard to stomach was the suggestion that they should fight the Communist bandits, who after all were Chinese and many of them natives of the area, in preference to the Japanese interlopers. But Chang Hsueh-liang was still—at the end of 1934—loyal to Chiang Kai-shek. And much against his own inclinations, he was still responsive to the Generalissimo's orders.

He began to change his mind in the winter of 1935 when the North-Eastern Army fought a major battle with the Red Army while the Young Marshal was attending the Fifth Congress of the Kuomintang in Nanking. The Reds suffered heavy losses; but so did the North-Eastern Army, which lost two whole divisions. If this was to be the price of suppressing "bandits", Chang would soon, at this rate, have no forces left to fight the Japanese. From the Communists themselves came a message that they wished to end the civil war and unite to fight Japan. It was as a result of this overture that Chang Hsueh-liang began to negotiate with Mao Tse-tung's representatives.

Having digested intelligence reports about the growth and rebirth of the Red Army, Chiang Kai-shek decided to visit Chang Hsueh-liang in his Sian headquarters to discuss the sixth bandit-suppression campaign, which he had been planning. For the first time, the Generalissimo found Chang unwilling to listen. He knew, he explained, that the Communists were now prepared to cooperate and take orders from Chiang Kai-shek in applying an anti-Japanese national policy. He called for an alliance with the Soviet Union and a joint programme of resistance against Japan. Chiang was "deeply hurt" (writes Lu Pi). How could a subordinate, hitherto loyal, advise him to unite with the Communists? His mood turning to fury, Chiang Kai-shek berated the Young Marshal, declared that Chang had lost his trust, and returned to his field headquarters at Loyang.

Although during this whole period, the Generalissimo was pressing on with his secret preparations for resistance to Japan, he was not yet ready to reveal himself either to China or to the invader. Nor was he to be deflected from his chosen order of priorities. Indeed, his first act on leaving Sian was to order the arrest of seven prominent leaders of the National Salvation Movement in Shanghai and close down fourteen popular magazines guilty of advocating resistance. He then turned to a very public piece of private business—the forthcoming celebrations of his fiftieth birthday by the Chinese reckoning (his forty-ninth, as most of the world would say). The date fell on 31 October 1936, and it had all the marks of an apotheosis. He himself chose to mark the occasion in simplicity in Loyang, an ancient capital of China. Two enormous birthday cakes had been provided, and after he had blown out the lighted candles, Mme. Chiang served slices of it to the local dignitaries and their wives and children. It was on this occasion that Chiang paid tribute to his mother in a message to the Chinese people.

Elsewhere, the celebrations were less reticent. A birthday fund, declared open a year earlier, had raised enough money to pay for the purchase and shipment of 100 American planes. At Nanking, a crowd of 200,000 gathered in the Ming Palace aerodrome to watch the aircraft fly in formation, dipping in salute before an enormous likeness of the Generalissimo. Three times the great crowd bowed heads in Chinese obeisance. It was a great day for Chiang Kai-shek. Yet only weeks away, the strangest and almost the most humiliating episode in his life awaited him: the Sian kidnapping.

The news that reached Chiang Kai-shek in late November was bad on all counts. He had sent one of his best formations, the famous First Army, under General Hu Tsung-nan, to seek out and destroy the Red Army in Kansu province. The first news was of success for Hu and flight for the Communists. But the unsuspecting First Army allowed itself to be surrounded: the Reds fell on them and destroyed and disarmed two infantry brigades and a regiment of cavalry, capturing thousands of rifles and machine guns. For good measure, one government regiment defected intact to the Red Army. The date was 21 November 1936, and four days later Germany and Japan signed the Anti-Comintern Pact. Could war now be far away?

The news, far from deflecting Chiang to a path of national unity, merely strengthened his resolve to finish the Communists once and for all. As though nothing untoward had happened in October, the Generalissimo flew to Sian on 7 December 1936 with the clear object of forcing the Young Marshal to join in the sixth bandit-suppression campaign by the sheer weight of his will and authority. In advance, he had sent some 1,500 members of the "special service" regiment of the Blue Shirts, commanded by his nephew, General Chiang Hsiao-hsien. Well organised and operating from secret headquarters, Chiang Hsiao-hsien started arresting and kidnapping all those suspected of being Communists. Overriding all objections, Chiang Kai-shek summoned all his commanders to a General Staff Congress on the 10th, to finalise plans for the Sixth Campaign. He let it be known that if Chang Hsueh-liang declined to attend or to obey orders, he would face dismissal from his command and the disarming of his forces.

Instead, a bizarre attempted *coup d'état* frustrated the Generalissimo's plans. Caught in their sleep, the Blue Shirts were disarmed and arrested, most of the General Staff were gaoled, the police surrendered, and fifty planes and their pilots were grabbed by the rebels.

What happened next was (as Edgar Snow pointed out) a *coup de théâtre* rather than a *coup d'état*. The Generalissimo was staying at Lintung, a hot springs resort ten miles from Sian. At 5:00 A.M., the commander of the Young Marshal's bodyguard, Captain Sun Ming-chiu, age twenty-six, led about a dozen lorry-loads of troops to Chiang's hotel, and his men opened fire when challenged by sentries. The Generalissimo's bodyguards, though taken completely by surprise, resisted long enough for Chiang himself to escape. According to his own later account, he was already up and was dressing after his early morning exercises. Realising what had happened, and accompanied by two of his men, the Generalissimo scaled a wall ten feet high, then fell thirty feet on the other side, into a moat. He felt a sharp pain, and found later that he had severely injured his back. He had also (although his own account does not record this undignified detail), lost his dentures. Helped to his feet, he clambered up the mountain that adjoined the hotel, having been joined by some of his bodyguards. At the top, they were fired upon, and several bodyguards were shot dead. Realising he was surrounded, he walked down the mountain again, and had a second fall—this time into a cave concealed by shrubs. There, in broad daylight, Captain Sun and his men found him, with only a loose robe thrown over his nightshirt. Snow had been falling, and he was shivering; his bare feet and hands had been cut while clambering up the mountainside. Shaking now with rage rather than the cold, the Generalissimo shouted: "Shoot me and finish it all." Sun's reply was: "We will not shoot. We only ask you to lead our country against Japan."

Chiang Kai-shek asked for a horse to take him down the mountain. Instead, Captain Sun offered him his own broad back. Farther down the slope, a servant arrived with the Generalissimo's shoes. On level ground, a car was waiting to take him into Sian, where he was conducted to the offices of the Pacification Commissioner of Shensi, General Yang Hu-ch'eng. Shortly after, Chang Hsueh-liang came in and stood to attention. He addressed Chiang Kai-shek respectfully as "Generalissimo", to which Chiang retorted: "Since you call me Generalissimo, then you are my subordinate. If you recognise me as your superior officer, you must immediately escort me back to Loyang. Otherwise you are a rebel. If I am in rebel hands, then you can kill me immediately. Apart from that, there is nothing more to be said." And he sank into a silence that was to last several days.

The news soon came out that General Yang's troops had killed or wounded more than forty of the Generalissimo's bodyguards, while seventeen high officials and officers of the National Government had been arrested. The Young Marshal presented Chiang with a list of eight points, of which he refused to take cognisance. His captors then telegraphed the points to Nanking, appending the unauthorised signatures of a number of the captured National officers and officials. They read as follows:

1. Reorganise the Nanking government and admit all parties to share the joint responsibility of national salvation.
2. End all civil war immediately *and adopt the policy of armed resistance against Japan.*
3. Release the leaders of the patriotic movement in Shanghai.
4. Pardon all political prisoners.
5. Guarantee the people's freedom of assembly.
6. Safeguard the people's rights of patriotic organisation and political freedom.
7. Put into effect the Will of Dr. Sun Yat-sen.
8. Immediately convene a National Salvation conference.

It is instructive to note that the words italicised in point 2 of the list do not appear in the Kuomintang versions, or indeed anywhere except in Edgar Snow's *Red Star Over China* (p. 409). Curiously, even Snow italicises them, but evidently to emphasise their importance. Indeed, there is nothing inherently improbable in proposing "armed resistance against Japan": this, after all, was the purpose of kidnapping Chiang Kai-shek in the first place. The omission of the words, even in Communist sources, is puzzling, however. As Snow rightly pointed out, seven of the eight points corresponded exactly to the programme of "national salvation" advocated by the Chinese Communist Party and the Soviet government on 1 December 1936. The Young Marshal was, of course, in collusion with the Communists at the time of the Sian incident. Not unexpectedly, then, the Soviet government, the Chinese Communist Party, and the Chinese Red Army immediately announced their support for the eight-point programme.

The news that Chiang Kai-shek was being forcibly detained stunned China and plunged the population into deepest gloom. This much is admitted even by hostile witnesses, and confirmed by the impartial. Eric Chou, at that time a student at Peiping Normal University, recalls the occasion in these words:

When the news of Chiang's kidnapping reached Peiping in the late afternoon on 12 December 1936, the whole campus was stunned. Both politically disinterested professors and students suddenly felt concerned about what had happened. Peiping was never a pro-Chiang city, but in the ensuing days there was anxiety everywhere over Chiang's safety. Perhaps because of this atmosphere, the left-wing groups were unusually quiet throughout the Sian incident.

Eastman, a writer with little sympathy for the Kuomintang, put it this way: "A pall of gloom had fallen over most of the nation. Children, it was reported, could not sleep; soldiers wept; and illiterates badgered those who read the newspapers in order to learn the most recent dispatches from Sian."

This generalised unhappiness had a close bearing on the bizarre war of nerves that followed. The kidnappers—Chang and Yang— had assumed that all the warlords who had suffered from Chiang Kai-shek's unitary ambitions would rally behind them and condemn the Generalissimo. The opposite happened. Feng Yü-hsiang, the followers of Hu Han-min—who had just died—and even the

Kwangsi generals, all proclaimed their support and loyalty for Chiang and called for his release. It dawned on the discomfited conspirators that they stood alone.

In Nanking, the Central Government appointed H. H. K'ung as acting Premier, placed Feng in command of the National Military Council, and Ho Ying-ch'in of troop movements. Chang Hsueh-liang was deprived of all his posts and referred to the National Military Council for punishment. On the night of 12 December, Dr. K'ung and Mme. Chiang took the express from Shanghai to Nanking.

In Sian, meanwhile, Chang and Yang had been browsing through the Generalissimo's diaries, where to their surprise they learned of his secret plans to resist the Japanese invaders. Repentance came fast. On the third day, the two men called on the silent Generalissimo and Chang made a little speech which Hsiung records as follows:

> We have read your diary and all your important documents and from them we have now learned the greatness of your character. Your loyalty to the Revolution and your determination to bear the responsibility of saving the country far exceed anything we could have imagined. Haven't you in your diary scolded me for having no character? When I reflect on it today, I really feel that I have no character. But you have been too silent with your subordinates. If I had known but ten or twenty percent of what you have said in the diary, never would this rash act have happened. Now I sincerely realise that my own views were mistaken. Since I know the greatness of your leadership, I feel I would be disloyal to our countrymen if I did not do my utmost to protect you.

Now it was General Yang Hu-ch'eng's turn to speak. A rough soldier who had risen from the ranks, he was barely literate, and his language was less flowery: "At first our idea was not like this. Later on it all went in a very bad way. Indeed we are very sorry. Now we will obey whatever orders you care to give."

"Send me back to Nanking," said the Generalissimo. Yang—no doubt thinking of the problem of "face"—said they would have to consult their colleagues, and left.

Down in Nanking, Ho Ying-ch'in was breathing fire. His proposal was to launch a punitive expedition against Sian, with air bombardment to soften up the target. When Mme. Chiang pointed out that bombs do not discriminate, and that Chiang Kai-shek himself might be killed, General Ho reluctantly withdrew his proposal.

The Communists were in a quandary. The Russians were taken by surprise by the kidnapping, or at all events behaved as though they were. On 14 December, the Soviet press severely condemned the kidnappers and imaginatively accused Chang Hsueh-liang of being in the pay of Japanese imperialism. In Soviet eyes—by the visible evidence—Chiang Kai-shek and his party were alone capable of uniting China in resistance to Japan.

The Chinese Communists understandably found it difficult to accept this view. Their first intention was probably to bring the Generalissimo to trial, then execute him. But now came Moscow's firm order: the Chinese party was to press for a national coalition government under Chiang Kai-shek. One of history's little ironies happened at this point. Chou En-lai, who had narrowly escaped the firing squad in Shanghai in 1927 during the Generalissimo's purge, was now sent from Yenan to Sian to save Chiang's life. Chou arrived in mid-December and immediately went to see Chiang. Still weak and in pain from his back and in psychological turmoil from his ordeal, Chiang turned pale on seeing Chou En-lai—remembering no doubt that he had once put a price of $80,000 on his visitor's head. But Chou was disciplined, and therefore friendly. With him was the Young Marshal, and both men acknowledged him as Commander-in-Chief. In frigid silence, Chiang listened as Chou En-lai expounded the Communist point of view. The first talk was inconclusive, and there were daily talks after that until 25 December.

Neither in his diary nor in his book, *Soviet Russia in China*, did Chiang Kai-shek make any mention of his meetings with Chou En-lai. From his close associate Ch'en Li-fu many years later, I learned some relevant background. Before the Sian incident, Chiang Kai-shek had sent Ch'en there to talk with Chou En-lai (who had been recalled to Yenan immediately after the capture of the Generalissimo), and with the Russian representative Bogumulov.

Chou took the line: "If you fight the Japanese, we shall cooperate with you." To this, Ch'en Li-fu retorted: "If we fight the Japanese, you should cooperate with *us*." He went on to enumerate four points that could form the basis of a KMT–Communist agreement:

1. The Chinese Communist Party should observe the Three Principles of the People.
2. The Communists should obey the orders of the Generalissimo.
3. The Red Army should be abolished.
4. The Chinese Soviet organisation should be abolished; however, under a special treaty with Yenan, the Communists could have their own autonomous government, as part of the Chinese local government structure.

Chou En-lai complied (says Ch'en Li-fu) because the Comintern ordered him to. Ch'en also discussed a non-aggression pact with the Russians. The Russians were to agree not to help the Chinese Communists. Chou En-lai agreed to see the Young Marshal and tell him and his followers to stop making a nuisance of themselves, since the National Government was preparing to fight the Japanese anyway.

In his conversation with me, Ch'en Li-fu went on to claim that it was Stalin himself who had ordered the kidnapping of Chiang Kai-shek, while at the same time he had directed the Japanese Communist Party to take a "patriotic" line in support of Japanese military action. The second of these points is likely enough; I know of no other evidence to support the first. It must be admitted, however, that Stalin did stand to gain from the capture of Chiang Kai-shek, since there seemed no other way of speeding up his decision to resist Japan.

Another influence now came on the scene—the Australian W. H. Donald. Having served Chang Hsueh-liang, Donald now offered his services to Nanking as a mediator; they were gladly accepted. He arrived in Sian on 14 December (whether a day after or a day before Chou En-lai's arrival is obscure). Back in Loyang on the 15th, he telephoned his report to Nanking. He was able to provide reassurance, in the face of desperate and often circumstantial reports of the Generalissimo's death, that he was alive and being well treated. This news further strengthened Mme. Chiang's hand against those advocating a military solution. It was clear now that a peaceful settlement was possible.

Mme. Chiang's brother, T. V. Soong, who knew the Young Marshal well, flew to Sian and arranged for Mme. Chiang herself to come. It was a wise arrangement. The Generalissimo's wife, at the height of her beauty and charm, was all tact and diplomacy: her role was that of conciliator, and she played it well. In her own account, she describes the Young Marshal as looking "very tired, very embarrassed, and somewhat ashamed", and Yang Hu-ch'eng as "obviously very nervous". She greeted both in a friendly way as though nothing had happened, and on 22 December—the day of Mme. Chiang's arrival (says Hsiung)—Chiang Kai-shek was reading a chapter of Jeremiah, and fell upon these words: "Jehovah will now do a new thing, He will make a woman protect a man." And so it came to pass. On Christmas Day 1936, the Generalissimo and his wife were driven to Loyang, then flown to Nanking. In a self-sacrificing mood, the Young Marshal accompanied them all the way as a guarantee of their personal safety. He had long years ahead of him in which to repent of his decision. The Generalissimo had him court-martialed and sentenced to ten years' gaol and five years' deprivation of civil rights. Later, the sentence was rescinded, but Chang Hsueh-liang remained under house arrest not only until the Nationalist defeat in China in 1949, but after that in exile on Taiwan (where he was still not being allowed to move freely when these lines were written in mid–1975).

His treatment must have been deeply embarrassing to T. V. Soong, who (according to an eyewitness) had personally guaranteed that Chang would not be punished in Nanking. Chang himself evidently did not expect punishment, for he regarded his readiness to accompany the Chiangs to Nanking as proof of his continuing loyalty to the Generalissimo. As for Yang Hu-ch'eng, he, too, was imprisoned, and the vindictive Generalissimo had him murdered in Chungking in 1949 when the Communists were about to take the city. There is now a general consensus that it was Yang's idea to kidnap Chiang Kai-shek, and that he talked Chang Hsueh-liang into seeing it through.

A great explosion of popular joy greeted the news of the Generalissimo's release throughout China. In Eric Chou's words:

On the evening of 25 December 1936, about 6:00 P.M., when the news of Chiang's safe return to Nanking came through, the whole city of Peiping erupted with joy. Firecrackers were set off everywhere and the streets were packed with cheering crowds. Many people gave parties to celebrate the occasion, and the occasion they had in mind was Chiang's release, not Christmas, which meant nothing in those days to the residents of the northern capital.

The balance-sheet of the Sian incident is by no means one-sided. The Generalissimo could rightly claim—and did—that he had not formally accepted the eight points presented to him by his captors; and certainly he declined to the end to sign any document. Events were soon to show, however, that tacitly at least Chiang did accept most of the eight points. The Generalissimo stopped his attempts to "suppress" or "exterminate" the Communists, and stopped calling them "bandits". Chiang's lifelong friend, General Chang Ch'ün, who was alleged to be pro-Japanese, lost his job as Foreign Minister; and the Communists were invited to send a delegation to the National People's Congress scheduled for November 1937. Preparations went ahead for a united front against the Japanese.

In the curious triangular play of forces of the Sian incident, only the Young Marshal and his followers had lost everything. The Communists had gained much. No longer were they being harassed; indeed, they had gained a new national and international respectability. Moreover, they could reflect that history was moving in their direction. For war with Japan was central to their plan: they knew it would mean the defeat and humiliation of the Nationalist armies, the loss of vast areas, and the destruction of Chiang's administration. In this dreadful situation, they themselves would gain their opportunities. They would fight the Japanese behind the lines and claim the credit of undefeated patriotism. They would consolidate their underground administration in defiance of the Kuomintang. And the war would leave them strengthened and ready to conquer China. For outside observers, this is the wisdom of hindsight, but there can be no doubt that Mao Tse-tung foresaw this sequence of events.

In the short and medium term, Chiang Kai-shek himself emerged enormously strengthened from his ordeal. He had minimised his loss of face by signing nothing and standing on his rights. He had humiliated and punished his captors, never forgiving the Young Marshal for forcing him to resist Japan before his secret plans were ready. He was now at the height of his authority and popularity, at last the undisputed national leader of all China.

15. | Japan Strikes

T he consequences of the Sian incident were complex. The immediate effects were misleadingly reassuring. The spectacle of the Kuomintang and the Chinese Communist Party no longer at war and apparently willing to put aside their differences in the national interest brought comfort to peasants and intellectuals alike. But there was more to it than that. Almost certainly, the Sian incident hastened the Japanese decision to launch a full-scale war on China. So long as Chiang Kai-shek kept his preparations for anti-Japanese resistance secret, and visibly gave priority to exterminating Communists, the Japanese could proceed with their plans of pressure and annexation calmly and leisurely. But now, it suddenly became clear that the order of priorities had changed. Already in November 1936 a Japanese Army pamphlet, recounting in detail the course of the Long March, had predicted that the government forces and the Red Army would soon unite. Early in the New Year, the Japanese had noted the departure of a thousand young people from Yenan to enroll in the Anti-Japanese Political-Military University° and a large batch of Peiping students enlisting in the Twenty-ninth Army. Seeing these things, the Japanese militarists decided to speed up their timetable for war.

The bizarre circumstances in which the Generalissimo was kidnapped played into the hands of Communist propagandists writing long after the event. It was easy and plausible to claim that Chiang had been made to change his mind about resisting Japan while in captivity—and especially under the persuasive pressure of Chou En-lai. It would have been truer to say that Chiang's exposure to the charm of Chou had made him decide to give the Communists the benefit of the doubt and prove that they were capable of patriotism in the face of the common enemy.

"I really believed that the Chinese Communists had repented," wrote Chiang many years later, "and were sincere in their expressed readiness to join the rest of the nation in the fight against aggression. Besides, even when directing military campaigns against the Communist troops, I regarded them as Chinese and hoped that eventually they would become loyal to the nation again." In time, Chiang Kai-shek would bitterly regret this decision, in the conviction that at the time of the Sian kidnapping, the Communists were gravely weakened and that just one more "extermination campaign" would be enough to finish them off. In this, he was almost certainly mistaken, in that he could not hope to gain widespread support for a civil war at a time when he was still refusing to fight the Japanese. But it is true that at the time the balance of military advantage was heavily in his favour, and in later years he could not be shaken in his belief that the post-Sian reconciliation was the great error of judgment that was responsible for the humiliation of 1949.

On 10 February 1937, the Central Committee of the Chinese Communist Party sent a telegram to the KMT's Central Executive Committee proposing the following five principles:

° The Anti-Japanese Political-Military University—also known as Kangta from its shortened name in Chinese—was originally called the Red Army University. Its original Director was Lin Piao, and it was in the Yenan area. Its formation was announced in February 1936, and it was opened on 1 April 1937. Its stated purposes were to train cadres for the "Anti-Japanese National Revolutionary War" and save the Chinese nation from annihilation as a result of Japanese imperialism and the actions of "the chief traitor Chiang Kai-shek". (Eric Chou; see also Stuart Schram, *Mao Tse-tung*, p. 207.)

1. To stop all civil fighting and concentrate national resources against foreign aggression.
2. To guarantee freedom of speech and release all political offenders.
3. To convene a meeting of all parties, factions, and armies for national salvation.
4. To complete, as quickly as possible, all preparations to resist Japanese aggression.
5. To improve the living conditions of the people.

If (the Communists added) the Nanking government accepted these five points, then the Communists in turn would abide by the following pledges:

1. To end armed anti-government action.
2. To abolish the Communist Party's own government, turning it into a "special administration".
3. To put democratic principles into effect in the Communist zone, and especially to hold elections.
4. To end confiscations of land.
5. To place the Red Army under the orders of the government and its Military Affairs Council.

It would have been un-Chinese and uncharacteristic of Chiang Kai-shek to accept these points as they stood. To have done so would have meant a loss of face for the Generalissimo, for it was open to the Communists to claim that these were the points—more or less—that Chiang had agreed (admittedly under duress) to accept at Sian. The Communist telegram reached the Central Executive Committee as it was meeting in plenary session. The outcome, eleven days later, was a "Resolution for Complete Eradication of the Red Menace". Many summaries of the Resolution exist; I have preferred to quote Chiang's own version, which he probably drafted himself:

1. The organisation and command of the nation's armed forces must be unified before there can be any effective control and operation. The simultaneous existence of armed forces that follow entirely incompatible political ideologies is impermissible. Therefore, the so-called Red Army and its units

under various specious names should be completely abolished.

2. The unitary administrative power is a prerequisite to national unification. The existence of two administrations side by side is impermissible. Therefore the so-called Soviet government and other organisations detrimental to unification should be completely abolished.

3. Communism is absolutely incompatible with the Three People's Principles, which are dedicated to saving the nation and the people. It is against the interests of the Chinese people, their opportunity of livelihood, and their way of life. Therefore, it must cease its operation.

4. Class struggle is based on the interests of a single class. Its method is to divide society into so many opposite classes and then set them hating and killing one another. It necessarily resorts to fighting over the control of the masses and to armed uprisings, resulting in social disorders and general sufferings. Therefore, it must cease.

The prospect of a reconciliation between the Communists and the Nationalists, and indeed of a united front between them, caused Stalin to lift his long-standing ban on the return of Chiang's son Ching-kuo to China. Only a few months earlier, Ching-kuo had placed duty to the Soviet regime above filial duty, and denounced his father in a very un-Chinese way. Now, in April 1937, he went home again, with his Russian wife. He had been away for twelve years. Deeply worried over the effects of this lengthy exposure to Stalinist indoctrination, Chiang Kai-shek set about (when time permitted) to re-educate his son. In his book, *My Father*, Chiang Ching-kuo gives this account of his father's requirements:

After my return to our country, Father demanded that I should study General Tseng Kuo-fan's *Letters to His Family*. . . . [General Tseng was the man who broke the T'aip'ing Rebellion.] Father thinks that Tseng Kuo-fan's teachings for his children are equally good for us. Whenever I wrote my father, he would instruct me to read a certain letter by Tseng Kuo-fan if he himself did not have the time to favour me with a reply.

Father also frequently passed on to me what he had just

read. These books were full of his own written comments and their important passages were underlined.

With a view to the fact that I went abroad as a young boy and stayed in a foreign country too long, Father feared that I lacked deep understanding of China's moral philosophy and national spirit. He specially instructed me to study Dr. Sun Yat-sen's works.

In his letter of 12 May 1937, he pointed out: "Hereafter, in your reading, you should pay more attention to China's moral virtues, national spirit and philosophy. The Political Theory of Sun Wen [Sun Yat-sen] is the foundation of Chinese philosophy which cannot be fully expounded in translations. The Russian version in particular has discarded the gist of the original text. So you should read the Political Theory of Sun Wen twice before you proceed to read the Three Principles of the People—all in Chinese, of course. You should also put your comments and remarks on paper, ready to be checked by me. In the chapters concerning the People's Livelihood, the criticisms of Marxism are particularly important."

Apart from studying the Three Principles of the People and books of a similar nature, I was also instructed by my father to read classics and history books extensively, as well as Chinese philosophers.

More than that, Father repeatedly asked me to re-read what I had read before, memorising many classical pieces by heart.

When Chiang Kai-shek addressed these didactic words to his son, Ching-kuo was twenty-nine and a married man. But his father was making up for lost time and felt there was much unfortunate education to be unlearnt.

During the first few weeks of 1937, Chiang Kai-shek was still in acute pain from the back injury he had sustained in his attempt to escape his Sian kidnappers. However, fitted with a brace, he began to recover and soon threw himself into the preparations for war with his customary energy. In the spring of 1937, China's regular army totalled about 1,700,000 men, supported by a navy of 59 units totalling only 15,288 tons, and an air force misleadingly claiming 200 first-line planes. About this time, Chiang had appointed an

American ex-fighter pilot, Captain Claire Chennault, as his air adviser, and as soon as Chennault had a chance of seeing the machines he was supposed to use, he pronounced only 91 of them to be truly "first-line". Wiry, tough, and with the single-mindedness of dedication or fanaticism (according to whether one was for him or against), Captain Chennault had been grounded from the American Air Corps because of deafness. This was in 1936, when he was forty-six years old; and he jumped at the chance of a job in China. In time, he would play a major part in China's war effort. But he was in no position to work a miracle in time to withstand the first wave of Japanese hostilities.

Henceforth, the key to events in a rapidly worsening situation was in Tokyo, where the military clique was daily growing stronger. The militarists were not in favour of waiting around until China's newfound "unity" could be consolidated. Their solution was to strike now and talk later. On strategic grounds, their reasoning was sound. They did not forget that in 1905, their predecessors had taught Tsarist Russia a military lesson. They were convinced that another showdown was on the way, and that when Soviet Russia had had time to build up its military strength, it would resume imperial Russia's traditional role as the great rival of Japan in continental East Asia. They reasoned, therefore, that it would make sense to deal with China as swiftly as possible, then strike at Russia while Japan retained the military edge.

The militarists were willing, however, to give the politicians and diplomats a last chance to bring the Chinese to their senses. The Japanese ambassador in Nanking, Kawagoe, never tired of reminding Chiang's Foreign Minister, Wang Ch'ung-hui, of Hirota's Three Principles of 1935. Hirota, at that time Japan's Foreign Minister, had called for: (1) the thorough suppression of anti-Japanese thoughts and activities in China; (2) conclusion of a Sino-Japanese anti-Communist military pact; and (3) achievement of "Economic cooperation" between Japan, Manchukuo, and China. Although the Nationalists and Communists had not yet formerly sunk their differences, there was close liaison between them at this time. Nationalist officials went to northern Shensi for talks with the Communists, and Chou En-lai visited Chiang Kai-shek at Kuling.

At the end of April, Kawagoe went home to report to his government. The cabinet heard his facts and views at a fateful meeting on 10 May 1937—then made its intentions clear by announcing that Japan was sending three divisions to the Chinese mainland. On the 19th, the war minister, Sugiyama, publicly complained of China's "over-confidence" and its adoption of an attitude "insulting to Japan". Five days later the Foreign Minister, Sato, declared that if Japan's honour and prestige were injured, there would be no alternative to war.

Against the mounting tension, Chiang Kai-shek secretly sent his son Ching-kuo to Shensi to negotiate with Chou En-lai for changes in the Chinese Communist Party that would enable the Nanking authorities to give it legal status.

In Tokyo on 5 June, a more hawkish cabinet than ever came to office. Back at the Foreign Ministry was Koki Hirota, who now declared that the Three Principles he himself had spelt out in 1935 were no longer practicable.

Clearly, the Japanese were waiting for an "incident", or preparing to provoke one. Provoked or not, it came on Wednesday, 7 July. That night Japanese troops on manoeuvres knocked at the gates of Wanping, a small walled town near the Marco Polo Bridge, fifteen miles south-east of Peiping. One of their soldiers was missing, they said, and they wanted him back. The Chinese garrison commander said he knew nothing about the missing man. According to the Chinese version of the incident, the Japanese thereupon opened fire; according to the Japanese version, it was the Chinese who fired first. But it mattered little: the Japanese militarists now had their "incident", and they were going to exploit it to the full. Within six days, 20,000 Japanese troops were assembled in the Peiping area. To Chiang Kai-shek, it was clear that the second Sino-Japanese war had begun.

On 17 July, at a conference at Kuling (Lushan), the Generalissimo stated that peace was in the hands of the Japanese. "We seek peace," he said, "but we do not seek peace at any cost. We do not want war, but we may be forced to defend ourselves."

Chiang Kai-shek's peace terms were defiantly conveyed to the Japanese government. Japan was to acknowledge responsibility for the hostilities in North China, express official regrets, and pay indemnities. The next day at Lushan, Chiang announced that China would not retreat from four principles: (1) no settlement should impair China's territorial integrity or sovereign rights; (2) no change in the status of the Hopei-Chahar council would be allowed; (3) no Chinese local officials could be removed by outside pressure; (4) no attempt was to be made to restrict the movements of the Chinese Twenty-ninth Army (in the Peiping area).

The Japanese replied with several attacks on Chinese garrison towns. When the Chinese Peace Preservation Corps counterattacked at Tientsin on 29 July, the Japanese retaliated with a devastating air bombardment. They then entered and occupied that city and Peiping, announcing that they had come to "protect" the people.

Now that the fighting had begun, Chiang Kai-shek demonstrated national leadership. In a statement to the nation, he declared that his government would lead it "in a struggle to the bitter end".

In the north, the Communists too had been breathing defiance. The party's line was thrashed out and defined at an important conference at Loch'uan in August 1937. At that time, Mao Tse-tung had not yet gained full control. There was unanimity on last-ditch resistance to Japan, but Mao opposed Moscow's policy for a united front between Communists and Nationalists. He was opposed and out-voted, though with typical Communist discipline, he accepted the majority verdict. Later speeches and events were to show, however, that he had made mental reservations and was determined to reverse the line as soon as he could. His hand is clearly visible in the so-called Loch'uan Declaration, with its passionate and intransigent style. The Communists called for the overthrow of Japanese imperialism and for a fight to the finish. The whole nation was to be mobilised and the people were to be armed. Guerrillas were to be created and traitors were to be liquidated. There was a call for freedom for all political parties (from which the Communists could be expected to benefit), for a genuinely representative national assembly, and for the elimination of corruption. The rich were to be taxed and speculation to be combatted. The taxation system was to be simplified and living conditions improved. The Communist Party would cooperate with the Kuomintang to set up a National Anti-Japanese United Front.

On 21 August a pact of non-aggression was signed in Nanking by representatives of the Russian and Chinese governments; and on 23 September, a Kuomintang declaration formalised the new alliance with the Chinese Communists. This important document was the outcome of a series of moves that owed as much to Chineseness on either side as to ideological differences between them. On 15 July, the Communist Party had handed a manifesto to the Kuomintang, but the Kuomintang did not immediately publish it. On the 19th, according to Feng Yü-hsiang, Chiang Kai-shek and Chou En-lai met at Lushan with senior colleagues. The Generalissimo is said to have acknowledged the administration set up by the Communists in certain frontier districts. Silence followed until the Loch'uan Declaration of 15 August. Then, on 22 September, the Kuomintang suddenly published the Communist manifesto of 15 July, then endorsed it in its declaration the following day. On paper, at least, the Communists were now willing to make all the concessions they had previously resisted. Their manifesto stated three aims and recognised four obligations. The aims were:

1. Launch the war of resistance, take back lost territory, struggle for independence, liberty, and national emancipation.
2. Establish a democratic regime.
3. Improve the living standards of the people.

The four obligations which the Communist Party now pledged itself to carry out were these:

1. Apply the Three People's Principles of Sun Yat-sen.
2. Not to overthrow the Kuomintang by force, and not to confiscate landlords' lands.
3. To reorganise the government of the Red Zone to become the Democratic Government of the frontier regions.
4. To change the name of the Red Army to National Revolutionary Army and submit it to the control of the Military Council of the National government.

Taking note of these pledges, the Nanking government declared rather smugly that "national consciousness has prevailed over all other considerations".

In October the Central Political Bureau of the Communist Party passed a resolution which made it clear that in Communist eyes the alliance with the Kuomintang was at best a wartime expedient, to be abandoned in favour of resumed hostility when the time had come. Under the title "The Future of the War of Resistance and the Chinese Communists' Line of Action", the resolution laid down this two-point programme:

1. To expand and to strengthen the United Front by removing the veils covering secret Communist organisation and activities and by extending regional operations to a nationwide scale for the purpose of obtaining for the Communist Party a legal and equal competitive status.
2. Force being the determining factor in China's politics, emphasis should be put on expanding the Communist Party's armed forces in the course of the war of resistance to lay the foundation in the struggle for political power in the future.

Both Chiang Kai-shek and Mao Tse-tung had thought long and hard about the situation that now faced them and their country. Each had a plan and a strategy, and both had considered the appropriate tactics. But Mao saw farther than Chiang. The Generalissimo's was a strategy for survival—for China, for his government, for himself. Mao wanted above all to use the war with Japan to put himself in a winning position once it was over; his was a strategy for ultimate political victory. Therein lay the difference between them.

Much impressed by Tsarist Russia's successful containment of Napoleon's invasion in 1812, the Generalissimo had elaborated a strategy that became known as "trading space for time". As the enemy advanced, the central armies would retreat, scorching the earth behind them and abandoning areas without either food or shelter for the invaders. There would be no quick campaign of conquest: Japan would be drawn ever deeper into the vast interior of China, so that in time the Japanese front would be spread out as thin as beaten gold, its communication lines extended up to and beyond the limits of logistics. The time would come, he reasoned, when the all-conquering Japanese would be exhausted by the unending struggle and would crack under the strain.

Given the disparity in strength between the invading and the defending forces, Chiang's strategy made sense—but in military terms alone, in psychological and political terms, it was bound to be disastrous. The Generalissimo failed to understand that his policy of trading space with time by constant retreat would play into the hands of the Communists by leaving vast areas open to their infiltration and creating opportunities for patriotic heroism in the harassment of the invaders. The war was the opportunity Mao Tse-tung had waited for. From being a band of outcasts and "bandits", the Communist Party had gained recognition through its alliance with the Kuomintang, thereby breaking the latter's monopoly of political power. By judicious reforms in the areas under their control, even far behind the front line of the advancing Japanese, the Communists would rally the people to their banner, swimming in the population (as Mao said in a memorable phrase) "like a fish in water".

It is doubtful whether these possibilities crossed the Generalissimo's mind. True, he had always wanted to eliminate the Communists before standing up to the Japanese, and he could later claim that he had been right all along. But the social and strategic opportunities which Mao so clearly foresaw evidently lay beyond his political imagining. He knew the Communists would be a problem to him once Japan had been defeated (as he was confident it would be), but if indeed victory came his way, surely the aura of glory and success would guarantee his own political victory at home. And indeed he was right in supposing that his side would be stronger by far than the Communist side at the end of the eight years of war that followed. But he could hardly foresee the circumstances of Japan's defeat—with Stalin's armies in control of Manchuria. Nor could he see that he would be presiding over a sullen, corrupt shell of a nation, with a disillusioned American government strongly inclined to support the Communist side. Least of all could he foresee that Mao would have created an invincible peasant army, thoroughly politicised and eager for his destruction.

But these dire calamities lay far in the future. For the moment, the reality was the ruthless advance of the Japanese forces. Peiping and Tientsin fell quickly, in the early days. Chiang had decided that northern China was expendable; his major forces would be concentrated along the Yangtze line. Apart from the north, he was determined that the Japanese would have to fight for every inch of territory they took.

For moral and political reasons he considered overriding, he decided not merely to make a stand for Shanghai, but actually to seek battle. Militarily the decision made no sense, and was taken against the advice of Chiang's German military advisers. It was obvious to everybody that the poorly armed and equipped Chinese forces were going to be mauled by the technologically superior Japanese war machine. It was surely a major strategic error to risk some of his own best-trained troops and not preserve them for the more vital battles that undoubtedly lay ahead. This was the reasoning of military orthodoxy. But Chiang Kai-shek wanted to demonstrate, to the Japanese and to the world, that this was going to be no easy option. This time, unlike 1931 and other previous incursions, the Japanese must be made to understand that they were up against the resistance of the entire Chinese people.

The battle for Shanghai started on 8 August 1937 and did not end until 8 November—three months of carnage, the price of which ran into several hundreds of thousands of Chinese casualties. The exact figure will never be known; the Japanese themselves lost some 60,000 killed or wounded. The fighting took place only five miles from the International Settlements, much of it in the Chinese quarters. One day a Chinese airman, aiming for the Japanese battleship *Idzumo*, at anchor on the Whangpoo River, misjudged his target and dropped his bombs on the crowded shopping district of the Settlement, killing more than 1,000 people. There were three distinguished casualties. One of them was Sir Hughe Knatchbull-Hugessen, the British ambassador, who was disabled by a machine-gun bullet in the spine fired by a Japanese airman while he was being driven from Nanking to Shanghai. Another was Mme. Chiang Kai-shek, who was severely injured when her car went off the road while the driver was trying to avoid enemy guns. With her in the car was W. H. Donald, who was also badly hurt.

During the battle for Shanghai, the Generalissimo kept in constant telephone contact with each of his commanders. Averaging three or four hours' interrupted sleep a night, he twice visited the battle front in person. Finally, the Japanese outflanked the Chinese defenders to the south, and swept them away in confused retreat towards Nanking. The battle, though lost, had astounded the Japanese invaders, and shown the world that the Chinese could fight as well as they, in defence of their homeland.

In an interview with Tillman Durdin of *The New York Times* on 19 November, the Generalissimo dictated these ringing words: "The enemy never realises that China's territory is not conquerable. She is indestructible. As long as there is one spot in China free from enemy encroachment, the National Government will remain supreme."

A few days later, a press conference over tea was interrupted by a Japanese air raid, and the foreign correspondents present reported how the Generalissimo went into the garden and looked on

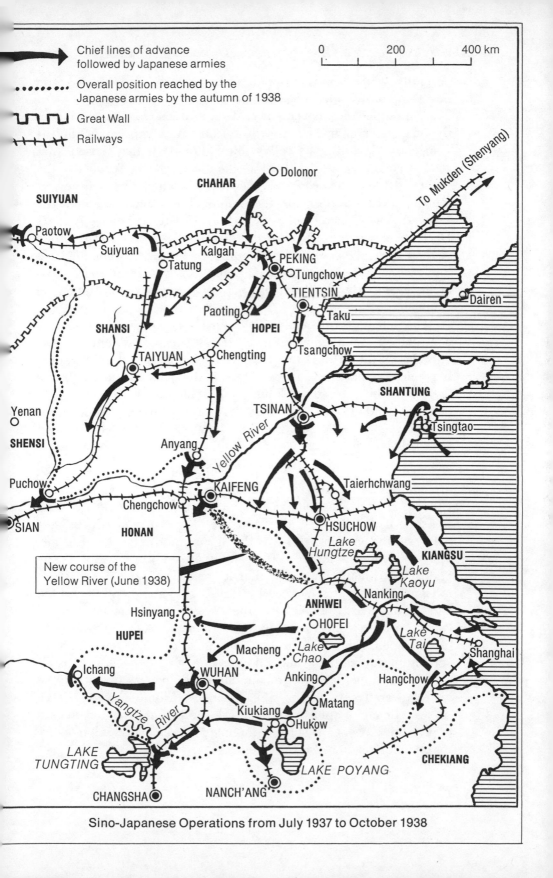

Sino-Japanese Operations from July 1937 to October 1938

curiously while bombs dropped close to him. Physical fear was never one of his defects of character.

The outflanking movement that had driven the Chinese out of the Shanghai area had been made possible by a Japanese landing at Hangchow Bay, bringing collapsible motor boats that ferried their reinforcements across the Tai Hu, the inland lake at Soochow—the natural defence between Shanghai and Nanking. The swiftness of the Japanese advance on the Nationalist capital stunned the Chinese. The Generalissimo and Mme. Chiang left the city on 7 December, two days ahead of the Japanese. Before leaving, in one of those symbolic gestures he favoured, he visited the mountainside tomb of Sun Yat-sen and pledged himself to fight to the end for Dr. Sun's ideals. He then set up his temporary administration in Hankow.

The defenders of Nanking held out for two days, in the face of constant air bombardment, after the Japanese had entered the outskirts on the 11th. Drunk with their bloodlust, and unrestrained by their commander, General Matsui, the Japanese forces threw themselves into an orgy of killing, raping, looting, and burning. As many as 100,000 Chinese civilians may have been massacred. World opinion was outraged, and even the Japanese cabinet felt the need to recall General Matsui.

The first five months of this second Sino-Japanese War had brought not only catastrophic military reverses, including the fall of China's capital, but bitter diplomatic disappointments. Chiang Kai-shek had hoped for aid from the Western democracies, but none was forthcoming: this was the age of appeasement in Europe, and of splendid isolation in the United States. On 6 October, the State Department announced that it considered Japan's behaviour in China to be contrary to the Kellogg-Briand Pact of 1928 and the Nine-Power Treaty of 1922. But there was to be no American aid to China; private American shipments of scrap steel continued to reach Japan. The League of Nations also condemned Japan's actions, but did nothing; and a conference of the Powers at Brussels on 15 November decided on an indefinite postponement of the Nine-Power Treaty in the Sino-Japanese dispute. Aware of the pacifist climate of opinion in the West, the Japanese had taken care to give the Powers a legalistic loophole for their moral dilemma by simply not declaring war on China.

Britain sold Chiang a few aircraft, but declined to supply the guns to go with them. Australia refused to fly a single Boeing plane that had been sent to America, on to China. So great was the determination of the British and Americans not to be drawn into the China conflict that they took no action even in the face of extraordinary Japanese provocations. A British steamer, for instance, was sunk by Japanese bombers, and H.M.S. *Ladybird* was bombarded by shore batteries. Then came the notorious Panay incident, when the U.S. gunboat of that name was sunk by Japanese airmen on 12 December. Flying low, they machine-gunned survivors as they tried to row away, killing three Americans and wounding seventeen.

The German attitude was ambiguous. The German-Japanese Anti-Comintern Pact had been signed in November 1936, but the German military training mission was still on duty with Chiang Kai-shek's forces. At the end of November 1937, the Japanese approached the German ambassador to China, Dr. Oscar Trautman, and asked him to convey Japan's terms to end the conflict to the Generalissimo. Chiang received Dr. Trautman on 3 December in Nanking. He had little faith in any Japanese terms, but heard them in silence. The Japanese called for the recognition of Manchukuo; the establishment of demilitarised zones; Chinese cooperation with the anti-Comintern bloc; the signing of an economic agreement between China, Japan, and Manchukuo; revision of customs barriers; and the payment of "necessary indemnities" by China to Japan. Chiang Kai-shek made it plain that these terms were of no interest to him. In any event, they were withdrawn as the Japanese drew near Nanking, when they began to think that they would soon be in a position to impose a dictated peace.

Only one great power offered to help China in its hour of need: the Soviet Union. The non-aggression pact of 21 August had paved the way, as indeed had the reconciliation between the Chinese Communists and Nationalists. Stalin had no more intention than the Western leaders to be drawn into the Chinese conflict; but he was fully aware of Japan's aggressive plans against his own Far Eastern territories, and it seemed to be a good idea to enable Chiang Kai-shek to kill as many Japanese as he could. Learning of Stalin's intentions through the Chinese ambassador in Moscow, General

Yang Chieh,° Chiang Kai-shek sent his confidant and former Education Minister, Ch'en Li-fu, to the Russian capital to negotiate an arms deal. Early in 1938, the Russians granted China credits for $100,000,000. Shortly afterwards, Soviet arms and ammunition, transported overland through Central Asia, began to reach the Generalissimo's forces. In due course, the Chinese paid for what they had received with shipments of tungsten, wool, and tea. There was a further credit of $150,000,000 in July 1939. The Russians also sent five wings of Soviet aircraft with pilots to strengthen China's air defences. After Trautman's unsuccessful attempt at mediation, the German military mission was withdrawn, apart from some individuals who elected to stay in China in a private capacity.

A very substantial Soviet military mission also came to China— some 500 of them, among them generals destined to achieve world fame in the later years of the Second World War: Zhukov and Chuikov. In Russia itself, at that time, the Great Terror was in full swing. Towards the end of December, Stalin offered, with murderous generosity, to give the Generalissimo the benefit of his current experience. He convened General Yang Chieh and asked him to convey to Chiang Kai-shek his recipe for achieving national unity: "Tell the Generalissimo that if he wants to do away with any manifestation of disloyalty on the part of his people while the fight continues, he should arrange to shoot at least 4,500,000 persons. Otherwise I fear that he will not be able to bring the war of resistance to a successful conclusion." Any Russian suspects, he explained, were immediately apprehended and sent to the Ministry of the Interior; and once they entered there were only two exits: to Siberia or to the grave.

For all his bursts of ruthlessness, however, Chiang Kai-shek was never a mass murderer in the Stalinist mould. But he soon showed that in the interests of discipline, swift death was an expectable punishment. Disobeying a direct order from the Generalissimo, the old Shantung warlord, General Han Fu-chü, handed the province to the Japanese by withdrawing with all his forces. Chiang had him arrested, court-martialed, and executed on 24 January. Nine more officers faced the firing squad that month, and thirty others were dismissed for suspected disloyalty. Other warlords, however, were

---

° Tong wrongly romanises this name as Yang Chi (says Eric Chou) because of his Shanghai accent. (Tong, p. 251.)

promoted and played a major part in the war. They included Yen Hsi-shan and Feng Yü-hsiang, Li Tsung-jen, and Pai Ch'ung-hsi, who became Chief of Staff. Feng, in particular, benefited from General Han's execution in that Han's niece became his concubine —until Feng's wife threw her out of the household.

After the fall of Nanking, Chiang Kai-shek gave up all his political posts, handing over the Presidency of the Executive Yüan to H. H. K'ung. Henceforth, at least for some time, he had decided to concentrate on military operations. Some of these were spectacularly successful. At Taierhchwang, in southern Shantung, for instance, the Japanese army suffered its first serious defeat in a straight battle in modern times, for the loss of 42,000 men. At Chengchow, the Chinese dynamited the breakwaters of the flood-swollen Yellow River, drowning thousands of Japanese and sinking vast quantities of artillery and other equipment.

Innocents, too, were drowned—how many will never be known. Two million Chinese peasants lost their homes in the eleven cities and 4,000 villages overrun by Chiang's man-made flood. It was incidents like these that gradually alienated China's silent millions from Kuomintang rule and predisposed them to welcome the Communists.

Although Chiang Kai-shek had abandoned the day-to-day running of affairs, he wanted formal recognition of his overall leadership, and the Kuomintang Congress, meeting at Hankow from 29 March to 2 April 1938, duly gave it to him. He was elected Party Head (*Tsung-t'sai*) and wielded final authority or power of veto over all KMT decisions. Needing a deputy, he unhesitatingly chose his old rival Wang Ching-wei, who was as able as he was untrustworthy—and safer by far in office and under supervision than at large and conspiring.

The Hankow period lasted until October 1938 and the foreign eyewitnesses who lived through it recorded it as a high point of Kuomintang history. Under the threat of death and the pressure of invasion, all was harmony and unity in the midst of confusion. China's best writers and journalists, its most qualified technicians, had gone to the industrial temporary capital to do their bit for the war effort. Communists and Nationalists worked side by side, cooperating on civil and military plans. Chiang himself lived in Wuchang, crossing the river by ferry every morning to reach the government offices in Hankow. A bombing raid on his own home killed ten of his armed guards, causing him to abandon the relaxed way of life he had previously adopted, walking the streets unconcerned with a light or non-existent bodyguard. The occasion of the raid had been an informal press conference for foreign correspondents, but the probability that one of them had leaked the fact to the Japanese made him reluctant, for some months, to receive any foreign visitors.

The war had already brought great economic loss and dislocation to China. The shortcomings of the Kuomintang period have been pointed out often enough. Yet in the face of the constant civil wars and natural disasters, great progress had nevertheless been made. Chinese capitalism had produced a thriving industry of textiles and consumer goods, clustering mainly around Shanghai and other coastal cities. But there was little heavy industry, and when the war broke out, the total output of steel was no more than 100,000 tons a year. Before the war began, Chiang Kai-shek called in his outstandingly efficient Minister of Economic Affairs, Dr. Wong Wen-hao, and instructed him to draw up plans for the wholesale evacuation of factories and industry. Smiling, hard-working, and signally uncorrupt, Dr. Wong drew up his plans in time, and the great evacuation began as soon as the Japanese attacked in July 1937.

The industrialists and businessmen of Shanghai were slow to move, hoping to preserve what they owned. Only 14,000 tons of equipment could be moved before the city fell. Machinery from the modern Shanghai Machine Works and other factories was loaded into rowboats and camouflaged with leaves and branches, then punted up the Yangtze River, sheltering in reeds when the Japanese bombers were out. Elsewhere, the removal of equipment was done with greater speed and efficiency. Thousands of miles to the east, the factories and steel works were reassembled in Szechwan, with some munitions plants hidden in the deep caves. Schools and universities, too, moved westward, and enrollment at colleges reached 40,000 by the autumn of 1939—8,000 more than in the last academic year before the war. It was a staggering achievement of primitive muscle power and equipment.

After the fall of Nanking in December 1937, the Japanese armies had paused, in the hope that Chiang Kai-shek would soon surrender. When it became evident that his defiance was no mere passing phenomenon, they resumed their advance. As they moved ever deeper into the interior, many millions of ordinary Chinese people clogged the roads ahead of them in one of the most gigantic mass migrations of all time. Amoy and Soochow fell in May, and Kaifeng and Anking in June. Meanwhile, farther north, the Japanese had decided to test the strength and resolution of the Soviet Far Eastern forces. On 20 July 1938, the Japanese ambassador in Moscow called on the Russians to withdraw their forces from an area in the border region of Korea, the Soviet Union, and China, claiming that it belonged to Manchukuo. In the military clash that followed, the Japanese were successful at first, then beaten back on 11 August.

For Chiang Kai-shek, the worst news that year, for symbolic and emotional reasons, was the fall of Canton—the cradle of the Revolution—on 21 October, after unhindered air raids in which 3,000 people lost their lives. Four days later, the temporary capital of Hankow fell to the Japanese. That day—25 October—the Generalissimo declared in a message to the people: "Even though the enemy has occupied Wuhan temporarily, it has taken him eleven months and cost him casualties running into hundreds of thousands. What he has acquired is merely scorched earth and empty cities. . . . Henceforth, we shall develop our all-front resistance."

Chiang Kai-shek had thought to establish temporary headquarters at Yochow, halfway between Wuchang and Changsha, but found the city almost burnt to the ground, with the fires of scorched earth still raging. Deciding the destruction had been premature, he court-martialed two high-ranking military officers and had them shot.

With their tiny air force, the Chinese could do little to counter the constant Japanese air bombardment. On 24 February 1938, however, Chinese pilots destroyed forty Japanese planes at Taipei's airfield on Formosa (Taiwan). And on 20 May, giant monoplanes showered Japan with leaflets—to demonstrate that the Japanese were not necessarily immune to attack from the air, and that the Chinese were less interested in killing civilians than the invaders.

It had been a hard year, not only for the retreating Chinese, but also for the advancing Japanese, who had been suffering dreadful losses from cholera and dysentery. At the end of 1938, however, the Japanese could claim to control 1,500,000 square kilometres of territory with a population of 170,000,000. Less convincingly, they claimed that the Chinese had suffered 800,000 killed in battle for the loss of 50,000 Japanese killed. But the great advance had halted, and for the next six years the Japanese undertook no further major military operations. The Chinese government settled in Chungking during the early stages of the lull. Their armies were now cut off from access to the sea. Except for Soviet supplies overlanded across Central Asia and the Burma Road, they were in complete strategic isolation.

In military terms, Chiang Kai-shek's strategy had been outstandingly successful, and the fact has not been sufficiently recognised. An interesting "enemy" evaluation was made in the 1970s by a Japanese military writer, Masanori Ito, in his book *Japan's Bloody Wars*:

> Although inferiority in weapons and lack of training had caused the Chinese forces to suffer heavy losses, this did not prevent the Chinese army from maintaining a first-line strength of 7 million, harassing the Japanese army to exhaustion.
>
> Actually, the great headache for the Japanese army was the Chinese army's strategy of "retreating instead of advancing". There were localised battles and small-scale clashes. But generally speaking, the Chinese army retreated (not advanced) to conform with its strategic needs. China's territory was "wide and deep", and the Chinese troops moved very fast. The weary Japanese forces had no way of catching up with them, especially since the supply lines were often cut.
>
> Therefore no devastating blow had ever been dealt on the main force of the Chinese army. The Japanese army merely succeeded in occupying towns, points and railways. . . . As far as the Japanese army was concerned, this was undeniably a defeat. From the angle of the Chinese army, this was certainly not a victory; but on the other hand, it was not a defeat either. The Chinese were extending the war to the interior in order to fight a decisive campaign there.
>
> The traditional tactics of the Japanese army were to drive through the opponent's front line, cutting his forces into two halves, to be outflanked and annihilated one after the other. But such tactics proved useless in fighting the Chinese army. For the Chinese army moved to another position before the Japanese

breakthrough. Technically speaking, the Chinese army was full of flexibility. . . .

At that time, some suggested that the Japanese army should contract the war areas, merely garrisoning north China, Nanking and Shanghai. But the Chinese army observed the principle of "retreating in lieu of advancing". Once the Japanese army drew back, they would give chase. . . . Consequently, a tactical confrontation was maintained in the vast country for four and a half years.

When the Pacific War broke out, the Japanese army had already paid the huge sacrifice of 1,150,000 lives, including the victims of war illness.

This Japanese account is a useful corrective to the military claims made at the time by the invaders; although the author was mistaken in supposing that Chiang Kai-shek intended to fight a "decisive campaign" in the interior.

The year ended with further Japanese peace feelers—this time made public in a speech by the Premier, Prince Konoye, on 22 December. China, he declared, was ready for a "rebirth" and could now take part in a new economic order for East Asia. Earlier that month, Wang Ching-wei, who had been in secret contact with the Japanese, had tried to convince Chiang Kai-shek to accept the Japanese terms. He had made two attempts—at a meeting of the Central Political Council on 9 December, and again in what turned out to be a stormy private interview with Chiang on the 16th.

A friend of Wang's, Ch'en Kung-po, later revealed that Wang had twice taken him into his confidence about his intentions—in early and late November 1938. On the first occasion, Wang had said to him that peace with Japan was in the offing; and it was clear from the context that Chiang Kai-shek knew nothing about it. He added that he would leave Chungking when the time was ripe.

On the second occasion, Wang—having brought Ch'en from Chengtu to Chungking with a telegraphed request—told him that conditions were now ripe for peace between China and Japan. The Japanese Prime Minister had laid down the following principles:

1. Recognition of Manchukuo.
2. A mutual anti-Communist pact with Inner Mongolia.

3. Economic cooperation in north China.
4. Abolition of foreign concessions and consular jurisdiction.
5. No indemnities to be paid on either side.

If China agreed to these principles, Japan would withdraw its troops within two years. On 20 December 1938, Wang Ching-wei left Chungking, ostensibly for Kunming; but aware that he had burnt his boats, he went on to Hanoi in French Indo-China.

There was one particularly puzzling aspect of Wang's departure. According to Feng Yü-hsiang, Wang's wife had left by air two weeks earlier with their family and luggage. At that time, all communications in and out of Chungking were completely controlled by Tai Li of the Military Bureau of Investigation and Statistics. Ordinary travellers by air had to register for investigation and approval, while high officials had to get Chiang Kai-shek's personal sanction. Since Wang Ching-wei and his entourage had flown to Kunming by a chartered plane, how could Tai Li have failed to report the facts to Chiang before their departure? There was no way for Wang to "creep out" of Chungking by air, and Chiang could have stopped him had he so wished. Later, therefore, nobody could accept the claim that Chiang had no inkling of Wang Ching-wei's ultimate plan to form a puppet regime in Nanking.

On 1 January 1939, the Central Committee of the Kuomintang decided to expel Wang Ching-wei.

A few days earlier—on 26 December—the Generalissimo had rejected the Japanese terms with these defiant words: "We must understand that the rebirth of China is taken by the Japanese to mean destruction of an independent China and creation of an enslaved China. The so-called new order is to be created after China has been reduced to a slave nation and linked up with made-in-Japan Manchukuo."

The terrible year had ended in stalemate, but more trials were on the way.

The young Kai-shek, with his
iron-willed mother

Cadet in Tokyo's Shinbo
Gakyo Academy, Tokyo

The young officer: Chiang at twenty-eight

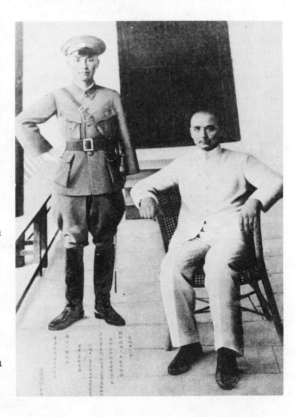

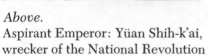

Above.
Aspirant Emperor: Yüan Shih-k'ai,
wrecker of the National Revolution

Above right.
"Father of the Revolution,"
Dr. Sun Yat-sen

Right.
Sun and disciple in 1924: Chiang
was about to take over as
Commandant of the new Whampoa
Military Academy

The scholarly Wu P'ei-fu, master of Peking area

The
Warlords

The "Young Marshal": Chang Hsueh-liang of Manchuria, later Chiang's lifelong prisoner

The "Christian General," Feng Yü-hsiang, who baptised his troops with a hose

Feng and Chiang as "brothers": at other times, they fought

Chiang's rivals for Sun's successio.

The rightist: Hu Han-min, exiled to Moscow

The leftist: Liao Chung-k'ai,
murdered by rightists

iddle-roader Wang Ching-wei, who
ecame Japan's "puppet" Premier

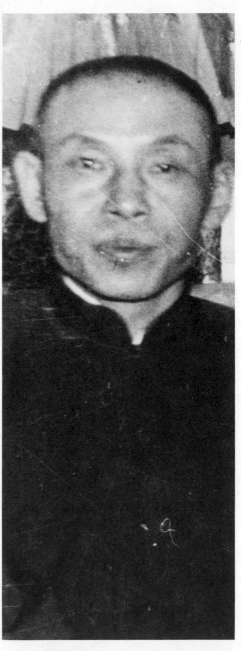

Chiang's protector, the banker-gang-
ster Tu Yueh-sheng

Chiang's men

Corrupt Chief-of-Staff:
General Ho Ying-ch'in

Corrupt Finance Minister:
H.H. K'ung

Dynamic Premier, T.V. Soong—
but he too printed money

The "Model Governor" of Shansi,
Yen Hsi-shan—briefly Premier
in the hour of Kuomintang's defeat

Li Tsung-jen, from Kwangsi rebel
to Acting President when
Chiang stepped down in 1949

Sun Yat-sen's son Sun Fo,
not always at Chiang's command

Above. The Big Three in Cairo, 1943: Chiang Kai-shek, Roosevelt and Churchill (with Mme. Chiang)

Right. Chiang's third wife, the beautiful and influential Mme. Chiang (T.V. Soong's sister)

he allied enemies: the Generalissimo with General ("Vinegar Joe") Stilwell

Chungking, 1944

The work of Japan's bombers

Shanghai, 1938

Governor Ch'en Ch'eng, author of Taiwan's land reform

The Generalissimo's elder son, Premier Chiang Ching-kuo

Family reunion in Taipei, 1959

III | World War and Civil War

(1939–1949)

16. Japan Bogs Down

Chungking, as remembered by those who were there when it was the wartime capital of China, is no more. Before the great Chinese exodus of 1938, it was what it had always been: the trading outpost for the rich produce of Szechwan province, on the confluence of the Yangtze and the Chialing rivers, linking China with the high plateaux of the Himalayas. Then came the refugees in their hundreds of thousands, sending the population up from 200,000 to more than 1,000,000. The newcomers—officials, students, merchants, bankers, servants, and the rest—learned for six years to share with the locals the chill, damp climate of Chungking's winter, the humid, enervating heat of its summer, and the stink of its open sewers. The Szechwanese became the minority, as the Pekingese, the Nankingese, the Shanghainese, and the Cantonese poured in. Then in the end, with Japan's defeat, they all left again, and Chungking reverted to its traditional status as a remote provincial city nobody visited.

Two or three hundred thousand of the newcomers—the poor ones—crowded within the old city's walls. The rest—the rich or the less poor or the more resourceful—built themselves dwellings or villas of varying splendour on the surrounding hills. One of the most splendid of these—at Huangshan across the Yangtze—was occupied by Generalissimo and Mme. Chiang Kai-shek. But he also had a town house in his headquarters compound; and later, he built a group of villas on the other side of the city, which he used to entertain State guests. In the town house on 28 December 1938, the American military attaché, Colonel Joseph W. Stilwell, called on the Chiangs.° It was a brief meeting—only fifteen minutes—and was very cordial, unlike the acrimony that was to prevail in their later relationship. Stilwell had already met Mme. Chiang in the last days of Hankow and had been both charmed and impressed, but this was his first meeting with the Generalissimo. Despite the cordiality, he formed an unfavourable view of the Chinese leader, which he recorded in a report a month later. He held Chiang "directly responsible for much of the confusion that normally exists in his command", and criticised his distrust of subordinates, which he (Stilwell) attributed to Chiang's desire to hold as many strings as possible in his own hands, so that his own position could not be threatened.

Stilwell was a shrewd but cantankerous career soldier who knew China well and spoke the language. No respecter of the exalted, he was a man of few spoken words, rarely chosen for reasons of tact. His nickname of "Vinegar Joe" fitted him. At the time of his first meeting with Chiang, he was nearing the end of his tour of duty; their monumental clashes belonged to a later phase of the war.

During the first few months of 1939, the Japanese ceased to be Chiang's most immediate worry. Instead, two more domestic preoccupations claimed his attention: Wang Ching-wei and the Communists. In January, the Generalissimo sent a young man named Wang Lu-chiao, then twenty-five and a graduate of the Police Officers' Academy in Chiang's home province of Chekiang, to Hanoi in pursuit of the other Wang. His job was to assassinate Ching-wei. He found his target, but missed, hitting a friend of

---

° Tong (p. 262) says Chiang moved his headquarters to Chungking in January 1939, but this approximation needs to be matched against Stilwell's meticulous diary entries. (See Tuchman, pp. 250–51.)

Wang's instead. Later, he followed Ching-wei back and forth from Hanoi to Shanghai, but never succeeded. For his pains, he was gaoled by the French for six years.°

The Communists were a bigger problem. Under the "united front" policy, they had been allocated a quota of seats in the 200-member People's political Council, which Chiang had set up in April 1938 as a supreme policy-making body for the duration of the war. First in Hankow, then in Chungking, they had a permanent delegation, led by Chou En-lai. With General Chang Chih-chung as Minister of the Political Department of the Military Council and Chou En-lai its Deputy Minister, the Department employed many intellectuals with left-wing affiliations. Kuo Mo-jo (later President of the Chinese Academy of Sciences in Peking) was the Director of the Department's Third Bureau, with overall control over plays and films to be written, staged, and produced. Professor Chang Shen-fu of Peking University, a German-trained philosopher of Marxist sympathies, was the editor of *Wartime Culture Monthly*, the organ of the Political Department. According to Eric Chou, who worked for him as an assistant editor for seven months from December 1938, he was frequently in contact with Chou En-lai and hired only people of left-wing views (including Eric Chou at that time) for his editorial staff. He was also an active delegate to the People's Political Council.

At that time, some underground Communists had successfully infiltrated key KMT organisations. For instance, Chi Ch'ao-ting held an executive job in the Central Bank, and enjoyed H. H. K'ung's unreserved trust. He went on, however, to become the first Director-General of the People's Bank of China in 1949. Then there was Wang Ping-nan, who was responsible for organisational work in the Ministry of Social Welfare, a stronghold of the CC clique. Later, he turned up as Chou En-lai's chief spokesman during the Nationalist-Communist peace talks and became Peking's ambassador in Warsaw, where he was involved in prolonged negotiations with American representatives in the late 1950s over the status of Taiwan and other contentious issues. Wang's German wife, Anna, was Mrs. Sun Yat-sen's secretary, frequently mixing with foreign

---

° Wang Lu-chiao later became Police Chief in Taipei, Chiang Kai-shek's headquarters in his Taiwanese exile. He died in a traffic accident in 1974, when the local press recounted his near-exploit.

correspondents and Western diplomats, to "feed" them news and political rumours.

For a while, Chiang tolerated the Communists—as they tolerated him—because anything else would have been inconsistent with the aid the central government was getting or hoped to get from Russia. A bonus, while the honeymoon lasted, was that Moscow's vast army of propagandists set a new fashion of adulation for the Generalissimo. Not only did he cease to be "fascist" and a "reactionary"; he was now a hero and a great leader. A horde of leftist writers from various countries turned up in Chungking to contribute to this image-building. The same people would later turn against Chiang and create an opposite stereotype as a hate-symbol, while simultaneously fostering a belief that the Chinese Communists were mild agrarian reformers and not really Communists at all.

There had been friction in Hankow, and in the autumn of 1938 all Chiang's old (and justified) suspicions of Communist intentions boiled up again when Chou revived the old idea of permitting dual membership of the Communist Party and the Kuomintang. He rejected Chou's proposal out of hand, but (as we have seen) he was not strong enough to force the disbandment of the Red Army and the incorporation of its troops, as individuals, into the National forces. Instead, the Shensi Red Army, under Chu Teh with P'eng Teh-huai as his deputy, and with 20,000 men under arms, had become the Eighth Route Army of the National Revolutionary Forces in August 1937. On paper, Chu Teh's force was responsible to General Yen Hsi-shan in northern Shansi; but in practice, it took its orders from Mao Tse-tung. Later, in the spring of 1938, the remnants of the Red Army south of the Yangtze were allowed to constitute the New Fourth Army, under Yeh T'ing but on paper taking its orders from the Nationalist General Ku Chu-t'ung.

The Eighth Route Army and the New Fourth Army were supposed, of course, to take part in the national war effort against Japan. Instead, from the start, they took advantage of their unity and autonomy to eliminate any Nationalist forces in their way and extend their clandestine political control over ever-expanding areas. The first incident was the disarming of the Nationalist Seventh Regiment at Poyeh, in Hopei province, in December 1938. The pretexts and the tactics were constant. Proclaiming that a Nationalist force was collaborating with the Japanese, the Communists would surround them and either liquidate the troops or win them over. Some engagements involved thousands of men and lasted several days. There was much brutality, and burial alive was a favoured form of torture.

According to the official Communist history of the "patriotic war", the Eighth Route Army grew from 45,000 in 1937 to 400,000 by 1940, and the New Fourth from 15,000 to 100,000 in the same period. These starting figures are probably exaggerated, but there is less reason to doubt the greater ones of 1940. Wherever they went behind the Japanese lines, the Communists introduced their well-tried techniques of mass organisation. In most places, the peasants had been alienated by Japanese brutalities and willingly joined the Communists, who, in turn, were careful not to alienate the peasants and kept political doctrine almost entirely out of their standard exhortations.

While the Communists were extending their political power, in effect by mobilising the peasants, their propaganda fostered the claim that they were bearing the brunt of the war of resistance. With the help of anti-Kuomintang writers, of whom there was no shortage, this picture gained extraordinarily wide acceptance. Yet it was a grossly exaggerated one. Even Theodore H. White and Annalee Jacoby, who much admired Mao Tse-tung's provisional regime but tried to report the war honestly, wrote: "The Communists fought when they had an opportunity to surprise a very small group of the enemy and to capture more than enough rifles and ammunition to make up what they had spent in the fray." And again: ". . . during the significant campaigns, it was the weary soldiers of the Central Government who took the shock, gnawed at the enemy, and died." Certainly the Japanese took the Nationalists more seriously than the Communists as an enemy and concentrated 70 percent of their forces against the former.

In May 1939, when the fogs that shrouded Chungking during the cold season lifted at last, the Japanese began to bomb the city from the air. The first raid took place on the 3rd and caused 5,000 casualties. The defenders had neither anti-aircraft guns nor proper shelters. The Generalissimo and his wife were on the scene as soon as the raid stopped. Typically Chiang Kai-shek berated the commanders of his tiny air force for gross inefficiency. Ordering the creation of a mass evacuation service, under Ho Ying-ch'in, he retired to the nearest mountain for silent meditation on China's problems.

The raids continued through the summer and resumed on a heavier scale in the spring of 1940, by which time dug-outs and shelters had at last been built in adequate numbers. But the worst year of bombardment was 1941, when the longest interval between raids was five hours and the shortest an hour and a half. Like London during the German blitz, Chungking took it.

Also in May 1939, the Japanese army made another attempt at testing the Soviet will to fight, with an attack on the frontier of Soviet-protected Outer Mongolia. The Russians hit back hard. General Zhukov, bored with his idleness in China, led the Russians and Mongolians and on 20 August inflicted a stinging defeat on the Japanese. Now Tokyo had the answer to its question. Only three days later came an event that shook the Japanese, and the rest of the world, to the core: the Nazi-Soviet non-aggression pact. Now the Japanese knew not only that the Russians would fight if attacked, but also that they could expect nothing from the Germans—certainly no concerted strategy—despite the anti-Comintern pact. The disappointment was the more bitter because discussions were going on between the Germans and Japanese at that time towards an alliance against the Soviet Union. They ended abruptly.

As we have seen, the united front was already breaking down, but the German-Soviet pact was the signal for the Communists to abandon even the pretence that it still existed. From September on, the Eighth Route Army and the New Fourth Army intensified their drive to supplant the Nationalists in Shensi, Hopei, and Shantung in the north, and in Kiangsu and Anhwei in the Yangtze valley.

On 28 August 1939, the Indian nationalist leader, Pandit Jawaharlal Nehru, visited the Chiangs in their mountain home, and the three talked for hours against the noise of a Japanese air raid. From then until the end of the year, Chiang's forces lost, then regained Changsha, and drove the Japanese out of Kwangsi in a battle in which the Kunlun Pass in south China changed hands three times, remaining under Chinese control with the final assault on 31 December.

The Generalissimo's forces had given a good account of themselves, and morale stood high. China's well-wishers abroad, and Chiang's supporters at home, wondered why they did not go over to the offensive. Later this passivity would infuriate Stilwell. But Chiang Kai-shek's strategy, having exhausted the Japanese *élan*—as he had rightly calculated—by his retreat into the interior —was masterly inaction. He had no plans for victory; only for survival, for outsitting the enemy. In time, he had guessed, the Americans would be drawn into the war; then he would be rewarded for tying up a million or so Japanese soldiers. Perhaps even the Russians, too, would be sucked into this conflict in which, so far, the Chinese armies had served Stalin's interests by diverting the bulk of Japan's power away from the Soviet giant. In these circumstances, why should Chiang exert himself militarily and fritter away the strength he would need for the forthcoming confrontation with the Communists?

Once again, the man's stubbornness was to prove his later undoing. While he sat and waited for the Japanese to attack, the Communists were pushing ever deeper behind the Japanese lines, not always fighting the Japanese but fighting them sufficiently to acquire the aura of those who take the offensive. Every now and then, the Japanese would burn villages and commit sundry punitive atrocities; each time, the Communists emerged stronger, their hold upon the popular imagination the greater. Sitting in Chungking, or indeed striding energetically, and always keeping his own council, the Generalissimo was oblivious to the fact that his inertia was paving the way for his downfall.

Even after the war had begun, Chiang was still plagued by his failure to break the feudal autonomy of the warlords in their respective provinces. As the military historian General Ch'en Hsiao-wei put it in conversation with Eric Chou in Hong Kong in 1957, he had divided the entire war theatre into separate war areas, with the object of creating independent fighting units, each of which could take on the advancing Japanese forces on its own. (What this really amounted to was making the best of the fact of warlordism.) The farther the Japanese pushed inland, the more counter-attacks they would face from the war zones they had crossed. The weakness of the plan was that the commanders of various war zones failed to do what had been expected of them. The provincial armies performed adequately enough in defence of their home towns, but they were not prepared to fight the Japanese in places far from their own provinces. This alone made it impossible for the National Armies to go over to the offensive, even if Chiang Kai-shek had not been reluctant to use the Central Army—that is, the better-trained and better-equipped troops under his direct command—to attack rather than to defend.

In general, the Nationalist troops could not compete with the Communists in guerrilla operations. Chiang had initiated a training school for guerrilla units in the Heng Shan mountain area of Hunan province, with the object of harassing the Japanese from the rear. Feng Yü-hsiang visited this area, where he found about 5,000 village workers—young and full of spirit—being trained for guerrilla warfare under the provincial governor. But their enthusiasm did not compensate for the inadequacies of the training provided. The duration of the course was too short, not enough attention was devoted to combat training. General Feng predicted therefore—and correctly—that the guerrillas would not be very effective.

A more ambitious Nationalist attempt at guerrilla action was in Hopei province. On Feng Yü-hsiang's recommendation, the Generalissimo appointed Lu Chung-lin as governor of Hopei and Commander-in-Chief for that province and Chahar. At that time the Hopei provincial government had retreated to Loyang. From Loyang, Lu crossed the Yellow River to go north. On arriving in Hopei, he gathered between 300,000 and 400,000 militia men with their own rifles and ordered them to harass the Japanese and inflict heavy casualties on them. But Chiang spared no more than $6 Chinese per month per head, at a time when a plain meal cost not less than $100. Even if patriotism was assumed, this was not a living wage. The experiment was a failure.

In one area, however, the Nationalist guerrillas did become a force to be reckoned with. This was in the north-west province of Shansi, which was particularly attractive to the Japanese because of its coal and mineral wealth. Early in the war, the Japanese had seized the provincial capital, Taiyuan, and the railways, but they never conquered the guerrillas operating from the mountains, who descended almost at will to inflict losses upon the Japanese throughout the war. Altogether, about 500,000 Japanese forces were tied down. The credit for these operations goes to the experienced Shansi warlord, General Yen Hsi-shan.

The most startling news in the early months of 1940 was not military but political: the emergence of Wang Ching-wei as a full-fledged puppet of the Japanese. When he had fled to Hanoi at the end of 1938, Chiang Kai-shek's only public action had been his statement of 7 January 1939, which merely said (untruthfully) that Wang and he had not previously discussed peace with Japan. Years later, Hollington Tong was encouraged to say that Chiang wanted to leave the way open for Wang to reconsider his actions. In fact, as we have seen, Chiang sent an assassin after him. When it was clear that the assassin was not going to succeed, Chiang's government—on 8 June 1939—issued a mandate for his arrest and punishment. On 9 July, Wang Ching-wei accused Chiang of doing the work of the Reds by leading China to destruction. He then proclaimed himself head of the "Orthodox Chinese Nationalist Party". This bogus Kuomintang held a "Sixth Congress", which elected Wang as chairman. Towards the end of January 1940, the Japanese Premier, Admiral Mitsumasa Yonai, announced yet another "peace" offer. He referred indirectly to the organisation of a government by Wang Ching-wei, in which "even General Chiang Kai-shek" would be acceptable, along with other Chungking leaders. A month later, it was reported that Wang's government had signed "eight agreements" with Japan. The climax to these moves came on 30 March 1940, when Wang's government was solemnly inaugurated in Nanking. It was a curious, almost farcical business. Not only did Wang Ching-wei's party call itself the Kuomintang, and adopt all the KMT slogans, it even used the same "blue-sky, white-sun, red-earth" flag designed by Sun Yat-sen. The same flag thus flew from the offices of both administrations in Chungking and Nanking. Wang's government even conscripted an army, by giving captured Chinese soldiers the choice between serving in it and being shot. Not surprisingly, there were many desertions—until in September 1941, some 30,000 of Wang's soldiers in northern Honan killed their Japanese officers and came over to Chiang's side.

Japan waited until 30 November before recognising its own puppet government. Manchukuo was next; then on 1 July 1941 Germany and Italy followed suit with their Axis satellites: Romania, Bulgaria, Slovakia, and Croatia. Spain did likewise.

In Chungking, Chiang Kai-shek reacted to the news by having one of Wang's co-plotters, General Shih Yu-shan, court-martialed and executed. His secret police seized 155 people considered to be clandestine supporters of Wang Ching-wei.

The conventional picture of Wang Ching-wei is inevitably that of a typical traitor and puppet—a quisling. But all such cases are more complex than they appear to men at war. Wang Ching-wei was the closest of Sun Yat-sen's disciples. He had been out-manoeuvred and pushed aside by Chiang Kai-shek in the struggle for power. But his personal bitterness against Chiang does not alone account for his actions during the war with Japan. According to his friend Ch'en Kung-po, his first misgivings about fighting the Japanese began as early as 1932. He had been advocating resistance, but the battle of Kupeiko on the Great Wall upset him deeply. From the returning Chinese generals, he learned that the soldiers simply could not stand up to the Japanese because their fire-power was so inferior to that of the enemy. This made Wang think that peace was better than resistance.

Hu Lin, the co-founder of the newspaper *Ta Kung Pao*, told Eric Chou in 1946 that Wang Ching-wei had become staunchly anti-Communist after his European tour in 1932. Thereafter, in private conversation, he frequently criticised himself for having led the left wing of the KMT. Europe, he believed, had more to fear from communism than from fascism. He saw a "genuine Sino-Japanese cooperation" as a stabilising factor for Asia. However, fearing to split the Kuomintang, he kept his thoughts to himself until 1935, when he set up the *Titiao* ("Low Tone") club in Nanking, to spread his principles for peace with Japan among members of the political, business, and cultural communities.

Then came Japan's all-out war of aggression against China. Admittedly with less justification than Pétain and Laval after France's defeat—since China had not yet been defeated—Wang seems nevertheless to have been honestly convinced that China could not win against Japan's overwhelming strength and that negotiations in 1939 or 1940 would yield more lenient terms than a peace dictated after total defeat. For him, and those who thought like him, Prince Konoye's statement of 16 January 1938, declaring that henceforth the Japanese government would refuse any further dealings with China's National Government personified by Chiang Kai-shek, seemed to block all possibility of peace. If the Japanese failed to overthrow Chiang, yet would not deal with him, the prospect was one of interminable war.

The only way out seemed to be to replace Chiang with a head of government with the right history and prestige who was *persona grata* with the Japanese. Only Wang Ching-wei himself filled these qualifications. Initially, the Japanese themselves had picked the old warlord Wu P'ei-fu as their puppet, but he spurned all their advances. The Japanese had given Wang to understand that they would be prepared to withdraw their armies from China two years after the end of hostilities. But once he was in "office", they were unwilling to make any such pledge, and in increasing frustration he spent the rest of his time trying to get the Japanese to live up to their promises. History might possibly have proved him right, had it not been for Pearl Harbor. Indeed (according to Hu Lin) Wang Ching-wei would not have taken the plunge in forming the Nanking puppet government had he been able to foresee Pearl Harbor. But the Japanese did sink the American fleet, and it was Chiang Kai-shek who was proved right for having chosen defiance.

From first to last, 1940 was largely a political year for Chiang Kai-shek and China. The disasters of the war in Western Europe had unpleasant consequences for China. Taking advantage of the collapse of France, the Japanese delivered an ultimatum to the French, requiring them to close the railway from Hanoi to China. The British, too, were weakened by the retreat from Dunkirk, and stood alone. Taking advantage of their plight, the Japanese threatened war unless they immediately closed the Hong Kong border and the Burma Road. Desperately, Winston Churchill appealed to President Roosevelt: if war came, would the Americans help Britain against Japan? But the Americans themselves were weak at that time, and it was politically unthinkable for Roosevelt to involve his country in war to save British imperial possessions. On 12 July, Britain closed the Burma Road—salving conscience with a proviso that the closure would last only three months, to give Japan and China a further chance to reach a peaceful settlement. For the Generalissimo and his government, this was one of the bitterest blows of all. For by that time, the Burma Road was China's only link with the outside world.

Chiang issued a statement, formally charging that the British decision violated existing Sino-British treaties; but the Chinese were in no position to take the matter further, for they and the British had this in common, that they were fighting alone, without allies, against dreadful odds. In Japan, the Yonai cabinet fell that month, and Prince Konoye was back as Prime Minister. To give him credit, he did—as promised to the British—come out with a further peace offer. This time, the Japanese proposed a special status for the five northern provinces of Chahar, Suiyuan, Hopei, Shansi, and

Shantung, recognition of Wang Ching-wei's regime, and deferment of any decision on the future status of Manchukuo. As usual, the Generalissimo took no notice. There were further peace feelers from time to time.

On 12 October, seeing that peace efforts in China had come to nothing, the British re-opened the Burma Road. For Chiang Kai-shek, this reversal of a harsh decision was the signal for a fundamental reappraisal of China's position. By now, the Generalissimo was convinced that a clash between Japan and America was not merely inevitable but approaching rapidly. He therefore announced China's outright alignment with Britain and the United States in standing up to Axis aggression. Henceforth, even if the Japanese offered honourable terms, the National Government would refuse to discuss them. These decisions were announced in November 1940, and among all Chiang's generals and advisers there was not a single dissenting voice.

The next bitter external blow to Chiang Kai-shek's war effort came from an unexpected quarter. On 13 April 1941, the Soviet Union unexpectedly signed a five-year neutrality pact with Japan. For Chiang, the duplicity of Stalin's policy passed belief. He had been sending military supplies to the Chinese, for use against Japan. And now, in cynical disregard of the Sino-Soviet Agreement of 1924 and the Sino-Soviet non-aggression pact of 1937, the Russians were giving the Japanese a free hand in China by relieving them of the threat of military action from Soviet Asia. The blow to Chiang was the worse for the fact that only two days earlier, on 11 April 1941, the Soviet ambassador to China, A. S. Panyushkin, had assured the Chinese government that Russia would not sacrifice the interests of a friendly country for selfish considerations. The Chinese had been concerned at the visit paid to Moscow the previous month by the Japanese Foreign Minister, Yosue Matsuoka, after a visit to Germany. But the Soviet government, said Panyushkin, was merely extending to Matsuoka the usual diplomatic courtesy. In the new pact, Japan recognised the Soviet-protected Republic of Outer Mongolia, and Russia recognised Manchukuo. In his account of these events many years later, in his book *Soviet Russia in China*, Chiang Kai-shek claimed that the neutrality pact of April 1941 was only a small part of a grandiose conspiracy between Russia and Japan, under which Outer Mongolia, Sinkiang, Tibet, and the mountain pass of Tungkwan in Shensi province were to be given to the Soviet Union.

More than ever, Chiang needed America's help. In a farewell dinner to U.S. Ambassador Nelson T. Johnson on 10 May 1941, the Generalissimo declared with encouraging flattery: "I am prepared to express the conviction that any country in the world matching itself against the American democracy will meet certain destruction."

Stalin's pact with Japan made perfect political and strategic sense: it complemented the Nazi-Soviet pact, which had initially driven a wedge between the anti-Comintern partners, and gave Russia a further guarantee of a sort against attack on a threatened border. But it did not save Russia, any more than the pact with Hitler had, against Hitler's decision to invade Russia on 22 June 1941. As Hitler's armies drove towards Moscow, Stalin called on the Chinese Communists to give battle to the newly reinforced Japanese divisions in northern China. This diversion, he reasoned, would enable him to withdraw Soviet forces from the eastern border for the defence of European Russia. But Mao Tse-tung, unwilling to risk the destruction of his Eighth Route Army, flatly declined.

In September, the desperate Russians transferred Far Eastern divisions to the European front anyway, and Zhukov was enabled to halt the Nazi advance in the suburbs of the capital. But the Japanese had no thought, at this time, of aggression in the Soviet Far East. Instead, their plan was to strike at the American fleet and overrun South-East Asia. The rub was that the "China incident" had already lasted more than four years, and was still tying up the bulk of the Japanese army. Yet another peace feeler came from Tokyo in September 1941. This time it took the form of a hint that the Japanese would accept a settlement between Wang Ching-wei and Chiang Kai-shek. But Chiang, once again, was not disposed to play their game.

The Generalissimo was finding America's attitude hard to fathom. In the summer of 1940, the United States Government had placed an embargo on the export of iron and steel scrap to a number of countries, including Japan. If Japan attacked America, there seemed no doubt that China would get its full share of American aid. But which China? A disquieting message from President

Roosevelt had been brought to Chiang in February 1941 by an administrative assistant to the President, Lauchlin Currie. Currie had no fewer than ten meetings with the Generalissimo, in the first of which he gave Chiang an oral message from the President to the effect that China's Communists seemed more like socialists to him, and surely the aim ought to be for Communists and Nationalists to work together.

Currie expressed a desire to meet Chou En-lai, to which the Generalissimo raised no objections. But he gave the President's envoy a stern lecture on the behaviour of the Chinese Communists and their relations with the Third International. It was obvious to Chiang Kai-shek that misleading information—of the kind we would now call "disinformation"—about the Chinese Communists had been reaching President Roosevelt for some time.

As 1941 wore on, President Roosevelt began increasingly to stand up to the Japanese. In July, he froze Japanese assets in the United States; in August, he warned Japan that any further policy of military domination in Asia would force the United States "to take immediately any and all steps" to safeguard American rights and interests: On 17 October, Prince Konoye stepped down and was replaced by the arch-militarist, General Hideki Tojo. The abortive Japanese-American negotiations followed in Washington. And on 7 December, the Japanese struck without warning against the American fleet in Hawaii and the British forces in Hong Kong and Malaya. That day in Pearl Harbor, the Americans lost 5 battleships and 3 cruisers, together with 177 aircraft. There were 2,343 dead, 876 missing, and 1,272 injured. The next day, the United States and Britain declared war on Japan, and China declared war on Germany and Italy. The Generalissimo cabled President Roosevelt: "To our new common battle we offer all we are and all we have, to stand with you until the Pacific and the world are freed from the curse of brute force and endless perfidy."

The "China incident" had merged into World War II.

17. | Chiang and His Allies

No sooner had Pearl Harbor ended China's isolation than Chiang Kai-shek tried to help his new British and American allies. The day after the Japanese attack, he sent identical messages to President Roosevelt, Winston Churchill, and Stalin, to propose an immediate joint military conference. Stalin replied that Russia was not yet ready to take part in the Pacific war; Roosevelt and Churchill declared themselves in favour, and the conference was in fact held in Chungking on 23 December. The results were gratifying to Chiang and useful to the Allies. A Joint Military Council was set up in Chungking, to coordinate strategy for East Asia. For Britain, General Sir Archibald Wavell argued that top priority must be given to save Burma, then under threat of imminent Japanese attack. It was agreed that action should be taken from China. The Burma Road, which had been re-opened in October 1941, was indeed a vital supply line for China, and the Generalissimo was anxious to help keep it open. Apart from Burma and the overland route from Russia, China's only bridge to the outer world was now Hong Kong.

But Hong Kong itself was now under growing Japanese pressure. In December 1941, Chiang Kai-shek offered to send substantial Chinese forces to help the British defend their Crown Colony. Although the offer was declined, he nevertheless sent a considerable force to attack the Japanese from the mainland side. It was a quixotic gesture, for on 18 December the British withdrew from Kowloon and Hong Kong fell on Christmas Day. The Chinese force, under General Tsai T'ing-k'ai—who had stood up to the Japanese in Shanghai in 1932—were left at the mercy of the Japanese, who gradually crushed them between Kowloon and Canton.

Next, Chiang offered to help the British in Burma by sending Chinese reinforcements. Again he was rebuffed, the British fearing that the arrival of Chinese troops would go down badly with the Burmese population. But as the Japanese pressure mounted, they changed their minds and the Generalissimo sent the Fifth and Sixth Chinese Armies to the Burma front. There, on 16 February 1942, they first clashed with the Japanese.

About that time, Chiang made an unheralded trip to India. His motives were mixed. On the one hand, he genuinely thought that he could use his influence to swing popular opinion in India behind the Allied cause, at a time when the prestige of imperial Britain stood particularly low. A less altruistic, though perfectly honourable, motive was to stake a claim for himself as a great Asian leader in the post-war world. Roosevelt thought the trip was a good idea, but to Churchill it was an unwarranted intrusion.

The trip was shrouded in deep secrecy and the Generalissimo's presence, with Mme. Chiang at his side, was not announced until they had been in India five days. Immediately, they ran into a curious problem of protocol. Chinese courtesy required the Generalissimo to go to Wardha, near Bombay, where Gandhi was staying. But Indian custom obliged Gandhi to make the effort to meet his visitor where he was staying—in this instance, at New Delhi. A Viceregal plea supported the Indian custom. The Viceroy of India was Lord Linlithgow, and the British ambassador to China, Sir Archibald Clark-Kerr, brought a letter from him to Mme. Chiang to say that if the Chiangs travelled to Wardha the Viceroy would suffer "grave political embarrassment"; and he begged most earnestly that the plan should not go ahead. The Prime Minister, Winston Churchill himself, now cabled the Generalissimo to appeal to him not to go against the wishes of the Viceroy of the King Emperor. To do so, he said, "might impede the desire we have for rallying all India to the war effort against Japan", and "might well have the unintended effect of emphasising communal differences at a moment when unity is imperative". The Generalissimo bowed gracefully to these simultaneous pressures, and Calcutta was chosen as a compromise meeting place. He was much impressed to learn that the Indian leader had made the journey in a third-class railway carriage to share the hardships of the lowly. Much talk of solidarity against imperialism followed.

On the last day of the visit, 21 February, Mme. Chiang broadcast an English translation of a message from the Generalissimo to the people of India. Not altogether to Britain's liking, he expressed the hope that India should be granted self-administration as speedily as possible, but he also called on the people of India wholeheartedly to support the world-wide struggle against aggression.

Not long after his departure, Gandhi and some of the other Congress leaders were gaoled, as happened periodically in their long conflict with the British Raj. Not wishing to offend his erstwhile British hosts, the Generalissimo called on President Roosevelt to mediate, an honour which the President declined.

Within a few days of Chiang Kai-shek's return to Chungking, on 6 March 1942, General Joseph Stilwell arrived in the wartime capital of China, and the great Sino-American misunderstanding got under way. So much has been written on the American side of the Stilwell-Chiang dispute—especially since the publication of Stilwell's acrid diaries—that it is as well to remember there was a Chinese point of view, too. In fact, friction was built into the portfolio of overlapping jobs General Stilwell brought with him from Washington. He informed the Generalissimo at their first meeting that he was to command all the American forces in the China, Burma, and India theatre (which is usually called simply the CBI), to represent the U.S. Government on all international war committees in China, to control and supervise Lend-Lease and all other American defence aid schemes in China, and also to be Chief of Staff to the Generalissimo as Supreme Commander in China. Moreover, he was charged with liaison between Chiang Kai-shek and General Wavell, who commanded the British forces in Burma and India. As Chief of Staff to the Supreme Commander, Stilwell was at the Generalissimo's orders. But in all other respects, the President's commands naturally took precedence over Chiang Kai-shek's. His job as Lend-Lease administrator was particularly irksome to Chiang, for if Stilwell felt that it was not in America's interests to release a consignment to the Chinese forces, he would simply withhold it.

To make matters worse, China was "less equal" than the others when it came to Lend-Lease. The British, the Russians, or other recipients could allocate the American bounty as they saw fit in their own countries. Only Chiang Kai-shek was required to submit his needs on a project-by-project basis to General Stilwell. This humiliating procedure, it became clear, had been devised by supporters of the Soviet Union in Washington who did not want to give Chiang any right of veto on supplies intended for the Chinese Communists.

The situation would have been difficult enough if Stilwell had been a paragon of tact and diplomacy, but even he would not have claimed these qualities. In his despatches to Washington, "Vinegar Joe" referred to the Generalissimo as "Peanut" and "the little rattlesnake". But then, his diaries later disclosed that he referred to Roosevelt as "Old Softie", and had favourite invectives for other distinguished contemporaries. Moreover, he returned to China nursing an ambition which he concealed initially but later did not bother to hide—to take over from Chiang Kai-shek himself as Supreme Commander of the Chinese forces. It should have been obvious to Stilwell that this aspiration was only a dream, but Stilwell saw only the evidences of Chiang's strategic shortcomings, and had infinite confidence in his own military genius.

Nor was Chiang Kai-shek the only person with whom General Stilwell clashed. Another was Chennault, who had been reintegrated into the American forces after Pearl Harbor, with the rank of Major-General. Already his volunteers—soon known as the "Flying Tigers" and passing into legend—and Chennault had had a stimulating effect on Chinese morale. The Chinese had been defenceless against Japanese air attacks, and now they felt defended. Chennault's volunteers became the U.S. China Air Task Force, and later the Fourteenth Air Force. Under the strategic plan worked out by Stilwell and Chiang, Chennault was to take command of a series of air bases in Hunan, Kwangsi, and Yunnan, to be built with American aid and supplied by air from India over the Himalayan "Hump".

But Stilwell did not take the same view as Chennault of the priority to be given to allocation of the Hump supplies. Chennault wanted them for his air bases; Stilwell wanted them for the training of new Chinese armies at Ramgarh in India, and at Kunming in Yunnan. These were the armies on which Stilwell counted to roll the Japanese out of Burma.

Unlike Stilwell, Chennault got on very well with Chiang Kai-shek. In conversation with Eric Chou in Nanking in 1947, the Generalissimo's secretary-general at that time, Wu Ting-ch'ang, listed a few reasons for this rare harmony. Chennault, he said, displayed no interest at all in China's internal politics and was invariably very respectful to Chiang. With rare exceptions, he talked only about the subject he knew best—the air force. Another point that helped was that Chennault had great faith in the Chinese pilots he was training, and therefore had very little criticism to offer. Moreover, Chennault appealed to Chiang as one professional military man to another; at that level, of course, Chiang also appreciated Stilwell's qualities, but this appreciation was not reciprocated.

Stilwell was primarily a fighting field general, and as such one of the best in World War II. His first Burma campaign, in the early months of 1942, ended in May in bitterness and retreat. When it became clear that withdrawal was inevitable, he did not bother to inform the Generalissimo. Instead, he sent two cables to his assistant in Chungking, General Magruder, to say that his troops had broken up into small units and could not be brought together again, and that he was leaving Burma for India. The Generalissimo had ordered that in the event of defeat, the Chinese forces should be withdrawn to Myitkyina in north Burma, and thence back to China. Without consulting him, Stilwell had countermanded the order, and proposed to evacuate the Chinese to India. On hearing of Stilwell's order, the Generalissimo immediately cabled the commander of the Chinese Fifth Army in Burma, General Tu Yu-ming, who managed—despite Stilwell's pessimism—to rally three divisions together. They succeeded in fighting their way back to China. Stilwell was incensed, and on his return to Chungking wrote to the Generalissimo saying that he should not have written directly to a general under his command. For an old China hand, Stilwell had been strangely obtuse in ignoring Chinese military psychology. For the Chinese army tradition has it that (as Tong puts it), "when cornered, Chinese troops will not degrade themselves by seeking shelter in a foreign country".

Although Stilwell was not the most welcome of President Roosevelt's gifts to Chiang Kai-shek, there were other things to be thankful for. One of the most welcome was a loan of $500,000 early in 1942. A telegram from the President telling Chiang the good news reached the Generalissimo while he was in Delhi: "The gallant resistance of the Chinese armies against the ruthless invaders of your country has called forth the highest praise from the American and all other freedom-loving peoples." There was more in this vein. A delighted Chiang Kai-shek cabled back: "Your far-sightedness in this world's greatest crisis is deservedly the envy of all real statesmen." Article II of the loan agreement that followed on 8 March deferred final settlement until after the war, on terms that would be "in the mutual interest of the United States and China and which will permit the establishment of lasting world peace and security".

The British immediately came in with a parallel loan of £50,000,000. A Joint Stabilisation Board was created, with American and British participation. Recording these facts, Tong added that "the result of the joint efforts was to place the Chinese currency on a sound foundation for the remaining war years", but this was pure fantasy. The great Chinese inflation was already well entrenched when Stilwell arrived, about the same time as the American and British loans were announced, and he was struck by the fact that "coolies go around with $50 bills". And as the war went on, the value of money kept on dwindling. Towards the end (wrote White and Jacoby) an entire month's earnings could be spent on a single evening's party. The government ensured the survival of its minions by monthly allocations of rice, cloth, cooking oil, salt, and fuel at frozen prices. Two years after the creation of the Stabilisation Board, each convoy of supplies flown painfully over the Hump included tons of paper money printed abroad to feed the insatiable appetite of the great inflation.

Money was not all the Chinese looked for in life, however. "Face" mattered still more, and on the Double Tenth anniversary— 10 October 1942—the Generalissimo made an announcement that did more for Chinese face than anything that had happened since the 1911 Revolution. He disclosed that the United States and Britain had voluntarily renounced all their extra-territorial rights under the notorious "unequal" treaties. Although this major concession by China's allies was voluntary in the sense that their renouncement was not wrested out of them under duress, they were not unprompted. At first, they had been inclined to postpone any decision until the end of the war. But Chiang pointed out to them that an early announcement would have a tonic effect on the Chinese people; whereupon they yielded.

While Chiang Kai-shek was emerging as one of the Allied war leaders, Mao Tse-tung was gaining complete control over the Chinese Communist Party. The "united front" between the Nationalists and Communists had finally broken down early in 1941, and the break helped Mao in the struggle for power. The decisive event—still hotly contested and blurred by the propaganda of either side—was the "New Fourth Army incident" of January 1941. At the time, the New Fourth Army had been operating south of the Yangtze River, not far from Shanghai. In September 1940, Chiang's Chief of Staff, General Ho Ying-ch'in, ordered it to cross the river then move north, cross the Yellow River, and take up new positions in concert with the Eighteenth Group Army (the Nationalist term for the Communist Eighth Route Army). The Communists hesitated, partly because crossing the Yangtze under Japanese fire was perilous and partly because they had plans of their own to set up a new operating base in the Nanking-Shanghai-Hankow triangle south of the river. Chiang Kai-shek extended the deadline for the crossing to 31 December, but still the New Fourth Army stayed where it was.

Suddenly and secretly, the Communist Chief of Staff, Hsiang Ying, began to move his force southward. On 4 January 1941 the New Fourth Army clashed with the government's Fortieth Division, which heavily outnumbered it. What followed is obscure. What is certain is that Hsiang Ying was killed and the army commander Yeh T'ing was wounded and taken prisoner. The Communists lost about 1,000 men.°

° The casualty figure of 1,000 is given by Guillermaz (p. 352), quoting Communist sources, including two declarations to be found in Mao Tse-tung's *Selected Works*. Yet Richard C. Thornton, in *China: The Struggle for Power*

On 17 January, the National Military Council ordered the disbanding of the New Fourth Army. In any case, it had ceased to exist as a fighting force. But in Yenan, the Communist Party decided not only to ignore the government's order, but to proclaim that the New Fourth Army would be reconstituted under the same name, with seven divisions in place of the original one. For weeks, Communist propaganda violently denounced the Nationalists for disarming the New Fourth Army, attributing the decision to the "pro-Japanese clique" as part of a plan to conclude a peace treaty with Japan and join the anti-Comintern pact. On 6 March, Chiang Kai-shek sent a long message to the People's Political Council, charging the Communists with bad faith and adding, not entirely truthfully:

> I need scarcely assert that our government is solely concerned with leading the nation against the Japanese invaders and extirpating the traitors, and is utterly without any notion of again taking up arms to "suppress the Communists". It desires never again to hear of that ill-omened term which now has a place only in Chinese history. Let them obey orders, give up their attacks on their comrades-in-arms and cease all their provocative acts; the government will then treat them with all possible consideration.

Earlier, Chiang Kai-shek said privately, "The Japanese are a disease of the skin. The Communists are a disease of the heart."

Evidence that came into his hands after the New Fourth Army incident strengthened his long-standing view of Communist duplicity. General Yeh T'ing, the commander captured by the government forces, confessed that under the Comintern's directive to the Chinese Communist Party, it was to do everything within its power to prolong the war and prevent the conclusion of a peace in order to

---

1917–1972 (p. 123), writes: "In over a week of pitched battle, the Nationalists annihilated the entire unit of 10,000 men." Clubb (p. 237) says the Communists "suffered several thousand casualties". And White and Jacoby (p. 78) mention "several thousand" troops dead and "several thousand more in captivity", although they say earlier that only 5,000 men were involved on the Communist side. For good measure, they add an atrocity story involving the rape of all the women on the Communist side by Nationalist troops, and live burials. It is improbable, however, that the Communists themselves would understate their casualties.

eliminate the Japanese threat to the eastern frontiers of the Soviet Union. Meanwhile, the Communist forces were to remain in the areas they occupied, while as far as possible avoiding an open break with the government.

More startling evidence came to the Generalissimo some time after the incident, when a copy of Mao Tse-tung's secret directives to the Eighth Route Army came into Nationalist hands. It read:

> The Sino-Japanese War affords our party an excellent opportunity for expansion. Our fixed policy should be 70 percent expansion, 20 percent dealing with the Kuomintang, and 10 percent resisting Japan. There are three stages in carrying out this fixed policy:
>
> The first is a compromising stage, in which self-sacrifice should be made to show our outward obedience to the Central Government and adherence to the Three People's Principles; but in reality this will serve as camouflage for the existence and development of our party.
>
> The second is a contending stage, in which two or three years should be spent in laying the foundations of our party's political and military powers, and developing these until we can match and break the Kuomintang, and eliminate the influence of the latter north of the Yellow River.
>
> The third is an offensive stage, in which our forces should penetrate deeply into Central China, sever the communications of the Central Government troops in various sectors, isolate and disperse them until we are ready for the counter-offensive, and wrest the leadership from the hands of the Kuomintang.°

Even after the New Fourth Army incident, contact between the Kuomintang and the Communist Party continued. On 28 March 1942, Chou En-lai and Lin Piao (who had been one of Chiang's pupils at the Whampoa Military Academy) presented four demands in the name of their party:

1. Legal status for the Chinese Communist Party over the whole national territory, where only limited tolerance now exists.

° The Communist secret directive is quoted by Tong (p. 324); a slightly different translation of it appears on p. 85 of Chiang Kai-shek's *Soviet Russia in China*, but in a context that leaves the chronology totally obscure.

2. Official recognition for the administrative structures in the "liberated" areas.
3. Enlargement of the Eighth Route Army from three to twelve divisions.
4. Authorisation for the reconstituted New Fourth Army to remain south of the Yellow River until the end of the war.

The government naturally rejected these demands, which, however, were revived a year later.

In the wake of the New Fourth Army incident, anti-Chiang activities gained momentum in cities such as Kweilin and Kunming. With Li Chi-shen as Director of the Kweilin headquarters of the Generalissimo, left-wing writers and playwrights (originally based in Hong Kong) flocked to that city. Li gave willing shelter to these cultural refugees, finding them jobs and offering them financial assistance. At that time the Provincial Institute of Dramatic Arts was headed by Ouyang Yü-chien, who had previously participated in the Fukien People's Revolutionary Government. Under his guidance, historical plays with anti-establishment themes were staged with great success. Although Chiang was never mentioned by name, it was clear to the audiences that he was the target. People saw him through characters such as Ch'in Shih-huang—the first emperor of the Ch'in dynasty—or that nineteenth-century soldier-statesman whom Chiang admired so much: Tseng Kuo-fan. Magazines with a scarcely veiled anti-Chiang line flourished.

But the real mischief was done by underground Communists, such as Miss Yang Kang, Sa K'ung-liao, and Chin Chung-hua, who were regular guests at the cocktail parties hosted by the U.S. Office of War Information (OWI) and the American consulate in Kweilin. Miss Yang later became deputy-chairman of the Foreign Policy Committee of the Chinese Communist Foreign Ministry in 1949, and Sa became deputy-chairman of the National Minorities Commission of the State Council; while Chin emerged under Communist rule as deputy-mayor of Shanghai. In 1942, however, they worked assiduously to "win over" the Americans, as the party required them to do under the principle of "international United Front" work.

In Kunming, the South-West Associated University and Yunnan University were havens for anti-Chiang people and Communist sympathisers. Although the Democratic League did not come into the open until the National Political Consultative Conference met early in 1946, it was already very active in Kunming in 1943. Some of the leading figures in the League were lecturing at the time in Kunming and later emerged in Peking under the Chinese People's Republic. One was Lo Lung-chi, later to serve Peking as Minister for Light Industry, and another was Wu Han, who was to be the deputy-mayor of Peking, and whose play *The Dismissal of Hai Jui* sparked off the Cultural Revolution in 1966. Other Democratic League personalities in Kunming at that time were Wen Yi-to and Li Kung-pu, both of whom were later assassinated by KMT agents. The Yunnan provincial governor, Lung Yun—a former warlord— condoned or deliberately ignored their activities among the students. He, too, later turned up in Peking as a "democratic personage" and as such was used by the Chinese Communists during the Hundred Flowers period in 1957 publicly to air Chinese grievances against the Russians.

In the South-West Associated University, wall-newspapers were first used to express grievances against or criticisms of the Nationalist government. Although these texts fell short of direct attacks on Chiang Kai-shek, they included bitter criticisms of the Chungking government in general, and of Chiang's trusted subordinates in particular.

In Chungking, the OWI (later re-styled the U.S. Information Service) hired a good many left-wingers. These included Liu Tsun-ch'i (who became Director of the International Propaganda Bureau of the Peking regime in 1949) and Meng Yun-ch'ien (later Director of the Bureau of Industrial Cooperatives). Another man who worked for the OWI was Chin Chung-hua, after he had left Kweilin. The part they played in exaggerating the evils of the Kuomintang regime and denigrating Chiang Kai-shek was considerable, for diplomats and foreign correspondents alike cultivated them as important sources of information.

The dissolution of the New Fourth Army undoubtedly served to consolidate Mao Tse-tung's power. It was the end of the united front policy as expounded by one of his principal rivals, Wang Ming, who returned to China from Moscow at the beginning of 1938 as the Comintern's designated representative. Mao had never liked the united front, but had gone along with it, partly under Moscow's pressure at a time when his hold on the party was still insecure, and partly because of the realities of the Japanese invasion. If even Chiang Kai-shek had agreed to reverse his order of priorities and resist Japan rather than exterminate Communists, then Mao had no choice but to do the same. In the north, the united front policy had never, in any case, inhibited him in his own extermination policy against any government troops that fell into Communist traps. Now the united front was seen to be irrelevant as well as unpractical.

Almost immediately after the signing of the Soviet-Japanese neutrality pact in April 1941, the Japanese launched their notorious "three-all campaign" (kill all, burn all, destroy all). Their immediate target was the Eighth Route Army, and Mao was forced to reduce the party's military presence all over the north China plain, withdrawing forces to the Shansi plateau and the hills of Shantung. This suited Mao, who used the period of relative military inactivity that followed to tighten his grip on the party machine. He altered the "percentage" into which he liked to divide activity. The new proportion was 10 percent against the Japanese, 20 percent to the protection of bases, and 70 percent to expansion of political influence. His first concern was to appoint his own men to various key positions, including those in the reconstituted New Fourth Army. He then convened about a thousand "delegates" from various areas, ostensibly to take part in the much-delayed Seventh Congress of the Chinese Communist Party. The Congress did not meet, however: instead, Mao took advantage of their presence in Yenan to launch a *"cheng-feng"*, or rectification campaign. By then it was February 1942. "Rectification" was a euphemism for a party purge, which went on until September. From then until the spring of 1945, he systematically reorganised the entire party structure.

During 1942 and 1943 (according to estimates by Guillermaz) between 40,000 and 80,000 party members were expelled; there were numerous executions of "traitors", "collaborators", and "Kuomintang special agents". From the time of the *cheng-feng* until the Communist victory in the Chinese civil war, Mao Tse-tung's power was never again seriously challenged.

While Mao Tse-tung was consolidating his power in the north, Chiang Kai-shek's regime was degenerating fast. The Generalissimo himself was becoming more and more authoritarian and unapproachable. Officials sometimes had to wait for weeks to see him,

and when they got through the barriers, owed their good fortune
to a whim of Madame's. His position as *Tsung-t'sai*, or Director-
General of the Kuomintang, gave him virtually unlimited power to
dictate to the Executive Yüan, bully the Legislative Yüan, and
by-pass the Judicial Yüan. In practical terms, these bodies were
ornamental. He had his own system, which divided the administrative chores between three men: Ch'en Li-fu for party affairs, Ho
Ying-ch'in for military ones, and H. H. K'ung for the actual business
of government. Each represented a clique, for the real secret of
Chiang's power was his manipulation of rival groups.

By common consent, the most impressive of the Generalissimo's
three henchmen was Ch'en Li-fu (who indeed remained impressive
when I met him, by then an old man, in Taiwan many years later).
He has already come into this story. With the refined features of a
mandarin and aristocrat, his hair prematurely grey for a Chinese, his
eyes black and piercing, he was the arch-upholder of traditional
China, of the Confucian values, and of the infinite superiority of
Chinese culture. His intelligence and energy were beyond question.

As Secretary-General of the KMT, he was the wheeler-dealer of
wartime China. As a nephew of Chiang's early protector, Ch'en
Ch'i-mei, and himself a protégé of Chiang's with his elder brother
Ch'en Kuo-fu, Li-fu was untouchable. Together, the two brothers
ran the so-called CC (Central Club) clique.° They had alternated in
key jobs, such as the directorship of the internal security service
(CBIS) and of the Organisation Department of the KMT, and singly
or jointly were the scourge not only of the Communists but of
dissidents of all kinds. In addition, Li-fu—the younger by eight
years, and fitter than his tubercular elder—was Education Minister
for some years and as such the implacable guardian of doctrinal
purity, not hesitating to send doubtful students or professors to gaol
or the firing squad. Both the Ch'ens were austere and personally
uncorrupt: it was power that interested them, not money.

General Ho Ying-ch'in, the War Minister for fourteen years,
naturally led another powerful group, the military clique, which
would have been even more powerful than it was, had it been
united. General Ho personified the older generation of military

---

° The founder and original leader of the Central Club was Tai Ch'i-t'ao. Later,
Buddhism claimed him, and the two Ch'en brothers became joint leaders of
the clique.

bureaucrats—the soldiers who had made Chiang Kai-shek's rise to power possible. But there was a younger group—a clique within a clique—more fiercely loyal to Chiang than their elders, and determined to wipe out the corrupt inefficiency that clogged the war effort. These younger men were known as the Whampoa clique, and the best-known among them was General Ch'en Ch'eng, one of the greatest men of modern China, who went on to become Vice-President of the exiled National Government in Taiwan and to preside over a spectacularly effective land reform programme. Just over five feet in height and of very slight build, he was full of nervous energy and rapidly became the most popular of the KMT military leaders with the Americans in China. A graduate of Paoting Military Academy in the 1920s, he had been one of Chiang's young instructors at Whampoa. The other members of the Whampoa clique had graduated there when the Generalissimo was Commandant.

Ho, whom Ch'en Ch'eng was to supplant as War Minister in 1944 under intense American pressure, was a round-faced, courteous man of stocky build. He came to symbolise the gross corruption and inefficiency of an army in which the pay packets of dead men went straight into the pockets of local commanders, while the conscripts literally starved. The Premier and Finance Minister, K'ung Hsiang-hsi—usually known under the Americanised form of H. H. K'ung—represented a clique of another kind: that of the powerful Soong family. Having married Mme. Chiang's imperious elder sister, Eiling Soong, he was automatically in a position of privilege and influence. A plump, amiable, bespectacled man with a clipped moustache, he showed himself adept at adding to his personal fortune, and equally at ruining the nation's finances. Perhaps his greatest distinction came to him at birth, for he was a direct descendant of Confucius (K'ung Fu-tse in Chinese) in the seventy-fifth generation. White and Jacoby quote one of his friends as saying that 90 percent of the gossip heard about him was not true, and adding: "Ten percent is even worse than the gossip."

It has often been alleged—and never been denied or made the subject of a libel action—that Mme. K'ung speculated successfully on tips that could only have come to her through her husband in his official capacity. Since the grain tax collectors in the villages tended to keep the proceeds for themselves, H. H. K'ung's invariable solution to the regime's financial problems was to print more money. On V–J Day, prices were 2,500 times as high as when the war began. Yet Chungking's dollar reserves were enormous, thanks to K'ung's insistence that the Americans should get only $20 Chinese for each U.S. dollar, at a time when the black market rate was $400, then $600, and in time $800.

There were other cliques, too, and some individuals of outstanding stature. The group most favoured by the Americans was the Political Science Clique, consisting of modern-minded technocrats (though the term was not yet in use), many of them educated in America or Japan, most of them English-speaking and determined to turn their country into a technologically efficient industrial state.° Among them, two men stood out: Sun Fo and T. V. Soong. As the son of the father of the Revolution, Sun Fo was sacrosanct; a scholar and a reformer, he had the courage to speak up but not the personal drive to break with the KMT and build a personal following. Although he was President (Speaker, as the British would say) of the Legislative Yüan, he could do nothing against the party machine manipulated by Ch'en Li-fu. Chiang Kai-shek feared and shunned this liberalising voice and refused to see him for months on end. The same treatment was meted out to T. V. Soong, who was Foreign Minister from 1942 to 1945. He, too, was untouchable and could speak his mind, and did. But the Generalissimo preferred yes men and "T. V." was rarely in favour. There has been an unfortunate tendency to link his name with K'ung's as another reprehensible KMT type, but the two men were very different. T. V. Soong had made a great fortune, but unlike his brother-in-law, he had made it by dynamic, entrepreneurial capitalism, creating wealth for China and jobs for tens of thousands.

The greatest blot on the KMT's reputation was surely the army. Rich men's sons could buy their way out of military service for a fat fee, pocketed by the official who sold the exemption. Poorer men of the right age groups were kidnapped by press gangs, roped

---

° Those who belonged to this "clique" called it the Political Science Group. Its original name was the Forum of European Affairs, and it was founded by Huang Hsing in the United States, after he had left Japan in 1913 when he had broken with Sun Yat-sen over a regulation that party members should have their fingerprints taken. The change of name came after the end of World War I. In the early 1930s, the leader was Yang Yung-t'ai, but he was assassinated in Hankow in 1936; thereafter the group lacked an identifiable leader, although its best-known member was General Chang Ch'ün, a close associate of Chiang Kai-shek.

together, and dragged off to the military fate—all too often death from starvation. Many thousands of conscripts died even before reaching the units to which they had been assigned. White and Jacoby quote horrifying figures for the Chinese troops sent to Burma. One unit lost 30 percent of its effectives on the 500-mile march, and of those left—presumed to be strong—15 percent were pronounced to be consumptives by an American doctor. Apart from tuberculosis, dysentery, malaria, scabies, beri-beri, and worms took a heavy toll—along with typhus and influenza. For most of the sick, there was no medical attention available. On average, there was only one Chinese doctor for a whole division. But one major scourge of Western armies was missing: venereal disease—possibly because the conscripts were too devitalised to resort to prostitutes and too poor to pay them if they felt capable. The wonder was that such an army fought heroically and died in battle.

Conditions were bad enough at the outset, but they rapidly became worse as inflation gained momentum. In the autumn of 1939, Eric Chou worked briefly in the Military Council as a translator with the honorary rank of major. His monthly pay was $60 Chinese, at a time when a pair of shoes sold at $80. By 1943, a pair of shoes fetched between $900 and $1,200, but a major's pay had not risen at all.

In this respect as in so many others, the remarkable General Yen Hsi-shan, the "model governor" of Shansi, set an example which others were reluctant or incapable of following. In the spring of 1939 (according to his own memoirs) he had led more than 300,000 troops to a mountainous area in the western part of the province. "The land was almost barren and the local population extremely poor. . . . In June 1940, he started a system of farm tax levies in kind, and introduced a rationing system for food and other necessities among troops, civil servants and school teachers." In his area, at least, the army was well-fed. In the summer of 1941, the Central Government ordered the whole country to follow suit; but self-seeking KMT generals continued to line their own pockets.

The Christian General, Feng Yü-hsiang, who also had a reputation for caring for his troops, describes a typical incident at Chihchung, where he was welcomed by the district commissioner. Local people crowded around them and appealed to Feng, saying that their boys—800 or 900 of them—had been drafted and were on their way to their training camps. But the commissioner had told the new conscripts to remove their quilted uniforms before they left. "In such cold weather, they would freeze to death!" they exclaimed. Feng intervened on their behalf and the commissioner sent the quilted uniforms to catch up with the new conscripts who had left two hours ago. Feng continues:

> The following day, I went to review the troops at Paishihyi. The regimental commander there showed me the roll-call book of his soldiers. I discovered that it was at full strength last week, but that now every battalion was short by thirty or forty men. I asked him the reason. The commander replied: "When the conscripts came from their homes, they were deprived of food on the way. Once they got here, they over-ate to burst themselves to death." But in fact, they were starved to death.

On another occasion in Sapingpa, about fifteen miles from Chungking, the Christian General asked one regimental commander where his sick soldiers were. He was taken to a small village some miles away where there were indeed more than twenty sick soldiers. Feng writes:

> I went in and found these poor youths feverish. They lay on doors which had been taken down to be used as beds, covered with hay. I felt their foreheads and asked whether they had taken any medicine or drunk any water. These innocent youths wept. They said: "No one has come to see us since we were ill. We cannot even get a mouthful of boiled water."

Brutalised by their superiors, the Kuomintang forces were often brutal in their turn to the peasants whose villages they encountered. Even without a thousand other reasons, this one alone would account for the final victory of the People's Liberation Army. The Communists were as brutal as the Nationalists, but more selectively. They made the peasants feel wanted and gave them a cause to fight for; and by and large, once in uniform, the men of the PLA refrained from raping and looting, paid their way, and helped with the harvest. The contrast was glaring.

Oblivious of the sufferings of his people—except when specific examples were brought to him and would send him into one of his uncontrollable rages—Chiang worked in increasing insulation. One reason why he had become so unapproachable, however, had nothing to do with an authoritarian disposition or aloofness of temperament. For about four months, from November 1942, taking advantage of a prolonged absence in the United States of Mme. Chiang, her sister, and her niece, the Generalissimo was writing a book. With the despatch that comes from absolute priority, it was published on 10 March 1943 in Chungking, under the title, *China's Destiny*. It was clearly Chiang's answer to Mao Tse-tung's book, *On the New Democracy*, which had appeared in January 1940 and which adapted Marxism-Leninism to Chinese conditions. It is often said that in fact the book was ghosted by a former secretary and ex-professor, Tao Hsi-sheng, and it is certain that Tao played an important part in the drafting.* But much of it was probably dictated by Chiang himself. In any case, the Generalissimo was fully responsible for—and indeed proud of—the contents. It was intended to be the ultimate statement of Chiang's political philosophy, and was hailed in Chungking as the most important book written since Sun Yat-sen's *Three Principles of the People*. Although there was an acute shortage of paper, 200,000 copies were printed for the first edition, and by the end of 1943 more than 200 printings had been issued. *China's Destiny* immediately became obligatory reading in Chinese schools and colleges, for all army officers and all civil servants, for all students at the Central Political Training Institute, and for all members of the Kuomintang Youth Corps.

Shortly after, Chiang brought out another and much shorter book, *Chinese Economic Theory*. This, too, was at least partly ghosted by Tao Hsi-sheng, but much of the technical economic material was contributed by Ch'en Pao-ying, who was a professional economist.

Both books were deeply nationalistic in tone—*China's Destiny*

---

* Tao Hsi-sheng's main job was as Chiang's speech-writer. He went on to become a member of the Central Committee of the Kuomintang and when this book was written, he was Chairman of the Board of Directors of the *Central Daily News*. Chiang had three other speech-writers during his long political career. The first was Yang Yung-t'ai, leader of the Political Science group, who was assassinated in the 1930s during one of the "bandit-suppression" campaigns against the Communists. The second one was Ch'en Pu-lei, a journalist mentioned in this chapter, who committed suicide in Nanking in 1948 (see p. 322). The fourth speech-writer was Chin Hsiao-yi, deputy Secretary-General of the Central Committee, who drafted Chiang's Will.

even more than *Chinese Economic Theory*. Chiang Kai-shek attributed China's problems exclusively to the depredations of the foreign powers and the effects of the unequal treaties. The main purpose of *Chinese Economic Theory* was to evolve a specifically Chinese solution to economic problems, based upon the teaching of Sun Yat-sen.

There are a number of curious aspects about these two books. One is the personality of the principal ghost-writer, Tao. Between 1934 and 1937, he was Professor of Chinese Social History at Peking University, as well as a lecturer at Peiping Normal University. In 1928, he had been Chiang Kai-shek's secretary, but he later became a close associate of Wang Ching-wei, with whom he fled to join the Japanese. In January 1940, however, Tao broke with Wang and escaped to Hong Kong, bringing the text of a secret treaty between Wang and the Japanese. His return was accepted as evidence of loyalty, and in Chungking he lived with Chiang's then secretary, Ch'en Pu-lei, and was on close and cordial terms with the Generalissimo.

Odder still was the absence of an English-language version of *China's Destiny*. It had been announced that a translation was being prepared for publication in April or May 1943. But the months and even the years went by without an English version. The most likely explanation is that the project was abandoned because it was realised in time that to make *China's Destiny* available to English-speaking readers at a time when the Kuomintang propagandists were building up the image of Chiang Kai-shek as a great democratic leader would have a shattering effect on public opinion, especially in America. The tone of the book is consistently anti-Western and anti-liberal. The curious situation thus arose that at a time when *China's Destiny* had sold more than 1,000,000 copies in China and was compulsory reading, the KMT censors deleted all references to the book in foreign correspondents' despatches. As late as January 1946, six Congressmen were refused access to the State Department's own translation on the ground that it was a "top secret" document. *Chinese Economic Theory* was published that month in the Communist "front" New York magazine, *Amerasia*, with a commentary by a left-wing American writer, Philip Jaffe, who later edited and annotated an English-language translation of both books in one volume in 1947. But this, of course, was part of the world-wide campaign to discredit the man who had been a wartime hero.

In 1943, however, the great American public was quite unaware that Chiang Kai-shek was not the great democratic leader he was portrayed to be. Mme. Chiang had captivated the American public on her mission to the United States, addressing enormous crowds and winning great personal popularity. In private, her imperious manner was less welcome to those of her hosts who saw her at close quarters. Roosevelt, who was afraid she was going to "vamp" him, gave in to her peremptory demand for more planes by ordering the immediate delivery of new Curtiss Wright C-46s before the test flights had been completed. Several of them crashed when flying over the Hump.

While Mme. Chiang was away, Chungking gossip linked the Generalissimo with a young nurse named Miss Ch'en, who—it was said—shared his bed and cooked his favourite dishes from his native Chekiang province. The gossip was unfounded, but it so enraged Chiang Kai-shek that when his wife returned he summoned foreign correspondents, cabinet ministers, and missionaries, and proclaimed his Christian and monogamous love for his lawful spouse, and utterly denied the rumours of his infidelity. At that time—the incident must have taken place in March 1943—the Nationalist armies were suffering disastrous reverses. But the Generalissimo's public avowal of virtue took precedence over military news for days. According to White and Jacoby, "semi-official transcripts of the Generalissimo's denial could be obtained from the government on request"

On the whole, Mme. Chiang's prolonged visit to America was a great propaganda success for Chungking, and the build-up of Chiang Kai-shek as one of the top war leaders proceeded apace. In October 1943, Vice-Admiral Lord Louis Mountbatten, Supreme Allied Commander, South-East Asia Command, arrived in Chungking. He brought a letter of introduction from Winston Churchill, who described him as a friend of twenty-five years' standing. With his handsome appearance and easy charm, Mountbatten brought a natural talent for diplomacy as well as outstanding strategic competence. He immediately ingratiated himself with Mme. Chiang by presenting her (writes Barbara Tuchman) with a Cartier vanity case bearing her initials in diamonds and by introducing himself to the Generalissimo as a relatively young commander eager to "lean on his vast experience". The object of his visit was to confer with the Generalissimo and with General Marshall's personal representative, General B. B. Somervell, on the strategy for Burma and other theatres in the war against Japan.

But Mountbatten was soon involved in the great Stilwell controversy; for he arrived at the precise moment when President Roosevelt, swayed by the combined complaints of the Chinese government and General Chennault, had virtually decided that Stilwell would have to be recalled. This was little to Mountbatten's taste, as Stilwell was his deputy, and he did not fancy losing the services of a man with so extensive a knowledge of things Chinese and making do with a less qualified successor. Mountbatten told Stilwell his job could be saved, but only on condition that he went to Chiang and apologised for his mistake. Inwardly fuming, Stilwell accepted Mountbatten's advice and did as he was told. The Generalissimo graciously accepted his apologies, and reconciliation was swift.

The climax of Chiang Kai-shek's wartime career in international eyes followed almost immediately, when he attended a summit conference in Cairo in November as one of the Big Three with President Roosevelt and Mr. Churchill. And he came with the formal title of President of the Republic of China, for on 11 October he had been inaugurated to the presidency in succession to Lin Sen, who died on 1 August. The three statesmen met at Mena House Hotel for four days from 22 to 26 November.

The joint communiqué that ended the conference was a personal triumph for the Generalissimo, for it recorded the resolve of the three Allies to strip Japan of all the territories "stolen from the Chinese, such as Manchuria, Formosa, and the Pescadores"—all of which were to be restored to the Republic of China. Moreover, Roosevelt pledged his support for a major combined land, sea, and air offensive in Burma in the spring of 1944 to break the blockade of China, and to arm and train ninety Nationalist divisions. He went on to support China against "foreign aggression" after the war by a joint U.S.–Chinese occupation of the Port Arthur–Dairen naval complex in Manchuria, these pledges being clearly aimed at preventing any Soviet move to grab Manchuria. In return, the President extracted a promise from Chiang to settle the Communist problem.

Elated, Chiang Kai-shek went home with his prestige higher

than ever. He was not to know that President Roosevelt would go on to a conference with Churchill and Stalin at Teheran (27 November–2 December), at which he would make pledges to the Soviet dictator in direct contradiction to those he had given Chiang Kai-shek. Indeed, the Americans failed to honour any of Roosevelt's Cairo commitments to the Generalissimo. Roosevelt cancelled the Burma joint offensive in 1944, and did not make sure that ninety Nationalist divisions were armed and trained. And his successor, President Truman, failed to support the Republic of China against the Russians after the war, although he did make a belated attempt. One thing Roosevelt did stick to, however: the determination that Chiang should honour his own commitment to settle his differences with the Communists.

18. | One War Ends

"'For me," said Chiang Kai-shek, "the big problem is not Japan, but the unification of my country. I am sure that you Americans are going to beat the Japanese some day, with or without the help of the troops I am holding back for use against the Communists in the north-west. On the other hand, if I let Mao Tse-tung push his propaganda across all of Free China, we run the risk—and so do you Americans—of winning for nothing. I say this because behind Mao there is the religion of Communism—and in consequence, Russia."

Like the Tanaka Memorial, this statement attributed to the Generalissimo comes into the category of things that are essentially true even if their authenticity is in doubt. It is quoted by the French Air Force General Lionel Max Chassin in his history of the Chinese civil war, and he places it in the context of a discussion between

Chiang and Stilwell.° Although Stilwell himself does not appear to quote precisely these words, they are certainly consistent with the arguments Chiang was known to use in private conversation. They sum up his attitude in the climactic years of World War II and explain better than any analysis the reasons for American exasperation with the Generalissimo.

What President Roosevelt, General Marshall, and other American war leaders found incomprehensible was the fact that Chiang Kai-shek was less interested in killing Japanese than they were, and more interested in killing Communists than Japanese. For five and a half years, since the end of 1938, the Japanese had left the central armies more or less alone, without launching any major fresh offensive. And Chiang on his side was quite content to sit and wait upon events. His best troops—the best armed, trained, and equipped—were in the north-west, confronting the Communist forces on the approach to Yenan. True, the Chinese central armies had suffered enormous losses at the hands of the Japanese during the early stages of the invasion of China, at a time when the Americans were comfortable in their peaceful isolation. But what was Roosevelt to make of their passivity in this greater war in which they were now involved? Were the Americans doing the right thing in supporting and materially aiding this unsatisfactory government? Would their aid not be better employed if directed to the Chinese Communists, who, by all accounts, were people of austerity and virtue and "Communists" in name only?

The messages and accounts reaching the White House or publicly available in the American press were both numerous and contradictory. There were the sour despatches of General Stilwell, full of complaints about the inefficiency and disorder of the Kuomintang's military bureaucracy, and the personal obstructiveness of the Generalissimo. There were the sceptical reports of the American ambassador in Chungking, Clarence Gauss. It was Gauss who, at one time, had referred in a despatch to the concept of

---

° L. M. Chassin, *The Communist Conquest of China* (London, 1966), pp. 17–18. In this English edition, the translators add a footnote: "The source of this account is a highly-placed Nationalist general officer whose identity the author cannot disclose." Chassin himself was not in China during the events he describes, but wrote his account from French intelligence sources available to him as Vice-Chief of Staff for National Defence in Paris. For a general confirmation that these were indeed Chiang's views, see Tuchman, p. 613.

Chiang as a great leader energetically directing China's resistance to Japan, and commented that "looking the cold facts in the face one could only dismiss this as rot". Then there were the views of Lauchlin Currie, President Roosevelt's administrative assistant, who came to China in 1941 with ready-made opinions on the Chinese Communists, which time has shown to have been fanciful.

Then on 1 October 1942, the defeated American presidential candidate, Wendell Willkie—a large, gregarious, gullible man—had come, seen, and been conquered. The wartime capital had been given a face-lift in his honour, and he was quite carried away by the warmth and splendour of Chinese hospitality, Mme. Chiang's insidious charm, and the Generalissimo's air of scholarly wisdom. A visit to the "front" on the Yellow River—on a site well provided with "captured" Japanese weapons and equipment including helmets (all of which, it is said, were moved from place to place to impress distinguished visitors)—had planted a tiny seed of scepticism in him, which he soon swept away as unworthy. It was he who had suggested that Madame would be the perfect ambassador, with her "brains, persuasiveness, and moral force . . . with wit and charm, a generous and understanding heart, a gracious and a beautiful manner and appearance, and a burning conviction". As we have seen, Mme. Chiang took this flattering advice.

There are, then, more ways than one of misleading. Willkie's was the generous and expansive kind, but there were more sinister influences at work. And others, whose motivations were reasonably pure, but who misled nevertheless because they were persuaded that since the Kuomintang was obviously evil, it followed that the Communists must necessarily be good. In February 1941, the Generalissimo had told Lauchlin Currie that he wished the U.S. President would send him a political adviser enjoying Roosevelt's personal confidence. Instead, Currie recommended to President Roosevelt that he should send Owen Lattimore as "political adviser" to the Generalissimo.

Lattimore, a distinguished Sinologist who in later years took a Chair at the University of Leeds, had not met President Roosevelt before his appointment. Nine years later, the former leader of the American Communist Party, Louis F. Budenz, who by then had abandoned Communism, was to testify before the Tydings Committee that Lattimore was at the time an agent of the Communist Party. He would later become one of the leaders of the anti-Chiang group in the American Institute of Pacific Relations. The circumstances of his appointment were given in detail in the Report by the Senate Judiciary Committee, filed in the Senate on 2 July 1952. In fact, after the great build-up of Chiang Kai-shek by leftist writers during the united front period, a vast disinformation operation was in progress in the 1940s. It was not so much a question of vilifying Chiang and the Kuomintang regime: the unfortunate facts spoke for themselves, even without the epithets showered on the Generalissimo's head by the disinformers. Where the disinformation came in was in the idyllic picture painted of the Communist state within the state. The campaign was powerfully furthered, in all liberal innocence, by yet another special envoy of Roosevelt's, Vice-President Henry Wallace. In four long conversations with Wallace from 21 to 24 June, the Generalissimo listened while the Vice-President came out, yet again, with the carefully fostered theory that the Communists were "agrarian democrats", and countered with his habitual lecture on the virulence and orthodoxy of their Marxism-Leninism. When Wallace insisted on visiting Yenan, the Generalissimo at first said no, then changed his mind. On his return, Wallace duly reported that the Communists were indeed "agrarian democrats". He did, however, back Chiang's reiterated request for the recall of Stilwell.

On the military side, Chiang was forced to fight the Japanese again in 1944 because the Japanese resumed their offensive. For China, it was to be the most terrible year of the long conflict. The first attack came, in fact, in November 1943, when the Japanese seized Changteh in northern Hunan after a fifteen-day battle in which the Japanese clinched the issue by poison gas. So severe was the bombardment that only 30 of the city's 10,000 buildings were left. The entire population had fled. Chinese reinforcements arrived within seven days, however, and the Japanese were forced to retreat. But it soon became clear that the offensive was of major importance to Japan. In the Pacific, the war of the islands was going badly for the Japanese. The nightmare that haunted the Japanese high command was the landing of an American expeditionary force on the south China mainland. If this came about, the Americans would get full air support from the string of bases set up by General Chennault's Fourteenth Air Force. It was imperative to gain control of the entire railway from Peking to Canton, thus cutting China in two and isolating Chungking.

Secured from Russian attack both by the Soviet-Japanese neutrality pact and, now, by the gigantic scale of hostilities in European Russia, the Japanese transferred ten divisions from Manchuria to Hunan in March 1944. The Red guerrillas did not trouble to harass them. Indeed, the International Communist Movement chose this time of acute peril for China to cause maximum embarrassment to Chiang's government in China itself and elsewhere. In January, Mao Tse-tung and his colleagues had accepted an invitation to send representatives to a meeting with the Kuomintang to discuss an overall settlement of differences. Mao immediately returned to the theme of a coalition government, demanding equal status for the Communist Party. A month later, American Communists and sympathisers with the Yenan regime launched a propaganda campaign calling on the U.S. Government to put pressure on Chungking to allow an American mission to visit Yenan and to force the lifting of the Nationalist blockade.

In March, Russian planes bombed Sinkiang. On 2 April, the Soviet government accused the Sinkiang authorities of sending troops to Outer Mongolia, and claimed that Nationalist planes had strafed refugees. These fabricated charges were held to justify the Soviet bombing attack. In mid-May, the Russian ambassador to Chungking, Panyushkin, was recalled to Moscow, along with the entire group of Soviet military advisers. By that time, the Chinese Communists and Nationalists had held several meetings at Sian, where their talks had rapidly reached deadlock over Communist insistence on recognition of the autonomy of the Communist-controlled areas and fighting units.

By then, too, the great Japanese offensive was under way. For the attack, the Japanese now had 1,800,000 men. These were not necessarily the best Japanese troops, many of whom were fighting on other fronts; but they were well-equipped, well-led, and fiercely disciplined—more than a match for Chiang's 6,000,000 men, many of them ill-fed, ill-led, ill-equipped, and reluctant.

From Honan province, north of the Yangtze River, the news was of a pitiful and disastrous famine. First news of it had come in February 1943 when the *Ta Kung Pao,* a newspaper that tried against all odds to maintain its independence, carried a full report of the sufferings of the people. For its initiative, it was suspended for three days, and censorship thereafter kept the news out of the press. Theodore White, in his unforgettable eyewitness report, attributes the famine to prolonged drought after the government had commandeered most of the 1942 grain crop for taxes in a bad year. Famine relief was hopelessly inadequate and hampered both by the rivalries of better-off neighbouring provinces and the callousness of local grain hoarders. Probably 2,000,000 or 3,000,000 people had fled the province, and about the same number died of hunger and disease.

In mid-April 1944, 60,000 Japanese troops struck at the Chinese defences in the famine province. One of the Chinese commanders, T'ang En-po, was absent when the attack came and did not get back in time to meet the Japanese onrush. T'ang En-po was one of the most disreputable Kuomintang military men. There is no reason to disbelieve Feng Yü-hsiang, who wrote that all the units under his command were under strength, so that the officers could pocket the pay destined for non-existent soldiers. Moreover, he and his men were heavily involved in trading with the enemy. All of them purchased Japanese goods at Chiehshou on the Honan border and transported them to the interior for sale. On their way back, they brought Chinese goods for sale to the Japanese. These contacts were a gift to the Japanese intelligence service.°

T'ang En-po's absence was only one of a number of instances of criminal negligence in the Nationalist defence of Honan. A Chinese

---

° Throughout the war, Chinese firms did a brisk trade in imported luxury goods in big towns such as Chungking, Chengtu, Kunming, and Kweilin. Wartime profiteers spent their money freely on Swiss watches, British suiting materials, and French cosmetics. It was understood that these goods came from Shanghai via the areas garrisoned by T'ang En-po's troops. T'ang also grew tobacco in Honan to be sold to inland cigarette manufacturers. Commercial travellers frequently went to Shanghai and Kuangchouwan (Fort Baya) on the southern tip of Kwantung to purchase goods, later sold at huge profits in Chungking and other places. What appears to be an odd misconception of T'ang En-po appears in *Japan's Bloody Wars*, by the Japanese writer Ito, who describes a major Japanese defeat at Chihkiang (Hunan), which he attributes to a new army corps under T'ang En-po, which (writes Ito) was even better equipped than General Stilwell's Chinese units. "They were so strong that the Japanese troops were scared." But Nationalist sources make no mention of a victory at Chihkiang; nor do they credit T'ang with a victory. One can only speculate that Ito, writing long after the event, may have relied on contemporary Japanese intelligence reports that later turned out to be erroneous.

headquarters staff was mopped up when the Japanese saw them playing basketball. The Chinese Twelfth and Thirteenth Armies suspended their flight to fight each other. Armed with pitchforks, the local peasants disarmed 50,000 Chinese troops. It took the Japanese three weeks to smash a Chinese army of 300,000 men and seize the railway down to Hankow.

In this hour of disaster, President Roosevelt dealt China a severe blow by draining it of forces badly needed for home defence. He had been badgering the Generalissimo to send 20,000 men of the Y–Force trained and equipped by the United States to north-west Burma, where a Japanese offensive threatened Imphal across the border in India. Twice Chiang Kai-shek turned down the President's request, with pointed references to the Cairo agreements, under which Stilwell was to lead his Chinese and American land forces in an offensive against the Japanese on the North Burma Road, to coincide with a British amphibious landing with 50,000 troops in south Burma, with Rangoon as the main objective. Churchill went along with this idea, but with a visible lack of enthusiasm, on the ground that it was marginal to Britain's strategy. Chiang shared this view for different reasons. He warned the President that he expected the Japanese to mount a large-scale offensive in east China at that time. His reminder of the President's commitments at the Cairo conference was, of course, in order. But in the end, and unaccountably, Chiang agreed to Roosevelt's entreaties and committed himself on 14 April to sending the American-trained troops to Burma.

Within days, Chiang's apprehensions were proved well-founded, when the Japanese launched their well-planned offensive in Hunan in May. Late that month, Changsha fell. Three times before, General Hsueh Yueh ("Little Tiger") had recaptured the city; this time the Japanese drove him out again. In mid-June, the Communists in north Shensi, on the pretext of safeguarding Sian, persuaded the Kuomintang troops to lift their blockade. Thereupon, the Communists attacked the Nationalists from the flank.

Fortunately [writes Chiang Ching-kuo], the Japanese had already been routed at Shouhsiang. . . . At this point, many of our comrades [KMT] behaved most disgustingly. Seeing how the outsiders were mounting a slanderous campaign against our party and leader, they looked on with their arms folded. Some wavering elements even harped on the same tune, serving as the guiding spirit for the tiger.

A string of Japanese victories followed throughout the year, and by late November they controlled Kiangsi province and had deprived the Fourteenth Air Force of its bases at Hengyang, Lingling, Paoching, Tanchuk, Kweilin, and Liuchow. Only the hills of Kweichow now separated the conquerors from Chungking two hundred air miles away.

The only Nationalist stand had been made by Hengyang in southern Hunan, where General Hsueh Yueh, though denied reinforcements (perhaps because he was not a favourite of Chiang's), held out for forty days while heavily outnumbered. Writing of these disasters, Chiang Ching-kuo said: "Father felt great pain at the fall of Kweilin. He wrote in his diary: 'Kweilin had strong fortifications, with food and ammunition in abundance. All telecommunication sets and arms were used there. It collapsed without a single day of fighting—extremely painful for me.'"

There were, however, valid reasons for the fall of Kweilin, and of Liuchow. As the military historian Ch'en Hsiao-wei put it in conversation with Eric Chou, the Chinese military authorities had been taken completely by surprise. All along, they had presumed that the Japanese would be too concerned about the forthcoming American landings on the coast to push farther inland. Most units of the Kwangsi Army were out of the province. Civic leaders and local businessmen had discouraged the garrison forces from fighting around Kweilin for fear that the city might be destroyed. Moreover, the fall of Hengyang after its gallant stand had demoralised the forces responsible for the defence of Kweilin and Liuchow.

Through the disastrous past few months, Chiang had been gathering as many troops as he could for a desperate stand. Some of them had marched on foot from places 2,000 miles away on either bank of the Yellow River; others had been flown in from the Burma front. And now, in December 1944, this Nationalist force stopped the Japanese before the city of Kweichow and drove them back into Kwangsi province. This was the turning-point of the long war.

Intent on the fighting, Chiang Kai-shek was oblivious to the tragic realities of China. Was he ignorant because the facts were not brought to his notice, or because his sublime self-confidence automatically discounted whatever news might call for caution? It is hard to say, and doubtless both elements were at work. Himself uncorrupt—unless the corruption of power be counted—but lacking for nothing, he had surrounded himself with yes men because he could brook no opposition, preferred flattery to the truth, and disliked facts that discorded with his optimism. In Chungking, before the return to the national capital, it was widely believed that his aides regularly faked newspaper editorials and reports to reassure him that all was well. Nobody told him of rocketing commodity prices, food shortages, and the daily miseries of ordinary people. Junior civil servants, professors, teachers, and students were all on the starvation line. These educated members of the Chinese middle class were as willing to accept wartime sacrifices as more humble people, but the flagrant enrichment of those in power and those around them caused understandable resentment. The privileges were for high Kuomintang officials, for those with the right connections, and for war profiteers. The intellectuals, in particular, supported the Democratic League. They were not necessarily pro-Communist, but they detested the degenerate body the Kuomintang had become. The secret service agents could do no wrong, and arrested political suspects on flimsy evidence or at their whim. Indeed, the "secrecy" of these agents was a fiction, for they tended to reveal their identities to cast fear around them.

Yet something of the mounting chaos and dissatisfaction must have reached even the insulated ears of the Generalissimo—or it could have been a desire on his part to please the Americans—for towards the end of 1944, he made a number of changes in the interests of efficiency. The corrupt and inefficient H. H. K'ung went, at last, and his brother-in-law T. V. Soong, who held him in deep contempt, was brought in as President of the Executive Yüan. His departure from the Foreign Ministry created a vacancy which Chiang filled in the person of the modest, moderate, and hard-working Wang Shih-chieh. Even the entrenched General Ho Ying-ch'in, who on the military side competed with K'ung in the self-seeking disorder he created around him, was pushed to one side. His successor as War Minister was the able and energetic General Ch'en Ch'eng; General Ho was not, however, deprived of all power to keep the effectiveness of the army as low as he could make it, for he remained Chief of Staff.

Once Soong was back in high office, the Generalissimo could hardly ignore what went on out of sight, for his brother-in-law,

Harvard-educated, burly, and outspoken, was one of the few men in China not afraid to speak his mind in the presence of the man at the top.

But it made no difference. As Chiang Kai-shek had explained to General Marshall, China's agrarian economy was unaffected by the ordinary laws of economics. K'ung had printed money because that was the handiest way of keeping the affairs of state moving, at least for a while. For all his drive and bustling efficiency, Soong was powerless against the central fact that the Generalissimo was bent on further hostilities, which progressively ate up more and more of the national budget, reaching 80 percent in 1947. So T. V. Soong also printed money.

In Burma, while the battle for Kweichow was in progress, Stilwell had had brilliant, though hard-won, successes against the Japanese, the credit for which mostly went to his Chinese forces. By late January 1945, the Ledo Road in north-west Burma had been linked with portions of the old Burma Road running into Kunming. At last, the long Japanese blockade was broken, and on 28 January the first land convoy of 500 lorries reached China. With a sense of historic justice, Chiang renamed the highway the Stilwell Road.

General Stilwell, however, was not there to enjoy this late triumph. His long quarrel with the Generalissimo had come to a head in the summer of 1944. The mounting drama was reflected in President Roosevelt's cables to Chiang Kai-shek. For some time, it had become apparent to the President that his exchanges with the Generalissimo were a dialogue of the deaf. This was because T. V. Soong—frank though he was about current Chinese affairs—thought it prudent, for his own foreign policy reasons, not to expose Chiang to the undiluted complaints of the White House and invariably intercepted Roosevelt's cables, deleting passages likely to offend the Generalissimo in the Chinese translation. Through his protector, General Marshall, Stilwell had returned to an old theme, hinting that the only way to bring China fully into the war would be for him (Stilwell) to take over from Chiang as Supreme Commander of all Chinese and American forces in China. In July 1944, Marshall recommended this proposal to Roosevelt, who cabled Chiang on the 6th to say that in his view Stilwell was the "one individual of the power to co-ordinate all of the Allied military resources in China, including the Communist forces". To make sure the message was not distorted, it was delivered in person by the senior American officer in Chungking, General Ferris, with the embassy's first secretary, John Service—whose anti-Chiang views were well-known—to go along as translator. The message was blunt, but Chiang read it imperturbably with his usual smile. To everybody's surprise, he replied two days later on an amenable note. However, he requested an intermediary with "full power" who could adjust relations between him and Stilwell. And as a hint of displeasure, he suggested that any future messages from the President should be entrusted to Dr. K'ung.

President Roosevelt was delighted, but some of his advisers thought it was too good to be true, and they were right. On 23 July, the Generalissimo followed up with three previously unstated conditions: the Communists could of course come under Stilwell's command, he said, but only when they accepted the authority of the Central Government; there was to be no further ambiguity about Stilwell's relations with him; and the Chinese government should have full authority over Lend-Lease. To confuse the issue still further, he instructed Dr. K'ung in Washington to say that when he referred to Chinese forces, he meant only those already under Stilwell's command in Burma.

Confused, the President thought that at least he could meet Chiang's position on one point: the appointment of a high-powered intermediary. His choice was Brigadier-General Patrick Hurley, a big, expansive Oklahoman whose carefully trimmed moustache bristled with self-confidence. The high point in his career hitherto had been as President Hoover's Secretary of War. As an afterthought, the President decided that Hurley should be accompanied by Donald Nelson, a businessman who had lately been chairman of the War Production Board. Nelson's special mission was to study China's economy. He, too, was a large, self-confident man, and the two of them arrived in Chungking, via Moscow, on 6 September.

By the time Hurley arrived, it was too late even to attempt to heal the breach between Chiang and Stilwell. Although "Vinegar Joe" was worshipped by his troops and junior officers, the Chinese generals resented his abrupt manner and air of arrogance. They would have preferred him not to notice the inadequacies of the military bureaucracy, or to keep his opinion of it to himself. In self-defence, even rivals in the military hierarchy, such as Ho Ying-ch'in and Ch'en Ch'eng, would gang up to denigrate Stilwell in front of the Generalissimo.

There was a further cause of misunderstanding in Chiang's Chekiang dialect. Stilwell spoke Chinese and scorned an interpreter. But even other Chinese—except from his own region—found Chiang hard to understand. When he said "hao, hao", what he meant was: "I see, I see." In Mandarin, however, this means: "Good, good." If this was the way Stilwell understood it, it would help to account for his accusations that Chiang was always "backing out of his promises".

There are other tales of the misunderstandings caused by Chiang's Chekiang accent. One of the best concerns Ho Hao-jo, Director of the Liaison Office of the Military Council, who was summoned to the Generalissimo's office in 1943 or 1944 and found himself at the receiving end of a rebuke. He defended himself as best he could, but turned pale when Chiang shouted: "Ch'iang pi!" which means "execution" in Mandarin. Trembling with fear, Ho went home to bid farewell to his family and friends. Days later, he was still alive. He regained enough composure to approach one of Chiang's bodyguards and find out what was happening. The news was comforting, but made him look ridiculous. For what Chiang had shouted in his heavy accent was: "Ch'iang pien!" (contrived argument). In this instance, misunderstanding had been mutual, for Ho was a Hunanese (like Mao Tse-tung) with a strong accent of his own, making his speech barely intelligible to Chiang Kai-shek. The story made the rounds of the cocktail circuit, and Ho found himself a laughingstock.

Apart from his accent, Chiang had another way of hindering communication: his habit of nodding his head even when he disagreed with the person he was talking to. This was Chiang's personal habit rather than a Chinese trait, and it may have added to the confusion in his dealings with Stilwell. But the last straw (according to Hu Lin of the newspaper Ta Kung Pao) was Stilwell's suggestion that Communist troops should be used to fight the Japanese, with the proviso that they should get American arms and ammunition. Although Stilwell was "correct" in declining to meet Chou En-lai, his American advisers were in close touch with Chou's assistants. (The part these American advisers played in the formation of American policy for China is dealt with later in this chapter.) Since the fact that Stilwell's political advisers were strongly in favour of Yenan, it would have been almost impossible—even if other reasons had not existed—for Stilwell to win the Generalissimo's confidence.

Hard-pressed on the military front in September 1944, Chiang politely requested Stilwell to divert some of the Chinese forces under his command to defend Lung Ling, a town in Yunnan astride the Burma Road and under pressure from the Japanese. Unnecessarily—since Chiang has respected the conventions by "requesting" not "ordering" the transfer of troops—Stilwell turned down the request, and in a rage, cabled Marshall demanding that a strong message should be sent to Chiang to bring him to heel. Marshall himself dictated the message, which went out under Roosevelt's signature on the 16th. The message went straight to Stilwell, who read it with relish. In harsh terms, it called for the appointment of Stilwell "in unrestricted command of all . . . forces", under a scarcely veiled threat that the United States might be forced to withdraw its support from Chiang Kai-shek. To enjoy his triumph and his enemy's discomfiture, Stilwell decided to deliver the message in person. Before entering the conference room, he showed it to Hurley, who advised him to soften the wording. But this was just what Stilwell did not want to do. He went into the presence and delivered the unexpurgated Chinese translation; then was deprived of his hour of triumph by the Generalissimo's total composure as he read it. He knew, however, that the blow had struck home, and in typically crude language recorded his thoughts in his diary. He had "handed this bundle of paprika to the Peanut". And he added: "The harpoon hit the little bugger right in the solar plexus and went right through him." Having declared the audience at an end, the Generalissimo duly exploded into the kind of monumental rage his entourage had often witnessed.

Chiang called in T. V. Soong for advice. The problem now was to get rid of Stilwell while retaining Lend-Lease. On 25 September, having decided to call Roosevelt's bluff, Chiang cabled the President to demand that Stilwell should be recalled and replaced. By now, Roosevelt realised that there was no point in keeping Stilwell in Chungking, where his usefulness was obviously at an end, but wanted to continue to use his military talents in East Asia. His compromise reaction was to reply on 5 October, agreeing that Stilwell should be replaced as Chiang's Chief of Staff, but proposing to keep him in Burma for the duration of the campaign.

Chiang wasn't going to let the President get away with that and on the 9th replied with a lengthy analysis of military developments since the Cairo conference, pointing out—correctly—that by sending his American-trained troops to Burma he had left himself dangerously short of men to resist the Japanese offensive in East China, of which he had given clear warning. Stilwell, he went on, had shown "complete indifference to the outcome in East China", and had refused to release Lend-Lease munitions for use there. "In short, we have taken Myitkyina, but we have lost all of East China." Since it was under intense pressure from Roosevelt that Chiang had agreed to send part of the Y–force to Burma, his message was an indirect criticism of the President as well as of the General.

This time, the President "got the message". Stilwell was recalled on the 18th. Before he left, the Generalissimo offered him the Special Grand Cordon of the Blue Sky and White Sun—the highest Chinese order on offer to a foreigner. Predictably, Stilwell turned it down, but he steeled himself to accept an invitation to a farewell tea which followed. The Generalissimo was graciously voluble; Stilwell, sourly silent. On the 27th, "Vinegar Joe" flew off, never to return to China.

With the departure of Stilwell in September 1944 and of Ambassador Gauss in November, the first phase of Sino-American misunderstanding ended. With the arrival of their successors, the second phase began—no less profound but subtly different in character. Stilwell had seen through Chiang Kai-shek's military pretensions, and Gauss through the democratic claims of his government. It is hard not to sympathise with "Vinegar Joe" in the frustrations imposed upon him by Chiang's refusal to take the offensive against the Japanese, but he was a man of narrow perspectives and no political awareness. It was foolish of him to nurse the illusion that—with Chiang still in power—he could ever hope to be in supreme command of all the Chinese as well as the American forces in China.

Both the General and Ambassador were heavily influenced by career Foreign Service advisers whose misapprehensions about the nature of Chinese Communism they accepted uncritically. Stilwell himself had requested the appointment of career man John Payton Davies, Jr., as "liaison agent for the duration of this mission". Davies was born in China of Protestant missionary parents. Of similar background was John Stewart Service, who arrived in China on the embassy staff in July 1944. Other career diplomats in China at that time held similar views, and their reports to the State Department were endorsed by their superior on the "China desk", John Carter Vincent. These names achieved brief fame—or notoriety—in the prolonged investigations to which their bearers were submitted during the "McCarthy era" in the 1950s. Their cases became a collective *cause célèbre* and their careers were broken. A reading of their despatches from Chungking many years after the events described does not provide proof that they were, in any conscious sense, agents of international communism. It is undeniable, however, that their reporting from China strongly and in the end decisively influenced the United States Government away from Chiang's regime (which it was official American policy to support) and towards Mao Tse-tung's Communist Party. But if they were not "Communist agents", this was not true of other American advisers who had the ear of the President or of the Secretary of State during those crucial years. An interesting instance was Miss Josephine Truslow Adams, who had access to President Roosevelt although at the time she was working closely with the leader of the American Communist Party, Earl Browder.°

In fact, the main themes pressed by the American embassy in Chungking under Clarence Gauss were both realistic and prescient.

° Despatches from Ambassador Gauss and named members of his staff are reproduced in the famous and bulky "White Paper", *United States Relations with China* (Department of State, 1949). In 1945, many of these despatches, together with a large number of classified documents, were made available to the pro-Communist magazine *Amerasia*, published monthly in New York. The *Amerasia* case, too, became a *cause célèbre*. Its editor, Philip Jacob Jaffe, who also edited the English translation of Chiang Kai-shek's *China's Destiny* quoted in these pages, was at the time teaching at the official academy of the American Communist Party, the Jefferson School of Social Science in New York. For a scholarly but hostile account, see Anthony Kubek, *Introduction to the* Amerasia *Papers: A Clue to the Catastrophe of China* (Washington, D.C.: The Committee of One Million Against the Admission of Communist China to the United Nations, 1970). For the personal story of a Foreign Service officer of that period, who was cleared after a lengthy investigation by the State Department's Loyalty Security Board, see O. Edmund Clubb, *The Witness and I* (New York, 1975).

The despatches rightly pointed out that Soviet intentions in the Far East were aggressive; that the Chinese Communists had been subservient to the U.S.S.R., but that nationalism was modifying their outlook; that the Kuomintang and National Government were disintegrating; that there would probably be a civil war, which the Communists would inevitably win. In March 1945, however, John Service visited Yenan, and his reports powerfully argued the case for a switch of United States' policy to all-out support for the Communist Party.

Ambassador Gauss resigned on 1 November 1944, and General Hurley, who had been in China since August as the President's personal representative, succeeded him on 8 January 1945. After Stilwell's departure, his command was divided into two sections: General Daniel Sultan took over the Burma–India theatre and General Albert Wedemeyer took command of the China theatre. Hurley and Wedemeyer stood in startling contrast to the men they had succeeded. Hurley, the hearty extrovert, had no time for the diplomatic subtleties of the career man, Clarence Gauss. Wedemeyer, with his undoubted intelligence and air of distinction, was as diplomatic as Stilwell had been tactless. Both men were determinedly anti-Communist, and as determined to support Chiang Kai-shek in the interests, as they saw it, of the United States. Both men, however, were saddled with the requirement to work towards a reconciliation between the Communists and the Nationalists—an objective that was ruled out by the Generalissimo's intransigence.

Hurley was immediately at loggerheads with his entire diplomatic staff, who were reporting things—hostile to Chungking and favourable to Yenan—with which he disagreed and did not wish them to report. Wedemeyer, too, was in disharmony with his political adviser, Davies, whom he had inherited from Stilwell; but less irritated by his advice than Hurley was with the work of his own staff. But he, too, in the end, was no less frustrated than the new ambassador, when he discovered as others did that it was impossible to bring the two sides together in China.

The Generalissimo was delighted with both appointments. On his appointment as ambassador, General Hurley had made it clear—both to the State Department and to anybody he met in Chungking—that his mission comprised the following objectives:

1. To prevent the collapse of the National Government.

2. To sustain Chiang Kai-shek as President of the Republic and Generalissimo of the Armies.
3. To harmonise relations between the Generalissimo and the American commander.
4. To promote production of war supplies in China and prevent economic collapse.
5. To unify all the military forces in China for the purpose of defeating Japan.

It was not immediately apparent to him that the fifth of these objectives was incompatible with the first three. He was soon to learn the hard way. His initial over-confidence had been based partly upon a naturally sanguine temperament and partly on his exchanges with Stalin and Molotov in Moscow on his way to China, in which the Russians had assured him that they had lost all interest in the Chinese Communists and wished to improve their relations with Chungking. A first attempt on his part to bring the Communist and Nationalist armies together failed, but on instructions from President Roosevelt, he made a more determined attempt early in November 1944, when he flew to Yenan for a conference with the Communist leadership. With the pride of instant achievement, he flew back to Chungking on 10 November with a five-point proposal calling mainly for the creation of a coalition government in which the Communists would serve. He was discomfited to learn that Chiang was not interested in a plan that would deprive the Kuomintang of its monopoly of power. On 22 November, he approved a three-point counter-proposal, agreeing to recognise the Chinese Communist Party as a legal party and to incorporate the Communist forces in the National Army. But there would be no coalition.

For the Communists, Chou En-lai initially accepted Chiang's counter-proposals, but on 8 December—when he was about to leave Chungking for Yenan—he suddenly reversed his stand and declared them unacceptable. In a telegram from Yenan on the 28th, he called for the release of all political prisoners, withdrawal of National forces surrounding Communist areas, the abrogation of all oppressive regulations, and an end to all secret police activity.

This sudden change of attitude worried and disappointed Hurley, though not the Generalissimo. Hurley soon discovered, however, that the American Office of Strategic Services (the wartime forerunner of the Central Intelligence Agency) had secretly offered to provide complete equipment for up to 25,000 Communist guerrillas for disruptive action behind the Japanese lines in North China. Thus favoured, the Communists no longer felt any great incentive to negotiate with Chiang Kai-shek. When Hurley and Wedemeyer found out what had been happening behind their backs, they made it clear to the Communists that their government would not deal with them at the expense of Chungking. Apparently seeing the light, Chou En-lai returned to the national capital on 24 January 1945 for another round of talks.

There seemed no easy way of bridging the chasm between the two sides. Chou kept on insisting on a coalition government, after which they would turn over their forces; while Chiang wanted the Communists to dissolve their military organisation first, before any talk of a coalition. Since Chou showed no signs of yielding, the Generalissimo now made it known that he would call a meeting on 4 May, in line with the Will of Sun Yat-sen, to start drafting a constitution, to abolish one-party rule, and to establish constitutional government. Suddenly afraid that his party would be left out of this momentous process, Chou En-lai thereupon put on his conciliatory face, and on 3 February a joint proposal was published, to convene a Political Consultative Conference—in lieu of a constitutional congress—to pave the way for constitutional government, to draw up a common programme and plan for military unification, and to determine ways for parties other than the Kuomintang to join the government.

At this precise moment, however, a still more momentous meeting was in progress thousands of miles away in Soviet Crimea. The last of the wartime summit meetings, which was to shape the post-war world, began at Yalta on 4 February and ended a week later. Exhausted, cadaverous, and literally moribund, President Roosevelt signed away China's territorial rights and handed Eastern Europe to Stalin, while Churchill watched and listened impotently. Under secret clauses disclosed exactly a year later, Stalin agreed to enter the war against Japan "two or three months after Germany has surrendered and the war in Europe has terminated". In return, the Soviet Union would get the Kurile Islands, hegemony over Outer Mongolia, South Sakhalin and neighbouring islands, and control over port and rail facilities in Manchuria. It was understood that the provisions affecting Outer Mongolia and Manchuria would require Chiang Kai-shek's "concurrence", which, however, President Roosevelt undertook to obtain.

The master-stroke on Stalin's part was his "readiness to conclude with the National Government of China a pact of friendship and alliance . . . to render assistance to China with its armed forces for the purpose of liberating China from the Japanese yoke". At a stroke, the Soviet dictator had achieved the traditional objectives of Imperial Russia—territorial aggrandisement in the Far East, the crippling of Japan, and the debilitation of China. Clearly, the provisions of Yalta—even more than those of Teheran—were in direct contradiction to the solemn pledges Roosevelt had committed himself to at the Cairo summit. One of the great purposes of the Nationalist Revolution of 1911 had been the passionate wish to end China's international humiliations. Chiang Kai-shek himself had entered the war, by resisting Japan in 1937, with the overriding objective of restoring China's territorial integrity. At Yalta, President Roosevelt, who had been China's guarantor, gave away all that he had pledged himself to support.

Yet at the time of Yalta, the great American air offensive against Japan was about to begin; the atomic bomb was about to go into production, and it was clear to the military commanders that the Japanese could now be defeated without Soviet help. But there was more: not only was the Generalissimo not consulted, but Stalin had extracted from Roosevelt a promise that he was not, for the time being, to be told. Asked when that time would come, Stalin replied: "When it was possible to free a number of Soviet troops in the West and move twenty-five divisions to the Far East . . . it would be possible to speak to Marshal Chiang Kai-shek about these matters."

So deep was the secret that the American Secretary of State, James F. Byrnes, later admitted that he did not become aware of the Far East provisions of Yalta—although he was present at the conference—until seven months later. On 2 March 1945, reporting to Congress on the Yalta conference, Roosevelt blandly declared: "Quite naturally, this conference concerned itself only with the European war and with the political problems of Europe, and not with the Pacific war."

Despite these precautions, rumours of a deal at his expense quickly reached Chiang Kai-shek. Greatly disturbed, Ambassador Hurley left Chungking for Washington on 19 February, about a week after the Yalta conference had dispersed. In the White House, the President showed Hurley the text of the Yalta agreement. Hurley was still in Washington on 6 March when Chiang's Foreign Minister, T. V. Soong, cabled him to request a meeting with the President. The reply was that there was no time for a useful meeting before the proposed San Francisco conference, which was scheduled to open on 25 April to set up the United Nations organisation. By this time, fairly precise intelligence reports on Yalta had reached Chiang Kai-shek, and on 10 March Soong sent another cable, this time to Roosevelt's personal assistant, Harry Hopkins. The cable to Hurley had made no mention of Yalta. The one to Hopkins spelled it out. Soong said he proposed to come as Acting Prime Minister and not as Foreign Minister:

> The President has already seen the Prime Ministers and the Foreign Ministers of the Big Three at Yalta. Since China was not present, I know it will help our war effort here and the future relations of the four sponsors of the San Francisco conference if I come now. . . . China's situation is one of desperate crisis. . . . We feel that never has it been so important that we obtain the President's advice now about our joint strategy, and this includes our relations with Soviet Russia, the Communists and plans we have for dealing as best we can with our desperate economic problems.

Soong's cable went unanswered, and his visit was deferred until after the San Francisco conference. Before that—on 12 April—Franklin D. Roosevelt died.

Chiang Kai-shek could now see the situation and his problems with extraordinary clarity. His mind was entirely concentrated on the post-war struggle for power in China. The end, he sensed, was near. To accept the Communist demands for a coalition government now—whatever the pressure from the Americans—would be disastrous, for it would amount to conceding defeat without a struggle. He had to gain time—enough time to be in a winning position after hostilities had ceased. Yet he had to reassure the Americans, who kept on complaining that his regime was undemocratic and who were showing such deplorable tendencies towards supporting his arch-enemies, the Communists. For some time now, the Generalissimo had been relatively inactive, presiding over the sloth and inefficiency of his regime. Now he showed that he had lost none of his political skill and power of swift decision. On 1 March, he announced that a National Assembly would meet on 12 November 1945 to begin the inauguration of constitutional government. Once inaugurated, there would be equality for all political parties. Even before that, the Chinese Communists and other parties could take part in the government, but the final power of decision and responsibility would still rest with the National Government.

Chiang thought in terms of territory and power. Once the Japanese had gone, most of China's national territory would be, at least nominally, under Kuomintang control. By retaining control over the government, he would thus be in a position to organise local administrations and therefore control the selection of delegates to the National Assembly.

Mao Tse-tung and his colleagues saw through this device, of course, and on 9 March condemned the whole programme as a "deceitful, China-splitting" device. The trouble-shooter, Chou En-lai, broke off the talks which Hurley had been sponsoring.

The Communists, however, could not entirely dissociate themselves from the political processes suggested by Chiang Kai-shek. But first, they had to decide on their policy in the crucial period ahead. On 23 April the Seventh Congress of the Chinese Communist Party met in Yenan under Mao's chairmanship, and remained in session until 11 June. The party now declared itself ready to re-open negotiations with the Kuomintang, and even to take part in the political process, with reservations, on Chiang's terms. Indeed, Mao now accepted the plan to convene a National Assembly. Until the Assembly could meet, however, he proposed Communist participation in a provisional coalition government.

With an eye to Chinese and world opinion, Mao publicly claimed that the Chinese Communist Party now controlled "liberated areas" with a population of more than 95,000,000. He went on to claim that in those liberated areas, "local coalition governments have been or are being elected by the people". This sop to democratic sentiment in the West was no more truthful than his claim to control 95,000,000 people. The best estimates are that no more than 35,000,000 people were at that time in any sense controlled by the Chinese Communist Party. Mao also claimed that his Red Army now totalled 910,000 men, plus a militia of 2,200,000. But these figures, too, were undoubtedly exaggerated. Chiang's own estimate was that the Communists had 300,000 men under arms;

American intelligence estimates placed the Communist strength at 475,000 men, with 207,000 rifles.

While the Communist Congress was still meeting, the Kuomintang convened its own Sixth Congress, which met on 5 May and remained in session until the 21st. Not unexpectedly, Chiang Kai-shek was re-elected *Tsung-ts'ai* of the party. The date of 12 November was confirmed for the opening of the National Assembly. Some important concessions to the Communists were made, however: laws were passed to give legal status to all political parties. The important question of membership of the National Assembly was to be decided by the People's Political Conference, "on which it is anticipated that all parties will be represented". On 1 July, a delegation of Kuomintang members and representatives of the Democratic League flew to Yenan. The reply they brought back from the Communists was, however, unsatisfactory to Chiang Kai-shek. Mao proposed that the National Assembly should be deferred and that all major political parties in China should meet to discuss the formation of a provisional coalition government. The deadlock continued.

Chiang Kai-shek's next problem was to salvage something from the wreckage of his international hopes. President Truman, who had succeeded Roosevelt, sent Harry Hopkins—himself a dying man—to Moscow on 26 May. Stalin told him the Russians would be ready to begin operations in China on 8 August. But they would not do so until a treaty had been concluded between China and the Soviet Union. He declared his support for Chiang Kai-shek as the only man qualified to lead China; as for territorial ambitions, he had none either in Manchuria or Sinkiang. He was even prepared to allow Kuomintang representatives to organise local governments in areas of Manchuria occupied by the Soviet forces. On 15 June, Hurley called on Chiang and formally reported to him on the Yalta agreements. His revelation that the United States was committed to supporting the Russians in Manchuria at China's expense visibly shook the Generalissimo. But he remained calm, and proposed that America and Britain should be party to any Sino-Soviet agreement, that the Port Arthur Naval Base should be at the joint disposal of all four powers, and that America and Britain should join Russia and China in the discussions on the transfer of Sakhalin and the Kuriles to the Soviet Union. The content of Hurley's reply—if not the manner—was freezing. The United States' government stood by the Yalta agreement. None of Chiang's proposals was acceptable.

Chiang now summoned T. V. Soong, briefed him, and sent him to Moscow, where he arrived in late June. Reflecting the Generalissimo's stand, and despite China's weakness, the Foreign Minister was in no mood for concessions. A week of talks with Stalin and Molotov left the two parties as far apart as at the beginning. On 14 July, Stalin left for the Potsdam conference, and Soong went back to Chungking. Less inclined towards conciliation than Roosevelt, Truman sought to give America a voice in Manchuria and called on Stalin to agree that Dairen (Port Arthur) should be a "free port". When Chiang learned of these exchanges, he was comforted at this evidence that Truman was disposed to meet some of his proposals, which Hurley had rejected outright.

On 7 August, T. V. Soong led a new Chinese delegation to Moscow. This time, he went as Prime Minister, accompanied by the new Foreign Minister, Dr. Wang Shih-chieh. Events were now moving rapidly. The day before, on 6 August, an American atomic bomb had been dropped on Hiroshima. And on the 8th, the Soviet Union declared war on Japan. Two days later, the second bomb fell on Nagasaki. In the belief that Truman was with them, Soong and Wang initially stood firm. In Taipei, nearly thirty years after these events, Wang Shih-chieh told me that he had asked Stalin for a specific pledge. Stalin replied with two questions: "What do you want me to do? To fight against Mao?" Wang had countered that all he required of the Russians was that they should pledge themselves not to provide political or material aid to the Chinese Communists. All such assistance should be reserved for the legal government of the Republic of China. Stalin agreed. But at the last minute, T. V. Soong declined to sign the new treaty, the draft of which had been prepared by Molotov. Dr. Wang, feeling he had no choice in the matter, signed on the dotted line.

It was a harsh treaty for China. The Chinese agreed to allow the Soviet Union to use Port Arthur as a naval base, to declare Dairen a free port, to allow the status of Outer Mongolia to be determined by a plebiscite (which, however, the Russians would police), and to joint Sino-Soviet ownership of the Chinese Changchun Railway in Manchuria. In turn, Stalin made some unenforceable pledges: to recognise the National Government as the legitimate government of China, and to refrain from interference in its internal affairs.

Belatedly—and in fact too late—Truman decided to make a military bid to pre-empt Soviet control of Manchuria. On 11 August he instructed the Joint Chiefs of Staff to arrange for American occupation of Dairen and Seoul in Korea "immediately following the surrender of Japan if those ports have not at that time been taken over by Soviet forces". But the order was cancelled within a week, for the Soviet forces had won the race for Dairen and were irremoveably in control of Manchuria.

The Japanese cabinet had offered to surrender while the Sino-Soviet talks were still in progress in Moscow. The offer was accepted on 14 August—the day the Sino-Soviet treaty was signed —and on 2 September the instrument of surrender was signed on board the USS *Missouri* in Tokyo Bay.

For China, one war was over, and another was about to begin.

19. | The Marshall Mission Fails

The collapse of Japan was so swift that it found Chiang Kai-shek and his government totally unprepared. A story recounted by Eric Chou illustrates the point. In August 1945, he was personal secretary to the Mayor of Tientsin, Hsiao Cheng-ying. On the 15th, Hsiao was playing mahjong in his country residence, with the then Nationalist Chief-of-Staff, General Ch'eng Ch'ien, and two other men, when the telephone rang. The call came from the Generalissimo's residence, and the speaker asked for the Chief-of-Staff. Ch'eng Ch'ien rose from the mahjong table, grumbling about the interruption of the game. The others listened, trying to guess the tenor of the conversation from Ch'eng Ch'ien's responses. But all he said was yes, repeatedly. After replacing the receiver, he turned round and burst out: "It was him, all right. Why did the —— Japs have to surrender today? Now I have to go and take part in the victory parade, just when I was getting interested in our mahjong game."

The others chimed in: "You're right, victory has come too soon. We haven't made any preparations at all yet."

More excited than the rest, Hsiao Cheng-ying declared: "Mark my words, the biggest headache is going to be the takeover of the north-east."

He was referring to Manchuria, and indeed during the next few days, his country home was crowded with Manchurian politicians. Except for Hsiao Cheng-ying himself, there was general agreement that the Young Marshal should be released and appointed overlord of Manchuria. For them, the key argument was that nobody else could command as much support in Manchuria as Chang Hsueh-liang.

But they had counted without Chiang Kai-shek's life-long vindictiveness towards the man who had "rebelled" against him and—worse—kidnapped and humiliated him.

Having decided not to release Chang Hsueh-liang—or rather, refusing even to discuss the idea—the Generalissimo was faced with the awkward fact that there were virtually no north-eastern politicians of calibre and renown who were also personally loyal to him. As there was no obvious "overlord", Chiang decided to divide and rule. In fact, he re-divided the three original Manchurian provinces into nine, with Harbin and Changchun as special municipalities under the direct control of the Executive Yüan. He had thus created "vacancies" for nine provincial governors, which he filled with minor north-eastern politicians with CC clique connections, but virtually unknown to their fellow-Manchurians. Not only was the Young Marshal neither released nor given a job, but not one of his former associates was allowed to return to his native province, even in an unofficial capacity. (Out of the blue, Eric Chou—who is Manchurian-born—was approached by the new Mayor of Harbin, Yang Cho-an, whom he had not previously met, but who offered him a job as his principal secretary. He declined politely. Yang, too, was a faithful KMT man—a member of the Political Science Group.)

An overlord was still needed, and Chiang appointed another Political Science Group man, Hsiung Shih-hui, as High Commissioner for the Nine North-eastern Provinces—to the dismay of the CC and Whampoa cliques. On Hsiung's recommendation, the Generalissimo appointed his son Ching-kuo as Special Commissioner for Foreign Affairs, with the specific task of dealing with the Soviet occupation authorities.

Some weeks later, Chiang Kai-shek invited the veteran journalist Hu Lin to an off-the-record talk in Chungking, to seek his advice about post-war rehabilitation and reconstruction. Hu Lin's recommendations (as he outlined them later to Eric Chou) are seen in retrospect to have been eminently sensible; but the Generalissimo ignored them all. His suggestions were these:

1. Remove the National capital to Peiping and rename it Peking. The object would have been to attract support for the KMT from the people north of the Yellow River. Since the party had chosen Nanking as the National capital, northerners had felt that they were left out of the political mainstream and had become second-class citizens.
2. Either negotiate seriously with the Communists, or openly proclaim that they were going to be fought, and ignore advice from the U.S. Government.
3. The take-over of areas evacuated by the Japanese should be conducted with fairness and compassion. There should be no witch-hunt, for most collaborators had been unwilling supporters of the puppet regime, most of whom had been left behind unprotected by the Nationalists as they retreated in haste in the face of the Japanese advance.
4. Special care should be paid to Manchuria, since it had been under Japanese occupation for more than fifteen years—since 1931.
5. Introduce rural reforms in country areas evacuated by the Japanese.
6. Give high priority to the problem of re-educating young people in the evacuated areas.

Unfortunately for his country and for his own future, Chiang Kai-shek was insensitive to such enlightened advice. Just as the Young Marshal could not be released because he had been a "rebel", so nobody who had served under the Japanese, or even merely lived under Japanese occupation, could be given the benefit of the Generalissimo's doubt.

The people had thought that they were being liberated; they

soon discovered that they had exchanged one set of conquerors for another. No thought of compassion or rehabilitation inhabited the minds of the officials sent from Chungking immediately after Japan's surrender to take over the administration of Nanking, Shanghai, Peiping, and Tientsin. The conquering liberators descended on them like locusts. Everything was for confiscation: gold, houses, cars, women. On their lips, the word "Chungking" meant: "Open, sesame", giving them rights without limit. Collaborators were rounded up and thrown into gaol, but only after bribes in cash or kind had been extorted from them as a guarantee of freedom from arrest. The friends and relatives of true collaborators—that is, those who had actually worked for Wang Ching-wei's regime— were marginally luckier. They, too, had to pay up but in their case the bribes usually worked, and they stayed out of gaol.

Nor were the Chungking officials alone in doing well out of the take-over. One British official flew between Chungking and Shanghai once a week, bearing cases of Chinese National currency to Shanghai for exchange against foreign bank notes *at the official rate*. After several trips, he resigned his official post, having (it is alleged) made a profit of about U.S.$100,000. In his capacity as an "Allied" official, he also took possession of two attractive houses in the former French Concession in Shanghai. On leaving for a comfortable retirement in Hong Kong, he is said to have parted with the houses for a substantial sum in "key money".

Then there was Liu Tsun-ch'i (later Peking's Director of International Propaganda), who at that time worked for the U.S. Information Service. In the name of USIS, he is reported to have approached the Administration of Enemy Properties—a branch of the "take-over" organisation—and obtained vacant possession of twelve houses in a lane off Diswell Road in the Honkew district, which had been occupied by Japanese residents in Shanghai. Normally, each of these British-styled, three-storey houses, with gardens and verandahs, would have fetched 200 ounces of gold as "key money". Liu got them for nothing. He picked the best one for his own use, and allowed his left-wing friends to take the others.

In the eyes of the Shanghai people, the British official and Liu Tsun-ch'i were "officials from Chungking". At that time, a little ditty went the rounds, and even small children sang it:

We've been expecting the Central Government,
We've been longing for the Central Government.
But once they come, they are worse than the plague.

Manchuria's turn came later. When the Han Chinese moved in in the wake of the Russian looters, they stripped the workshops of their tools and the hospitals of their equipment, much of which turned up later on the stalls of street vendors. Homes and office buildings were deprived of roof tiles, panelling, and plumbing. As in Manchuria, so in Formosa (Taiwan), the most prosperous colony of the Japanese empire, which the Kuomintang hordes looted for their private benefit. In all these places, the behaviour of the KMT officials and officers shocked and alienated the local population. The words "Central Government" became a term of contempt on the lips of ordinary people. After a while, those working for the government became reluctant to mention the fact.

Chiang Kai-shek was ignorant of all these excesses. On the morrow of Japan's surrender, his mind was on higher politics—especially on the need to retain American support while keeping the Chinese Communists at arm's length. The problem was that the Americans wanted him to embrace his deadly foes. Well, then, he would go some way to meet their wishes. For eighteen years, he had not met the man who—more than any other apart from himself—held China's fate in his hands. And now, on 28 August 1945, Chiang Kai-shek and Mao Tse-tung shook hands in Chungking. Pressed by the State Department, the Generalissimo had invited Mao three times in quick succession after V–J Day. At first, Mao, fearing for his personal safety, had been reluctant to come, but he agreed to make the journey if Hurley came to fetch him and personally guaranteed his security.

Mao had already met Hurley, of course, when the American had gone to Yenan the previous year. In Chungking as in Yenan, he had startled his Chinese hosts with his sudden impulse to break into Indian war dances, punctuated by high-pitched "Yahoos", reputedly in the Choctaw Indian dialect which he had learnt as a young Oklahoman. With his simplistic mind, and his reluctance or incapacity to study the problems of China, he had thought initially that he would have no trouble in bringing the Communists and Nationalists together. His failure to do so in 1944 when he thought success was "in the bag" had barely dented his self-confidence. This time, he was convinced, agreement really was on the way.

Hurley's self-confidence was the product of ignorance. The infinite self-confidence of Mao and Chiang was different in kind: each was convinced that he was in the right and that he personified China. And of course each had solid reasons for distrusting the other. In these circumstances, talks between them were bound to fail.

The Russians held the key to the situation. Although Chiang—through T. V. Soong and Wang Shih-chieh—had negotiated the Sino-Soviet treaty from weakness, it did appear to give him a distinct political advantage over Mao, who was shown to be less important to Moscow than the Generalissimo. Mao, however, was better placed geographically to move his forces into Manchuria than Chiang was. On 9 August, the day after the Soviet invasion began, he had announced a "nation-wide counter-offensive" against the Japanese, and on the 10th General Chu Teh had invited the Japanese forces and their Chinese "puppets" to lay down their arms. Very few Japanese or "puppet" commanders surrendered to the Communists, however; most handed their arms in to the government forces. As a result, the Nationalist armies found themselves with enough Japanese equipment for forty divisions, in addition to thirty-nine divisions that were being trained and equipped by the Americans under General Wedemeyer.

The Russians, however, having overrun Manchuria, obstructed all American and Central Government efforts to gain a foothold in the great industrial province, while facilitating entry by the Chinese Red Army. With the Soviet forces entering Manchuria from the north and east was a "baggage-train" force of armed Chinese Communists, who were allowed to set up local administrations and defences in the small towns. Another Soviet army moving across Inner Mongolia and northern Hopei into southern Manchuria met a Communist force under Lin Piao and provided it with railway transport. Lin's men soon set up administrative and defence installations in the south to match those already set up in the north.

Chiang's Russian and Chinese enemies were not the only ones to put obstacles in his way at this crucial moment: the obstructiveness of his American allies was no less damaging to his strategic position. His first concern, in August and September, had been to reoccupy the great cities of east China—Nanking, Shanghai, Hankow, and

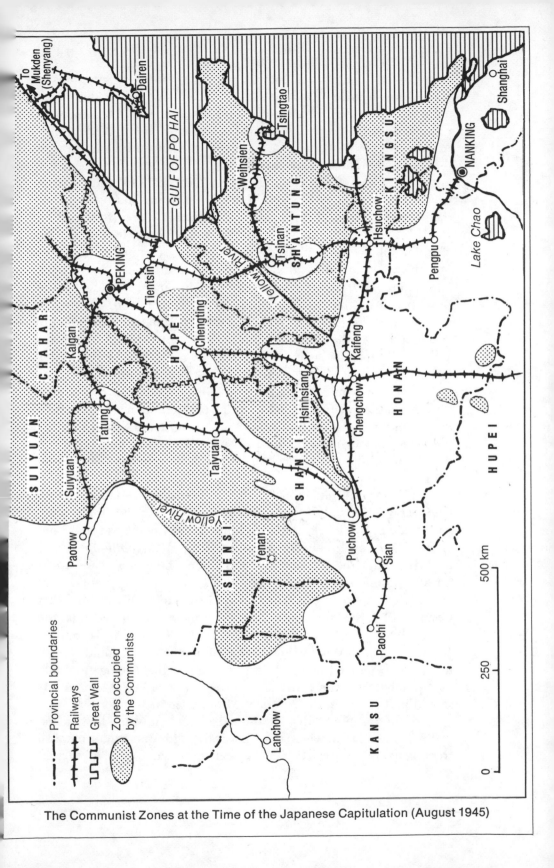

The Communist Zones at the Time of the Japanese Capitulation (August 1945)

Peiping—into which the central armies moved in that order in planes and ships provided by the Americans. Indeed, at this stage, he acted with the full approval and assistance of the American commanders, including General MacArthur, General Wedemeyer, Admiral Barbey, and the rest, to accept the surrender and arrange the repatriation of the Japanese troops. When Chiang's forces were just short of Kalgan and Chihfeng, west and north of Peiping—from which they could have blocked Mao's forces from entering Manchuria—General Marshall put heavy pressure on Chiang (to which he yielded) to order a cease-fire and to freeze his forces in their tracks. This fateful decision allowed the Chinese Communists to enter Manchuria. It was these troops that were later able to move back into China, after reorganisation, retraining, and rearming by the Russians, and complete their conquest of the mainland.

There is no doubt that General Wedemeyer was deeply concerned over the probable consequences of General Marshall's actions. His military assessment was that the central forces, after their long wartime ordeal, were inadequate even to attempt to take over Manchuria, and he advised the Generalissimo to consolidate his hold on the territory he held. But he realised the need to create a barrier in North China and Manchuria against the Soviet military presence, and to this end he pressed Washington to send seven American divisions to China. All he got, however, was two Marine Corps divisions.

Such was the situation in the early days of Mao's visit to Chungking. He stayed just over seven weeks and talks were conducted at two levels: between himself and Chiang Kai-shek, and at the lower level, between Chang Ch'ün, Wang Shih-chieh, and Shao Li-tze for the Nationalists, and Chou En-lai and Wang Jo-fei for the Communists. Immediately, all the old arguments were resurrected on either side. The Generalissimo inflexibly insisted that Communist forces should be dispersed and incorporated into the National Army, against representation in the National Government. Just as inflexibly, Mao insisted that Communist units should remain intact and under their existing officers while being formally incorporated into the National Army. Moreover, the Communists should participate in the National Military Council.

Ever optimistic, Hurley had hoped agreement would be reached by 22 September, on which day he was to go to America for medical treatment and consultations. He sent a message to Mao to that effect, then sat with Chang Ch'ün awaiting word from the Communist leader, after which he planned to board his plane. Word did come, but not of agreement. Instead, Mao simply appealed to Hurley to defer his trip until he had seen Mao back to Yenan in safety. Hurley turned to the Generalissimo, who said he would guarantee Mao's safe return, but this of course was not good enough for Mao, who insisted on—and was given—a written assurance from the Ambassador that he would guarantee his safe return. Disappointed, Hurley flew off.

Against Wedemeyer's advice, Chiang had decided to attempt to occupy Manchuria, as indeed was his acknowledged right under the Sino-Soviet treaty. Disturbing news was reaching the two men: everywhere, the Soviet forces were systematically stripping all industrial equipment and shipping it to the Soviet Union. On the face of it, this was a curious way to behave, if—as Chiang assumed—the Russians intended to hand over the province to his Communist rivals. In the absence of access to the Soviet archives, one may only speculate that Stalin, imputing guile of his own kind to the Americans, could not bring himself to believe that they would allow him to get away with his plans for Manchuria, and wanted to deny the Nationalists all industrial capacity on their arrival. On the American side, however, there was no real determination to support the Central Government's right to Manchuria, although Roosevelt had so pledged himself at the Cairo conference.

On 6 October, however (while Mao was still in Chungking), American naval forces did try to land Chinese troops at Dairen, but the Soviet authorities flatly refused to allow them to disembark, on the ground that this was a commercial port that could not be used for military purposes. Yet the Sino-Soviet treaty, concluded less than two months earlier, had given Chiang's government the right to administer the port. The Americans half-heartedly tried two other ports but did not insist when met with similar non-cooperation, not from the Russians but from hostile Chinese Communists. It was not until 1 November that Nationalist forces were able to land at Shanhaikuan, which gave them a modest foothold in the south.

On 10 October—the Double Tenth—Mao Tse-tung, Chiang Kai-shek, and their assistants drafted a joint communiqué, which barely cloaked the total lack of agreement between them. Here is a sample passage:

It was agreed that peace, democracy, solidarity, and unity should form the basis of the nation's concerted efforts. It was likewise agreed that under the leadership of President Chiang, co-operation should be perpetuated and resolute measures taken to avert internal strife so that a new China, independent, free and prosperous, might be built and the Three People's Principles be fully implemented. Both parties further agreed that political democratisation, nationalisation of troops, and the recognition of the equal legal status of political parties, as advocated by President Chiang, are absolutely essential to achieving peaceful national reconstruction.

The communiqué was not published till the following day when Mao—unmolested by the National authorities—flew back to Yenan. On two points, it appeared to enshrine progress of a sort. It was agreed, for instance, that local autonomy was to be extended; however, the government refused to recognise the Communist administration of the "liberated areas". As regards the armed forces, the Communists unexpectedly agreed to reduce their forces from between eighty and one hundred divisions to between twenty and twenty-four divisions for the whole of China. They would station their troops in assigned zones.

These arrangements were moot, however, as skirmishes between Nationalists and Communists broke out in various places within a couple of weeks.

The failure of the Chiang–Mao talks was the terminal blow to Patrick Hurley's ambassadorship. From the first, he had been at loggerheads with his staff of China experts, from George Atcheson —who was Chargé d'Affaires in Chungking during the Ambassador's absence—down. The main recipient of his ire was the most industrious member of his staff, John Service, who never lost a chance of denigrating Chiang and his regime and heaping praises on the Chinese Communists, whom he presented as the country's true democrats. Service took it upon himself repeatedly to recommend that the American government should switch its support from Chiang Kai-shek to Mao Tse-tung. On one occasion, Hurley had warned him in these terms: "If you confine yourself strictly to reporting, we will get along, but if you try to interfere with me, I will break you."

When Service ignored the Ambassador's warnings, Hurley had

him recalled to Washington. This was in April 1945. Shortly afterwards, he was arrested with three of his colleagues, when about 100 of his own despatches were found in the offices of the Communist-front magazine *Amerasia* (see footnote on p. 265).°

Another member of the embassy staff, John Davies, shared Service's views, and in a secret report dated 12 December 1944 he had gone so far as to recommend that the United States should cut off supplies to the Nationalist armies unless they ceased fighting to contain Communist forces. Davies had been seconded to General Wedemeyer's staff as his political adviser and Hurley insisted on having him recalled as well.

On 26 November 1945, Patrick Hurley wrote to President Truman to resign. In his letter, he accused the "professional foreign service men" in his embassy and in the State Department of siding with the Chinese Communists, advising them that Hurley's efforts to prevent the collapse of the National Government "did not represent the policy of the United States", and counselling Mao Tse-tung to "decline unification of the Chinese Communist Army with the National Army unless the Chinese Communists were given control".

The reasons for Hurley's misunderstanding with his staff and for his resignation are directly relevant to Chiang's loss of China, which is the central theme of this book. When he had met the Soviet leaders on his way to Chungking in September 1944, Molotov had told him that the Chinese Communists were not necessarily related to Communism in any way at all, but were just expressing dissatisfaction with their economic conditions, and would forget their political inclination when economic conditions improved. As Wedemeyer puts it, in an astute analysis: "Instead of realising that Molotov had deceived him about the Chinese Communists, Hurley grew angry. Instead of revising his estimate of the political situation in China and Soviet Russia's role, he blamed John Davies and John Stewart Service and their backers in the State Department." Wedemeyer continues:

> Whereas many Americans were deluded by clever propa-
> ganda into believing that the Chinese Communists were not real

---

° John Stewart Service was cleared six times by the Loyalty Security Board of the State Department, then summarily discharged in December 1951 by the Loyalty Review Board. After litigation, which went up to the Supreme Court, he was reinstated on 3 July 1957 with the rank he had held at the time of dismissal. He received about $60,000 in back pay, plus interest.

Communists but agrarian reformers, Pat Hurley would seem to have fallen for a contrary but equally pernicious myth. To him it seemed that Stalin, Molotov, and Co. could be relied upon, or their words believed, and that the villains of the piece were the Chinese Communists and the State Department in the person of the political advisers on my staff whom I had inherited from Stilwell.

In other words, during the whole of the critical period which ended the Second World War in East Asia, the American policy-makers were systematically misinformed—and also disinformed—about the true nature of the struggle for power in China. Hurley was at one with his diplomatic staff in swallowing the myth that the Chinese Communists were not truly Communists, but agrarian reformers, and the parallel myth that Moscow had no control over them (which did not become true until the 1960s). The career diplomats went further and advised their government to switch their support to Mao Tse-tung; Hurley, loyally upholding his government's official policy, went on supporting Chiang Kai-shek, but also tried loyally to square the circle by fostering a reconciliation between the two. The policy rested on false assumptions, but Hurley's successor was charged with carrying on as though nothing had happened.

On 27 November, President Truman announced his acceptance of Hurley's resignation and simultaneously his appointment of General George C. Marshall as his Special Representative in China, with the personal rank of ambassador. During the first two weeks of December, Marshall held a series of discussions, with the President, Secretary of State James Byrnes, Under-Secretary Dean Acheson, and others, to thrash out the next phase of America's China policy. Essentially, the policy was unchanged, but there were significant glosses to it. Marshall was to pursue his predecessor's policy of working towards political unification; however, if his efforts failed—and even if the cause of failure was Chiang's refusal to co-operate—the U.S. Government would continue to back the National Government. It was agreed, moreover, that the United States would assist the Generalissimo to move troops into North China "in order that the evacuation of the Japanese might be completed". The decision to back the Generalissimo, regardless of the success or failure of mediation, was to be kept secret; the stated reason for American readiness to help Chiang build up his forces in North China was for public consumption: in fact, it gave Marshall the power to make sure the Nationalists had superior forces in any confrontation with the Communists. The President also made it clear that generous American economic aid would be made available to China for national reconstruction, but only on condition that a coalition government emerged from General Marshall's mission.

Chiang Kai-shek hailed the appointment of Marshall by President Truman; and so did Mao Tse-tung and Stalin. All sides involved in the struggle for China felt the appointment could be turned to their own advantage. The President's Special Representative arrived in Chungking with three specific instructions. He was to work for a cessation of hostilities between the National Government and the Communists; for the absorption of the Communist armies into the Chinese National Army, in proportionate strength; and the convocation of a national conference of the Kuomintang, the Communist Party, the Democratic League, and other groups. The object of the conference would be to end the period of Kuomintang tutelage and bring the Communists into a coalition government.

General Marshall brought to his mission the prestige of a great soldier and one of the main architects of the Allied victory; an equable temperament and a courteous manner; and a character of notable uprightness. Although better equipped intellectually than Hurley, he was no better versed in the wiles and complexities of Chinese politics. As soon as he arrived, he was besieged on all sides—by the Kuomintang, certainly, since he was accredited to Chiang's government; but also by Chou En-lai for the Communists and Chang Lan and Lo Lung-chi, leaders of the Democratic League, which the Kuomintang considered as a Communist-front organisation. One of Marshall's first concerns was to make sure that Hurley's successor should be both worthy and acceptable. His initial recommendation was General Wedemeyer, because he enjoyed the confidence of the Generalissimo. It does not seem to have occurred to him that this alone would disqualify Wedemeyer in the eyes of the Communists. When he leaked the news of Wedemeyer's nomination at an off-the-record press conference, Chou En-lai was told immediately and forcefully protested to Marshall that Wedemeyer would be totally unacceptable to his side.

Embarrassed, Marshall cabled Acheson in Washington, appealing to him to drop the appointment. When Marshall asked Chou

En-lai for an acceptable name, the Communist leader suggested Dr. John Leighton Stuart, President of Yenching University. Dr. Stuart had spent most of his working life in China and commanded wide respect; but he was unversed in Chinese politics, and especially in the techniques of power practised by the Communists. The Kuomintang chalked up the Communist veto on Wedemeyer as a victory for their enemies.

General Marshall moved with soldierly briskness towards all three of his stated objectives. On the first of these—the cessation of hostilities—the National Government met him halfway, by proposing a committee of three. Marshall himself headed the committee, the other members of which were Chang Ch'ün for the government, and Chou En-lai for the Communists. On paper, a cease-fire agreement was reached on 10 January 1946. Both the Generalissimo and Mao Tse-tung instructed their armed forces to cease all troop movements and hostilities on the 13th. Executive headquarters were set up in Peiping, and eight truce teams were appointed, each consisting of an American, a government representative, and a Communist.

The hollowness of this arrangement soon emerged. While the talks were still in progress, the Communist forces went into action in Hopei, Shansi, Suiyuan, northern Kiangsu, and Shantung—more than trebling the localities under their control.

Chou En-lai had insisted that two strongholds on the border of Outer Mongolia—Chinfeng and Tuling—should be left in Communist hands under the truce. As a gesture of goodwill, the Generalissimo conceded this point, thereby giving the Communists the key to control of Jehol province. Immediately, the Communists took advantage of the truce by building up their strength in Manchuria. Some 46,000 troops moved from Shansi to reinforce Lin Piao's forces. In February, 10,000 more came from Hopei and 40,000 from Shantung. In March, another 80,000 were shipped from Shantung to Manchuria, disembarking at Soviet-held ports.

Unaware of these developments, General Marshall had been moving rapidly towards the second and third of his objectives. A military subcommittee of the Political Consultative Conference, at which both sides were represented with General Marshall in attendance, signed an agreement on 15 February 1946. The army was to be demobilised during the next twelve months, reducing the government's forces to ninety divisions and the Communists' to eighteen. During a further six-month period, there would be more reductions, to fifty and ten divisions, respectively. The Communists, however, rejected a proposal by the Generalissimo that the reductions should be supervised by a tripartite commission with American representation.

On the political side, the Generalissimo had called meetings of the Political Consultative Conference starting on 10 January. Precise plans were debated for a National Assembly and a permanent democratic constitution. During these meetings, the Communists appeared to go along with the government's proposals, so that Marshall was persuaded that harmony was within reach.

At this time, the Generalissimo's son Chiang Ching-kuo was in Moscow, where he had gone on Stalin's invitation on Christmas Day. He had two talks with the Soviet dictator, who expressed his hopes for peaceful coexistence between China and Russia and between the Kuomintang and the Chinese Communists. Stalin suggested that Ching-kuo's father should meet him either in Moscow or somewhere on the Sino-Soviet border.

This invitation presented Chiang with a painful dilemma. If he accepted, the outcome might well be the coalition government that the Americans were pressing on him, and "complete dependence on Russia". If he did not, a disappointed Stalin might be still more ruthless in his support of the Chinese Communists. He turned to Marshall, who said: "Anything that can help relations between China and Russia, I am for it." But Chiang took his own counsel and courteously declined the invitation.

On 13 March, General Marshall returned to Washington in triumph, in the belief that all his objectives had been met and with the new object of winding up his mission. Doubts must nevertheless have troubled his mind as he left China, for on 9 March, he had received a memorandum from Raymond Ludden, second secretary in the embassy, drawing his attention to the increasingly hostile attitude of the Communists in Manchuria. He mentioned his apprehension about possible collusion between the Chinese Communists and the Soviet Union. In fact, General Marshall could not have chosen a worse time for his return to the United States. On 7 March, the Russians had begun to withdraw from southern Manchuria, but without announcing the fact. Hard on their heels, the Chinese Communists moved in. When the news reached the Generalissimo, he immediately decided to occupy any towns evacuated by the Russians, regardless of Communist resistance. But in various places, the Communists had pre-empted him. On 15 April, Chou En-lai had killed the truce, by proclaiming a state of "all-out hostilities" in Manchuria. The Communists had seized Changchun, Harbin, and Tsitsihar. More importantly, they had taken Ssup'ingchieh, which gave them the power to block all land movements by Chiang Kai-shek's forces into Manchuria.

On 18 April, his policy in disarray, General Marshall returned to China. The Nationalists, counter-attacking, recaptured Ssup'ingchieh on the 19th and started pursuing Lin Piao's retreating forces.

In military terms, the catastrophic defeats of the Nationalist armies in the later stages of the civil war were made inevitable by the events of May and June 1946 in Manchuria. Despite their initial successes, it had become clear that the Communists were not going to be able to stand up to the Nationalists, who out-numbered them and out-gunned them. At this stage, the Russians were starving the Chinese Communists of military materiel. Apart from their rifles, most of their equipment came from raids on government arsenals. Appraising the situation from Moscow, Stalin invited Chiang Kai-shek to meet him there to discuss new arrangements for Manchuria, from which the Americans would be excluded. The wily dictator knew what he was doing. He knew, for instance, that the Americans would not at all mind being excluded from Manchuria: their main concern was avoiding excessive involvement. As he had calculated, both General Marshall and President Truman strongly urged the Generalissimo to accept Stalin's invitation. They were deeply worried, however, by the dreadful prospect of a Manchuria integrated into the Soviet economy. As they saw it, Stalin's proposal raised the possibility of a Nationalist-Communist administration of the province without the Americans, certainly, but without the Russians as well. In this situation, Marshall was to re-double his efforts to persuade the Generalissimo to form a coalition government with the Communists.

To these arguments, however, Chiang Kai-shek turned a deaf ear. He knew—although the Americans had not yet understood it—that it was no longer possible for his government and that of the United States to work out a joint policy towards the Soviet Union. He therefore took the momentous decision to "go it alone, if necessary, in resisting Soviet aggression". He would not accept the neutralisation of China through "the establishment of a coalition government". He therefore declined Stalin's invitation.

But for a series of American actions which he could not have foreseen, the Generalissimo's decision might have turned out to be justified. The immediate consequence, however, was fraught with danger for him. Stalin had made it easy for the Chinese Communists to move into Manchuria, but he had deprived them of an industrial base by looting the capital equipment, and he had done next to nothing to help them with arms and ammunition. And now, suddenly, he changed course. During the months that followed, the Russians handed the Chinese Communists 1,226 guns, and 369 tanks—all of Japanese manufacture. Also provided were 300,000 rifles, 4,836 machine guns, and 2,300 motor vehicles. All told, the arms and equipment handed over amounted to that for 594,000 Japanese and 75,000 Manchukuo soldiers. Moreover, the former Moscow-line leader of the Chinese Communist Party, Li Li-san, was sent back to China during the winter of 1946–47 to arrange for the incorporation of 100,000 North Korean troops into Lin Piao's army. Although these massive transfers were not initially decisive, because the Chinese Communist troops had to be trained in the use of their new and modern equipment, in time they gave the Communist side an overwhelming advantage over the Nationalists.°

American decisions during the second phase of the Marshall mission made it virtually impossible for Chiang Kai-shek to win the war in Manchuria, at the precise time when Stalin's decision to help the Chinese Communists made it possible for them to win. There was a curious blindness on the part of both the Chinese Nationalists and the American policy-makers during this crucial period. The

---

° There has been much controversy over the Soviet transfers of Japanese arms to the Chinese Communists in Manchuria. Some writers have dismissed these reports as unfounded Kuomintang propaganda. General Chassin minimises Soviet aid. Max Beloff, in *Soviet Policy in the Far East* (London: Oxford University Press, 1953) writes cautiously: "Since the Soviet Command had . . . the sole right to take the surrender of the Japanese in Manchuria, large dumps of arms could not have fallen into Communist control except through Japanese officers defying their orders, which is unlikely, or through Russian collusion." But later evidence makes it clear beyond a doubt that the Nationalist claims were true. A Peking publication in 1957 gave the exact figures that had been quoted earlier by the Kuomintang. And a Moscow radio broadcast to China on 3 September 1967 gave even higher figures, e.g., 1,800 pieces of artillery, and 700 tanks. (See Thornton, p. 367, source reference 71.)

Generalissimo was blind because it never seems to have crossed his mind that the Americans might not support him if he carried the war into Communist territory. The Americans were equally blind in that they failed to perceive that there had been a fundamental change of policy in Moscow, and that the Chinese Communists, when the policy began to take effect, lost all interest in Marshall's efforts at mediation.

On 18 April, the day Marshall returned to China, the battle for Ssup'ingchieh was at its height. He tried, but failed, to persuade Chiang Kai-shek to call off the offensive. Chiang could smell victory, and no amount of pacifying talk was going to make him stop in his tracks.

Yet the warning signs were there, if Chiang had chosen to see them. On 19 June 1946, Dean Acheson told the House Committee on Foreign Affairs: "Communist leaders have asked and General Marshall has agreed that their integration with other forces (the National Army) be preceded by a brief period of United States' training and by the supply of minimum quantities of equipment." Nine days later, he explained publicly that the United States was "impartial" between the Central Government and the Communists. He added:

> Too much stress cannot be laid on the hope of this government that our economic assistance be carried out in China through the medium of a government fully and fairly representative of all important Chinese political elements, including the Chinese Communists.

Congressional opposition halted plans to send sixty-nine American officers—who had actually been selected and assembled in Shanghai—to the Communist areas to provide military training. Impartiality could go no further.

During the preceding weeks, Marshall had been involved in an increasingly acrimonious discussion with Chiang Kai-shek, who wanted the American mediator to guarantee Communist observance of the January cease-fire and the plans for reducing and reorganising the Chinese armies. He explained that by "guarantee", he meant that Marshall should lay down a time limit for the Chinese Communists and make sure they complied with it. If Marshall did not do this, said Chiang, then the alternative would be for the Nationalist forces to occupy the Manchurian strategic centres.

The Generalissimo thereupon went to Mukden to direct operations. There, on 29 May, he received an angry message from Marshall, who threatened that unless the fighting stopped immediately, he would withdraw as mediator. When Marshall explained the situation to Chou En-lai in Chungking, Chou commented cryptically that "at that moment they were standing at the turning point in China's history". Chou knew that, even if Marshall did not. The mediator was shocked and surprised at a later conversation with Chou En-lai—on 23 June—to hear the Communist delegate accuse the United States of pursuing a "double policy" in China— supporting the Kuomintang while pretending to mediate. To anyone versed in the significance of a change of tone in negotiations with Communists, the implication would have been crystal-clear; but Marshall was not so versed and took the remarks as a personal insult.

The negotiations nevertheless continued, yielding a cease-fire for Manchuria on 26 June. But it was soon shown to be as empty as the previous one, although both sides proclaimed on 1 July that the cease-fire would continue indefinitely. On the 4th, Chiang Kai-shek announced that the National Assembly would convene on 12 November. It had been scheduled to meet in May, but was postponed when the Communists refused to present a list of their delegates. On the 7th, the Russians and the Chinese Communists issued simultaneous manifestoes denouncing American support for Chiang Kai-shek's government. This was the message Marshall was intended to receive when Chou En-lai had changed the tone of his conversation.

The Generalissimo could now see, though Marshall and his superiors could not, that there was no point in further negotiations. He ordered his armies to take the offensive. A string of Nationalist victories followed. By mid-September, the major railway network in North China was under Nationalist control and the Communist forces were trapped in the mountains of Shantung and Shansi. But the Generalissimo had his eyes on a more glittering prize—the Mongolian city of Kalgan, which was of symbolic as well as strategic importance. Symbolic, because the Russian occupation forces had turned it over to the Chinese Communists, who had decided to move their capital there from Yenan. Strategic, because it was a gateway between China's north-west and Siberia. The Communists, realising that they could not hold the city, took a diplomatic offensive instead, protesting to General Marshall and threatening that if the Nationalist forces did not stop, they would break off negotiations with the government. Increasingly exasperated by the Generalissimo's disregard for his efforts, General Marshall pressed him not to take Kalgan. But Chiang Kai-shek was in no mood to listen, and duly seized it.

In his fury, Marshall now inflicted a blow on Chiang Kai-shek, his government, and his army, from which they would never recover. He persuaded the United States government to impose a total embargo on military deliveries to the Chinese government. The pretext was a specious one—that such deliveries could only be made to a coalition government, and could be withheld if denial appeared to be "in the best interests of the United States". This fateful decision, however, was not made public or communicated to Chiang Kai-shek. The first the Generalissimo heard of it was on 30 August, when he learned that a request for military deliveries had been met with an American refusal to issue an export licence. Unknown to him, the embargo had already been in force since 29 July; it was not officially lifted until the following 26 May, and in fact no American ammunition was shipped to the Chinese Central Government until November 1948.

In the face of this depressing news, the Generalissimo was forced to admit to himself that he could not long press on with his offensive. Kalgan fell on 10 October—the Double Tenth—and that day, in his usual annual speech, Chiang declared himself ready to continue to seek a settlement by mediation and consultation.

In his naivety, Marshall now thought success was at hand. But he had reckoned without the Communists, who now made it clear that they were no longer interested in reaching a negotiated settlement. Instead of a truce, which would have left the National-ists in a strong position by virtue of their conquests, they demanded that the government armies should withdraw to the positions they held on 13 January in China proper and 7 June in Manchuria. Bewildered by these demands, Marshall told Chou En-lai that he now felt his efforts at mediation were "futile". "I told you some time ago," he went on, "that if the Communist Party felt that they could not trust to my impartiality, they merely had to say so and I would withdraw. You have now said so. I am leaving immediately for Nanking. . . ."

The last-minute attempt to bring the two sides together had caused Chiang Kai-shek to postpone the meeting of the National Assembly again, and it now met on 15 November, in Nanking (to which the government had returned on 1 May). Neither the Communist Party nor the Democratic League was represented. On the 16th, Chou-En-lai denounced the convening of the National Assembly and requested General Marshall to provide transport for himself and other Communist representatives to Yenan the following week.

Now there was nobody left for General Marshall to talk to except the Generalissimo, and the two men met on 1 December. The gap between them was unbridgeable. Marshall severely lectured Chiang Kai-shek for neutralising his mediation attempts by military actions, and for consuming 70 percent of his government's budget in military expenditures, thus dragging the country towards financial collapse, which could only create a fertile field for the spread of Communism. The Generalissimo replied that the Communists had never intended to co-operate with the National Government; indeed under Russian influence, their aim was to disrupt the government. The only thing to be done was to destroy the Communist military forces. This would take eight to ten months. As for the economic situation, he said with the sublime confidence of ignorance, there was no danger of a collapse since the Chinese economy was an agrarian one. On this note, the two men parted.

Now that it was clear to Chiang Kai-shek he was no longer going to be bothered either by General Marshall or (at least politically) by the Communists, he went ahead and on 27 November introduced a draft constitution before the National Assembly. It was approved on Christmas Day 1946 and it was agreed that it should come into effect exactly a year later. On paper, the new Constitution was all that Sun Yat-sen would have wished. There were provisions for the equality of all citizens and racial groups; universal suffrage and the secret ballot; voting rights for men and women aged twenty or over; a guarantee of rights and liberties; and the election of the President for six years, with the right to be re-elected for a second term only. As laid down before Sun Yat-sen's death, there were to be five branches of government: Executive, Legislative, Judicial, Examination, and Control. By implication, the period of Kuomintang tutelage—that is, dictatorship—was to end, although neither the Communist Party nor the Democratic League, by their own choice, would enjoy the benefits of a Constitution to which they had not contributed. Apart from the Kuomintang, only two small parties were partners to the constitutional process: the Youth Party and the Democratic Socialist Party, under Carson Chang, who had led his followers out of the Democratic League in 1945, in protest against its deferential attitude towards the Communists. As far as the Chinese mainland was concerned, the provisions of the new Constitution remained largely moot; they were applied, more or less, in Taiwan after the Nationalists had been driven into exile.

Seeing that no hope at all now remained, General Marshall requested his recall and returned to the United States on 7 January 1947, to become Secretary of State. That day, he issued a lengthy "personal statement", in which he attributed his failure mainly to the "almost overwhelming suspicion" with which the Nationalists and Communists viewed each other. Each side, he said, had been spurred on by extremists—a "group of reactionaries" in the Kuomintang, and "dyed-in-the-wool Communists" in the Chinese Communist Party. Among the Communists, he thought, was a liberal group, especially of young men "who have turned to the Communists in disgust at the corruption evident in the local governments", who would put the interest of the Chinese people above Communist ideology. But he did not explain how such people could hope to impose their views upon the fanatics. Nor did his statement contain any reference to the Russians, as though the intransigence of the Chinese Communists from the middle of the year was unrelated to Stalin's decision to abandon cooperation with the United States and build up Mao Tse-tung's forces.

American post-mortems on the failure of the Marshall mission—including General Marshall's own views—have been well-publicised. Chinese interpretations have attracted less attention, but throw a fresh light on the reasons for his failure.

The terms proposed by the Nationalists and Communists were irreconcilable: they were like parallel lines that would never meet. Overestimating Chou En-lai's importance in the Communist hierarchy, General Marshall tended to be deceived and persuaded by his eloquence. He was unaware that Mao Tse-tung did not necessarily reveal his plans to his chief negotiator, who worked to a careful and restrictive brief.

Both sides deceived the American mediator, the Communists more successfully than their rivals. The Nationalist negotiators did not carry much weight. Their leader, Chang Chih-chung, did not enjoy the backing of either the army or the party; nor did he rate highly in Chiang Kai-shek's confidence. One of his assistants, Chang Li-sheng, was supposed to represent the CC clique, but was not empowered to speak for it: he had to defer, and indeed refer, to the Ch'en brothers. Another, Shao Li-tze, was of no consequence; he was picked as one of the negotiators because of his reputation as a "moderate". None of the three had access to the Generalissimo, and could only report to him indirectly through Chang Ch'ün.

Chang Chih-chung was fully aware of the American government's hope for a peaceful settlement, and played on that hope by often presenting Marshall with an excessively optimistic picture of the peace prospects. Himself politically ambitious, he personally favoured a coalition government, in which he presumed he would play an important part. On occasion, he must have been strongly tempted to misrepresent the Generalissimo's intentions to the mediator.

Throughout the negotiations, Ch'en Li-fu and his group maintained an incessant flow of verbal attacks on the Communists, calling in question the usefulness of any negotiations.

On the propaganda front, however, the Communists undoubtedly outsmarted the Nationalists in every way (according to Eric Chou, who covered the talks). The Communist delegation at 5 Mei Yuan (Plum Garden), a few hundred yards from the building of the National Government (later to be the Presidential Office after the institution of constitutional government), was the only source of information available to both foreign and Chinese journalists. Chou En-lai was always available for comments (Eric Chou once called on him at 3:00 A.M. and was received without delay), while his spokesmen, Wang Ping-nan and Mei Yi, were invariably most obliging to the newsmen. It is fair to say that all the news despatches about the peace talks filed from Nanking were based on Communist hand-outs. Ironically, even those mouthpieces of the KMT, the Central News Agency and Central Daily News, had to rely on the Communists for their information on the peace talks; for the negotiations were supposed to be secret, and the Nationalist negotiators and spokesmen were afraid to say anything for fear of Chiang Kai-shek's displeasure. When cornered, they would consent to see the journalists, but refuse to say anything. This gave the Communist side the monopoly of information.

The military were divided. The Central Army—that is, the forces under Chiang's direct control—were essentially against the idea of talking peace with the Communists. The localised clashes between them and the Communists during the Sino-Japanese War were still fresh in their minds. Besides, they had been taught to hate the Communists for too long to aspire to love them at this late hour. The various local armies under the command of the ex-warlords were in general indifferent. True, they disliked the Communists, but equally they resented the Central Army's "superior" claims on equipment and privileges.

The one exception was Yen Hsi-shan (the "model governor" of Shansi). To all who would listen, he insisted that the Communists were not really interested in peace. Unlike some of the other generals, he was perceptive enough to see that Mao Tse-tung and his followers would not abandon their plan to communise the whole of China even if a coalition government could have been formed. He declared this publicly as well as privately, making this point at a press conference he gave in Taiyuan in 1947, before the peace talks broke down.

In June 1946, General Marshall had invited Hu Lin of the newspaper *Ta Kung Pao* to his residence at 5 Ninghai Road, Nanking, for a long talk. The American ambassador, Dr. Leighton Stuart, was present and Eric Chou was the interpreter. When Marshall asked Hu for his frank opinion on the prospects for the peace talks, he made the following points:

1. The Chinese Communists were not "land reformers", and the Americans were misled if they thought so. "The crows are black all over the world," said Hu, quoting a Chinese proverb. "So why not in China?"
2. To form a coalition government would be like setting up a "United Republic of Germany and France". There was no basis on which the Nationalists and Communists could work together.
3. At best, Marshall might be able to obtain a temporary peace. But first, he had to make sure that the cease-fire worked. And without international supervision, it would never work.
4. A practical possibility would be to give Manchuria to the

Communists, so that they could set up some form of autonomous government there. But the problem was that neither the KMT nor the Communists would wish to incur the odium of dividing up the country. Nor would it be fair to the people of Manchuria, who had undergone the Japanese occupation, to be asked now to submit to a communist system.

5. The minor parties, such as the Democratic League, the Young China (Youth) Party, and the Democratic Socialist party, had no popular support and no public appeal. They should not be taken seriously.

6. Democracy in the American sense could never be established in a country like China, or indeed in any other Asian State.

7. The emergence of a Communist regime in China would do the United States more harm than good.

8. There was every possibility that the Russians would consolidate their power base in Manchuria, with the object of giving secret help to the Communists.

Unfortunately, General Marshall ignored these words of wisdom, the truth of which was soon proved by events. Hu Lin had been even more explicit than General Yen Hsi-shan, who had tried earlier, and with equal unsuccess, to disabuse the mediator of his first illusions. Marshall had gone to see Yen in Taiyuan on 3 March 1946. The next day, Yen had driven Marshall to the airport, and on the way, Marshall had said, "I want to mediate, and I am sure I can solve the conflicts between the Nationalists and Communists. For the terms I offer the Communists are better than those the Soviet Union would offer." Yen replied: "You are talking about a deal. If the Communists do want a deal, you will be successful. But if their aim is to take over the factory, no deal can be made."

Marshall asked: "You think the Chinese Communists will really not compromise?"

Yen: "This I cannot say for sure. It all depends on whether the Communists are prepared to give up their aims of world-wide revolution and dictatorship of the proletariat."

Marshall: "As regards China, the United States will see how the mediation works. If it is unsuccessful, the United States will withdraw everything."

To be fair to Marshall, he was at a disadvantage in that the background he got from the State Department and the American Embassy in Chungking was heavily slanted against the Nationalists and in favour of the Communists. He tended therefore to place greater credence in Chou En-lai than in Chiang Kai-shek. Meanwhile, now that he had gone, the Communist build-up continued, while Chiang was starved of military supplies. It was against this background that the Chinese civil war moved into a new and virulent phase in the spring of 1947.

20. | Chiang Steps Aside

C hiang Kai-shek faced his enemies in a condition of catastrophic economic weakness, for the great Chinese inflation got out of hand in 1946. In Shanghai, wholesale prices were seven times as high at the end of the year as they had been at the beginning. The American dollar, more realistically priced now than the pegged wartime rate of 20 to one, fetched 3,350 to one Chinese dollar (*fapi*). But the open market rate was much higher, and hit 6,500 to one in December 1946.

Meanwhile, China's reserves of gold and dollars were declining fast. On V–J Day, they had stood at the astonishing level of U.S.$900,000,000, but at the end of 1946 they had dropped to no more than half of this figure. Throughout the year, however, foreign aid had continued at a generous rate. The United Nations Relief and Rehabilitation Administration (UNRRA) began shipping supplies to China in November 1945, and the programme continued into 1947. China's total share of the UNRRA programme amounted to

$658,400,000, of which the American share was $474,000,000. Most of the supplies consisted of food and clothing, but there was also a wide variety of capital equipment, and many technically qualified people to help the Chinese distribute commodities and set up factories. To the UNRRA programme should be added American Export-Import Bank credits of $82,800,000 from V–J Day to 1947; and a long-term Canadian credit of $60,000,000. But many of the supplies and much of the cash went into the private stores or bank accounts of Kuomintang officials or ministers.

The race towards total insolvency might have been at least slowed down if not halted had the country returned to normal economic activity. But the greatest industrial area, Manchuria, had been stripped bare by the Russians, and what the Russians had left was looted by the swarms of Han Chinese who reached the province as the Russians departed.

One bright spot was the textile industry, which had expanded under Japanese occupation. But the collapse of the transport system made trade exceedingly difficult. The railways were devastated, with tracks destroyed, bridges ruined, and rolling stock decimated. The main arteries of north China were under constant Communist assault. Thanks to American aid, the shipping tonnage was satisfactory, but protectionism and high freight and port charges were unnecessary burdens. In this situation, the "capitalists" of Shanghai and other great cities preferred to speculate rather than to construct or produce. At the end of 1946, interest rates on bank loans were running at 15 to 28 percent *per month*. T. V. Soong had decreed that the banks should make "productive credits" available to industrial entrepreneurs at "only" 5 to 8 percent per month, but these rates were still far too high for productive investment and were passed on to private banks at 15 percent, for a profit of up to 10 percent monthly. Desperately, at the beginning of 1947, Soong imposed import restrictions and stopped all sales of gold. But money was still being printed, and the inflation got worse, not better. A poor crop contributed to the general misery. The dollar exchange rate touched 12,000 to one by February 1947.

On pay days, potato sacks were filled with almost worthless paper money, which those receiving it would immediately convert into rice, paraffin, oil, or coal, before a further price rise within the next few hours. The living standards of wage earners dropped by one-third in 1947, as compared with the previous year.

On 12 March that year came news of great importance that caused Chiang Kai-shek to believe mistakenly that the Americans had at last changed the policies which he blamed for his current difficulties. That day President Truman, in an address to both houses of Congress, did indeed announce a major policy change. Immediate assistance, both military and economic, was to be given to Greece, at that time in imminent danger of being taken over by Communist revolutionaries. Turkey, too, was to be aided, as part of a new policy to "support free peoples who are resisting attempted subjugation by armed minorities or by outside pressures". This was the first statement of the famous "Truman Doctrine".

It was perhaps natural for the Generalissimo to assume, given the undeniable parallels between his country's situation and that of Greece, that Truman's words would apply to China as well. It might, however, have occurred to him that in this event, Truman would have said so.

At all events, he took the President's goodwill for granted and immediately ordered his forces to resume the offensive on the 14th. The next day he convened the Kuomintang's Central Executive Committee, which at his behest proclaimed that relations with the Chinese Communists were now broken. It was decided to "suppress the armed rebellion". This seemed a good moment to get rid of T. V. Soong, whom he continued to dislike and who had shown himself no more capable than his predecessor had been to stem the inflationary flood. So Soong was out, and in came General Chang Ch'ün, dapper in appearance, moderate in his opinions, a converted Christian by religion, and popular with the Americans. Against this, his amiability was greater than his technical competence. He well understood that the Generalissimo would require of him, above all, to bow to his will without question. To show that he was in earnest about ending the period of Kuomintang tutelage, however, Chang gave four cabinet seats to the Youth Party, two to Democratic Socialists, and two to independents; the Kuomintang kept fourteen. The new government took office on 18 April, on a caretaker basis until the new President could be elected under the Constitution. On 24 March, the Central Executive Committee had voted to abolish the Supreme National Defence Council; in its place, a State Council was created. The office of Vice-President was inaugurated, with Sun Fo as the first holder.

From Washington came a cold shower shortly after President

Truman's announcement. Before the House Foreign Affairs Committee, Under-Secretary of State Dean Acheson declared that "the Chinese government is not in a position at the present time that the Greek government is in. It is not approaching collapse. It is not threatened by defeat by the Communists." There would therefore be no military assistance to China. It was a disappointing spring, after all. Morale was boosted temporarily on 19 March with news of the capture of the former Communist capital, Yenan; but the Communists had evacuated it, and no prisoners were available. Uncertain now whether his forces would be adequately supplied for an offensive, Chiang Kai-shek discovered that it was the Communists who had moved over to the attack in Manchuria, Jehol, and Shensi. From Taiwan came disquieting and unfortunate news. An orderly local demonstration by the Taiwanese had turned into a riot when mainland troops had opened fire. The governor was General Ch'en Yi—not to be confused with the Communist General Ch'en Yi. A brutal and insensitive man, he had sent for reinforcements and widespread massacres followed, in which at least 10,000 Taiwanese were killed, including many of their leaders. The American embassy in Nanking protested and on 22 April, the Generalissimo appointed Wei Tao-ming, a former ambassador to the United States, as Ch'en Yi's successor. Ch'en Yi himself was later executed.

About a fortnight later, the Communist general Lin Piao, with a force of 400,000 men and 200 guns, launched a general offensive, with Ssup'ingchieh and Mukden as objectives. The Communists had swarmed across the Sungari River, at their fifth attempt.

The news from China alarmed Truman and his administration. The Americans didn't want Chiang Kai-shek to wage war; but they did not want him to lose China either. As a short-term measure, they temporarily lifted the embargo on arms deliveries to China. The Central Government was enabled to purchase 130,000,000 rounds of ammunition—enough to meet the Communist offensive, but not enough to counter-attack. The Kuomintang troops now found that they were up against the new Japanese equipment which the Russians had turned over to the Communists. On 1 May 1946, Mao Tse-tung had renamed his forces the People's Liberation Army (PLA).° This new phase of the unending hostilities was termed the

---

° That the name "People's Liberation Army" (PLA) was indeed adopted on 1 May 1946 is confirmed by *The Concise History of the People's Liberation War*

"Third Revolutionary Civil War". By June, the PLA had driven 150 miles to the south. In Manchuria, they had seized the initiative, and they were never again to lose it.

On 4 July 1947, the National Government solemnly declared that the Communists were in a "state of rebellion". Fatuously, in the prevailing circumstances, Chiang Kai-shek renamed his military headquarters the "Bandit-Suppression Headquarters", but the days of bandit extermination were long over. General mobilisation was decreed, nevertheless, and in speeches on 6 and 7 July, the Generalissimo called for immediate reforms. In his second speech, on the tenth anniversary of the outbreak of the Sino-Japanese War, his words were: "Unless drastic reforms are introduced, China may not be able to exist in the family of nations." Between his two speeches, on 6 July, Ambassador John Leighton Stuart had handed him a message from Secretary of State Marshall. In effect, what Marshall said was: "I told you so." Military aid alone would not cure China's ills.

When Chiang asked the ambassador what Marshall meant, Stuart said that authority had to be delegated, civil liberties protected, and a closer relationship established between government and people. "I understand," the Generalissimo replied. But as usual, nothing actually happened.

On the 9th, President Truman decided to send General Wedemeyer back to China (and to Korea) on a fact-finding mission. The news was formally announced on the 11th, and greeted with some enthusiasm in Nanking, where Wedemeyer was rightly considered to be a friend, and a bitter enemy of the Communists.

During the next eight weeks, Wedemeyer travelled extensively

(Peking: Chinese Youth Press, 1961). Various authors (e.g. Guillermaz, p. 389 and Clubb, p. 277) erroneously date the change of name in July 1946. The first public mention of the People's Liberation Army, however, was in an order issued by the Central Committee of the Chinese Communist Party on 4 May that year, spelling out the rules governing the confiscation of land from traitors, local gentry, and rogue landlords. The order called on the peasants to give full support to the "Liberation Army in its efforts to nullify the Kuomintang offensive" (op. cit., p. 36). Earlier, the Communist troops had been referred to as the Eighteenth Group Army, as when Mao Tse-tung wrote to Chiang Kai-shek on 13 August 1945. They were also called "anti-Japanese troops in the Liberated Areas" (op. cit., pp. 10 and 18). In October 1945, the terms "Eighth Route Army", "New Fourth Army", and "East River Column in Kwangtung" were still being used in CCP documents (op. cit., pp. 22–24).

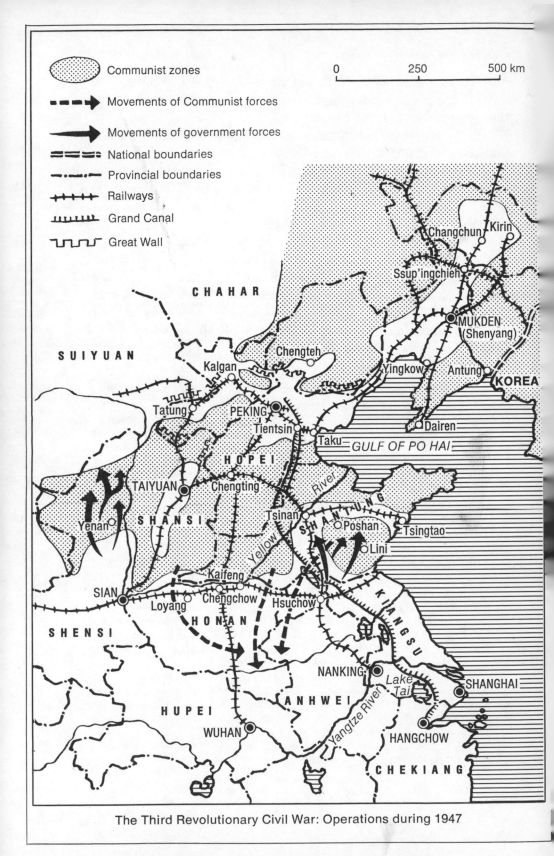

The Third Revolutionary Civil War: Operations during 1947

—to Mukden, Peiping, Tientsin, Formosa, Shanghai, and Canton. Back in Nanking, the Generalissimo invited him to address government officials and military officers, urging him to speak frankly and without compunction. Wedemeyer had "grave misgivings" about accepting, and consulted Ambassador Stuart. The ambassador, however, insisted that he should do as he was bidden. When the day came, on 22 August, General Wedemeyer spoke his mind before a joint meeting of the State Council and all the ministers of the National Government. The American ambassador was present; and so were the Generalissimo and Mme. Chiang. In a hushed silence, he spoke of maladministration and corruption, defects of organisation, shortcomings of officials, inefficiency, and ineptitude. Wedemeyer's account of what happened next differs sharply from Stuart's. "At the conclusion of my talk, the Generalissimo, with Mme. Chiang and a few other officials shook my hand warmly and thanked me. On the ride back to my quarters with Ambassador Stuart, he complimented me and assured me that what I had said could not possibly offend, and that no one else he knew could have presented the information so convincingly and with such beneficial effects." He added that an old and respected member of the Executive Yüan had dissolved into tears on hearing his words because he knew Wedemeyer was a friend of China and had spoken the truth.

The ambassador, however, reported that those present had found Wedemeyer's remarks offensive, and that President Chiang had also been "apparently offended".

Two days later, on the point of departure from Nanking, Wedemeyer issued a public statement complaining of "apathy and lethargy, abject defeatism", and a lack of "inspirational leadership". He did not name the Generalissimo, but the reference was clear.

Unexpectedly, perhaps, in the light of these critical observations, Wedemeyer's report recommended a new programme of military and economic aid to China over five years, to include measures to stabilise the currency, and military advice and supervision. China was to be enabled to purchase military equipment and supplies and to obtain ammunition immediately.

The Wedemeyer Report, which was submitted to President Truman on 19 September 1947, was immediately suppressed by Marshall, presumably because the author had strongly criticised America's China policy and because the Secretary of State had no intention of recommending acceptance of Wedemeyer's proposals. In retrospect, Wedemeyer was to express bitter regret at his public criticism of the Chiang regime in his Nanking statement of 24 August. His press relations assistant, Mark Watson, had strongly advised him against issuing it. His speech two days earlier before the assembled Kuomintang elite was acceptable because it was made in private. But the public statement inflicted humiliation and loss of face on the Generalissimo and his followers, without corresponding benefits. It was a gift to the Chinese Communists and further depressed Nationalist morale, which already was low enough. While Wedemeyer had been touring China, the Chinese Communists had infiltrated about 150,000 men in small groups in half a dozen areas of Central China. Although this operation did not directly threaten the centres of government power, it obliged Chiang Kai-shek to keep most of his strategic reserve south of the Great Wall.

Chiang Kai-shek reacted to the Wedemeyer visit in anger, not so much against the United States as against his own party. On 9 September, while Wedemeyer was writing his report, he called the Central Executive Committee to a meeting in Nanking. Scathingly, he denounced the Kuomintang for failing to solve China's problems; the responsibility was not his, he declared. The Communists had proved themselves abler and more devoted: unless the Kuomintang reformed and rejuvenated itself, it was doomed to extinction. Never again, the Generalissimo asserted, would China be dependent on the United States for assistance.

The American embassy nevertheless reported that the CC clique emerged stronger than ever from the meeting, while the Central Government continued to look to the United States to extricate China from its problems.

A few days later Ambassador Stuart recounted with approval that President Chiang was at least trying to do something about corruption. He had ordered that the son of an old friend of his, charged with flagrant speculation, should be punished according to the law, regardless of other considerations.

In general, however, the anti-liberal and anti-reformist trends in the KMT continued to wax. The Foreign Minister, Wang Shih-chieh, was taken to task for his allegedly "servile" policy towards Washington; and the able General Ch'en Ch'eng lost his job as Chief of Staff (from which he had finally displaced Ho Ying-ch'in).

On 28 October, Chiang issued a decree banning the Democratic League, on the ground that it was subservient to the Communists. Doubtless it was, but the ban left its liberal and intellectual membership with no refuge but the Communist Party. The effect on public opinion, especially in America, was deplorable. The leaders of the Democratic League were not arrested, but its offices were wrecked by the police, and many of its writers and ordinary members were detained.

And always, the vertiginous fall of the exchange rate continued. At the beginning of the year, the face value of the bank notes in circulation stood at $3,500,000,000,000 Chinese; by July, it had tripled. In September, the exchange rate reached 38,000 to one U.S. dollar; and by November it was hitting 73,000. Despite this chaotic and depressing situation, Chiang Kai-shek ordered the elections for the proposed National Assembly to go ahead. They were in fact held from 21 to 23 November through most of China. Inevitably, in a country at war, there were great disparities in the electoral turnout. In many rural areas, it was very low; in most of the cities under KMT control it was reasonably satisfactory, although only 100,000 voters out of 3,000,000 went to the polls in Shanghai. There were, of course, no elections in the Communist-held areas, and the party simply nominated deputies for those areas. Of the 1,744 deputies either elected or nominated, 48 percent, or 847, were described as "independents"; 42 percent represented the Kuomintang (725 seats); while the Youth Party and Democratic Socialists were allocated only 10 percent, or 172 seats.

The year closed with a ringing and virulently confident statement by Chairman Mao, on 25 December 1947. The turning point had come, he boasted. The Communists had now passed from the defensive to the offensive. He denounced the United States as the great enemy of the world and as the agent responsible for continuing the civil war in China. As for Chiang Kai-shek, he was "the running dog of American imperialism".

Mao Tse-tung was right: the tide had indeed turned, and 1948 was the year in which it became clear to everybody—except perhaps to Chiang Kai-shek—that the defeat of the Central Government was now inevitable. The People's Liberation Army had become an irresistible force, growing in size, power, and ardour as it advanced against the dwindling, disunited, and demoralised Nationalist armies. And yet (as General Chassin has pointed out), on 1

January 1948 the Nationalists still outnumbered the Communists by nearly two to one—1,250,000 men to 700,000. But it had long ceased to be a question of numbers alone; although the American unwillingness to keep the Nationalists supplied with weapons and ammunition had a bearing on morale.

Contemplating the dismal situation at the turn of the year, the Generalissimo had an agonising choice to make. Strategically, the wise course would have been to abandon Manchuria to the Communists, consolidate the defences of China proper, and negotiate while he still had something to negotiate with. But Manchuria had great symbolic meaning in his eyes: it was there that the dismemberment of national territory had begun with the Mukden incident in 1931. To withdraw from Manchuria was more than he could bear: more than a loss of face, it would have been a betrayal of his deepest instincts and emotions. Besides, he reasoned, how could his will to resist remain credible in the eyes of his people if he gave up China's greatest industrial centre without a fight to those whom he had been denouncing once again as "Communist bandits"? What Chiang did not or would not understand was that at the beginning of 1948, morale had already collapsed and credibility had gone.

The Generalissimo moved to Peiping to plan and direct his strategy. His plan was to hang on at all costs to the main cities of Manchuria—Kirin, Changchun, and Mukden—defeat or reduce the PLA in China proper, and then go on to the offensive in Manchuria. On paper, it was not a bad plan, if one accepted the need to keep Manchuria. But there were too many "ifs" about it: *if* the Communists had not continually broken the rail links between Manchuria and China proper; *if* the Nationalist air force had been strong enough to supply its garrisons when deprived of the railways; *if* the Americans had resumed military deliveries earlier than they did; *if* individual Nationalist commanders had not preferred surrender to combat; and *if* the economic situation had not continued to deteriorate.

There was nothing to raise the Generalissimo's spirits in the American attitude. On 18 February, President Truman called on Congress to approve an appropriation of $570,000,000 for "financing, through loans or grants, essential imports into China". But there was no mention of military assistance. In a statement of uncompromising severity, Secretary of State Marshall reminded

Congress that he had consistently warned the Generalissimo and his advisers that "the odds were too heavy against them" to settle their differences with the Communists by force. His most damaging words were these:

> The Chinese Communists have succeeded to a considerable extent in identifying their movement with the popular demand for change in present conditions. On the other hand, there have been no indications that the present Chinese government, with its traditions and methods, could satisfy this popular demand or create conditions which would satisfy the mass of Chinese people and prevent further violence and civil disobedience.

Marshall made it clear that in these circumstances the United States had no intention of underwriting the Nationalist effort in the civil war. The China lobby rallied to the Generalissimo's defence, however, but with limited success. An amendment was forced through specifying that there should be a "special fund" of $125,000,000, which the Chinese Government could use as it saw fit—to obtain military supplies, for instance. The Secretary of State had in fact been arguing that the provision of economic aid would free Nationalist funds so that Chiang's government could buy its own military equipment. His main concern, which he spelled out, was to keep the United States out of the Chinese civil war. President Truman's proposals emerged in April as the China Aid Act, providing for $400,000,000 in aid, including the "special fund" of $125,000,000.

The public expressions of American disapproval, especially in Marshall's statement, undoubtedly weakened the Generalissimo's hold even on the Kuomintang, which he had dominated for so long. His loss of prestige was reflected, albeit indirectly, when the elected National Assembly met in Nanking on 29 March. Chiang Kai-shek went through the motions of half-resigning by announcing that he was not a candidate for re-election as President. But however disillusioned his followers might have been, the thought of choosing somebody else as their leader appalled them. Deputations implored him to change his mind, which he did with no great difficulty, and to no one's surprise he was elected with an overwhelming margin (2,430 votes to 369) against an opponent of no great stature.

It was in the election of a Vice-President that the party faithful

allowed themselves to show their displeasure. Chiang had nomi-
nated Sun Fo, son of Sun Yat-sen, as his running mate. But the vote,
by a small margin, went to General Li Tsung-jen, the former
Kwangsi warlord and rebel, who for good reasons had never enjoyed
Chiang's utter trust. It was the first round in what was to develop
into a protracted struggle for power between Li and Chiang, and it
had gone to Chiang's rival.

Li Tsung-jen had built up a national reputation—for the first
time—as Director of the Peiping Headquarters of the Generalissimo
in 1946–47. He had met Dr. Leighton Stuart before the latter's
appointment as American ambassador, and had impressed Stuart
with his sincerity and "enlightened attitude" on China's civil strife.
Gradually, the word got around that Li would be the American
government's alternative choice as China's leader if Chiang Kai-
shek failed to make peace with the Communists. When rumours to
this effect reached the Generalissimo, he became intensely suspicious of Li.

Li's success in the Vice-Presidential election disturbed Chiang
deeply. He had set his heart on Sun Fo as Vice-President for two
very good reasons: now that the war with Japan was over, he
reckoned that his government would present a more normal image
with a non-military figure as his deputy; moreover, as the son of the
Father of the Republic, Sun Fo had a strong appeal to the whole
membership of the Kuomintang. The thought that Sun Fo might be
rejected had not crossed Chiang's mind, for the National Assembly
was dominated by the CC clique, and had Ch'en Li-fu not assured
Chiang that Sun Fo would be duly elected? What shocked him now
was the realisation that Li, this rather mediocre general from
Kwangsi, had majority support in the Assembly. Then there was a
serious loss of face, for he had promised Sun Fo that the job was his
and the election a formality. Worst of all, Li Tsung-jen had
deliberately challenged Chiang's authority, and of all "crimes", this
was always the one Chiang found completely unacceptable.

This first exercise in constitutional government was not going
well in other respects. Some of the elected deputies had been
turned away at the doors of the National Assembly by party
functionaries who had allocated their seats to Kuomintang nom-
inees. Some of the rejected parliamentarians had declared a hunger
strike, and one of them settled down in an antechamber with the
coffin he threatened to occupy if he were not allowed to take his

seat. The Archbishop of Nanking, Paul Yü Pin, persuaded the "strikers" to improve their longevity with a ration of water, orange juice, and milk, while discussions went on. In the end, the elected deputies were allowed to take their seats, and the Assembly was enlarged to accommodate them. Perturbed by their Vice-Presidential failure, the old guard of the KMT tried to regain lost ground by proposing General Ho Ying-ch'in as Premier. But they were too weak to carry the day, and the job went to the able, uncorrupt Dr. Wong Wen-hao. The advent of Dr. Wong gave the new cabinet a more liberal-looking tinge, but it was now too late for cosmetic surgery.

In the face of all setbacks, the Generalissimo continued to present to the world an image of sublime unflappability. Taking office as President of the Republic of China on 20 May 1948, he declared:

> I cannot deny that the path before China is beset with troubles. Much less can I deny that the task of rebuilding our nation is a difficult one. Our basic conditions for democracy are still deficient. But the forces of the times have already pushed us onward on the road to constitutional democracy. . . .
>
> My experience, after having been in the service of the nation for the last forty years, has led me to believe firmly in Dr. Sun Yat-sen's axiom: "Success will come to any measure that conforms with the natural laws, that follows the course of human understanding, that keeps in step with world trends, that answers the people's needs, and that has been discovered by men of superior intelligence".

It was truer than ever that Chiang Kai-shek's outward serenity hid an inner turmoil. The Nationalist hold on Manchurian strong points was becoming untenable. Kirin had been evacuated on 12 March, for a reason well described in the military cliché, to shorten lines of communication. Its garrison had been evacuated to Changchun, where its presence added to local difficulties in the besieged city. All food supplies to Changchun were being blocked by the Communists, and soon the daily deaths from starvation topped 100. The hotly contested Ssup'ingchieh fell three days later than Kirin, leaving Mukden open to Communist assault. In vain, the head of the American military advisory group, Major-General David

G. Barr, pleaded with the Generalissimo to evacuate Mukden, but Chiang—obstinate in his pride—refused.

On 24 April, the Communist General P'eng Teh-huai recaptured Mao Tse-tung's former capital, Yenan, after a hard battle. Nationalist successes followed, but were short-lived. By this time it was clear that the People's Liberation Army had ceased to be a guerrilla force, and was capable of deploying large armies. For the battle for Kaifeng in north Honan in June, General Ch'en Yi had assembled nearly 200,000 men. A similar number of Nationalist troops faced him; the city fell on the 22nd and was recaptured on the 25th.

That month, the great Chinese inflation leaped forward again alarmingly, as measured in the money market of Shanghai. Within a few days, the exchange rate for the Chinese yuan soared from 2,000,000 to the American dollar to 4,000,000. A few weeks later, its value was halved again, when the unofficial rate reached 8,000,000, and in August the incredible figure of 11,000,000 was reached. Yet in June, at the start of this new inflationary flight, the Generalissimo had declared in a speech that the financial situation was satisfactory and that inflation resulted exclusively from Communist propaganda, the calumnies of foreigners, and speculation in Shanghai.

Certainly, Chiang Kai-shek was less worried by inflation than by the military situation. In July, the centre of his anxieties was Taiyuan, where the Nationalist defenders of the north-west province of Shansi were hemmed in. Ever since 1912, except during the Japanese occupation, the wise old warlord, Yen Hsi-shan had maintained his effective rule in the province. With coal and iron mines in the surrounding country, Taiyuan had developed steel mills and arms factories—enough to supply Yen with his normal military requirements. The thought crossed the Generalissimo's mind that now he was hard-pressed, Yen might make a deal with the Communists. But his loyalty remained unshaken. On the 22nd, Chiang Kai-shek made a hazardous air trip to Taiyuan, landing at the only one of the provincial capital's three airports still under government control. There, at any rate, morale was high, and was enhanced by Chiang's arrival.

Earlier, the Generalissimo had flown—at great personal risk—to Chengchow in Honan, then under immediate threat of occupation. Further flights to boost morale followed—to Tsinan and to Mukden. For these exertions, and a continuing attempt to keep all threads in his own hands, Chiang's reward was insomnia. Sleeping tablets gave him little relief. His nights were no longer for sleep, in any case, for they went mostly in long-distance consultations with his field commanders. Still, some sleep was needed, and in the end Chiang Kai-shek found it by drinking a glass and a half of whisky every night before going to bed.

And now, the Generalissimo was forced after all to take note of the runaway inflation, and do something about it. On 19 August 1948, he issued a Presidential mandate establishing a new national currency, the Gold Yuan. By then, the old *fapi* had sunk virtually to zero. The Gold Yuan was convertible to the American dollar at 4 to one. The people were ordered to turn in their old paper money at 3,000,000 to one, and to deliver all private holdings of gold, silver, silver coins, and foreign currencies by 30 September, against appropriate issues of the Gold Yuan. Heartily sick of worthless money, the people responded enthusiastically—at least in the beginning. The Generalissimo appointed his son Ching-kuo, now a general, to administer the currency reform with unlimited powers. It was the first time Ching-kuo's forceful personality had had a chance to display itself. He moved to Shanghai, where he declared war on the black marketeers and speculators. Nobody was spared, and one of the top police commanders, known to be one of the major black marketeers as well, was among several hundreds arrested. An emergency tribunal passed frequent death sentences, which were immediately carried out. For a brief moment, Chiang Ching-kuo was enormously popular with the workers of Shanghai.

Then a curious incident put a brake on his successes. One evening in September, word reached Mme. Chiang by telephone from Shanghai that her stepson had seized large quantities of goods on the premises of the Yangtze Development Corporation, apparently destined for the black market. This powerful company was the property of the K'ung family, and Mme. Chiang learned to her great anger that Ching-kuo now planned to arrest her nephew, David K'ung, the general manager. On hearing the news, and while the Generalissimo meekly left the field to her, she took off for Shanghai. David K'ung was not arrested: instead, he left China for a visit of several months in the United States. The Yangtze Development Corporation was not molested anymore, but began to wind down its activities in Shanghai; soon, the head office was moved to Florida. In the 1950s, a branch was opened in London under a different name, and operated for about ten years until it closed down.

Halted in his tracks, Chiang Ching-kuo suffered a severe loss of face. But there was worse to come: the government had attempted a financial reform in an economic vacuum. It could neither increase its revenues nor decrease its expenditures; nor could production be increased. The Gold Yuan fell. Prices started their upward spiral and on 31 October wages were allowed to find their level. After the first brief flush of confidence, the people had ceased to obey Chiang Ching-kuo's injunction to turn in their American dollars and valuables in exchange for the Gold Yuan. Some people had lost confidence too late. One of them was Chiang's biographer, Hollington Tong, who told Eric Chou over lunch in a Nanking restaurant that on his insistence, his wife had agreed to exchange their life savings of U.S.$4,000 for 16,000 Gold Yuan notes—now utterly worthless. An invisible wall of passive resistance had sprung up around Ching-kuo and his team. His workers were men who had worked for him in Kanhsien, and they were out of their depth in sophisticated Shanghai. A sense of doom was in the air, and it was clear to all that the days of the Nationalists were now numbered.

With true Confucian humility, Chiang Ching-kuo resigned and apologised in these words:

> After the past 70 days of my work, I feel that I have failed to accomplish the duties which I should have accomplished. . . . In certain respects I have rather deepened the sufferings of the people. . . . Today, aside from petitioning the government for punishment so as to clarify my responsibility, I wish to take this opportunity of offering my deepest apology to the citizens of Shanghai. . . . I sincerely wish the citizens of Shanghai to use their own strength to prevent unscrupulous merchants, bureaucrats, politicians and racketeers from controlling Shanghai. . . .

In late September, the Generalissimo finally conceded that Mukden could no longer be held. On the 25th, he ordered the garrison commander, Wei Li-huang, to evacuate the city and relieve the hard-pressed garrison at Chinchow. But Wei did not fancy his chances against Lin Piao's victorious forces. For a fortnight, he hesitated, then obeyed, and paid the penalty of hesitancy, for his twelve divisions were attacked by superior PLA forces and routed. Wei himself escaped by air and was later court-martialed. He kept his life, however, and joined the Communist regime in 1955. (When he died four years later, his soul was rewarded with a splendid funeral.)

Thoroughly demoralised now, the Nationalist commanders began to change sides. The defender of Tsinan, the capital of Shantung, General Wu Hua-wen, surrendered with most of his garrison to Ch'en Yi's attacking force. The provincial governor, General Wang Yao-wu, soon followed suit.

In Manchuria, the collapse followed rapidly after Wei Li-huang's defeat. On 23 October, starving Changchun was evacuated, and Mukden itself fell on 2 November. Some 300,000 Nationalist troops were in Communist hands.

In conversation with Eric Chou in Hong Kong shortly after the fall of Manchuria, the veteran journalist Hu Lin made a penetrating analysis of the reasons for the Nationalist collapse, which he attributed unreservedly to major psychological blunders on Chiang Kai-shek's part. The Generalissimo's treatment of the Young Marshal, Chang Hsueh-liang, had disgusted the population of Manchuria. Chang's long captivity had made him more popular than ever, and deepened Chiang's own unpopularity and the mistrust in which he was held. If he had had the sense to release Chang Hsueh-liang and send him home, the Young Marshal could have rallied popular support for the Nationalist cause.

There were other reasons for Chiang's unpopularity: the arbitrary re-division of the province of Manchuria had offended native sentiment, since the Manchurians themselves had not been consulted. Moreover, the new governors appointed from Nanking with authority over the re-divided provinces were generally rejected by the natives, who regarded them as representatives of the "Southerners"—that is, the Central Government. Again, many non-natives had been appointed to key posts, so that the advent of the Nationalist Government was felt as a form of occupation. The looting, the corruption, the bribery and brutalities of the Kuomintang "take-over" had made many Manchurians wish the Japanese were still there. The witch-hunt conducted by KMT officials for collaborators and "puppets" had driven many people to turn to the Communists. But the worst blunder of all was probably the disbanding of 300,000 Chinese troops of the puppet regime in Manchukuo by General Ch'en Ch'eng on Chiang Kai-shek's orders.

Without means of support, they had flocked to the Communist banner, and Lin Piao had welcomed them with open arms. Indeed, they became the backbone of his "United Democratic Army".

Some years later (in Hong Kong in 1957), Ch'en Hsiao-wei gave Eric Chou his military historian's gloss on Hu Lin's analysis. He, too, thought the disbanding of the 300,000 "puppet" troops was the worst blunder—for which (probably unfairly) he blamed Ch'en Ch'eng rather than Chiang Kai-shek. Once they had joined the Communists, they became the "local forces" defending their own territory, whereas the Central Army forces were the "outsiders" in the eyes of the peasants. The ex-puppets knew the geography of Manchuria intimately; not only were Chiang's new divisions ignorant of the territory, but they were given no time to acclimatise themselves. Highly trained and with American equipment, they had proved themselves in the steaming jungles of Burma. Most of them were southerners, and they suffered intensely in the severe cold.

There was another and purely military reason for the great Nationalist débâcle. Strategically, the Nationalists had been thrown on the defensive from the outset. The Russians had handed the cities back to them, but abandoned the countryside to the Communists. In Chinese military parlance, the Nationalists merely held the "points", while the Communists controlled the "plane". The "points" could be isolated and encircled; but the Nationalists could not hope to sweep over the "plane". All they could do was to try to keep the "points" linked by safeguarding the "lines"—that is, the railway and the roads—so that their strength, already numerically inferior, was stretched to the breaking point.

Desperately, Chiang Kai-shek sent his wife to the United States on 1 December to plead for further American aid. She saw Marshall on the 3rd, and Truman on the 10th, but neither man was sympathetically disposed. She had brought with her demands of a magnitude to match the scale of her country's disasters. They included a request for an economic and military aid programme totalling $3,000,000,000 over three years. In fact, Paul G. Hoffman, head of the Economic Cooperation Administration, whom Truman had sent to Shanghai, returned on 20 December with negative recommendations; and on the 21st, the Americans suspended their reconstruction aid programme for China. Disinclined to come home in failure, Mme. Chiang remained in America for nearly a year, pleading the Nationalist cause with unflagging ardour. But to no avail.

Earlier, but without malice, the Americans had delivered an unwitting but cruel blow to Nationalist hopes in North China. Perhaps the best of the Nationalist generals, Fu Tso-yi, defended the Peiping-Tientsin area with eleven well-trained armies. Of these, however, four entirely lacked equipment and three were inadequately armed. In the summer of 1948, American aid officials, increasingly disenchanted with Chiang Kai-shek, negotiated separately with Fu Tso-yi, whom they proposed to arm so that he could stabilise the defence of North China. Ultimately, they thought, he could open a relief corridor to the Nationalists in Manchuria.

Early in July, they recommended that $16,000,000 in military supplies should be sent to General Fu in Tientsin. Although the Joint Chiefs of Staff concurred, the first shipment did not arrive until 29 November. When it did, it was discovered that most of the arms on board were unusable, for lack of vital parts.

Although Fu Tso-yi had been regarded as one of the most steadfast and capable of Nationalist commanders, the fiasco of the arms deliveries shattered the morale of his forces. Tientsin fell on 14 January 1949, leaving Peiping defenceless, and without a sea route for evacuation. Rather than subject the northern capital, with its great Chinese cultural heritage, to Communist bombardment, Fu handed the city over on 21 January, surrendering that day with his armies.

After the fall of Tientsin, General Yen Hsi-shan had wired Fu Tso-yi six times, urging him to "sacrifice and struggle, giving up any idea of survival". But Yen knew nothing of the pressures to which General Fu had been submitted, nor of his inner psychological stresses. In fact, Fu Tso-yi's surrender was one of the outstanding successes of Mao Tse-tung's United Front policy. The Communists had offered Fu a post in the future government, and had done so astutely through Teng Pao-shang—a north-western warlord operating in Shensi and Kansu—who was the father-in-law of Fu's daughter. Assurances that the people of Peiping were all in favour of surrender had been pressed on him by members of the Democratic League, headed by Professor Chang Tung-sun of Yenching University. The business community, led by Hsu Hui-tung, the chairman of the Municipal Assembly—a member of the CC clique—had pleaded with Fu not to do anything to destroy the historic city of Peiping, and urged him to be "sensible".

Militarily, too, Fu Tso-yi felt isolated. Now that Chiang's best troops had been destroyed in Manchuria, he knew he could not count on the promised assistance of the Central Army. By then, his right-hand man, General Tung Ch'i-wu, had surrendered Suiyuan to the Communists. Apart from these specific points, Fu Tso-yi was operating in a climate that was overwhelmingly unfavourable to continued resistance. The highly vocal student population of Peiping and Tientsin was overwhelmingly anti-Chiang, though not necessarily pro-Communist. And so, the old capital fell.

Further south, the Generalissimo had lost some 400,000 of his remaining troops in a fruitless defence of Hsuchow and the Yangtze River line. When Hsuchow fell on 3 December, the road to Nanking and Shanghai was wide open. The Battle of Hsuchow was indeed one of the greatest military defeats in modern history. It lasted rather less than three months and sealed the fate of Chiang Kai-shek's Central Government on the mainland. Eric Chou covered the campaign from beginning to end, and interviewed one of the army commanders who had escaped to Nanking. This was General Li Mi (he later turned up in Burma at the head of KMT remnants who took to opium-growing). From this interview and from his own observations, Eric Chou analyses the reasons for the Nationalist defeat as follows:

1. Liu Ch'ih, Commander-in-Chief for the Hsuchow Theatre, enjoyed Chiang's personal trust—a reward for unswerving loyalty—but had never won a battle in his life; he was a laughingstock among his fellow-generals.
2. The Nationalist troops were outnumbered by more than three to one: 450,000 Nationalists faced 1,500,000 Communists.
3. The defection of Ho Ch'i-feng's division opened a gap in the left flank, and the Communists drove through without needing to fire a shot. Ho's division was formerly a unit of the Twenty-ninth Army under Sung Cheh-yuan, who had won much renown in the Marco Polo Bridge incident which sparked off the Sino-Japanese War in 1937. The defection was a blow to the morale of other units.

4. There was no unified command, in that the Nationalist forces consisted of troops from Kwangtung, Szechwan, and Yunnan, as well as Chiang Kai-shek's own troops. There was more rivalry than co-operation among the various units.
5. The Generalissimo interfered too much. He gave orders to every army commander by telephone from Nanking almost daily, often failing to take into account the latest developments on the front.
6. The Communists were kept fully informed of Nationalist plans throughout the operation by Liu Fei, who was Chiang Kai-shek's military assistant at headquarters, and who later defected to the Communist side when Li Tsung-jen sent him to Peiping as a member of the peace delegation in April 1949.
7. Because of the runaway inflation, the Nationalist troops were underpaid and poorly fed. When surrounded, whole companies or battalions handed their arms to the Communists in exchange for *man-tou* (Chinese steamed bread) and bowls of rice.
8. The Nationalists no longer had air support, since the Americans were denying them new planes and even parts for the ones they had.

The military historian Ch'en Hsiao-wei, in conversation with Eric Chou in Hong Kong in 1957, added to this dismal list:

1. One of the ablest Nationalist generals, the former Kwangsi rebel Pai Ch'ung-hsi (who was offered the job of over-all Commander-in-Chief in the Hsuchow–Pengpu theatre only at the eleventh hour, and turned it down) was against Chiang Kai-shek's plan to fight a decisive campaign around Hsuchow. His own proposal, which was turned down, was to plan for a major stand at Wuhu (in Anhwei province south of the Yangtze), on the sensible ground that by the time the Communist forces reached that point, their lines of communication would be overstretched.
2. General Chennault had told the Generalissimo that he was confident of turning the tide at Hsuchow with a mere forty fighter-bombers. But as we have seen, the American government turned down Nationalist requests to that end.
3. The Nationalists' mechanised units were immobilised by

deep trenches, which the Communists had dug extensively as tank traps. (Mao Tse-tung's slogan of the 1970s, "Dig the trenches deep", to resist a possible Russian onslaught, may well have originated from Hsuchow.)

4. On the whole, the Nationalist units in the Hsuchow campaign were inferior to the enemy in equipment and firepower.
5. The Nationalists fought a defensive positional war, while the Communists pressed their attack with superior mobility.
6. While they attacked, the Communists forced civilian refugees to march ahead of their fighting units to confuse and frustrate the Nationalist forces in their defensive positions.

After Hsuchow, the Communists lost all interest in peace talks with the Nationalists. This, at least, Chiang Kai-shek saw clearly, even if others—led by Li Tsung-jen—allowed their thinking to be clouded by false hopes.

At about the time of the great Hsuchow defeat, Chiang Kai-shek suffered an intimate psychological blow. His private secretary, Ch'en Pu-lei, committed suicide. Having interviewed him two weeks earlier, Eric Chou had found him very depressed. He had blamed himself for having failed to serve the country better. Looking deeply distressed, Chiang attended the funeral service. In Ch'en's diary, there was a short passage ending: "I have now reached the stage when the oil in the lamp has dried up." His health had been collapsing: an insomniac for years, he was deeply depressed. The last straw had been the discovery that his only daughter was an underground Communist, who could have passed vital state secrets to her party. He could sense that the KMT was now doomed, and blamed himself for not having been able to influence Chiang's policies and decisions.

As the dreadful year of 1948 drew to its close, a peace group came to the fore within the Kuomintang government. Initially, the leader of it was one of Chiang's best generals, Pai Ch'ung-hsi; but soon enough the group crystallised around Vice-President Li Tsung-jen, Pai's old Kwangsi comrade. That December, Pai and the Governor of Hunan, General Ch'eng Ch'ien, went into rather frequent secret huddles. The two men agreed that only by negotiating with the Communists could they delay the Red offensive. Pai went into action with a flurry of telegrams. The first was a circular one, advocating peace negotiations. He followed up with telegrams to Chang Ch'ün and Chang Chih-chung, requesting them to suggest to Chiang Kai-shek that the time had come for peace talks with his enemies. Next, the chairmen of the Provincial Assemblies of Hunan, Hupei, Honan, and Kwangsi jointly signed a circular telegram, condemning President Chiang and calling on him to come to a quick decision about his personal future so that the peace negotiations should be neither delayed nor jeopardised. From the governor of Honan, Chang Ch'en, came yet another circular telegram calling on the Generalissimo to retire.

These signs of defeatism and insubordination, as the Generalissimo saw them, shook him deeply. At that time, Pai Ch'ung-hsi had 500,000 troops under his command, and his was a voice not lightly to be ignored—even by Chiang Kai-shek. He therefore sent his faithful friend Chang Ch'ün twice to Hankow to discuss the situation with General Pai and try to disperse any misunderstandings. It soon emerged that Pai, at least, was no defeatist. While the telegrams had been bombarding Chiang Kai-shek, the Communist armies were pushing southward inexorably towards the Yangtze River in the wake of their crushing victory at Hsuchow. The point, as Pai saw it, was to negotiate a halt, so that the Nationalist armies could reorganise their defences in Hunan, Hupei, Kiangsi, Kwangsi, Yunnan, and Kweichow. But the peace group also had men who were truly defeatist or even pro-Communist. Both descriptions were true of Chang Chih-chung, who wanted to force Chiang to resign, so that Li Tsung-jen could negotiate peace immediately.

On the strength of Chang Ch'ün's report, Chiang Kai-shek had thought that some understanding would be reached with Pai Ch'ung-hsi, but he was disabused and angered when a telegram from Pai reached him on Christmas Day, urging him to start peace negotiations immediately under joint American-Soviet mediation. From Hong Kong, too, came irritating news—that a "Kuomintang Revolutionary Committee", controlled by the Communists, was "negotiating" with an emissary of Vice-President Li Tsung-jen. Moreover, even Chang Ch'ün now told him that he favoured peace talks; and so of course did the American ambassador, Dr. Stuart.

By nature, Chiang Kai-shek was a last-ditcher. He was also, as he had shown so often, a resigner—but on his own terms. To retire on request and under pressure was hurtful. Yet how could he fight on without the support of his political colleagues? On 31 December, as he was about to deliver his New Year's message, he invited about forty members of the Kuomintang Central Executive and Supervisory Committees to dinner. He listened to their guarded words in silence, then exploded: "I did not want to quit, but you members of the Kuomintang wanted me to resign. I intend to leave, not because of the Communists, but because of certain sections of the Kuomintang." He had already prepared his New Year's statement, declaring himself willing to negotiate for peace, but on the usual terms which he knew the Communists would not accept: "If the Constitution is not violated . . . , if the democratic form of government is maintained, if the entity of the armed forces is safeguarded". But the key sentences were these: "If peace can be secured, I am not at all concerned about my own position. In this I will follow only the consensus of popular feeling." While his guests resumed the discussion, Chiang ordered his statement to be released.

Within hours, the peace group—whose leader, it now emerged, was Vice-President Li—began harassing the Generalissimo with slogans in the press and on city walls: "Unless President Chiang retires, the Communists will not talk peace"; "Unless President Chiang retires, there is no hope of American aid." And indeed, the American embassy, consistent to the end in its support of negotiations, favoured Li and the peace group.

And now, on 14 January 1949, Mao Tse-tung intervened with a shattering statement. The Communist radio broadcast eight conditions for peace negotiations. The statement began with an indictment of Chiang Kai-shek as "China's number-one criminal," "Chieftain of the Kuomintang bandit gang", "Bogus President of the Republic", who had "sold out the national interest wholesale to the U.S. government". Before the end of the year, the Communists had already published a list of forty-three top "war criminals", headed of course by Chiang Kai-shek.

The Communist conditions were these:

1. Punish the war criminals.
2. Abolish the bogus constitution.
3. Abolish the bogus "constituted authority".
4. Reorganise all reactionary troops on democratic principles.
5. Confiscate bureaucratic capital.

6. Reform the land system.
7. Abrogate treasonable treaties.
8. Convene a political consultative conference without the participation of reactionary elements, and form a democratic coalition government to take over all the powers of the reactionary Nanking government and of its subordinate governments at all levels.

Humiliating though these terms were, the peace group decided that it had no option but to accept them, and on 19 January the Executive Yüan declared itself ready "to cease-fire simultaneously with the Communists, and both sides send representatives to start peace negotiations."

Now Chiang Kai-shek's mind was made up. He would withdraw from the scene, but not resign. If Li Tsung-jen thought he could negotiate successfully with the Communists, let him try. And whether he failed or succeeded, let him bear the odium. As for Chiang himself, the struggle would go on after a suitable interval. Before issuing his New Year's statement, he had decided that at all costs, Taiwan should be held as the ultimate redoubt. To this end, he had appointed Chiang Ching-kuo as head of the Kuomintang on the island, and General Ch'en Ch'eng as governor. On 21 January, Chiang Kai-shek now announced his retirement, saying:

My earnest prayers will have been answered if the Communist Party henceforth realises the grave situation confronting the country, orders a cease-fire and agrees to open peace talks with the government. Thus the people will be spared their intense sufferings, the spiritual and material resources of the nation preserved, and its territorial integrity and political sovereignty maintained. Thus, also, the continuity of the nation's history, culture and social order will be perpetuated and the people's livelihood and freedom safeguarded.

In fact, as the Generalissimo well knew, there was no provision for the President's resignation under the new Chinese Constitution. Chiang merely turned over his powers to the Vice-President under Article 49, which provided for such devolution "in the event of the President being unable for any reason whatsoever to attend to his functions". To mark the point that he had not necessarily gone forever, he remained *Tsung t'sai* of the Kuomintang.

As on previous withdrawals from public life, on leaving Nanking, Chiang Kai-shek headed for his native village in Chekiang province.

21. Chiang Loses the Mainland

Chiang Kai-shek took his son Ching-kuo with him into "retirement" at Chi Kou, his native village. As they arrived, the first order Chiang gave his son was to see to it that the Air Force General Headquarters should complete the building of the airfield at Tinghai without delay. At the time, he gave no explanation, and neither Ching-kuo nor the Air Force officers to whom the order was transmitted knew what was in his mind. But it became painfully clear before very long. Tinghai is in Chekiang province between Chi Kou and Shanghai. The Generalissimo's order showed in fact that he already had no illusions about the possibility of holding onto China's greatest port. In his "retirement", he kept on inquiring about the progress of the construction work. Four months later, when Shanghai fell, its defenders relied on Tinghai airfield to evacuate to Taiwan.

Later that day, Chiang Kai-shek said to Ching-kuo: "We will be here three months." His forecast was correct to the day. Except for

327

his absence from the seat of government, it was almost as if he had not gone through the formality of retiring from the Presidency.

The acting President soon discovered that his ministers would not take his orders, nor would the army or police. Moreover, he had no money. From his village retreat, Chiang Kai-shek had sent instructions to the Governor of the Central Bank of China, O. K. Yui, to transfer the entire gold reserve of 500,000 ounces to Taipei. By that time, Chiang lacked the constitutional authority to give any such order, but he was obeyed because he was Chiang Kai-shek and because he invoked his authority as Director-General of the Kuomintang. His main object in so doing was undoubtedly to finance continued resistance to the Communists, should they complete their conquest of the Chinese mainland, as Chiang now held to be inevitable. But he was not averse to the side-benefit of depriving Li Tsung-jen of the financial means of governing. The transfer was completed by 20 February 1949. Had the gold remained where it was, there is no doubt that Li would have used it as a bargaining counter in his peace negotiations with Mao Tse-tung.

On hearing of the transfer, the acting President flew into a rage and forbade Yui to transfer any further assets to Taiwan. The embargo came just in time to prevent the shipment of a large quantity of pearls, diamonds, and other precious stones confiscated by the Central Government during the war and deposited in the vaults of the Central Bank in Shanghai. When the Communists captured the city later in the year, they took possession of the entire haul. For Li, the immediate situation was that the Central Bank disregarded his requests for cash to meet administrative outgoings. Deprived of its gold backing, the Gold Yuan resumed its vertiginous descent.

By the time Li discovered that his government had no money, he had already found out the limits of his personal authority. One thing seemed clear to him: he had a mandate of sorts to talk peace with the Communists. His first move was to talk the problem over with the Soviet ambassador, General V. I. Roshchin, who readily agreed to offer his good offices—on condition that the Chinese government would undertake to be neutral in the event of a future conflict between America and Russia, and that steps should be taken to eliminate American influence from China. With the naivety of diplomatic inexperience, he then sent a memorandum on his talk with Roshchin to the American ambassador, Dr. Stuart, on 23 January, requesting that the United States should publicly pledge its support of the National Government. In Chi Kou, the Generalissimo learned of this curious move with wry amusement. He was not surprised when the State Department rejected this attempt to persuade the United States to agree to the elimination of its own influence in China.

Intent on peace, Li Tsung-jen was wide open to the persuasions of the "peace brokers" who swarmed in Nanking and Shanghai as the winter ended. One of them was Professor Wu Yü-hou of the Central University; and another was a certain General Li Ming-yang, who had been associated with Wang Ching-wei's "puppet" regime. Then there was a member of the Legislative Yüan, Wu Ho-hsuan. All three, and the others, claimed to have "very influential connections" in the Communist hierarchy. However, apart from the instant publicity their claims brought them, and the money they extracted from the acting President, their "brokerage" came to nothing. The "peace brokers" included two members of Li Tsung-jen's own staff: Liu Chung-jung and Huang Ch'i-han, who both claimed to be members of "the Third Influence"—half-way between the Nationalists and the Communists. In time, however, both men turned out to have been underground Communists.

On 22 January, Li Tsung-jen had appointed a committee of five to negotiate with the Communists on behalf of the National Government. Two days later, he proclaimed the end of martial law, the release of political prisoners, and the disbandment of the secret police. And on the 27th, he followed this conciliatory gesture with a telegram to Mao Tse-tung agreeing to the eight-point Communist proposal as the basis of peace talks.

It was at this point that the acting President discovered that he was governing in a vacuum. Indeed, he had failed to consult either the Executive Yüan of the KMT's Central Political Committee; nor had he thought fit to inform the Prime Minister, Sun Fo. Furious, Sun Fo repudiated the telegram, declared that he would not be responsible for the acting President's policy before the Legislative Yüan, and announced that he was moving to Canton with his government. The removal duly took place on 5 February, and all government departments were transferred from Nanking except the acting President's office. All governments accredited to the Republic of China were requested to move their embassies to Canton on that date. Stuart declined the request, and so did most of the embassies of the larger powers. To everybody's stupefaction, the only important exception was Roshchin, who found himself, once in Canton, in daily contact with the "bitter enders" of the Kuomintang, including the then Foreign Minister, Wu Tieh-cheng, while the peace group remained in Nanking with Li Tsung-jen.

In other ways, too, the absent Generalissimo had crippled his "acting" successor. He had transferred some 300,000 of his most faithful troops to Taiwan, together with "his" navy of twenty-six gunboats and "his" air force. About 900,000 Nationalist troops remained on the mainland, but of these only General Pai Ch'ung-hsi's 120,000 men were at Li Tsung-jen's disposal, for reasons of ancient comradeship. Both the ordinary police and the secret services took their instructions from the redoubtable Ch'en Li-fu, on behalf of the invisible Chiang Kai-shek. It followed that the acting President's amnesty for political prisoners and disbandment of the secret police remained a dead letter. Li Tsung-jen had thought to gain popularity by releasing the Young Marshal, Chang Hsueh-liang, who had remained in detention since the Sian kidnapping of 1936. But the Young Marshal could not be found: the Generalissimo had had him sent to Taiwan, still in captivity.

Having ensured his return (in line with his life-long rule that resignations were not meant to be permanent), Chiang Kai-shek was enjoying his "retirement". Accustomed to living at the expense of the State, he had had to borrow 1,000,000 Gold Yuan—worth about U.S. $10,000 at the official rate—from the Farmers' Bank on personal loan, to cover his expenses. This was an "easy touch", since the bank was controlled by Ch'en Li-fu. Apart from Chiang Ching-kuo, his staff consisted of one secretary and another assistant. He and his son went on long walks in the fields, and he stirred nostalgic memories by revisiting the temples and shrines his mother had introduced him to as a boy. At first, much as was General de Gaulle's habit at Colombey, he declined to receive any official visitors. The acting President was one of those whose request for a talk was rejected. Letters and telegrams from well-placed informants, however, kept him abreast of developments.

One telegram came from Chang Chih-chung, whom the acting President had named as head of the peace talks delegation to Peiping. Chang said he proposed to go to Chi Kou to see the Generalissimo for instructions. But Chiang, with a lifetime's experience of struggling with the Russians and the Chinese Communists, was indifferent to the forthcoming negotiations. The optimists had not bothered to hide their delight at the removal of Chiang Kai-shek, whom they regarded as the main obstacle to the peace talks. Well, then, let them get on with it and not bother him. On reading the telegram, Chiang Kai-shek said to Ching-kuo: "It doesn't matter whether he comes or not."

The next day, Chang Chih-chung arrived in Chikou. But the Generalissimo pointedly made no reference to the peace talks, and changed the subject when his visitor showed signs of mentioning them. Instead, he insisted on showing Chang the local beauty spots. That evening, Ching-kuo told Chang the reasons for his father's scepticism and lack of interest in the peace talks. But Chang said he was going ahead anyway, and he left on this note.

Chiang Kai-shek learned without surprise of the escalating difficulties Mao Tse-tung was placing in Li Tsung-jen's way over the peace negotiations. The acting President, his mind on the feudal China of the warlords in which he had risen to power, nursed the illusion that he could make a deal with the Communists enabling the Kuomintang, or his section of it, to keep China south of the Yangtze. But he soon discovered that Mao was not interested in deals of this kind: he wanted all China.

The peace talks began in Peiping on 1 April. The Communist team was led by Chou En-lai and Lin Piao, and the Nationalists—as announced—by Chang Chih-chung. Chou had done his homework, and presented the Nationalists with twenty-four supplementary requests, on top of Mao's original eight points. Moreover, said Chou En-lai, the thirty-two points were not negotiable: it was all or nothing, if the Kuomintang wanted peace. The Nationalist negotiators were shaken. Not only were they required to hand over the forty-three "war criminals" named earlier by the Communists, plus two, and including the Generalissimo and his wife, General Ho Ying-ch'in, T. V. Soong, Ch'en Li-fu, and Chiang Ching-kuo—but the new points amounted, if complied with, to unconditional surrender. The Communists were now demanding unhindered military access to the south bank of the Yangtze, the reorganisation of the national armies under Communist control, and a hand-over of administrative powers in preparation for a coalition government. Moreover, the preamble to the Communist document would have obliged the National Government to accept the moral responsibility for the civil war. All the Nationalist delegation could do was to plead for concessions. This they did for a fortnight, with little visible progress.

On 4 April, Mao Tse-tung startled his visitors and the world with the announcement that in the event of a third world war, the Chinese Communists would side with Russia against the United States. On the 15th, Chou En-lai delivered an ultimatum: either the National Government accepted the Communist peace draft by 20 April, or the Communist armies would cross the Yangtze. One of the Nationalist delegates was sent to Nanking to explain the position to the acting President. As he explained the situation, it was even worse than it looked on paper. Not only were the central armies required to surrender, but those that did would have to help the Communists to disarm the rest. Moreover, the ultimatum was make-believe: the Communists were going to cross the Yangtze River anyway.

Li Tsung-jen talked the problem over with his close associate Pai Ch'ung-hsi, who found the terms totally unacceptable. Chang, the leader of the Nationalist delegation, had sent an urgent message to Li advising acceptance of the Communist terms. But Li felt he could not "go it alone", without Pai. The situation was getting out of control. It was in fact even more out of control than the acting President knew. From the beginning of the talks, he had realised that he could place no reliance on Chang Chih-chung, whose opportunism had become conspicuous. He had therefore relied heavily on other members of the delegation, especially Huang Shao-hung, who had belonged to the Kwangsi Clique in the old days, and Liu Fei, a Vice-Minister in the Nationalist Defence Ministry. But Huang turned out to be no less of an opportunist than Chang, and once in Peiping, he spent more time angling for a post in the proposed "coalition government", which the Communists proposed to set up, than in negotiating with them. As for Liu, it turned out that he had worked secretly for the Communists in the Defence Ministry for some years. In the end, not only did the whole delegation capitulate to Mao Tse-tung and Chou En-lai, but they stayed in Peiping for good, throwing in their lot with the Communists.

On 17 April, the acting President wired Chiang Kai-shek, asking him to resume the Presidency and his leadership of the nation. Chiang wired back, proposing an emergency conference in

Hangchow with acting President Li and General Ho Ying-ch'in, whom the desperate Li had appointed Prime Minister in succession to Sun Fo. Other familiar Kuomintang figures were there, including Wang Shih-chieh, Chang Ch'ün, and Pai Ch'ung-hsi. Referring to the Communist ultimatum, Chiang Kai-shek asked Li: "What attitude do you think we should adopt?" Li Tsung-jen replied: "I am prepared to send someone to Peiping to negotiate the terms."

According to Chiang Ching-kuo, the Generalissimo said: "There is no point in doing this. The Communists agreed to peace negotiations, but only because they had not yet deployed their forces to cross the river. Now that their preparations are complete, there is no room for negotiations. Besides, the first item of the peace terms puts all the blame on our party, writing off the party's glorious history of sixty years. This is totally unacceptable!" And Chiang Kai-shek produced a draft he had prepared for a circular telegram. "This telegram," Chiang explained, "can be signed jointly by ourselves—by you as the acting President, and by me as Director-General of the KMT." The draft declared that the peace negotiations with the Communists had broken down, and announced the removal of the government to Canton to continue resisting Communist aggression. Li Tsung-jen had no further comments to offer, and agreed to sign the telegram.

One practical measure that emerged from the Hangchow meeting was that the new Prime Minister should also be Minister of National Defence, with over-all authority over the armed forces. To mark the point that his "retirement" was not yet over, Chiang Kai-shek thereupon returned to Chikou. Li, who was exhausted, went to Kweilin, capital of his Kwangsi stronghold, for a two-week rest.

The ultimatum had expired, but seven hours earlier the Communists opened fire with the artillery they had massed on the north bank of the Yangtze. That night General Ch'en Yi led his People's Liberation Army troops across the broad river—two miles wide at that point—with ease in the face of token resistance from a few Nationalist river gunboats. In panic, the acting President ordered the evacuation of Nanking, which the Communists occupied on the 24th. With the Red forces came a "peace preservation committee" to handle the take-over. In silence, the inhabitants watched as the Communist forces set an example of discipline in victory which the Nationalist armies might well have envied. There was neither rape nor looting, and foreigners were left unmolested.

The fall of Nanking shattered the illusions of the diplomatic corps in Chiang Kai-shek's capital. Wishful thinking had injected euphoria into their reports. They included Dr. K. M. Panikkar, the Indian Ambassador; Dr. Copland, the Australian Minister; and Chester Ronning, the Canadian chargé d'affaires. All were under the illusion that the Chinese Communists, being "agrarian reform-ers", would be willing to compromise. Surely, they reasoned, the Communists would need trained personnel to run the cities and the economy. In this need, they saw the making of a coalition government, with Li Tsung-jen leading the Nationalists. The American ambassador, Dr. Leighton Stuart, put his faith in the notion that the Communists were bound to seek American aid and cooperation, even if Li Tsung-jen failed to reach an agreement with them in the peace talks. His naive faith was strengthened by Fu Ching-po, his protégé and "Chinese adviser", who lived in his official residence and whom he paid out of his own pocket. Fu had been Dr. Stuart's secretary at Yenching University, and talked with great conviction about the "old boys of Yenching" within the Communist Party and their "respect for the old man"—as if the mere sight of their former principal would make them reasonable and pro-American. Even Li Tsung-jen and his close associates (according to Eric Chou) were under the impression that Fu Ching-po was the "voice of the U.S. State Department". This misconception helps to account for Li Tsung-jen's stubborn belief that even when the peace talks had failed, he could make a deal with the Americans by getting rid of Chiang Kai-shek. Eventually, when all was lost, he would make a personal appeal to President Truman.

When the departing Nationalist government advised all the embassies to move to Canton, Ambassador Stuart stayed behind in Nanking in the vain hope of persuading the Chinese Communists, through his former students, to exchange diplomatic relations with the United States. In the eyes of many Nationalists, Dr. Stuart's attitude, by further demoralising their side, accelerated the collapse on the mainland.

Li Tsung-jen did not have a restful holiday in Kweilin, for a stream of visitors came to him urging him, among other things, to move to Canton, where all resistance efforts could be co-ordinated.

Li was in a quandary. Having failed to get peace, it seemed sensible to hand power back to Chiang Kai-shek; but the Generalissimo, not for the first time, was playing hard to get. An important meeting on 3 May helped him to clarify his ideas. That day, a special plane arrived from Canton, bringing Yen Hsi-shan (the old Shansi warlord) and others. They immediately went to Li's official residence, in Wen Ming Road, where they were greeted by Li Tsung-jen and Pai Ch'ung-hsi. Yen and his companions—who had been in touch with Chiang Kai-shek—reported that the Generalissimo was now ready to support the acting President without reservations.

A number of decisions were reached, which were to be presented to Chiang Kai-shek in the form of demands. The Minister of Defence and the military and political leaders should be given complete power to direct and move the armed forces in the areas under the Central Government's control. The acting President and the President of the Executive Yüan should have sole authority, as laid down by the Constitution, over all appointments and dismissals of military officers and civil officials. Local governments should be responsible only to the acting President and the President of the Executive Yüan. Neither the Kuomintang nor its Director-General (Chiang Kai-shek) should interfere in any of the matters listed. All the gold, silver, and foreign exchange sent to Taiwan must be brought back to the mainland to finance Li's government. As for the Generalissimo, it was hoped that he would leave China on a trip to Europe and America, ostensibly to raise money and support for China, but actually so that the proposed military and political reforms should not be hindered.°

° The chronology of this period is confused, as various Chinese writers contradict each other. For instance, Chiang Ching-kuo gives 24 April 1949 as the date of Mao Tse-tung's ultimatum to the Nationalist government; in fact, it was issued on 17 April. He goes on to say that on the 24th, his father sent Li Tsung-jen a telegram proposing a meeting in Hangchow. In fact, the meeting took place on 22 April. (Chiang Ching-kuo, *My Father*, ch. 4, pp. 2–3.) Similarly, another writer states that after Li's meeting with Yen Hsi-shan and others in Kweilin on 3 May, Yen flew to Taiwan to see Chiang Kai-shek. However, at that time Chiang was in Shanghai, having gone there from Chi Kou. (*The Inside Story of the Chiang-Li Power Struggle*, by Li Tsung-jen's personal secretary, Liang Sheng-chun, p. 134.) While I have drawn from these writers for interesting details, I have preferred Hollington Tong's more accurate chronology.

Chiang Kai-shek had ideas of his own, of course, which did not at all coincide with those of Li Tsung-jen and his colleagues. On 25 April—his three months having elapsed—he left Chi Kou and boarded a gunboat, allowing it to be known that his destination was either Amoy or Taiwan. But in fact he headed for Shanghai. There, as a young man, Chiang had found love, fame, and power. Now, in the hour of disaster, he nursed a mad dream. The local commander, General T'ang En-po, had been defying the acting President's orders to lift martial law and evacuate enough troops to reinforce the defenders of the triple city of Wuhan. Instead, he proclaimed a proud resolve to make Shanghai a "second Stalingrad". Chiang supported him. He ordered several armies to join the defenders of Shanghai, and made a speech forecasting "total victory within three years". Thousands of coolies were made to dig an enormous moat and erect a ten-foot bamboo palisade, of no apparent military value.

Chaos and brutality reigned everywhere. With him, T'ang En-po had brought the number of troops in Shanghai to 200,000. In return for "protection", his men had behaved as undisciplined conquerors. Offices and houses had been requisitioned, and the splendid trees on the grounds of the Golf Club had been razed to make way for a rifle range. The police forces—open and secret— were rounding up people by the dozen on allegations of black marketing or espionage, and executing them summarily with shots in the back of the neck in the street and in full view of the crowds, without the formality of a trial. The army had seized the Central Bank, which was printing money in large quantities—most of which went to high officials and officers to ease them in their flight to Canton or Taiwan, where many of them made fortunes by exchanging them at the official rate for harder currencies.

As usual, Chiang Kai-shek seemed oblivious to these excesses. With his normal disdain for physical danger, he moved about the city without bodyguards. Perhaps because, even in this extremity, he was less unpopular than his regime, nobody laid a hand on him.

During the eleven days he spent in Shanghai, full details of Li Tsung-jen's conversations in Kweilin were brought to him by a special plane. "Much saddened," writes Chiang Ching-kuo, Chiang Kai-shek wrote back to the acting President, saying: "You demand that I should go abroad. This I cannot do, for I am not a warlord!

But I shall agree not to concern myself with affairs of State. From tomorrow, I shall wash my hands of them completely."

Unknown to Chiang, the acting President chose that moment—5 May 1949—to write to President Truman to complain that the National Government had misused American aid. His letter was published, along with a mass of other documents, in the State Department's "White Paper", *United States Relations with China*, in the summer of 1949.

On 6 May, the Generalissimo left Shanghai for a secret destination, which turned out to be Taipei. The provincial authorities, alerted in time, met him and pressed him to set up house in the former Viceroy's residence. On the ground that he was now a private citizen, Chiang politely declined and moved into a former guest house of the Taiwan Sugar Company in the village of Tsaoshan (since renamed Yangmingshan), eight miles north of Taipei in the mountains.

In Shanghai, meanwhile, the bankers and businessmen were having secret talks with Communist emissaries. During the Sino-Japanese War, the Shanghai banking community, in particular Chou Tso-min of Kincheng Bank, had secretly provided General Ch'en Yi and his New Fourth Army with money and medical supplies. Now, with the Communist forces outside the city, these bankers wanted assurances from the Communists that it would not be destroyed. At the same time, they also approached T'ang En-po, offering him gold bullion and American dollars in return for a promise not to make a last-ditch stand around Shanghai.

In 1957, Eric Chou met one of the secret Communist emissaries in Hong Kong. He was Chou's old friend Ch'en Po-liu, one of the left-wing student leaders in Peking in 1935. When this book was written, Ch'en Po-liu held a senior post in the (Communist) Bank of China in Hong Kong.

In his village home near Taipei on 25 May, news of the fall of Shanghai reached Chiang Kai-shek. For all their heroic talk, the defenders had decided to surrender when the Communist forces drew uncomfortably close. Doubtless the bankers' money helped to deflect them from unnecessary heroics. T'ang En-po got out in time with about half his forces, but Ch'en Yi entered the great commercial metropolis virtually without a fight, taking more than 100,000 prisoners.

Unknown to the outside world, a great bonus awaited them. For this, they were indebted to one of the less famous defectors, Wu Shao-shu. A member of the CC clique, Wu was also on the staff of the Central Bureau of Investigation and Statistics. During the Sino-Japanese War, he had worked underground in Shanghai, as master spy for the Nationalists. It was part of his job to know the Shanghai underworld, and he was a member of the Green Society. After V–J Day, Chiang Kai-shek appointed him deputy mayor of Shanghai and gave him the job of organising the students. In this capacity, he ran the local branch of the *San Min Chu Yi* ("Three Principles of the People") Youth Corps. When the Communists entered the city, Wu handed them his complete files on the local business magnates, secret-society leaders, and Nationalist secret agents. Ch'en Yi was thus able to round up all "hostile elements" without delay. Before leaving the city, Chiang Kai-shek is believed to have personally seen to the organising of a Nationalist Underground Command in Shanghai (according to Eric Chou's sources); Wu Shao-shu's defection "blew" the whole set-up. As a reward, he was presented to Chou En-lai in Peking and appointed a counsellor to the Ministry of Communications in the People's Government.

The best of the old warlords, Yen Hsi-shan, plays a brief starring role at this point. He had built roads and railways in Shansi, which he had dominated since 1911. He had planted trees and developed agriculture, and he had not neglected education. Not for nothing was he known as the "model governor". On 24 April, Taiyuan, the old provincial capital, with its thirty-foot-thick ramparts, had fallen at last after a siege that began in the autumn of 1948. Lacking adequate support from the centre, Yen flew to Canton towards the end of May to confer with Li Tsung-jen. Li sent him to Taiwan, bearing a deferential letter from the acting President to Chiang Kai-shek, saying: "All our comrades here hope that you will come to Canton to lead us and I myself also sincerely hope that I shall be able to seek your daily advice and direction." But Chiang, who had other things on his mind, was not yet ready to resume office.

Chiang listened carefully, however, as Yen Hsi-shan forcibly outlined his views. Of all the Nationalist leaders, Yen was the most bitter about America's "non-intervention" in the Central Government's hour of need. He wanted Chiang to agree to suspend the Constitution, set up a military government, ignore American advice or reactions, reorganise the remaining provinces on a war footing, and take immediate steps to organise anti-Communist guerrilla units behind the Communist lines. But Chiang (according to Yen) refused to listen, on the ground that "the democratic system must be preserved". With contempt in his voice, Yen said:

> The Americans think they know what is good for China. But what do they know about China? They see China through the eyes of their missionaries and they learn about China from a handful of English-speaking Chinese intellectuals and compradores. They want to introduce their type of democracy in China without taking into consideration conditions in China. But we eat rice and they eat bread. Does this mean we have to eat bread to become a democratic nation? We do not profess to know what is good for America, and rightly so. When one lends money to one's friends, there should be no strings attached. It's absurd to lend money to your friend on the condition that he should run his household to your specifications.
>
> The Americans have done us enough harm; President Roosevelt sold us to the Russians at the Yalta conference, Marshall's ineffective mediation gave the Communists the time they needed to complete their deployment and preparations for the all-out offensive, and now they rely on their missionary-ambassador Stuart to convert the Communists into God-fearing Christians. If I were Mr. Chiang, I would forget about the Americans. How much is democracy worth when there isn't even a country in which to practise it?

But these fighting words (which were quoted to Eric Chou by Yen Hsi-shan's secretary) fell on deaf ears. So Yen flew back to Canton, where on 2 June, he succeeded Ho Ying-ch'in as Prime Minister.

Though old and irritable from diabetes, Yen was a strong personality and enormously popular. His appointment gave a temporary boost to Nationalist morale, which had already been stimulated towards the end of May by a rare victory. A dashing Muslim general, Ma Pu-fang, and his son, had unexpectedly defeated the Communist General P'eng Teh-huai, after Sian, capital of Shensi province, had fallen to the Reds. From Taiwan, the Generalissimo announced Ma's promotion to Commander-in-Chief in the north-west and promised to air-drop arms and ammunition to him. This Nationalist success was, however, short-lived: the arms and ammunition never came, and P'eng returned, driving Ma out of the province by 26 August.

There were two other things Chiang Kai-shek had on his mind: a new diplomatic offensive designed to force the United States to resume full support of Nationalist China, and a careful study of last-ditch defence possibilities in the wilder regions still under Nationalist control. On the diplomatic front, Chiang flew to Baguio in the Philippines on 10 July, to meet President Elpidio Quirino. He brought with him a plan for an anti-Communist alliance of all independent nations in East Asia. Quirino agreed, and next day a joint communiqué launched the plan. On 7 August, the Generalissimo followed up with a flight to Chinhai, in South Korea, where he met President Syngman Rhee. In a joint letter to President Quirino, the two statesmen called on the Philippine President to convene a conference at Baguio at which interested states could be invited to join the proposed union.

Nothing came of this late initiative. Later in the month, Quirino went to Washington, where Secretary of State Acheson firmly discouraged Chiang Kai-shek's proposal. Invitations to the conference were never issued.

Between his talks with Quirino and Rhee, Chiang Kai-shek had paid a fleeting visit to Canton—which he had not seen since 1936—where he delivered what turned out to be the first of a series of pep-talks. Addressing a meeting of the Central Executive Committee of the Kuomintang on 16 July, he declared:

I feel ashamed to be back in Canton in the present circumstances of retreat and failure. I cannot but admit that I must share a great part of the defeat. I am appalled at the existence of gambling and opium smuggling in Canton under the very nose of the government. But we must hold Canton, our last port—the last place from which we can use both our navy and air force.

Rhetorically, the Generalissimo added: "I am ready to perish with the city." But he rather spoilt his effect by leaving on the 21st. The day of his Canton speech may be said to mark his active resumption of a leading role in Nationalist politics, for that day the

Kuomintang set up the Supreme Political Council, with Chiang as Chairman.°

At the Canton meeting, Li Tsung-jen had clashed with Chiang Kai-shek on strategy in the dark period ahead. Li backed Pai Ch'ung-hsi's plan to hold Central China—Hupei, Hunan, Anhwei, and Kiangsi—with Kwangtung and Kwangsi as the rear. Li had therefore pressed for the return of the Nationalist air force from Taiwan. Chiang, however, was determined that if all else failed, Taiwan itself should be impregnable. He refused to authorise the transfer of the air force, and Li bowed to him.

At first General Pai's plan seemed to be working out as he had hoped, despite the crushing Nationalist defeat at Hsuchow. He pulled his forces back, according to plan, when Lin Piao attacked at the beginning of August, aiming south along the Canton Railway. Pai Ch'ung-hsi decided to make a stand at Changsha, and was much comforted when the volatile bandits of the Tapieh Mountains went into action against the Communists in the rear. Those same bandits had been anti-Communist in 1930, had fought the Japanese in 1940 and the Communists in 1945: like the Irish, they were traditionally "agin the government"—meaning whoever held the reins of power. Floods also delayed Lin Piao's advance.

Then treachery intervened to wreck Pai's hopes. Responding to secret Communist overtures for a "local peaceful settlement", the Nationalist commander of the Changsha garrison, General Ch'eng Ch'ien (the man who was playing mahjong on V–J Day), went over to the Reds. His successor, General Ch'en Ming-jen,† immediately followed suit, with 30,000 men. Both generals had been encouraged to think that they would be allowed to hold on to their local fiefs after the Communist victory; but, as with so many other Nationalist defectors, they were to be disillusioned. In time, they were "promoted" to the People's Congress.

Now Pai Ch'ung-hsi had no option but to surrender Changsha,

° Chassin's translators quote *The China Handbook, 1950* (New York: Rockport Press), pp. 134 and 239, as authority for the creation of the Supreme Political Council, also known as the Emergency Council, which became the "highest policy-making organ" of the KMT "during the period of Communist rebellion". The Central Executive Committee continued, however. (Chassin, p. 231, footnote.)

† This name appears (incorrectly) as Ch'en Ming-ch'en on p. 228 of Chassin's *The Communist Conquest of China.*

which he evacuated on 4 August. Two striking but short-lived successes nevertheless lay ahead for him. The Communist General Liu Po-ch'eng was now in southern Kiangsi, at Kanchow, and Lin Piao had driven beyond Hengyang in Hunan. With great *élan*, Pai Ch'ung-hsi now (in Chassin's words) "thoroughly thrashed" Lin Piao's Twenty-ninth Red Army, which hurriedly retreated north-wards to Changsha. A splendidly conceived diversionary manoeuvre by Chiang Kai-shek was, however, frustrated by the provincial egotism of the governor of Kwangtung, Yü Han-mou, who was determined not to part with his 50,000 regulars, and to keep Pai out of his province. Ch'en Ch'eng, who had landed an army from Taiwan at Amoy counting on help from Yü, and aimed at preventing the Communist General Liu from rescuing Lin Piao, was forced to re-embark.

Although the Generalissimo could still get his way in military matters, he had no immediate control over the government's decisions. In July the acting President and his ministers abolished the discredited Gold Yuan and introduced a new paper currency backed on the Silver Yuan. It was high time, for civil servants and soldiers alike demanded payment in something harder than worth-less banknotes. For three and a half months, the government ransacked the deposits of the Central Bank in Taiwan and paid out more than U.S.$120,000,000 in gold and silver coins and foreign currencies. The fall of Canton on 15 October ended this drain on Chiang Kai-shek's "survival fund". On the 11th, Li Tsung-jen had flown to Chungking, while Yen Hsi-shan had gone to Taiwan. Within the next few days, Swatow and Amoy fell as well, giving the Communists complete control of the great Chinese coastline.

But Mao Tse-tung had not waited for these inevitable victories to savour his northern triumph. From 21 to 28 September 1949, the Chinese Communist Party, the Democratic League, and various other anti-Kuomintang parties met in Peiping in a "Political Consultative Conference of the Chinese People". By the time they had disbanded, the name "Peiping" ("Northern Peace") had been discarded as a symbol of the decadence of the KMT, which had adopted it in 1928; instead, the great city reverted to its former name of Peking ("Northern Capital"), and was designated as the new capital of the Chinese People's Republic. The new republic was proclaimed by Mao on 1 October, and with him that day to celebrate the overwhelming victory were not only his comrades of the war years, but Mrs. Sun Yat-sen, a number of Nationalist generals who had changed sides in the latter days of the civil war—Fu Tso-yi, Ch'eng Ch'ien, and Chang Chih-chung—the widow of the "Christian General" Mrs. Feng Yü-hsiang, and sundry Shanghai and Singapore millionaires.

And so, very briefly, Chungking again became the capital of the Republic of China. The Generalissimo had gone there on 24 August, in his new capacity as Chairman of the Kuomintang Supreme Political Council. His followers planned a giant anti-Communist rally in his honour on 3 September, but the Communists had their fifth column well organised and on the 2nd Red arsonists lit a raging fire which destroyed a part of the city and wrecked plans for the demonstration.

With Taiwan as a last resort, Chiang explored other possibilities for a last stand. The almost inaccessible mountains of Sikang, between Szechwan and Tibet, attracted him most. But he soon discovered that the local forces would not necessarily be on his side when the crunch came. He made much the same discovery in Yunnan on the Indo-China border, and returned to Canton towards the end of September to a series of squabbles with Li Tsung-jen and his old Kwangsi comrade, Pai Ch'ung-hsi. On 4 October, with the black news of Mao's proclamation in Peking pounding inside him, he had flown back to Taiwan. Losing no time, the Soviet Union had recognised Mao's Republic on the 2nd, and on the 3rd the Nationalist Government—still in Canton—had broken diplomatic relations with Moscow. By now, Chiang Kai-shek had lost all control over events. All he could do was to breathe defiance—which indeed he would continue to do until his dying day nearly twenty-six years later. On 10 October 1949, in his first Double Tenth message from Taiwan, Chiang condemned what he still regarded as "Soviet aggression" in China, and reiterated his determination to fight communism to the bitter end. He was not going to sit in Taipei and watch the fall of Chungking from afar, however, and on 14 November he flew back to the temporary capital of his tottering Republic.

To his great displeasure, the Generalissimo discovered that Li Tsung-jen had left the previous day for his old Kwangsi stronghold of Nanning. Literally, Li had no further stomach for a fight. An abdominal disorder from which he had long suffered was giving him acute trouble, and he had told everybody he was off to seek surgery for it. He turned a blind eye to Chiang Kai-shek's entreaties to return. Meanwhile, his ailment did not rule out political ma- noeuvres. He went to see the vacillating governor of Yunnan, Lu Han, and ordered the release of about a thousand Communists and members of the Kuomintang Revolutionary Committee whom the governor had arrested on 10 September. On 19 November, Pai Ch'ung-hsi flew to Nanning, where the acting President told him he planned to denounce the Generalissimo publicly, then go to the United States for treatment. In an acrimonious discussion, Pai talked him out of issuing his anti-Chiang statement, but not out of going to America. Instead, he wrote to Chiang saying he was sorry he couldn't return to Chungking: he was very tired, and needed a check-up and possibly an operation in the United States. "Mean- while," he went on, "I shall sound out the attitude of the U.S. Government towards China. In view of the grave situation, I shall come back in a short time to take up my responsibilities. . . . As for government affairs, I have asked Premier Yen Hsi-shan to look after them." On the 20th, Li Tsung-jen left for Hong Kong on his way to America, leaving the Republic of China without a President.

The next day, with Chiang Kai-shek in the chair, the Supreme Political Council resolved to urge Li Tsung-jen either to come back to the temporary capital or to resign as acting President. The Generalissimo sent a four-man delegation to Hong Kong to assure Li that if he returned, his authority in the National Government would be unimpaired, and suggesting that he should bring a doctor and any necessary medical equipment with him. The one important thing was that he should not be thought to be abandoning China in this supreme crisis.

The four envoys returned empty-handed, without the acting President. A fierce debate then broke out within Chiang Kai-shek's entourage, with Ch'en Li-fu and others strongly urging Chiang to resume office, and Chiang Ching-kuo even more strongly urging that he should not. The Generalissimo listened to his son, who in fact was probably reflecting a mind already made up. To resume the Presidency, Ching-kuo had argued, would play into Li's hands in that any failure by Li Tsung-jen to raise money and support in America would be blamed on Chiang's disruptive role.

The standing committee of the Central Executive Committee, however, disregarded the Generalissimo and his son, and sent the envoys back to Hong Kong with a strong resolution calling on the acting President to return immediately despite his illness. "If his illness is so serious as to prevent his return," the resolution went on, "then a request shall be made that the Generalissimo resume the Presidency." After some wavering, Li said he was going to Washington as acting President of China, and would request American financial support. Whether he got it or not, he would be back in China in one month to continue the struggle. He left on 5 December 1949, but never came back.

Disregarding personal danger, the Generalissimo left Chungking by air for Chengtu—also in Szechwan—when a force of 30,000 Communist troops had already entered the city. Where else was he to turn? Kunming was a possibility, but Chiang did not trust governor Lu Han. On 7 December, he sent his trusted friend General Chang Ch'ün to Kunming to ask Lu Han whether the Executive Yüan could move to his provincial capital. Lu was uncooperative, but suggested that the Generalissimo should drop in and see him. Sensing a trap, Chiang sent Chang Ch'ün back to Kunming for further details. But the Communists had got in first, and the Generalissimo's emissary was promptly arrested. Unknown to Chiang Kai-shek, two Szechwan warlords, both leading figures in the Democratic League, had defected to the Communist side. They were Chang Lan (the Chairman) and Hsien Ying, who thereupon put the Communist emissaries, who included Teng Hsiao-p'ing (a native of Szechwan, who was Peking's deputy premier when this book was written) in touch with other warlords in the south-west. The main ones were in fact Lu Han himself in Yunnan province and Liu Wen-hui in Sikang. Both Lu and Liu were given to understand that the Communists would allow them to hold on to their own territories, with their private armies intact. What they had not understood was that Mao Tse-tung was not the same kind of man as Chiang Kai-shek. When the time came, both warlords were almost perfunctorily removed from their strongholds; Lu was later appointed deputy Chairman of the National Commission of Physical Education and Sports, while Liu was given a post on the Standing Committee of the People's Congress.

With these successive defections, Chiang Kai-shek's plan for a last stand in the south-west—in Szechwan, Sikang, Yunnan, and Kweichow—became meaningless. Three days after Chang Ch'ün's arrest in Kunming, the Nationalists intercepted a cable disclosing that Lu Han intended to place himself under Chairman Mao's orders, and planned to seize Chiang Kai-shek. But this intelligence arrived when the Generalissimo had already taken off for Taipei. Chang Ch'ün was released, and a Communist committee was set up in Kunming with Lu Han as chairman. On the 8th, the Executive Yüan in an emergency session chaired by Premier Yen voted to remove the capital to Taipei.

From the Soviet border to Indo-China, and from Tibet to the China Sea, the whole of the ancient Middle Kingdom was now in Communist hands. Chiang Kai-shek had "lost" the Chinese mainland.

IV | Chiang's Island Redoubt

(1950–1975)

22. A Place of Refuge

In utter defeat, Chiang Kai-shek decided to meditate. He found the peace and seclusion he needed at Sun-Moon Lake, in the mountains of central Taiwan, no less of a beauty spot for being man-made. With him was Ching-kuo. They had scarcely arrived when a telegram reached him giving the news of the final Nationalist collapse on the mainland. He stayed silent for one hour (writes Tong), then said to his son: "Let us go to the mountain and take a walk." After a further long silence, he suggested that they should go fishing. Ching-kuo hired a boat from a fisherman, and the Generalissimo went out alone. His thoughts elsewhere, he cast the net and caught a fish five feet long. On seeing it, the fisherman exclaimed that he had seen no such sight in twenty years. A good omen, thought Chiang Kai-shek.

Chiang's need for good omens was patent. True, there were points of resistance by guerrillas or scattered remnants in Chekiang (Chiang's birthplace), northern Anhwei, Szechwan, Kwangsi, Yunnan, southern Shensi, and in Sichang, on the Tibetan border. Otherwise, "Free China" survived only on Taiwan, the large island of Hainan—a logical base for a reconquest of the mainland—and the smaller islands of Chusan in the mouth of the Yangtze, Quemoy, and Kinmen, opposite Amoy, Tungshan, and the Pescadores south of Taiwan. The Generalissimo's military assets totalled about 800,000 men of varying quality, between 750 and 1,000 tanks or armoured cars, and an air force of between 300 and 600 planes— the lower figure if first-line aircraft alone are counted, the higher if the obsolete ones are included. About 70 major vessels had come over. All this, Chiang reflected, was not enough to reconquer the mainland, but it was enough—with luck—to defy the Communist regime indefinitely, and to damage it by air raids and an economic blockade.

In the days of his boundless self-confidence, Chiang Kai-shek had spurned the advice of those who wanted him to abandon Manchuria temporarily and concentrate on defence of China proper. That way, he had lost not only Manchuria, but also, in accelerating stages, the whole of the Chinese mainland. He had spread his forces too thinly and tried to defend everything. He had failed to understand that a strategic withdrawal is sometimes necessary for a long-term recovery. Now, in his extremity, he recognised his past errors. Of the islands still in Nationalist hands, only Taiwan was indispensable for survival. Hainan off the coast of Kwangtung was a prize he had no wish to give up. With its iron ore, its facilities for a potential submarine fleet, and its proximity to the mainland, it would have been an ideal base for a campaign of reconquest—if the Nationalists had had the means for an effective defence. But they did not. The garrison commander, General Hsueh Yueh (the "Little Tiger") had a well-trained force of about 40,000 regulars, but they were constantly harassed by a Communist guerrilla force in the interior, which was nearly as large as the Nationalist garrison. The mainland Communists made ten unsuc- cessful attempts to invade the island between February and April 1950. They succeeded in landing a substantial force on 16 April, and the defenders were quickly driven back to the south coast. The Generalissimo ordered Hsueh Yueh to evacuate his troops to Taiwan without delay.

The following month, a much larger Nationalist force—

150,000—was evacuated from the Chusan Islands in sixteen Liberty ships and some smaller vessels. Two more islands—Mansan on the approaches to Canton, and Tungshan off the coast of Fukien—were also abandoned. These withdrawals effectively ended the Nationalist blockade of Shanghai and Canton, which had been maintained in the face of stern British and American disapproval. Thereafter, Chiang entirely lacked an invasion base. Apart from the small islands of Quemoy and Matsu off the coast of Fukien, and the Pescadores, "Free China" was reduced essentially to Taiwan island, less than half the size of Scotland and less than one-third arable, with (at that time) a population of 10,000,000 or 11,000,000, including between 1,000,000 and 2,000,000 military and civilian refugees from the mainland. In this unpromising situation, Chiang Kai-shek had two minimum objectives: political survival and the preservation of the traditional Chinese way of life, threatened on the mainland by the imposition of an alien revolutionary ideology. From the time of his arrival until the day of his death, however, his publicly stated objective, reiterated *ad nauseam*, was the "return to the mainland". As time went on, this public objective became decreasingly credible to those who constantly heard it. It had begun as a fierce resolve; it became an aspiration, then a myth, then a liturgy. Yet it played a major part in sustaining and justifying Kuomintang rule over a population that was undoubtedly Chinese, but which had emerged from half a century of Japanese colonial rule and had evolved a traditional spirit of dissociation from continental China. On their arrival after the collapse of Japan, the Nationalists had initially behaved (as we have seen) as brutal and insensitive conquerors. This had to stop, and in appointing General Ch'en Ch'eng as governor of the island in 1949, Chiang had picked a man with the capacity to tackle an arduous job.

On taking refuge in Taiwan at the end of 1949, Chiang Kai-shek set himself two main tasks: the security of his home base; and abroad, recognition of the government of the Republic of China as the legitimate government of the entire Chinese people, in the face of the undeniable fact that Taipei exercised no control over the lives and destinies of hundreds of millions of Chinese under the rule of Mao Tse-tung's Chinese People's Republic. He achieved the first of these objectives by a paradoxical combination of ruthless security measures and determined reforms. He achieved the second objective, to an improbable degree, through an unlikely set of circumstances which caused the United States to continue to recognise the Nationalist Government instead of the Communist. By far the most important of these circumstances was the Korean War in the 1950s.

The most important of Chiang Kai-shek's stabilising measures in Taiwan was the land reform programme, which he directed Governor Ch'en Ch'eng to initiate as soon as he took office. In fact, as early as 4 February 1949, one month after Ch'en Ch'eng became governor, he launched the "land rent reduction programme". It was much needed. Traditionally, tenant farmers on the island had paid about 50 percent of the total yield of their main crops as rent, often to absentee landlords. In some areas, the proportion was as high as 70 percent. Moreover, rent had to be paid regardless of the weather and crop failures. Throughout the programme, the authorities had the devoted technical assistance of the Sino-American Joint Commission on Rural Reconstruction. On 25 May 1951, a Legislative Yüan resolution fixed a ceiling of 37.5 percent for rents on tenanted land. The aim was fulfilment of Sun Yat-sen's slogan, "land to the tillers". On 30 May, the Executive Yüan announced "Measures for Sale of Public Farmland", compelling absentee landlords to sell their lands to the State, which in turn sold it back to the tenants on ten-year mortgages repayable in instalments representing 25 percent of the annual crop output. Landlords in residence were allowed to keep no more than two hectares of irrigated land or four of dry land. Compensation was either in cash, in land bonds, or in stocks in publicly owned enterprises. Thus, many landlords were turned into industrial capitalists. By the time the programme was completed in 1953, nearly 80 percent of all arable land was owned by those who tilled it. No blood was shed, in striking contrast to the land reform programme initiated in June 1950 by the Communist regime, which involved the physical liquidation of the landed gentry as a class.

Ch'en Ch'eng's land reform programme was undoubtedly a major stabilising factor, and gave a great boost to the island's economy. The immediate security problem, however, had to be dealt with by harsher measures. During the flight to Taiwan, the Communists had planted many agents among Nationalist personnel. Some were of high rank: for instance, the deputy Chief of the General Staff, Lieutenant-General Wu Shih, and his wife. During the first six months of 1950, more than 300 cases of espionage were handled, involving an underground network of more than 1,000 agents. In May that year, Chiang promised immunity to all Communists who came forward. More than 400 did so. Those arrested without the benefit of the amnesty were usually executed.

While Communists were being executed and peasants were being given land, Chiang was reorganising and reforming the Kuomintang. Addressing an extraordinary session of the Standing Committee of the Central Executive Committee on 22 July 1950, the Generalissimo declared:

> We must make Taiwan the base for national recovery, a vanguard for the struggle of the free peoples of Asia, and a champion of world peace. To achieve this, we must thoroughly reform our party in order to reorganise our revolutionary machinery and to revive our revolutionary spirit. On the negative side, we must do away with the conflicts between the various cliques and factions, as well as between individuals in the party. We must not tolerate any longer the selfish behaviour and ideas which have caused the collapse on the mainland and may cause the collapse of Taiwan if unchecked.

The first thing to do, said Chiang, was to streamline the party organisation. The Central Executive Committee was swept away, and so was the Central Supervisory Committee. In their place, he created two much smaller bodies: a Central Reform Committee with executive powers, and an Advisory Committee of older party leaders. Prominent Kuomintang personalities who had gone over to the Communists, such as General Fu Tso-yi and Mrs. Sun Yat-sen, had already been expelled. Many others, who had not joined Mao Tse-tung but had declined to come to Taiwan—the fence-sitters— were now swept off the register of members. The army, too, was purged. On the Generalissimo's orders, Ch'en Ch'eng dismissed literally tens of thousands of officers. The battle orders of 181 armies, divisions, and smaller units were abolished: in fact, they had been paper organisations, with padded lists to fatten the payrolls of their commanders.

Next came currency reform. After the fall of Shanghai, Chiang's government introduced a new Taiwan dollar, backed by the gold and foreign exchange he had had the foresight to transfer to Taipei, and exchangeable at 5 to one with the American dollar.

It had not taken Chiang Kai-shek long to reassert his complete authority over the territory he controlled, and its inhabitants. For by now, not only was he Commander-in-Chief and Director-General of the Kuomintang, but he had resumed the Presidency of the Republic as well. On 21 February 1950, the Emergency Committee had issued an ultimatum to Li Tsung-jen, who of course was in America, to come to Taipei in three days or forego the acting Presidency. Li's reply was evasive, and on the 24th the Legislative Yüan petitioned Chiang to resume the Presidency. There was now no reason to refuse, and on 1 March, he was again President. His first act was to accept the resignation of Yen Hsi-shan, who felt himself too old and sick to remain premier. On the 8th, he handed the job to General Ch'en Ch'eng.

The day Chiang Kai-shek resumed his high office, Mao's Commander-in-Chief, Chu Teh, received members of the Taiwan Liberation League in Peking and told them that the "elimination of the Chiang Kai-shek regime from Taiwan has become the most pressing task of the whole country". A mighty military force was being assembled for the invasion, he added. At that grim moment, there seemed every chance that the Communists would carry out their threat. Chiang Kai-shek and his regime were saved, however, by the Korean War.

The key to Chiang Kai-shek's survival was the attitude of the United States. The Communist victory on the mainland had left the American people and government deeply and bitterly disillusioned with Chiang and his regime. But for some curious blunders on the part of Mao Tse-tung's government, the Americans were in a mood to recognise it, as the British did in January 1950. As early as 1 July 1949, however, Mao Tse-tung had set a keynote of permanent hostility towards America in his speech declaring that China would lean to the side of the Soviet Union. The highly disciplined soldiers of the People's Liberation Army had invaded the residence of the American ambassador, Dr. Leighton Stuart, and had even entered his bedroom, where he lay sick. No apologies had been forthcoming. On 13 January 1950, the Communist authorities had seized the American consular offices in Peking. Worse still, they had arrested the American Consul-General in Mukden, Angus Ward, and gaoled him for four weeks on trumped-up espionage charges. A wave of indignation swept the United States on the news of these insults and outrages, and on the 14th the State Department ordered the recall of 135 consular personnel with families from Peking, Tientsin, Shanghai, Nanking, and Tsingtao.

It was now politically impossible for Washington to recognise the Chinese People's Republic. But it did not follow that America would resume its support for the Nationalist regime. Indeed, on 5 January 1950, President Truman had made it clear that his policy for China was "hands off". The United States, he declared, would not get involved in the Chinese civil war; nor would it provide "military aid or advice" to Chinese forces in Taiwan. Spurred by one of the leaders of the China lobby, Senator William F. Knowland, in the wake of the anti-American outrages in China, Secretary of State Acheson on 24 January announced a programme of economic aid for Taiwan. But the turning-point was the invasion of South Korea by the North Korean army on 25 June 1950. Under the Yalta agreements, Korea had been divided at the 38th Parallel, with Russians in occupation of the north, and Americans of the south. The Americans had contented themselves with training a constabulary force in South Korea; whereas the Russians had trained and equipped a formidable North Korean army, which included the units that had joined the People's Liberation Army in Manchuria, where they had gained battle experience.

The change in American policy, when it came—as the Generalissimo knew it would—was less than satisfactory. Stalin had ordered his North Korean protégés to strike across the 38th Parallel on the assumption that the United States would not respond. There seemed to be good reason for this assumption, for in a speech in January, Secretary of State Acheson had specifically excluded Korea from the American security zone in the Pacific. The Commander-in-Chief of the U.S. forces in the Far East, General Douglas MacArthur, on the other hand, took a wider view of Pacific security, in which he saw both South Korea and Taiwan as playing an important part. The North Korean aggression shocked President Truman and Acheson out of their wishful passivity. And a curious Russian misjudgment enabled Truman to take action within the United Nations framework. The Soviet delegation had been boycotting the U.N. Security Council. Had the Russians been present, they could have vetoed any resolution proposing armed intervention. As it was, when the Security Council met on 25 June, it voted 9 to 0 (with the U.S.S.R. absent and Yugoslavia abstaining) in favour of a resolution calling on the North Korean authorities to withdraw their forces to the 38th Parallel. At the same time, all members of the United Nations were called upon "to render every assistance to the United Nations in the execution of this resolution and to refrain from giving assistance to the North Korean authorities". On the 27th, President Truman announced that he had ordered the American air and sea forces to help the South Koreans. Of more direct interest to Chiang Kai-shek, he also declared that Taiwan would be neutralised for the period of military operations in Korea. The Seventh Fleet was ordered to restrain the Chinese Nationalists from any operations against the Chinese mainland, and to stop any Communist attempt to invade Taiwan.

For the last of these provisions, at least, the Generalissimo could allow himself to feel relieved. Some weeks earlier, about 150,000 Chinese Communist assault troops had been massed on the coast facing Taiwan. Now it was clear that there was no immediate danger from that quarter.

The first few days of the North Korean invasion were disastrous for the southern defenders. Seoul fell, and the South Koreans retreated in disorder towards Pusan. Chiang Kai-shek chose this moment to offer General MacArthur 33,000 Chinese troops to help the United Nations forces being assembled under his command. MacArthur immediately advised the U.S. Joint Chiefs of Staff to accept the offer, although his advice did not become public knowledge until he revealed it the following year in testimony before Congress. Under strong pressure from Britain, which had recognised the Chinese People's Republic, the Joint Chiefs immediately turned down Chiang's offer.

However, the Joint Chiefs did recommend that military aid should be resumed to the Chinese Nationalists on the ground that Taiwan was of strategic value to the United States and that its defences should be improved. A new American Military Assistance Advisory Group was set up, although it did not take up its duties in Taiwan until early in 1951. Meanwhile, General MacArthur was to visit the island and report on the state of the Nationalist forces.

MacArthur flew to Taipei on 31 July and immediately went into conference with Chiang Kai-shek. It was the first time the two men had met. It was a cordial meeting, for they shared a common view of the nature of Chinese communism and of the need to counter it. There was a fairly detailed discussion on the possibility of a Chinese

Nationalist diversionary operation on continental China, but nothing came of it.

Caught by surprise by the speed of Truman's initiative while they were absent, the Russians now returned to the United Nations. On 1 August, it was Ambassador Malik's turn to preside over the Security Council, and he called in forceful terms for the exclusion of the Chinese Nationalist delegation, headed by Dr. T. F. Tsiang, and the immediate seating of a delegation from Peking. His draft resolution to that effect was supported by Britain, as well as by Norway, India, and Yugoslavia. The British defection on this issue shook the Americans but did not weaken their resolve. The resolution was defeated.

On 18 September, General MacArthur reported to the United Nations on Peking's assistance to the North Koreans. Between 40,000 and 60,000 of the North Koreans who had received training and battle experience with the Chinese Communists in Manchuria had taken part in the invasion, he disclosed. A fortnight earlier, General MacArthur had carried out a brilliant landing of the U.N. forces at Inchon, behind the North Korean lines. The military situation had been transformed, and on 1 October, MacArthur had ordered the North Korean forces to surrender. That day, the South Koreans had crossed the 38th Parallel, moving northward. That day in Peking, the Chinese People's Republic was celebrating its first anniversary. In a bellicose speech, Chou En-lai warned the United States that the Chinese people "cannot allow imperialists recklessly to take aggressive action against their own neighbour."

Chiang Kai-shek's intelligence showed that there was substance behind Chou En-lai's threat. The Communist Fourth Field Army of 500,000 men, commanded by Lin Piao, had been moving northward over the Canton-Hankow and Hankow-Peking railways since the beginning of June. On 28 October came the first American intelligence reports that units of the Fourth Field Army had crossed the Yalu River from Manchuria and were now moving into action in North Korea. By then, MacArthur's forces had reached the mountain ranges on the Korean side of the border, killing or capturing more than 200,000 North Korean troops on the way. It soon became known, however, that the Chinese Communists had committed 500,000 troops, euphemistically disguised as "People's Volunteers", to the Korean struggle. Now it was MacArthur's turn to give ground before the massive Chinese onslaught.

From his mountain retreat north of Taipei, Chiang Kai-shek watched these momentous events in well-suppressed frustration. His mode of life was austere now to the point of asceticism, and his demeanour was outwardly serene. With Mme. Chiang, he lived in a one-storey house with a green-tiled roof on the edge of the mountain. This gave them a magnificent view beyond the modest garden with its azaleas. The front door (wrote Burton Crane of *The New York Times*) opened straight onto a strange room, about 20 feet by 30, with four square stone columns in the middle. On the right was a dining table for about eighteen people, and on the left armchairs for relaxation. Servants' quarters and four little cubicles for aides and secretaries adjoined the house. The Generalissimo rose at daybreak, and dressed either in a traditional long blue Chinese robe or in a military uniform without insignia of rank. Mme. Chiang joined him in a dressing gown for morning prayers. His breakfast consisted of rice, pickled vegetables, and cold water. After breakfast he read the newspapers until 9:00 A.M., when his secretaries would bring him about a dozen folders—yellow for routine matters and red for urgent decisions. At 10:00 or 11:00, officials would call for conferences scheduled the previous day. Some would stay on for a simple lunch.

After eating, the Generalissimo took a nap of half an hour before resuming work. At 4:30, he would take a brisk walk with one of his assistants. Tea was served on his return. He would then work until 7:00 and retire for a second session of prayer and meditation until dinner. After dinner, he would either resume work or watch a film if persuaded that it was worth his time. Occasionally he would venture into town to attend a Chinese opera. The day invariably ended with a hot sulphur spring bath and an entry in the diary he still kept before going to bed.

It was becoming painfully clear to him that there was marked divergence of views about the conduct of the Korean War between General MacArthur and President Truman. Probably the greatest strategist of World War II, MacArthur stuck to the view that victory should be the aim of any war in which he was engaged. President Truman took a more cautiously political view of the conflict. An undeclared war, it was juridically a U.N. police action against aggression from the outside. In his exchanges with the Joint Chiefs of Staff, MacArthur had been calling for permission to bomb

military targets in Manchuria. On 23 March 1951, however, he
publicly declared himself ready to negotiate an armistice with the
Chinese Communist command. It became clear later that his aim
was to frustrate the diplomatic moves in favour of an armistice that
were going on at the time at United Nations headquarters by
provoking a rejection by the Chinese Communists. They duly
obliged him with a negative answer on the 29th.

And now, with dramatic suddenness, the world learned that the
cleavage between the President and his Commander-in-Chief in the
Far East was unbridgeable. On 5 April, Representative Joseph W.
Martin rose in the House and read out a letter from General
MacArthur. The Congressman had solicited the General's views and
MacArthur now spell them out unambiguously. The United States,
he wrote, should stop fighting a limited engagement and switch to
all-out war. The U.N. should accept President Chiang Kai-shek's
offer of troops and back Taiwan in launching a second front in
China. Anticipating the criticisms of those who felt that absolute
priority should be given to the European theatre, he argued that "if
we lose the war to communism in Asia, the fall of Europe is
inevitable".

If General MacArthur had kept his views to himself, or limited
them to his confidential exchanges with his military and political
superiors—or alternatively if Congressman Martin had kept quiet—
the matter might have rested there. But Truman was outraged at
MacArthur's attempt to meddle in political decisions. On 10 April,
President Truman relieved MacArthur of his command and ordered
him to return to the United States. General Matthew Ridgway was
appointed to succeed him.

Gone was Chiang Kai-shek's dream of a return to the mainland
with American military support. There was, however, a major
compensation in that the Americans abandoned the anti-Kuomintang and anti-Chiang attitudes that had dominated the "White
Paper" in 1949. On 18 May, the Assistant Secretary of State, Dean
Rusk, publicly declared that the Generalissimo "more authentically
represents the views of the great body of the people of China" than
his Communist rivals. In the Senate, fifty-six members pledged
themselves to oppose any recognition of Communist China or any
proposal that Taiwan should be turned over to Peking. In October
came a massive U.S. Mutual Security appropriation of $535,250,000

in military funds and $237,500,000 in economic aid, for the Asia and Pacific areas, excluding Korea. Much of this money was to go to Taiwan.

In material terms—and therefore in terms of survival—this news was the insurance policy Chiang Kai-shek needed. But in terms of prestige, it did nothing to remove a very recent humiliation: when the Japanese Peace Conference convened in San Francisco in September, the Republic of China was not represented. The Generalissimo's only consolation was that the Chinese People's Republic was also kept out. Britain had joined the Soviet Union in proposing that the Communist regime should represent China and had added, in a draft proposal in mid-April, that Taiwan should be returned to the Communist government. The Generalissimo was deeply wounded. For had he not been one of the wartime Big Four, with Winston Churchill as his ally? In June, President Truman's Republican roving ambassador had gone to London to resolve American differences on this issue with Kenneth Younger, Minister of State for Foreign Affairs in the Attlee Cabinet.

A compromise decision emerged. After the Japanese had regained their sovereignty, they should choose for themselves which government of China to recognise; meanwhile, neither Peking nor Taipei should be invited to the peace conference. The Generalissimo's Foreign Minister, George Yeh, issued a strong protest, and the Nationalist Government went on to conclude its own bilateral peace treaty with Tokyo. To Chiang Kai-shek's deep displeasure, the San Francisco treaty detached Taiwan from the Japanese empire but left its future status undefined. Once again, the Cairo Declaration to which President Roosevelt had pledged himself had been breached in Chiang Kai-shek's eyes.

In Korea, with MacArthur gone, a cease-fire was arranged in the summer of 1951 and interminable truce negotiations followed, which yielded an armistice in July 1953. This truce—it was not a peace settlement—was a satisfying moral triumph for Chiang Kai-shek. The Communists wanted the truce badly enough to bow before the insistence of the United Nations that prisoners of war should be free to decide where to go on being released. A neutral commission under Indian chairmanship administered the exchange of prisoners and 14,000 of the Chinese prisoners in U.N. hands—72 percent of the total—opted for Taiwan in preference to the People's Republic. (Twenty-one captured Americans chose to stay with the

Communists; they were among the first products of the then novel psychological process known as "brainwashing".)

The Chinese Communist intervention had restored the *status quo ante bellum,* and the North Koreans and South Koreans still faced each other on either side of the 38th Parallel. The great MacArthur controversy raged on. What Truman had feared above all was that any extension of the Korean War to the Chinese mainland might have caused Mao Tse-tung to invoke the treaty of alliance he had signed with Stalin early in 1950. Had Stalin responded, he might well have struck in Europe, instead of Asia, and World War III might have started.

The dismissal of MacArthur was unpopular in America, however, and the conduct of the Korean War was a major issue in the presidential election campaign of 1952. The Republicans criticised the Truman administration for adopting a negative policy that would neither bring victory nor a quick end to the war. Their candidate, General Dwight D. Eisenhower, won and immediately declared a change of line over Nationalist China. He announced the removal of the American prohibition on Nationalist operations against the mainland. If Chiang Kai-shek's government wished to order an invasion, the Americans would now no longer stand in their way. However, the Seventh Fleet would continue to protect Taiwan against a Communist invasion.

This again was not exactly what Chiang wanted. It amounted to no more than American approval of Nationalist guerrilla operations in continental China. Chiang knew his forces, though greatly improved in efficiency, were not strong enough to attempt an invasion of the country he had lost. And the Americans were not prepared to help him do it. The guerrilla operations were in fact on a fairly large scale. On 13 June 1950, Mao Tse-tung had estimated that some 400,000 "Kuomintang remnants" were in action— 1,000,000 others having been killed or rounded up since the fall of the National Government. These operations would continue, sporadically and on a diminishing scale, into the 1970s.

Chiang's diminishing hope was that World War III, which Truman had dreaded, might yet happen. He had put it in these words: "Our plan for fighting communism and regaining the mainland will necessarily form . . . an important link in the general plan of the free world to combat world-wide communist aggression." When the news from Korea made it clear that an armistice was on the way, on 20 July 1953, the Generalissimo called for a West Pacific security pact, in which Taiwan and neighbours of China would participate. Later that year—on 27 November—President Syngman Rhee visited Chiang Kai-shek in Taipei, and the two statesmen issued a joint communiqué calling on the free countries of Asia to form a united anti-Communist front with the backing of other "freedom-loving nations". The snag was that India, Burma, and Indonesia had all recognised the Peking government. And the biggest "freedom-loving nation" had less bellicose ideas.

Chiang's hopes rose in January 1954, when the American Secretary of State, John Foster Dulles, made a speech describing his new doctrine of "massive retaliation", which he said was already in effect in the Far East. When the French collapsed in Indo-China in the spring, however, the Americans failed to intervene. Instead, in September, the United States took the lead in setting up a new joint defence system for South-East Asia—SEATO—from which Taiwan was deliberately excluded.

Chiang's turn came on 2 December 1954, with the conclusion of a bilateral Mutual Defence Treaty (Security) with the United States. But this, too, disappointed the Generalissimo's hopes. Indeed, it represented a step back in comparison with President Eisenhower's initial declaration. Under the new pact, the United States pledged itself to defend Taiwan but not Quemoy and Matsu. The security of the island was thus guaranteed until further notice, but the Generalissimo was on his own if he tried his luck at unseating Mao Tse-tung's regime. Moreover, in an exchange of letters on 10 December between his Foreign Minister, Dr. George Yeh, and Secretary of State Dulles, Chiang's government gave a formal undertaking that its forces would not attack the Chinese mainland without prior consultation and agreement with the United States. From then on, his periodic threats to return to the mainland sounded increasingly like a ritual incantation.

23. | The Last Twenty Years

After the unceasing turbulence of Chiang Kai-shek's life until the fall of the Chinese mainland, his life in his island exile was relatively uneventful, almost static. Under his rule, Taiwan became something of a showpiece—not of democracy, but of prosperity, economic growth, relative contentment, and the preservation of China's cultural heritage. In microcosm, it showed what Chiang's regime might have achieved in continental China, if the progress of the decade from 1927 to 1937 had been allowed to continue unhindered—if neither the Communists nor the Japanese had faced it with problems so vast and intractable that they proved beyond the Generalissimo's powers to resolve. But history does not consist of might-have-beens: history is what happened, and how and why. In the end, this tiny plot of contested land was all Chiang had.

It is easy enough to claim, as some observers did, that Taiwan's achievements were those of other men, and of the hard-working population itself. But this would be unfair. Just as a commander-in-chief has the right to claim the credit or may be forced to take the blame for the victories and defeats of his subordinate commanders, so the success story of Taiwan must be credited to him in the final balance-sheet.

Chiang's situation on the island was highly anomalous, as of course was his government's. In juridical terms, it was unprecedented. With the remnants of his armies and his civil followers, he had taken refuge on an island which had emerged from half a century of Japanese colonial rule, and which the Cairo Declaration of 1943 had recognised as Chinese territory. But there were two Chinese governments. The Communist one in Peking undeniably controlled all China's national territory, apart from Taiwan itself and a few small off-shore islands. And Chiang Kai-shek's government of the "Republic of China" undeniably controlled Taiwan, which was recognised both in Peking and in Taipei as a Chinese province. De facto, there were "two Chinas"; but neither the Chinese People's Republic nor the Republic of China would even consider the proposition.

The world-at-large found it easier to understand Peking's claim. In the eyes of the uninvolved, Chiang's claim to sovereignty over the Chinese mainland was viewed as at best an absurdity and at worst an impertinence. In terms of power, however, it had an inescapable logic. For had the claim been dropped, what business did the Kuomintang have to rule over the Taiwanese majority of the population, who had never invited the mainlanders to take over, and whose wishes were not consulted? It was only by clinging to the claim that his government was the government of all China, and never for an instant weakening in his claim, that Chiang Kai-shek could "justify" his retention of power in the island province. And so, by the iron laws of this anomalous logic, a whole range of parallel anomalies had to be sustained. On this small island, with its population that had grown to about 16,000,000 by 1975, there had to be two governments: one for the whole of China and the other for the province of Taiwan. China's first general elections had been held on 21 November 1947—an incomplete and to some extent irregular exercise. Most of the members of the Legislative Yüan had come over to Taiwan and solemnly, year after year, until death claimed them, the ageing legislators sat on, claiming to represent the interests of distant "constituents" in the mainland provinces of China, with whom they had long since lost all contact.

The Taiwanese majority of the island had virtually no say in this "National" legislative process (although as was their "provincial" right, they had 100 percent control of the Provincial, Municipal, and County Assemblies). At best, they could aspire to useful but essentially minor positions in the Provincial Government. Until partial elections at the end of 1972 injected a little new blood into the aging legislative bodies, the great anomalies stood undiluted. At one level of understanding, it was utterly unreal: a fantasy for the outside world to laugh or marvel at. At another level, it was deadly real and earnest: this was Chiang Kai-shek's shrunken seat of power, and the Kuomintang's last place of refuge. To deny the essential reality of the unreal would be to abdicate by abandoning the basis of power. And Chiang was past the stage where resignations served a useful purpose. He was there, and there to stay—until such time as death claimed him or unforeseen but not unimaginable circumstances should restore him to his rightful seat of power in Nanking.

The high point of Chiang's hopes had come with the Korean War, and had faded when it was over. The Security Treaty with the United States had guaranteed his island base, and effectively prevented him from using it. Thereafter, his hopes flickered briefly into life with each international crisis or when the news from Communist China was encouragingly bad. Such moments meant more to the Generalissimo than all the record-breaking statistics of Taiwan's booming economy.

One such moment came in January 1955, when the Chinese Communists sent 20 warships and about 50 other assorted craft to land on the tiny island of Yikiangshan, north of the Tachen Islands. The Nationalist garrison—720 guerrillas—died to the last man. After heavy bombing attacks on the Tachens, Premier Chou En-lai declared on 24 January that his government was determined to "liberate" Taiwan and could not recognise the right of the United Nations or of any foreign country to intervene. That day, President Eisenhower asked Congress—in his capacity as Commander-in-Chief of the U.S. forces—to take whatever military action was necessary to repulse any Chinese Communist aggression in the Formosa Strait. Congress gave the President the authority he had sought, and Chiang Kai-shek's spirits rose correspondingly. But the crisis petered out after the U.N. Security Council had invited the Chinese People's Republic to send a representative to attend a discussion on a cease-fire proposal, and the Communists had duly and forcibly declined.

For consolation, the Generalissimo was soon to have proof that he was still important enough to attract the solicitous attention of the leading country in the Western world. True, Nationalist China was left out of the South-East Asia Defence Treaty, which the Americans and others had signed in Manila on 25 February 1955, but the American Secretary of State, John Foster Dulles, went on to Taipei on 3 March. There, in a lengthy discussion with Chiang Kai-shek, Vice-President Ch'en Ch'eng, Prime Minister O. K. Yui, and Foreign Minister George Yeh, he explored the implications and practical application of the Mutual Defence Treaty. In a press statement before his departure at the end of the long day, Dulles mentioned that the off-shore islands of Quemoy and Matsu "have a relationship to the defence of Taiwan". As far as it went, this was a comforting statement for the Generalissimo.

Three or four weeks earlier, Chiang had ordered the evacuation of the Tachen Islands in the face of heavy Communist air attacks. But there was no question, especially in the light of the Secretary of State's declaration, of giving up Quemoy and Matsu. Although the Chinese Communists renewed their attacks in March, the Generalissimo reinforced the garrisons, building up the force on Quemoy alone to 60,000 troops. The news continued ominous, however, and on 25 March the Communists announced that they were withdrawing a further six divisions from North Korea. Chiang's observers on the off-shore islands and his mainland intelligence network told him of a heavy build-up of troops in Fukien province opposite the islands. The Generalissimo had already stated—at a press conference on 14 February—that it had been made "perfectly clear" that the United States would defend the islands. In no case, he said, would they be abandoned to the enemy.

With his distant memories of Shanghai in 1927, and of his humiliation at Sian in 1936, it was galling to Chiang Kai-shek to read reports of Chou En-lai's outstanding personal success at the Bandung Conference of Asian and African States in April that year. With the sublime self-righteousness of the newly independent, the Ceylonese Premier, Sir John Kotelawala, had proposed "his" solution for the Taiwan problem. Matsu and Quemoy should be transferred immediately to China, he had proposed; the U.S. Seventh Fleet should withdraw from the Formosa Strait; Chiang

Kai-shek should go into "honourable retirement"; the U.N., or alternatively the Colombo Powers, should establish a trusteeship over Taiwan for five years; and at the end of that period, a plebiscite would decide whether the island was to remain Chinese territory or become independent.

In Washington, the State Department called on Communist China to show the sincerity of its professions of peace by announcing an immediate cease-fire and by immediately releasing American airmen and others, whom it unjustly held. But Chou En-lai merely declared that the future of Taiwan could be settled through the United Nations after China had been admitted to membership. He let it be known that he had proposed a "reasonable" solution to the question of Chiang Kai-shek's position. At Sian nearly twenty years earlier, Chiang had been glad to recover his freedom through the good offices of Chou En-lai. But he was not about to allow the Communist Premier to depose him with a "reasonable" solution. His government announced that it was not prepared to take part in negotiations with the Chinese Communists.

After all the disappointments and setbacks, the failure of the Marshall mission, the recriminations of the White Paper of 1949, and the dashed hopes of the Korean War, relations between the United States and Chiang Kai-shek's rump government on Taiwan had settled down to a prolonged period of amity and harmony. The great American bounty was flowing freely in Taiwan's direction— both for economic development and for the armed forces. Every year, the U.N. debated the question of China's representation; and every year, a comfortable majority followed the lead given by Chiang's American ally. Then suddenly, with explosive virulence, an outburst of anti-Americanism shattered the calm. The cause was relatively trivial: on 23 May 1957, Master-Sergeant Robert Reynolds, of the U.S. Army, was acquitted on a charge of the manslaughter of a thirty-year-old Chinese. The victim was said to have peeped through a window at the sergeant's wife when she was naked after a shower. Startled, Mrs. Reynolds cried out to her husband, who rushed out and killed the man with two shots. Court-martialed, Reynolds denied the charge and pleaded that he had feared the intruder intended to attack him. After acquittal, he was secretly flown out of Taiwan to the Philippines with his wife and child.

Incensed at the acquittal, an excited crowd gathered outside the

U.S. embassy, jeering and insulting Americans in the streets, while the Chinese widow marched up and down on hunger strike, bearing a placard demanding justice. The police stood idly by when the mob tore down the Stars and Stripes and ripped it to pieces. The Nationalist flag was hoisted above the building. By now, the mob had invaded the embassy, smashing desks and hurling steel cabinets out of the windows. American cars and lorries were set on fire and the building itself burned for a while, although the flames died down. More than a hundred rioters were arrested.

Ambassador Rankin of the United States, a staunch defender of Chiang Kai-shek, lodged a strong protest, to which Chiang Kai-shek responded with a message to President Eisenhower and Mr. Dulles on 27 May, expressing his "profound regrets" and his assurances that the incident "did not reflect in any way the expression of anti-Americanism" but had only been an expression of popular anger at the acquittal of Reynolds. Three senior police and army officers were dismissed, and the Chinese authorities promised full compensation. In Peking, the incident roused the press and radio of the Communists to new heights of vituperation. The Americans, said one Peking broadcast, regarded the people of Taiwan as "slaves and cannon-fodder to be ordered about at will". "All patriotic forces" should unite to drive the American aggressors out of the island. As it turned out in the long run, however, Chiang Kai-shek's assessment had been correct: the explosion of popular anger was an isolated incident, never to be repeated.

The following year brought a new and more disquieting Quemoy crisis to stir the Generalissimo's hopes and to show that he could still count on American help. On 23 August 1958, Communist shore batteries fired 50,000 shells at Quemoy within two hours. Over the next five days, the daily rate of bombardment averaged about 60,000 shells a day. By the end of the month, about 1,000 casualties, many of them civilians, had been announced. Food, ammunition, and other supplies rapidly ran short, and Chiang Kai-shek's government appealed to the United States. From 7 September, units of the U.S. Seventh Fleet helped Nationalist warships to escort supply convoys. Other supplies were air-dropped by Nationalist cargo planes from Taiwan. In an ominous statement on 11 September, President Eisenhower declared that if the Communists took Quemoy, that would not be the end of the story. "It is part of what is an ambitious plan of armed conquest," he said.

"This plan would liquidate all the free-world positions in the Western Pacific area and bring them under captive governments which would be hostile to the United States and the free world." He went on to accuse the Russians of working hand in hand with the Chinese Communists. A few days earlier, Chou En-lai had reiterated his government's claim to "liberate" Taiwan and the Pescadores.

The crisis, with its moments of drama, dragged on until late October, while the population of Quemoy settled down to a daily routine of intensive shelling. Tension was greatly relieved after John Foster Dulles declared on 30 September that the American government would favour a Nationalist evacuation of the off-shore islands if a "reasonably dependable cease-fire" were arranged. Peking suspended the bombardment on 6 October and did not renew it until the 20th, and then at a diminished rate. But it was already clear that if Chiang Kai-shek hoped for hostilities between the Americans and Chinese Communists, he was going to be disappointed. Indeed, the United States had made war virtually unthinkable by assembling what *The New York Times* described as "the most powerful air-naval fighting force in history" by mid-September.

On 22 and 23 September, the Generalissimo presided over a conference of Nationalist and American military representatives in Taipei. Admiral Felt, Commander-in-Chief of the U.S. forces in the Pacific, was there, and so was General Ch'en Ch'eng, Chiang's Premier. A month later—from 21 to 23 October—it was the Secretary of State's turn to fly to Taipei for talks with President Chiang Kai-shek. The final communiqué was so worded as to relieve feelings on either side, but without giving total satisfaction to everybody. There was a reference to solidarity; the U.S. Government reaffirmed its view that Chiang's government was the "authentic spokesman for free China"; and the Nationalist government stated that "its sacred mission" of restoring freedom to the mainland Chinese should be carried out, not by force but in accordance with Sun Yat-sen's Three Principles. Chiang then settled down to a further phase of his long wait.

The two Quemoy crises had in fact proved that Chiang Kai-shek and his regime, more than ever, were safe but circumscribed. Life did, however, offer ceremonial compensations, and one of the most gratifying came on 19 June 1960, when the Generalissimo welcomed President Eisenhower to Taipei. There was much mutual felicitation and talk of "lasting friendship".

Restrained though protected by the United States, Chiang Kai-shek continued to wage war on Communist China by the limited means open to him. There were air and naval battles, in which the Chinese Nationalists—with their American equipment— usually gave a good account of themselves; there were occasional raids on mainland territory; and from time to time teams of guerrillas and saboteurs were air-dropped. Most of the guerrillas and saboteurs were in Kwangtung province, scattered in villages and forever trying—though never with spectacular success—to set up local cells of resistance. Every now and then, Peking would announce the execution of Nationalist agents. And every now and then the Nationalists would claim successes, and sometimes admit losses. On 1 January 1963, for instance, the Nationalist China Central News Agency admitted that the Communists had killed 172 guerrillas in various skirmishes. And a few days later, Peking announced that 5 Nationalist agents had been executed and 10 others gaoled after trials in Canton and other towns in Kwangtung. Later that year, there were reports of widespread guerrilla activities in Chekiang, Kiangsi, Fukien, Kwangtung, Yunnan, and Hainan Island.

The activities of one group of Chiang Kai-shek's guerrillas aroused particular controversy for many years. These were the remnants of about 12,000 Kuomintang troops who crossed the border between Yunnan and Burma in 1949, when Mao Tse-tung's armies were overrunning southern China. On 8 December 1953, the U.N. General Assembly passed a resolution condemning KMT activity in Burma and calling on the Burmese government to report any infringements. After five months of negotiations with the Burmese, Chiang's government agreed to evacuate its troops from Burma's territory. Their commander, General Li Mi, announced on 30 May 1954 that his command had been dissolved. Nearly 7,000 Chinese were evacuated to Taiwan via Thailand at American expense. But this was not the end of the matter. Those evacuated included 1,400 dependants, and observers could not help noticing that many of those in uniform were either very young or very old. The ones who stayed behind were the able-bodied and the militant. Despite the prevalence of jungle fevers, and inadequate medical attention, they had strong incentives to stay where they were. Their

carefully tended poppy fields yielded handsome revenues in smug-
gled opium and paid for the import of arms flown in from
Taiwan—initially with Thai connivance—by General Chennault's
Civil Air Transport Corporation.

The KMT remnants undoubtedly carried on their lucrative
opium trade for many years, and the only point in doubt was
whether they were operating on their own account or by agreement
with Chiang's government. As recently as the late summer of 1973,
detailed information reaching me in London indicated that the
Nationalist government was itself involved in the opium traffic in
the "Golden Triangle" where Burma, Laos, and Thailand overlap.
Indeed, I had reason to believe that clandestine operations by the
KMT in Burma had lately been stepped up. I wrote two articles to
this effect in the London *Times* (they appeared on 28 September
and 10 October 1973). It is only fair to add that when I visited
Taiwan about a year later, the high officials of Taiwan's Intelligence
Bureau of the Ministry of National Defence (IBMND) categorically
denied government involvement in the opium traffic: any such
activities by KMT personnel, they added, were clandestine, strictly
prohibited and severely punished if detected. The IBMND continued to maintain stations in various Burmese towns, however, and
I have no doubt that much "normal" Kuomintang activity continued in the area, both in the gathering of intelligence and the
sabotaging of communications and installations in Communist
China. In such small ways, the Chinese civil war continued.

From the standpoint of the Chinese Communists, these raids
and guerrilla actions were a considerable nuisance, but no more.
From Chiang's point of view, they helped to relieve frustration,
boosted morale, and strengthened the claim to sovereignty over the
uncontrolled mainland. In this unsatisfactory situation, one of
Chiang's main concerns was to make and keep as many friends of
"free China" as possible throughout the world. His diplomatic
service, ably directed for many years by a learned and sophisticated
man, Dr. George Yeh, was extraordinarily active. The counting of
votes in the United Nations was vitally important to Chiang
Kai-shek, and warranted the meticulous care with which his
government cultivated relations with small anti-Communist countries, such as Nicaragua and Senegal. Yet year by year, the
majority in favour of retaining the delegation from Taipei as
representatives of "China" inevitably dwindled. In the Asia and

Pacific region, Chiang strengthened his bonds with nations that had reasons of their own to share his detestation of Peking. South Vietnam and South Korea were obvious examples; but so were two of the Asian members of SEATO, the Philippines and Thailand; and the Australasian members of that alliance, Australia and New Zealand.

All was well so long as the American administration stuck undeviatingly to the hard-line policy so energetically initiated and directed by Secretary of State Dulles. So long as the line remained unchanged, Chiang knew he could count on the support of the many countries, large and small, that were allies or dependants of the United States. True, there were exceptions, such as the United Kingdom, which had not waited long to recognise Communist China, though without visible benefit to itself. And of course, from time to time, the inevitable defections eroded Chiang's position. In January 1964, for instance, General de Gaulle shocked America—as was his intention—and Chiang Kai-shek himself, by opening diplomatic relations with the Chinese People's Republic. (Almost exactly two years later, the Generalissimo granted an interview to Eric Chou, and expressed his admiration for de Gaulle, while criticising him for having weakened the Western alliance. He added, incidentally, that Churchill was the only Western leader who had seen through Stalin.) But if the Americans themselves should weaken? This was the nightmare that haunted Chiang Kai-shek.

As in previous times of anxiety and danger, Chiang sent his wife on an extended visit to the United States in August 1965. She did not return until October 1966. In speech after speech, Mme. Chiang asserted that if only the United States would give it the tools, the Republic of China would do the job alone, "the job" being the recovery of the Chinese mainland. In case anybody had missed the point, the Generalissimo emphasised it in an interview with Stanley M. Swinton of the Associated Press, in which he said: "We can return to the mainland with our own forces alone. There is no need for American combat troops. We do not want to bring the United States into any war. On the mainland it is between us and the Chinese Communists. We have enough strength once we reach the mainland."

Within his intimate circle of family and advisers, Chiang Kai-shek—less prone to the prodigious rages of his younger years—frequently expressed his amazement at the timidity and incomprehension of his American allies. It was as though the bitter lessons of the Marshall mission and the Korean War had simply not been assimilated. Why couldn't the Americans understand that it is idle to expect Communists to be reasonable? Nor were the Chinese Communists the only Communists he had in mind. The Americans were fighting a losing war in Vietnam for precisely the same reason that had made them fail to win in Korea. Truman had ignored General MacArthur's wise advice to strike directly at Chinese power beyond the Yalu River, and victory had eluded the American-led U.N. forces. And now, they were making the same mistake all over again by failing to bomb Hanoi out of existence and destroy the main centre of Vietnamese Communist aggression. But the Chinese mainland was still more dangerous, now that the Communists had acquired atomic weapons. Couldn't the Americans understand that there would be no peace or security in East Asia so long as the centres of Chinese power were allowed to wax? Communist China's nuclear installations, mostly sited in Sinkiang and Szechwan, remained highly vulnerable to an American first strike. But this vulnerability could not be expected to last forever.

These were the arguments Chiang Kai-shek used constantly in his frustrated discussions at home and in the Presidential office. And he saw to it that, in suitably diplomatic language, they were passed on to the White House and the State Department. But all to no avail.

Chiang's spirits rose in April 1966 when the strange episode known as the Great Proletarian Cultural Revolution began in the Chinese People's Republic. Bands of young hooligans, known as the Red Guards, were turned loose on Mao Tse-tung's orders and encouraged to molest old people, deface or pillage historic buildings, humiliate government officials, and frog-march party leaders through the streets. By the time this turmoil decreed from above had begun to die down three years later, Mao had got rid of his main rivals—men like President Liu Shao-ch'i, officially until then the party's leading ideologist, the Secretary-General of the party's Central Committee, Teng Hsiao-p'ing, and the Chief of the General Staff of the People's Liberation Army, General Lo Jui-ching—a former Minister of Public Security.

Watching these troubled events from afar, Chiang Kai-shek was less concerned with the rise or fall of political personalities than with the opportunities the situation might offer for Nationalist exploitation. He did not, as some observers had guessed, conclude that the time had come for a military attack, however desperately lacking in air and naval support. On the contrary, in his New Year's message of 1 January 1967, he declared that a counter-attack was now secondary: the real need was to strengthen political preparations for a smooth transition once the Communist regime had crashed through its own internal dissensions. Not all Chiang's messages were as interesting as this one. In terms of measured vituperation to match the language of the mainland press, radio, and public speeches, he said:

> The important questions before us today are no longer how the military counter-attack on the mainland will be victorious or at what time the traitorous Mao bandits will be killed, because ever since the mainland's so-called "cultural revolution" and "Red Guards" appeared, not only has Mao's nerve cracked and the Communist Party split apart and disintegrated; in actuality, the bandit Mao long since was sent to the grave he dug for himself. . . . The question of the recovery of the mainland today is how to tidy up the calamitous situation which Mao has left behind; when to counter-attack the mainland, and how to bury Mao have become secondary questions. But by this so-called secondary question is not meant that, from now on, our preparations for military counter-attack can be relaxed even for a moment while we sit and wait for Mao to exterminate himself; rather, it is to point out that in the present anti-Mao war, political means are even more important.

A month later to the day, the China Central News Agency announced the creation of a new National Security Council for Mobilisation in the Period of Rebellion. This new body was charged with planning for defence strategy, for national reconstruction on the mainland and the political administration of "war areas". For all their propaganda, and the skilful use they made of defectors from the Communist regime, the Nationalists did not deceive themselves over the character of the upheaval Mao Tse-tung had unleashed. Faithful old Communists like Liu Shao-ch'i might now be described as "bourgeois" or "reactionary", but this did not make them any less

Communist in Chiang Kai-shek's eyes. Many Chinese were doubtless against the regime and against Mao Tse-tung; but what guarantee was there, apart from the inevitable claims of propaganda, that Chiang's Kuomintang would be welcomed with open arms by a people old enough to remember the excesses that had preceded its downfall in 1949?

It came as no surprise to anybody that the Generalissimo emerged as Chairman of the new National Security Council. Nor could it be overlooked that this powerful new body gave him the right to rule by executive decree and powers over the administrative organs of the Central Government and the nomination of civil officials which he could use not only in the hypothetical event of a return to the mainland, but in his island base as well, to bypass the Legislative Yüan at any time of his choosing. In fact, Chiang Kai-shek continued, as always, to rule as a dictator. As leader of the nation, Director-General of the Kuomintang, and Commander-in-Chief of the Armed Forces, all power in all domains inevitably flowed downward from him. The period of "political tutelage" of the KMT over the people had officially ended with the 1947 elections; but with the rapid deterioration of the Nationalist position on the mainland during the civil war, martial law had been imposed in 1949 and had not been lifted by the time of Chiang's death in 1975.

The 1946 Constitution was in practice moot, for the "Temporary Provisions Effective During the Period of Communist Rebellion", adopted by the National Assembly on 18 April 1948, enabled the President to act as he saw fit during the period of the emergency. These "Temporary Provisions" also enabled the President and the Vice-President to be re-elected beyond the two-term restriction prescribed in Article 47 of the Constitution. Moreover, they gave the President the sole right to declare that the "Period of Communist Rebellion" is over. As it happened, it was in fact not over by the time of Chiang Kai-shek's death; but if an unlikely historical good fortune had brought him and his regime back to the mainland, he could presumably have decided that the "Rebellion" was not over for many years after resistance had visibly ended.

This state of affairs naturally produced many anomalies and injustices, the most flagrant of which was the central fact that the great majority of the inhabitants of Taiwan were ruled under laws or decrees in the drafting of which they had no part. For that matter, they had had no part in the "Communist Rebellion". In the words of a prominent Taiwanese Nationalist dissident:

> Since the Nationalist government was exiled to Taiwan twenty-one years ago, any attempt to point out the fact that the war between the Nationalist and Communist Chinese has become verbal rather than military and the situation has become well stabilised, to urge the government to face and accept reality, to demand that the government normalise the situation and restore civil liberties, or to suggest that the political future of Taiwan should be determined in accordance with the principle of self-determination by all inhabitants in Taiwan has been regarded by the regime as the gravest of political offences and dealt with as sedition. . . .

The author of those words (which appeared in *China Quarterly*, London, July–September 1971), Professor P'eng Ming-min, formerly chairman of the Department of Political Science at National Taiwan University, was arrested in September 1964 with two former students after being denounced by printers whom they had engaged to make 10,000 copies of "examination papers" which in fact were political tracts urging Taiwanese to unite against the regime. On 2 April 1965, he was sentenced to eight years, and his co-defendants to ten and eight years respectively. Chiang Kai-shek, however, pardoned him on 3 November that year, and the two others—in a curiously selective exercise of clemency—had their sentences halved in 1966.

Nor was the P'eng case in any way isolated. On 4 September 1960, a well-known journalist, Lei Chen, was gaoled for ten years by a military court on sedition charges the gravest of which—in the eyes of the court—was his alleged failure to denounce an ex-Communist on the staff of his magazine, *Free China*. Lei Chen's major sin may well have been, however, the formation of an opposition group under the name of "Forum for the Improvement of Local Elections", which indeed he had formed on the discovery of alleged electoral irregularities. Late in 1965, a respected periodical, *Wen-hsing*, was suspended for a year after publishing an article in defence of the freedom of the press. A more disquieting case, perhaps, was the trial in 1970 of two brothers deported from the Philippines to Taiwan, where they were sentenced to relatively light terms of two and three years. They had been charged with publishing a pro-Communist paper in Manila. The International Press Institute—which by coincidence had been meeting in Hong Kong in mid-May—interceded on their behalf during a tour of Taiwan by 200 foreign newsmen after the conference. The point which many overseas Chinese wrily noted was that it was possible to be convicted in Taiwan for acts committed abroad. (To be fair to Chiang, this embarrassing case was forced on him by President Marcos of the Philippines, who insisted on deporting the brothers to Taiwan.)

In these and other respects, Chiang's regime was still burdened with Sun Yat-sen's "original sin" of organising the Kuomintang on Communist party lines. Between them, the Chiangs—father and son—controlled everything: the father because all power flowed from him, and Ching-kuo because he ran the Investigation Bureau, the all-seeing security organisation that made sure dissidents did not get out of hand. Although the most common charge levelled at dissidents was that of favouring communism, a frequent accusation —especially in the early years of KMT rule—was that of belonging to or supporting the Taiwanese Independence Movement.

The very able Taiwanese politician Kao Yü-shu (whom I met in 1957 when he was Mayor of Taipei) took part in an abortive attempt to form the China Democratic Party in 1960. He was driven out of politics for a while on threats of prosecution for alleged corruption—a favourite form of political pressure (according to Douglas Mendel). To be fair, however, Taiwanese independence was gradually reduced under Chiang's rule, by the rapidly increasing prosperity of the island, in which all shared, by the dramatically improved position of local-born candidates in the civil service and in various elections, and by an enlightened policy of educational assimilation resulting from the compulsory use of Mandarin Chinese as the medium of instruction in all educational establishments. Although it would be foolish to claim that Taiwanese resentment of the mainlanders had died down, the independence movement as such virtually collapsed in 1965 and 1966 with the return to Taiwan of its principal leaders, Dr. Thomas Liao and Cheng Wan-fu. Both men had spent many years in exile, mainly in

Japan, and both had been allowed to return unpunished on pleading for forgiveness and expressing repentance.°

Despite the favoured label of "free China" for Chiang Kai-shek's regime, it was, and remained to the end of his life, an authoritarian system. It was not, however, a *totalitarian* one, as was Mao Tse-tung's regime on the mainland. The distinction is important and is easily put to the test by a simple question: "Is it possible for ordinary citizens to opt out of politics?" In the Chinese People's Republic, no such possibility existed; in the Republic of China, it did. Except on certain questions, such as anti-Communism, the personality of the President, or Taiwanese independence, the press was remarkably free, and often critical of both the national and the provincial governments. In general, foreign visitors to the island are struck by the relaxed and generally contented atmosphere. In Taiwan (although to a lesser degree than, say, Spain) it is possible and indeed easy to live a full and happy life as individuals or families so long as one exercises care in keeping out of political controversy. The result—in the long run of problematic value—is a remarkably apolitical population.

One area in which Chiang allowed great and productive freedom—perhaps because he was not particularly interested in it—was economics. Here, the contrast with Communist China was striking. In 1953, the public sector accounted for 55.9 percent of industrial output; by 1974, the percentage had dwindled to 23.5 percent. It followed that the contribution of the private sector had risen in those twenty-one years from 44.1 percent to 76.5 percent. Of all the factors responsible for Taiwan's "economic miracle", the most fundamental was the combination of political order and economic freedom. Strikes were banned, but the combination of rising prosperity and paternalism would have kept industrial unrest low even without the ban.

There were other reasons for economic success, of course. One, in the early years, was American aid on a generous scale, for development as well as for military needs. The turning point came in 1965, when the U.S. government—by agreement with Chiang's

---

° Dr. Thomas Liao has been in charge of the Tsengwen Reservoir project since his return to Taiwan. Cheng Wan-fu kept his business interests in Japan, travelling freely and frequently between Tokyo and Taipei.

government and in view of the "healthy economic growth" already achieved—announced that economic aid to Taiwan would be discontinued in June, at the end of the American fiscal year. Military aid continued. Since 1949, the Nationalist regime had received $3,600,000,000 in assistance, which comprised $2,200,000,000 in military aid, $1,200,000,000 in economic aid, and $205,000,000 in agricultural products. The military side of the American aid programme continued after 1965.

In another important respect, too, 1965 was the turning point. That year Chiang's government decided to extend the period of compulsory education from six to nine years. In effect, this raised the school-leaving age to fifteen and marked the start of Taiwan's move into the age of sophisticated technology by spreading education wide enough to create the necessary skilled labour force. Ten years later, the island was exporting electronic calculators and colour television, and making its own jet planes. By then, Taiwan's foreign trade exceeded that of continental China, with fifty times the population.

In 1973, Taiwan's industrial growth rate reached the prodigious figure of 22.7 percent, and although it fell to about half that rate the following year (in a world trade recession), the industrial output continued to grow at a rate to be envied by more advanced countries. By the time Chiang died in 1975, the per capita income reached U.S. $697 a year, second only to Japan in all Asia. This phenomenal growth was accompanied, as in some other countries with similar experience, by rising prices. If 1966 is used as the base year, with an index of 100 for urban consumer prices, the 1974 index stood at 210.7. If one starts earlier, with 1952 as the base year, then the 1974 index reached 431. Although the parallel is not exact, if 1952 is taken as the base year for industrial production, the 1974 indices reached 783.5 in the public sector and 3,950.8 in the private.

Taiwan's economic achievement was the more remarkable in that it happened while the Nationalist Government continued to maintain 600,000 men under arms and to allocate 60 percent of its budget to defence, and while the population soared from a little over 8,000,000 in 1952 to nearly 16,000,000 in 1974.

In the absence of political freedom, scientific, technical, and economic expertise became a road to rapid political advancement. It was significant that when General Ch'en Ch'eng, the author of the land reform programme, resigned as Premier in December 1963,

Chiang Kai-shek chose as his successor the man who had been Taiwan's successful Finance Minister, Dr. C. K. Yen. Dr. Yen went on to be elected Vice-President of the Republic in March 1966 (by the very small majority of thirty-seven, after sick men had been wheeled in to the National Assembly to vote—an expression of widespread displeasure on the part of northern Assemblymen at Chiang's choice of yet another southerner as his running mate: Dr. Yen was born in Kiangsu).

Other able technocrats were Li Kuo-ting and Sun Yun-hsuan, who as Ministers of Finance and Economics respectively presided over the great economic surge of the late 1960s. When Chiang "recommended" his son's appointment as Prime Minister in May 1972, Li and Sun were two of the only three ministers who were kept in their previous jobs by Ching-kuo.

The changes of 1972 were significant in another sense, for they marked a breakthrough for the native-born politicians. Henry Kao (Kao Yü-shu), the former Mayor of Taipei who had got into political trouble in 1960, was brought in as Telecommunications Minister; and in December, "free China's" first general elections since 1947 gave Taiwanese candidates the chance, at last, to improve their tiny representation in the ageing, or dying, National Assembly. (To preserve the fiction of sovereignty over continental China, only 53 seats were up for election; the new members were elected for six years, while 1,376 members, elected in 1947, had life tenure.) One thing, however, did not change in 1972: Chiang Kai-shek was re-elected President, and on 20 May was sworn in, aged eighty-four, for his fifth consecutive six-year term as Head of State.

The forced growth of technocracy had a bearing on Chiang's foreign policy as well as on economic development. Year after year, the Republic of China had to muster votes to maintain its position in the United Nations. One way of making friends who would vote the right way was to help the emerging African nations with expert advice and technology. In increasing numbers, African officials were invited to Taiwan to look at agricultural work. Invariably, they liked what they saw. Next, Taiwan trained Africans in advanced planting techniques, and sent teams of specialists to African countries, usually for two-year terms. Between 1961 and mid–1966, Chiang's government sent more than 630 experts to 19 African countries. As a result, rice yields soared manifold in countries like Liberia, Rwanda, and the Ivory Coast. Taipei's reward came each year in the form of supporting votes when the U.N. debated that hardy annual—China's seat in the General Assembly and the Security Council.

What was astonishing was that it went on so long. With anybody less intransigent than the Generalissimo at the head of public affairs, the fiction that his government was the legitimate government of all China would long since have been discarded. But if it had been, Chiang's own claim to legitimacy of tenure in Taiwan itself would have been seriously impaired. There is reason to believe that the Generalissimo did not totally deceive himself about the prospect of recovering the mainland. In a little-publicised speech in 21 February 1966, he implied that his own forces could hope to do the job—with American help—only if they struck within two years. Thereafter, only the Americans themselves would have the capacity to dislodge the Communist regime; for by 1968, the Chinese Communists would have developed an effective nuclear weapons system.*

The year 1968 came and ended, and the mainland went unrecovered. Chiang continued to make speeches calling for the recovery of the mainland, but as time went on, with a decreasingly specific timetable. Events in continental China often provided him with material for his special brand of vituperation: the excesses of the Red Guards during the Cultural Revolution, the disgrace of P'eng Teh-huai, Liu Shao-ch'i, and even of Mao's chosen heir, Lin Piao—all these and many other events besides allowed Chiang to point to the contrast between the turmoil and barbarity of life under Mao's rule, and the relative contentment and infinitely greater prosperity on his little island.

But all this, although good for morale (his own and his people's), did nothing to change the facts of the power equation; and all the while America's strength and will were being eroded in the quagmire of Vietnam. The blow, when it fell, came from an unexpected source: from the man who had first made his national reputation as the scourge of the Communists and their real or supposed supporters during the McCarthy era—President Nixon.

---

* This speech was not included in the official selection of Chiang's speeches in 1966 (published by the Government Information Office, Taipei). It was quoted by Melvin Gurtov, of the RAND Corporation, in his interesting article, "Recent Developments on Formosa" in *China Quarterly* (London), July–September 1967.

It was not the least irony of Nixon's paradoxical career that he should have succeeded, where other Presidents failed, in extricating the United States from the Vietnam War. He did so, moreover, as part of a sweeping revision of America's international role—as it had stood since President Truman's age of "containment" and John Foster Dulles's system of alliances against communism. There were warning signs. Assiduous students of international affairs noted an article by Richard Nixon in the American quarterly, *Foreign Affairs*, of October 1967, written while he was in the political wilderness after his defeat in the 1963 elections for the governorship of California. In it, Nixon hinted that the time would soon come to end Communist China's isolation in the international community.

A further warning sign came on 25 July 1969 when, as President of the United States, he issued a press statement during a brief visit to the Pacific island of Guam. He made two points: that America would stand by its treaty obligations; but the United States would henceforth expect its Asian allies increasingly to handle their own problems of defence and security, except for a threat from a nuclear power (a clear reference to China).

Next came a political "bombshell", in the President's television broadcast of 15 July 1971, when he revealed that he had sent Dr. Henry Kissinger, his Assistant for National Security Affairs, on a secret mission to Peking for talks with Chou En-lai. He went on to say that he had accepted an official invitation to visit China before May 1972.

"The meeting between the leaders of China and the United States," said Nixon, "is to seek the normalisation of relations between the two countries and also to exchange views of concern to the two sides." Reassuringly, he added: "Our action in seeking a new relationship with the People's Republic of China will not be at the expense of old friends."

In Taipei, Chiang Kai-shek read these words, of which he had had no prior notice, with anger and dismay. He instructed his ambassador in Washington, Mr. James Shen, to make a strong protest to the American administration. There was little else he could do.

Inevitably, President Nixon's statement fatally undermined the Republic of China's already precarious position in the United Nations. The 26th session of the General Assembly was to meet in late October. As early as 2 August, Secretary of State William Rogers had disclosed that the United States would support the entry of the Chinese People's Republic into the U.N., but with a proviso that was wishfully unreal: that Taiwan should not be deprived of representation.

This was the "two Chinas" doctrine, abhorrent to Chiang as well as to Mao. With the writing now so clearly on the wall, the Generalissimo, remembering his foresight in removing some at least of his government's treasure before the collapse on the mainland in 1949, thought of another kind of "treasure": the Republic of China's automatic drawing rights from the International Monetary Fund, totalling $59,900,000 (at that time, £24,000,000). A week before the fatal U.N. debate on 25 October, Chiang ordered withdrawal of the full amount, lest it should fall into Peking's hands.

When the day came, seventy-six members of the General Assembly voted to admit the Chinese People's Republic to membership of the United Nations, including a permanent seat on the Security Council, and at the same time to expel "forthwith" the Chinese Nationalist regime on Taiwan. Thirty-five nations voted against, and seventeen abstained. The Nationalist delegation did not wait to face the humiliation of this bitter end, and on Chiang's instructions, walked out before the vote. Leading the delegation was Chiang's Foreign Minister, Chow Shu-kai, who said before leaving:

> I should like to take this opportunity to express the profound gratitude of my government to those friendly governments which have lent us their unstinting support throughout the years. My government will further strengthen these relations in the years to come. We shall continue to struggle with like-minded governments for the realisation of the ideals upon which the United Nations was founded and which the General Assembly has now betrayed.

By walking out, the Nationalist Government saved face, in its own eyes at any rate, and enabled it to claim that it had withdrawn, and not been expelled, from the United Nations. The reality of increasing isolation was unaffected by such gestures, however.

The sequel to the U.N. vote was President Nixon's visit to China from 21 to 28 February 1972. The final communiqué, issued in Shanghai on the 27th, was lengthy and inconclusive, but it contained an ominous paragraph:

The United States acknowledges that all Chinese on either side of the Taiwan Strait maintain there is but one China and that Taiwan is a part of China. The U.S. government does not challenge that position. It reaffirms its interest in a peaceful settlement of the Taiwan question by the Chinese themselves. With this prospect in mind, it affirms the ultimate objectives of the withdrawal of all U.S. forces and military installations from Taiwan. In the meantime, it will progressively reduce its forces and military installations on Taiwan as tension in the area diminishes.

These words were clear notice that from that point on, Chiang's government was "on its own". A considerable area of ambiguity remained, however, in that the Americans neither denounced the Mutual Security Treaty of 1954, nor—in the immediate future— took steps to exchange diplomatic relations with Peking (which would have necessitated withdrawing recognition from Taipei, unless Chiang's government, or its successor, should drop its claim to sovereignty over the mainland). In Taipei in September 1974, I discussed the implications of this situation with a prominent Kuomintang personality (whose name I cannot, for obvious reasons, reveal). He offered the following comments, which I noted verbatim at the time: "Chiang Kai-shek is unbelievably stubborn. He lost China. If he has his way, he will lose this island as well, by not recognising reality. He will not admit even the existence of Peking. If he did, we could have two American embassies" [that is, in Peking and Taipei].

The authorities on Taiwan reacted to the new situation with courage and characteristic ingenuity, compensating, wherever possible, for the withdrawal of diplomatic recognition by basically friendly countries, by opening "trade centres" or "cultural centres" in lieu of legations and embassies. A particularly ingenious example was Spain, which in common with many other countries, switched recognition to Peking (although the United States, whose actions had precipitated the switch other governments had made, did not itself make the switch). Taiwan opened a "Sun Yat-sen Centre" in

Madrid; and Spain opened a "Cervantes Centre" in Taipei. Life went on.

For Chiang Kai-shek, however, all was now over, bar death. Although he had accepted Presidential office for the fifth consecutive time in May 1972, he ceased, about that time, to be physically capable of carrying out his duties. Though not, it is said, senile, the cruelty of physical old age was upon him, and he had to be carried about or wheeled from room to room. More than ever, he became a recluse, seeing only his sons, his wife, and on occasion his top assistants.

Death came, at eighty-seven, on 5 April 1975. For several months, he had been in an almost constant coma. On the 9th, while his body lay in state, his Will (written for him by Chin Hsiao-yi, deputy Secretary-General of the KMT's Central Committee) was displayed in large characters above his coffin. His grandiose state funeral on 16 April attracted more than 300 foreign dignitaries to Taipei, among them the American Vice-President, Nelson Rockefeller.

The transfer of power was orderly and constitutional. The Vice-President, Dr. Yen Chia-kan ("C. K. Yen"), aged seventy, was sworn in as President of the Republic on 6 April. For form's sake, the man who held the real power, Chiang Ching-kuo, submitted his resignation as Prime Minister. It was duly declined.

It was a sad end to a life of extraordinary adventure, wild variations of fortune, and unfulfilled dreams.

V | An
Assessment

24. | An Assessment

Chiang Kai-shek belonged to that rare category of human beings: those who transcend the norm. His courage, his capacity for work, his will, and his stamina—his sheer staying power—were beyond ordinary expectations. Such men make history and leave the world not as they found it. Their influence on their contemporaries and on posterity varies according to the political context in which they operate, their heritage from history, and the size, power, or importance of their countries. We are still, all of us, suffering the consequences of Lenin and Stalin. Hitler created havoc for his generation. For his share in Hitler's defeat, Churchill left his mark on the future. Franco and Tito changed the face of their countries, as Mustapha Kemal had done a generation earlier. It was China's misfortune—and Chiang Kai-shek's—that historical accident forced him to share the Chinese scene and compete within it with a man still more exceptional than he: Mao Tse-tung. But then, Chiang lacked that prerequisite of enduring fame for generals and statesmen—luck. His ill-luck was monumental, as indeed were his blunders. Because he was what he was, he did nothing by halves.

It would be pointless in Chiang's case (as it is not in de Gaulle's) to attempt to deal with him in separate compartments as man, soldier, writer and philosophical guide, politician, and statesman. The motives, failures, and achievements are inextricably interwoven. He will undoubtedly go down in history as "the man who lost China", and my main object in writing this book was to narrate the circumstances of his stupendous defeat, in an attempt to analyse its causes. In fact, in the course of the narrative, I drew attention to Chiang's errors of omission or commission as they occurred, and pointed to the misfortunes that beset him, whether or not it lay within his power to prevent them. It may be useful now to gather all the threads together.

Most of Chiang Kai-shek's mistakes may be attributed to inherent defects of character and intelligence, and to a lesser degree to his upbringing. Deeply conservative by education and conviction, he yet considered himself a revolutionary, but interpreted revolution as essentially consisting of the overthrow of the Manchu dynasty, the abrogation of foreign privileges on Chinese soil, and the restoration of China's rightful place in the world through the revival of reverence for the traditional and Confucian virtues. Though not devoid of social ideas, he allocated them a lesser priority, in comparison with those other objectives. He was adept at playing off one individual or faction against another, but his view of power was narrowly military. He sought to impose his authority by force, and his way with rebels was to punish rather than convert. The greatest sin in his eyes was disobedience. It was a paradox in his character—one of many—that although he was capable of ruthless reprisals, usually in the form of summary trials and executions, he entirely lacked the sheer scale of ruthlessness that makes memorable tyrants. On this score, he cannot compare with Mao Tse-tung —let alone with Stalin or Hitler. True, he called his wars against the Communists "bandit extermination campaigns", but the exterminations were mainly in the heat of military action. He did not, as Mao was to do, systematically execute people in large numbers because they belonged to certain categories. It is possible, had he consolidated his power after World War II, or defeated the Communists in the civil war, that he would have had as many Communists executed as Mao executed "landlords", "feudal elements", and "Kuomintang remnants". But since history did not put him in this position, the question remains hypothetical.

Chiang's mind was greatly given to over-simplification. This can be useful for propaganda, but is counter-productive if the over-simplification forms the basis of political decisions. There was a time—in the early 1920s—when his description of the Chinese Communists as "puppets" was not far from the truth, but he went on terming them "puppets" long after it was self-evident that they acted independently of Moscow, and even years after the great Sino-Soviet rift of the early 1960s. He seemed impervious to the notion that a demonstrably untrue label rapidly erodes the credibility of those who affix it.

With his concept of overriding authority and the enforcement of obedience by punishment or the threat of punishment went a singular disinclination to follow his orders through and make sure his policies were being loyally applied. He had spoken, and that was enough. If a failure to execute his orders reached his attention, he would fly into one of his rages and order an execution or two or the launching of a punitive expedition. But there was no machinery at the grass roots to make sure policies affecting the people actually reached where they were supposed to reach. In this, perhaps, he differed most markedly from Mao Tse-tung.

In another respect, too, Mao undoubtedly had the edge over him: in ideology. Nobody who has read this book so far will suppose me to be an admirer of Marxism or Leninism; but the force of Marxism as a counter-religion, and of Leninism as a revolutionary technique, cannot be denied. In orthodox terms, Mao was far from being as good a Communist as some of the men he superseded or destroyed, such as Li Li-san or Liu Shao-ch'i. No matter. Mao grasped the possibilities of adopting Marxism-Leninism and adapting it to the Chinese reality of an overwhelming peasant mass. He grasped, too, the attractive potential of Marxian philosophies for a Chinese intellectual class that had lost its moorings. In contrast, Chiang and the Kuomintang alienated the intellectuals, who were left with nowhere to go but Mao and the Communist Party. It was Sun Yat-sen, not Chiang Kai-shek, who accepted the advice of Soviet agents, such as Borodin, and moulded the Kuomintang on Communist Party lines. Chiang inherited this instrument and welcomed its hierarchical structure, with all power flowing downwards from the top—himself. But he had nothing to match the technique of relentless mass persuasion which Mao developed. Mao won over the peasants; Chiang allowed them to be ill-treated and left the problem of land reform until too late. From the original Bolshevik model, Chiang borrowed the idea of an all-pervasive secret state security service, with the spying, the denunciations, and the fear. But this alone was not enough to ensure his continued hold on power in continental China.

He realised the need for an ideology, but his attempts to launch one were unconvincing and abortive. There was little popular enthusiasm for his New Life Movement, with its curious blend of Confucianism and Christianity, however zealously enforced by the semi-fascist Blue Shirts and a puritanical Y.M.C.A. Again, Mao was an easy winner with his *New Democracy*, and Chiang's book, *China's Destiny*, although rigorously enforced as bureaucratic doctrine, failed to capture the intellectuals, while the masses remained in ignorance.

It must be owned that Chiang faced enormous problems: the general turmoil that followed Dr. Sun's abortive revolution, the feudal disposition of the warlords, the challenge of the Communists and their Soviet backers, the Japanese invasion, and not least the ill-judgment, deceit, or outright treachery of his allies. But it cannot be claimed on his behalf that his problems were any worse than those that faced Mao Tse-tung initially, as leader of a persecuted minority party, beset by far more powerful official armies, unaided for years by the Russians, and bereft of American material assistance. But in the end, it was Soviet help that was decisive in tilting the scales on Mao's side, while Chiang himself was deprived of corresponding assistance.

The first and in a way the most fundamental of Chiang's misjudgments was his acceptance of the illusion of conquest during the Northern Expedition of 1926 to 1928. In Kuomintang annals, indeed, it is known as the "Northern *Punitive* Expedition", but Chiang was ready enough to accept a formal switch of allegiance to himself as a token of punishment and of the extension of his authority.

It was a spectacular achievement because he was content to do it the easy way. Perhaps he had no choice. Some of the warlords— such as Yen Hsi-shan and Feng Yü-hsiang—were too strong for frontal assault. Out for quick results, Chiang did not attempt to dislodge them from their strongholds and replace them by men of his choice. He wanted to get the Northern Expedition over and done with, so that he could turn to the real business that interested him—the extermination of Communists.

For the rest of his career on the mainland, he was to be plagued by the consequences of his facility. In the eyes of the warlords, he was just another among them—the biggest and most powerful, no doubt, but never unconditionally accepted as the supreme authority, even when he had achieved the Presidency in 1928. They would help him with troops when it was convenient but in general declined to operate outside their own territories. This was true during the Japanese invasion, and it remained true during the civil war.

In Chapter 10, I described the greatest of Chiang's many errors of judgment as his instructions to the Young Marshal in Manchuria, Chang Hsueh-liang, not to resist the Japanese invaders in 1931. From a military standpoint, Chiang had excellent reasons for this directive. The Japanese army was greatly superior to the Chinese forces in equipment, training, discipline, and leadership. Chiang's preparations were still in the initial stages; he wished to complete them and remedy the military deficiencies before standing up to the Japanese. Above all, he wanted to finish off the Communists while the going was good before dealing with the invaders. On all these counts, his policy of 1931 was disastrously mistaken. The stark message that reached the great Chinese people, as well as the intellectuals and the warlords, was that Chiang Kai-shek was prepared to pit Chinese against Chinese rather than to stand up to the invading foreigners. They could not read his hidden or deferred intentions, and under the misapprehension that Chiang had no intention of fighting the Japanese, the Young Marshal kidnapped him at Sian in 1936. Released, much humiliated, and ironically on the intervention of Chou En-lai, Chiang never forgave his captor, whom he kept under perpetual house arrest. This, too, was a major blunder, as we have seen.

Although Chiang was so often his own worst enemy, he had truly formidable "legitimate" enemies. His Fifth Extermination Campaign in 1934 broke the Communist experiment in Kiangsi and almost smashed the Communist Party forever. But Mao Tse-tung broke out of Chiang's iron ring, marched his men and their

dependants over 6,000 miles into the north-western province of
Shensi, and lived not merely to fight another day but to crush
Chiang's own power forever. At the time, the Fifth Extermination
Campaign was undoubtedly a victory; but the feat of the Long
March nullified Chiang's success over the longer term. So it, too,
must be counted among the causes of Chiang's defeat. But in the
balance-sheet, it rates a plus for his enemies rather than a minus for
himself.

The over-all failure of the extermination campaigns and the
fiasco of the Sian incident left Chiang with no option but to fight the
Japanese, although he would have liked still more time for
preparations. I have argued (with the Japanese military writer,
Masanori Ito) that the Generalissimo's strategy of withdrawal,
trading space for time, was both correct and successful. But it had
unfortunate long-term political consequences in that it left vast
areas of China open to penetration by Communist guerrillas, who
could plausibly claim the aura of heroism for fighting the Japanese
when the Nationalists had left the people to their fate. Chiang
might have countered the Communist challenge in this field had he
been more successful in creating rival guerrilla forces. But except in
certain areas—such as Shansi under the "model governor", Yen
Hsi-shan—it was an unfortunate fact that the Nationalists failed to
produce well-trained, successful, and steadfast guerrilla forces. As a
result, the end of the Sino-Japanese War found Mao's forces well
established in large areas of the north. Concentrating on his strategy
of the big battalions, and obsessed by great power politics beyond
China's borders, Chiang neglected the "micro-war" which gave
Mao and his followers the bases they needed for political as well as
military reasons.

Moreover, however correct Chiang's strategy may have been by
the standards of military orthodoxy and in the eyes of the frustrated
Japanese High Command, it was disastrous in a deeper sense for the
Nationalist side. Despite all the sufferings and hardships of the
exodus to the interior in the face of the ruthless invaders, morale
had remained high so long as the initial fighting lasted—from the
summer of 1937 until the beginning of 1939. Thereafter, a kind of
rot set in. Isolated in the unsuitable wartime capital at Chungking,
with its overcrowding, inadequate facilities, and foul climate, the
Nationalist regime degenerated quickly. Corruption set in and
became a way of life for the higher military and bureaucrats; the

great scandal of mass conscription, with tethered peasants led into starvation, disease, and death, ruled out the slightest chance that the peasantry—the overwhelming majority of the population— would ever support Chiang Kai-shek and the Kuomintang; finally, the great Chinese inflation, which first set in in Chungking, reached its extravagant climax in the post-war years, adding immeasurably to the sufferings of ordinary people and contributing to the general demoralisation of the regime. Chiang's failure to find out what was happening and do something about it was one of his monumental sins of omission. Secure in the conviction of his own moral rectitude, he turned a blind eye to scandals that enriched members of his family and his entourage.

The behaviour of the Kuomintang in power was a gift to his enemies and detractors. They would have done their worst to discredit his regime, anyway, but it was the regime itself that provided the raw material for the campaign of vilification success-fully launched and maintained by the International Communist Movement, and the "liberals" and "progressives" who, wittingly or otherwise, contributed to it. For it was the International Commu-nist Movement as a whole, and not simply the Chinese Communist Party, that was Chiang's enemy. He must, indeed, be given much credit for his prescience in understanding the nature of the Communist challenge from the time of his visit to Russia at the end of 1923. He grasped Lenin's intentions and the workings of the Comintern before most men of his generation. He warned his superiors, Sun Yat-sen included, but they would not listen. Later, he was stuck with his own simplistic view of monolithic communism, and was quite incapable of perceiving the burning nationalism in Mao Tse-tung's heart.

At the start of the Sino-Japanese War, it suited Stalin to be mildly helpful to Chiang's regime. The Sino-Soviet non-aggression pact of August 1937 was a sign of this momentary good favour. It was useful to the Soviet Union that Japan should be drawn into the China conflict and away from the Soviet Far East; the Russians therefore granted arms and credits to Nationalist China. In line with Stalin's wishes, Mao Tse-tung launched his United Front policy, involving expedient reconciliation between the Communists and the Nationalists. During this period, the world-wide propaganda appa-ratus of the Comintern went into high gear to build up Chiang Kai-shek as a great national leader and international statesman.

But there was much Soviet treachery in store for Chiang. The Soviet-Japanese neutrality pact of April 1941 was a major blow: it gave the Japanese a free hand in China, as far as the Russians were concerned. Now that it no longer suited Stalin to build up the Generalissimo's image, the great international propaganda machine went into reverse. With the disinformation techniques of the KGB's predecessor at that time—the NKVD—at its disposal, the Comintern launched a sustained campaign of vilification against Chiang. At the same time, a misleading notion was widely disseminated and almost universally accepted by leader-writers, commentators, and the intellectual establishment in general in the West: that the Chinese Communists were not really Communists at all, but agrarian reformers.

The influence of this two-edged campaign was immeasurable, especially on public opinion in the United States. It was supported by the wartime and post-war despatches of the American embassy, first in Chungking and later in Nanking. This coloured view of Chinese Communism became accepted doctrine in the U.S. State Department and the White House, nullifying Chiang's own propaganda efforts, tenaciously sustained by his wife's personal appearances in America, on his own regime's behalf and in favour of American support for anti-Communist actions.

Thus it can be said that the Comintern, through its conscious or unconscious allies, made a decisive contribution to the great Sino-American misunderstanding. It must be added, of course, that there would have been a misunderstanding in any case. General Joseph Stilwell, who represented the United States in China in various high capacities from March 1942 to September 1944, was immediately and totally incompatible with Chiang Kai-shek. From the time of America's forced entry into the war—as a result of the Japanese aggression at Pearl Harbor—the Generalissimo resumed his view that it was relatively unimportant for him to fight the Japanese (since the Americans would be doing it for him) and all-important to husband his resources for the decisive struggle for power with the Communists.

Stilwell was not the only American who found this attitude incomprehensible, and indeed intolerable. He communicated this view to his superiors—President Roosevelt and General Marshall in the Pentagon. On this point alone, there would have been tension anyway between Chiang and his American allies. But the misunderstanding was constantly deepened by the hostile reporting of American correspondents in Chungking, and later in Nanking, and by the assiduous efforts of the Chinese Communists and fellow-travellers in their "United Front" contacts with American individuals and organisations.

In the latter stages of World War II, President Roosevelt's conception of his country's national interest, both during the war and for the post-war period, led him into an unfortunate collusion with Stalin. At the Cairo summit conference in November 1943, Roosevelt committed himself to the return of Formosa to the Republic of China, to support for a major offensive in Burma in the spring of 1944 to break the blockade of China, and to supporting China after the war by preventing any Soviet move to grab Manchuria. In return, he extracted a promise from Chiang to settle his indigenous problems with the Communists.

The American President, however, went on to a further summit meeting with Stalin and Churchill (but without Chiang Kai-shek) at Teheran, in which he made pledges to the Soviet dictator that directly contradicted those he had given the Generalissimo. Indeed, the Americans failed to honour any of Roosevelt's Cairo commitments to Chiang Kai-shek. The great carve-up of the Yalta summit followed in February 1945, when President Roosevelt signed away China's territorial rights to Stalin, in return for Stalin's pledge to enter the war against Japan. Russia duly entered the war, occupied Manchuria, and frustrated the return of the Nationalist authorities, allowed the Chinese Communists to take possession of most of the countryside, and for good measure handed over vast quantities of captured Japanese equipment to the Communist armies.

These acts of treachery alone—on Stalin's part, but also on Roosevelt's—would possibly have sufficed in themselves to make Chiang Kai-shek's military defeat in the civil war inevitable. But Chiang compounded his misfortunes by some of the most monumental blunders of his entire career. His troops occupied the "liberated" areas with rapacious brutality, and he was powerless to control their behaviour. Still nursing his sense of outrage nearly ten years after the Sian kidnapping, he disregarded the advice of those who wanted him to free the Young Marshal, Chang Hsueh-liang, and send him back to Manchuria to make the area safe for the Nationalists. Instead, the long captivity went on. He disbanded 300,000 "puppet" troops who had served under the Japanese, turning them loose in Manchuria without pay, so that they brought a powerful accretion of manpower to the Communist side.

The sage advice of the best strategists was lost on Chiang. He might have done better to refrain from occupying Manchuria and consolidated his positions to the south. He wanted to defend everything, everywhere, and all the time. Stretching his forces too thinly, he lost control of city after city and province after province. The Marshall mission, dedicated to unattainable objectives—principally the reconciliation of the irreconcilables, that is, the Communists and Nationalists—not only failed but deeply damaged Chiang's chances of remaining in power on the mainland. The Soviet Union's decisive military gift of Japanese equipment to the Chinese Communists was matched by the decisive American ban on military supplies to the Nationalists from July 1946 to November 1948. Between them, these unconsciously complementary decisions tilted the military balance hopelessly against Chiang Kai-shek. Demoralisation and defeatism completed the job.

How, then, are we to assess this extraordinary career? As a soldier, Chiang Kai-shek proved himself a master tactician in the civil wars of the 1920s and 1930s; and demonstrated that he had a grasp of strategy as well during the first phase of World War II. But it was a strategy for the avoidance of defeat, not for the achievement of victory. His total defeat in the civil war was the graveyard of his military reputation.

As a politician and statesman, again, Chiang Kai-shek was a master of tactics rather than strategy. He was adept at keeping one jump ahead of his rivals and at out-manoeuvring them. But although he achieved great popularity in China, he had virtually no understanding of the social bases of permanent power. In world terms, he understood the menace of the International Communist Movement, but spoiled his own case by over-simplifying the problem and over-stating his view of it.

As a writer, unlike some other soldier-politicians, Chiang cannot be taken very seriously, since he did not write his own books or speeches. But he was responsible for the thought behind them, and in particular for the xenophobic note that permeates *China's Destiny*. As either ideology or history, it was neither original nor profound. He did not understand economics, and his (ghost-written) attempt at an indigenous *Chinese Economic Theory* was turgid and unsuccessful.

In the end, the summing-up must be that Chiang, with his courage and energy and his qualities of leadership, was not only a deeply flawed leader, but in the classical sense of the Greek tragedies, a *tragic* one. His tragedy was personal, but it far transcended the man himself, for he was a main instrument in one of the greatest tragedies of contemporary history: the fall of China to the most totalitarian system of government yet devised, still more totalitarian than Russia's in that the techniques of relentless mass persuasion developed by the Chinese Communist Party entirely rule out personal life and privacy, and make it impossible, as it is not in the U.S.S.R., for anybody to opt out of policies and politics imposed from above. It is more than ironical that Chiang, as the arch-enemy of communism, should have played a role contributing to the end which, above all else, he abhorred; and that is why his failure must be termed tragic.

Against this failure, the preservation of Chinese values in Taiwan, though not trivial, assumes smaller dimensions. His lasting monument was indeed one which he would have dismissed in earlier years as unworthy of his gifts and ambitions: the limited but undeniable success story of his island refuge.

NOTES ON SOURCES

INDEX

Notes on Sources

There is no really satisfactory way of giving sources in a work such as this. To give them at the foot of each page impedes the flow of the narrative; to collect them at the back is a worse irritant for those curious, diligent, and scholarly enough to wish to trace facts back to those originally responsible for their availability to the author. Since this biography of Chiang Kai-shek is intended primarily for the general reader I have thought it unnecessary in many cases to give the precise reference. In such cases, I give more general indications of the works I found most useful in each particular chapter. In selected instances, I refer (in the manner of Barbara W. Tuchman) to key words in the passage to be sourced. This method has the great merit of leaving the text unencumbered by numerous tiny figures. Where the source is Eric Chou, I have mostly said so in the text; where I have not, I indicate this source in the notes. "Private source" hides the names of informants who do not wish to be identified.

If the works mentioned in these notes are collated, they amount to a fairly large bibliography, but I do not claim that it is an exhaustive one.

PART I: THE ENIGMA OF CHIANG KAI-SHEK

Chapter 1: *Conservative Revolutionary*

PAGE

3   *Description of Chiang Kai-shek:* My own recollection of an interview in Taipei in January 1957.

4   *Letters to Chiang Ching-kuo:* Chiang Ching-kuo, *My Father* (Taipei, 1956). (Henceforth, *Father*)

4   *Chiang's wives, visits to brothels, etc.:* Ting Yi, "A Study of Chiang Kai-shek's Marital Life", in *The Perspective Monthly* (Hong Kong, January 1973). Ting Yi, a Chinese student of history, was living in the United States when this book was written. (Henceforth, *Ting*)

6   *The Green Society:* Eric Chou; also L. Z. Yuan, President of the Asia Foundation, Hong Kong, in conversation with me in that city in September 1974; Mr. Yuan witnessed Chiang's capture of Shanghai in 1927.

8   *Chiang's quick temper:* Theodore H. White and Annalee Jacoby, *Thunder Out of China* (New York: William Sloane Associates, 1946;

London: Gollancz, 1947; my references are to the London edition),
pp. 120, 125. Although the authors do not hide their dislike of Chiang,
their book is a gripping firsthand account of the World War II years in
China. (Henceforth, *Thunder*)

8–9   *Chiang's "drinking":* White and Jacoby reported Western accounts of
Chiang's drinking, which Eric Chou corrects: it was boiled water.

9   *Officers executed:* Lloyd E. Eastman, *The Abortive Revolution—China
Under Nationalist Rule, 1927–1937* (Cambridge, Mass.: Harvard
University Press, 1972), p. 19. (Henceforth, *Eastman*) This excellent
and scholarly account throws much fresh light on a confused period.
Hostile but well researched (my references to "China's Himmler" and
to the Blue Shirts are partly drawn from pp. 74 et seq. and 64 et seq.),
with material from Eric Chou. Eastman's description of the Chinese
bureaucracy (p. 12) was also useful.

While I was writing this book, the most objective available account of Chiang
Kai-shek's life (though one of the shortest) was the appropriate entry in Howard L.
Boorman and Richard Howard, eds., *Biographical Dictionary of Republican China*
(1967), which also offers a scholarly interpretative list of primary and other sources.

Chapter 2: *"Ripe for Revolution"*

As with my previous biographical histories (of Franco and de Gaulle) I made
good use of that wonderfully practical tool of the historian's trade, William L.
Langer, *An Encylopaedia of World History*, 5th ed. (Boston: Houghton Mifflin,
1972). I also consulted a number of the standard histories of China, both for this
chapter and for the linking historical narrative in subsequent chapters. The most
gracefully succinct account of China's difficulties in the twilight of the imperial era
known to me is C. P. Fitzgerald, *The Birth of Communist China* (London: Penguin,
1964 and subsequent editions; 1st ed., Cresset, *Revolution in China*, 1952), from
which I draw, in particular, the figure for the census of 1778 on p. 16. (Henceforth,
Fitzgerald, Birth) For a wider view of China in the Far Eastern context, I turned
from time to time to two impressive histories, well-known to me since they first
appeared: Franz H. Michael and George Taylor, *The Far East in the Modern World*
(London: Methuen, 1956; U.S. ed., Henry Holt); and Claude A. Buss, *The Far
East—A History of Recent and Contemporary International Relations in Asia* (New
York: Macmillan, 1955). Both are monuments of hard work; the former is written
with a special understanding of Communist methods.

PAGE

21–28   *References to Yüan Shih-k'ai:* Jerome Ch'en, *Yüan Shih-k'ai, 1859–1916*
(Stanford: Stanford University Press, 1961), ch. 7, pp. 115 et seq.
(Henceforth, *Ch'en, Yüan*)

26   *Reorganisation Loan:* Ibid.; also O. Edmund Clubb, *20th Century China*,
2nd ed. (New York, 1972), p. 48. This valuable and scholarly work is
the best general narrative for the period. Its author, formerly an
American Foreign Service officer in China, was penalised (unjustly, in
his case) during the late Senator Joseph McCarthy's purges, but with

some exceptions does not allow his experience to cloud his judgment. (Henceforth, *Clubb*) ·

27   *Description of Yüan:* Paul S. Reinsch, *An American Diplomat in China, 1913–19* (Garden City, New York: Doubleday, 1922), p. 1. An urbane memoir.

PART II: CONQUEST AND INVASION (1887–1939)

Chapter 3: *Student in Japan*

For the childhood, early years, and career of Chiang Kai-shek, the indispensable sources are: Hollington K. Tong, *Chiang Kai-shek: Soldier and Statesman* (London: Hurst & Blackett, 1937, Vols. I and II; henceforth, *Tong 37*); and S. I. Hsiung, *The Life of Chiang Kai-shek* (London: Peter Davies, 1948; henceforth, *Hsiung*). Although Tong's two-volume biography is a hagiography, it is carefully researched and accurate. He was the official biographer, and in the 1937 edition he takes the story through Japan's invasion of China. In a revised edition, published in Taipei in 1953, he incorporates the earlier material in abridged form and brings the story up to date at the time of publication. (Henceforth, *Tong 53*) My references in this chapter and the next few chapters are to *Tong 37*; in later chapters, I switch to *Tong 53*, and indicate the change. Hsiung, although an approved rather than an official biographer, includes much previously unpublished documentary material. This, too, is a hagiography, but Hsiung writes with a gentle and very Chinese irony, as befits the author of *Lady Precious Stream*, which enjoyed a long run on the London stage in the 1930s.

PAGE

31   *Reference to the Duke of Chou:* Eric Chou and *Father.*
33–34 *Chiang's fiftieth birthday: Tong 37*, Vol. II, pp. 435–41.
35   *Chiang's marriage: Tong* and *Hsiung* paint an idyllic picture, which I have corrected by reference to *Ting.*
41   *The Record of the Independence of Chekiang:* The name of the author is Ku Nai-ping; *Hsiung*, pp. 70–71.
43   *Shanghai garrison commander:* His name was Cheng Ju-cheng.
44   *Description of the Green Society: Thunder*, p. 118.

Chapter 4: *Chaos and Treachery*

Tong 37 and *Hsiung* are general sources.

PAGE

48   *Peasants forced to grow opium:* James E. Sheridan, *Chinese Warlord— The Career of Feng Yü-hsiang* (Stanford: Stanford University Press, 1966), pp. 24–26. (Henceforth, *Sheridan*) This scholarly account of the career of the most picturesque of China's warlords is also useful for the general background of the period.
48   *Commander of the First Fleet:* Ch'en Pi-kuang.

48   *Rival "President" in Peking:* Feng Kuo-chang.
52   *Ch'en Chiung-ming's list of titles: Clubb,* p. 103.
53   *A Kuomintang emissary:* Tai Chi-t'ao.
54   *Provisional President in Peking:* Hsu Shih-ch'ang.
55   *Presidential candidate in Peking:* Li Yüan-hung; *Clubb,* pp. 105–6.

Chapter 5: *Enter the Comintern*

General sources: *Tong* 37 and *Hsiung.*

PAGE

60   *KMT in trade-union movement:* Harold Isaacs, *The Tragedy of the Chinese Revolution* (Stanford: Stanford University Press, 1962), pp. 53–64. (Henceforth, *Isaacs*) A highly partisan but powerful account by a former Trotskyist.

60   *First Congress, Chinese Communist Party:* Stuart Schram, *Mao Tse-tung* (London: Penguin, 1966), p. 65. (Henceforth, *Schram*) Jacques Guillermaz, *A History of the Chinese Communist Party, 1921–1949* (London: Methuen, 1972), pp. 57, 73. (Henceforth, *Guillermaz*) Both *Schram* and *Guillermaz* are excellent and scholarly works; the latter is the more substantial. The English translation of *Guillermaz* is well done by Anne Destenay; the first edition in French was *Histoire du parti communiste chinois (1921–1949)* (Paris: Payot, 1968).

65   *Chiang disappointed in Comintern:* Chiang Kai-shek, *Soviet Russia in China—A Summing Up at Seventy* (New York: Farrar, Straus, 1957), p. 20. The *Hsiung* reference that follows is on p. 179. Chiang's spare, highly selective account gives details not found in *Tong* and *Hsiung,* who are reticent about Chiang's disagreement with Sun Yat-sen. (Henceforth, *Soviet Russia*)

66   *Official Archives of the Kuomintang:* Eric Chou.
67   *Chiang and Galen: Soviet Russia,* pp. 51–52.

Chapter 6: *Sun's Death, and After*

General sources: *Tong* and *Hsiung.*

PAGE

70   *Magna Carta of National Revolution: Soviet Russia,* p. 29.
71   *Franco at Saragossa:* Brian Crozier, *Franco: A Biographical History* (London: Eyre & Spottiswoode, 1967; American ed., *Franco,* Boston: Little, Brown, 1967), pp. 91 et seq. (Henceforth, *Crozier, Franco*)
72   *Yang and Liu:* Their full names are Yang Hsi-min and Liu Ch'en-huan.
75   *Wu, Chang, and Feng:* Their full names are Wu P'ei-fu, Chang Tso-lin, and Feng Yü-hsiang.
75   *Descriptions of Wu and Feng: Sheridan,* p. 19.
75   *Wu's man in Peking:* Ts'ao K'un.
76   *Canton merchants' rebellion: Clubb,* p. 125.

76 *Japanese gold: Sheridan*, pp. 141–42.
77 *Chiang's "provincialism":* Eric Chou, quoting a veteran KMT politician, Yü Yu-jen.
81 *Temple of the Azure Clouds: Guillermaz*, p. 98.

Chapter 7: *The Northern Expedition*

For my account of the preparations for the Northern Expedition and of relations between Chiang and Borodin, I have relied mainly on *Soviet Russia* and *Hsiung.*

PAGE

83 *Description of Yen Hsi-han:* Barbara W. Tuchman, *Stilwell and the American Experience in China, 1911–45* (New York: Bantam Books, 1972, 1st ed., New York: Macmillan, 1971), p. 93. (Henceforth, *Tuchman*)
86 *Communist in charge of Naval Forces Bureau:* Li Chih-lung.
86 *Arrests in Canton: Guillermaz*, p. 99.
87 *Feng on "March 20th incident":* Feng Yü-hsiang, *Chiang Kai-shek as I Knew Him* (*Wo So Jen Shih Ti Chiang Kai-shek*) (Hong Kong, 1950), p. 2. (Henceforth, *Feng*)
89 *Peasant Movement Training Institute: Schram*, pp. 89–90. The two ousted Communists were Lin Tsu-han and T'an P'ing-shan.
90 *Canton police commissioner:* Wu T'ieh-ch'en.
90 *Canton businessmen paid up: Tong*, pp. 102–3.
91 *Discrimination resented:* Yin Shih (pseud.), *The Li* [*Tsung-jen*]*-Chiang Relationship and China* (*Li Chiang kuan-hsi yü Chung-kuo*) (Hong Kong, 1954), p. 24. (Henceforth, *Yin Shih*)

Chapter 8: *Shanghai Incident*

PAGE

93 *Wu P'ei-fu's allies:* The main one was Sun Ch'uang-fang.
94 *Telegram to Wang Phing-wei: Hsiung*, pp. 263–64.
94 *Colleagues sent to France:* Chang Ching-kiang and Li Shih-tseng.
95 *Chiang's dictatorial powers: Guillermaz*, pp. 113 et seq.
95 *Teng (the disloyal associate):* His full name was Ten Yeng-ta.
97 *Mao's report on Peasant Movement:* Mao Tse-tung, "Report on an Investigation of the Peasant Movement in Hunan", *Selected Works* (Peking: Foreign Languages Press, 1965), pp. 23–30. (Henceforth, *Mao, Selected*)
98 *Browder, Doriot, Mann: Guillermaz*, p. 111 fn.
98 *Terror in Hankow and Changsha: Tong* 37, pp. 143–44.
98 My account of the Nanking incident draws heavily on *Soviet Russia* (pp. 46–47) and *Guillermaz* (pp. 116–17).
100 *KMT man named Wu:* His full name was Wu Chih-hui.

101   For the events in Peking, *Guillermaz* (pp. 124–26) is particularly useful. I
       have preferred his chronology to *Hsiung's*. In particular, Chang
       Tso-lin's decision to have the Soviet Embassy searched is dated 6 April
       1927; *Hsiung* dates it 4 April (p. 261).

101   *Telegram from Ho Ying-ch'in: Yin Shih*, pp. 26–28.

102   *"Bandit-soldiers" of the local warlord:* The warlord was Chang Tsung-
       ch'ang.

Accounts of the Shanghai coup are wildly contradictory. Chiang Kai-shek
himself is brief and reticent (*Soviet Russia*, p. 47). Among the pro-Chiang sources,
the most useful is *Hsiung* (pp. 270–71), but *Tong 37* is also useful. The hostile
sources consulted include: Edgar Snow, *Red Star Over China* (London: Gollancz,
1963; 1st ed., 1937; henceforth, *Snow*); Ch'en Po-ta, *Chiang Kai-shek—Enemy of
the People (Jen-min kung-ti Chiang Kai-shek)* (Hong Kong, 1964; Peking, 1962;
henceforth, *Ch'en Po-ta*); and the footnotes and commentary in Chiang Kai-shek,
China's Destiny, Philip Jaffe, ed. (London: Dennis Dobson, 1947; henceforth,
China's Destiny). On my trip to the Far East in September 1974, I also had the
benefit of eyewitness accounts by L. Z. Yuan in Hong Kong and Ch'en Li-fu in
Taipei.

My account of the "CC clique" is based on *Eastman* and on Eric Chou's
recollections.

Chapter 9: *Chiang's Re-marriage*

107   *Price on Chiang's head: Clubb*, p. 137.

108   *"All will be brought to nought": Tong 37*, pp. 149–51.

109   *Roy's telegram from Moscow: Soviet Russia*, pp. 50–51; *Guillermaz*, p.
       135.

109   *Communist declaration of 30 June 1927:* For full text see *Guillermaz*, pp.
       137–38.

110   *Chiang's farewell to Galen: Soviet Russia*, p. 52 (see last paragraphs of
       Part II, ch. 3).

110   *Second Revolutionary Civil War: Guillermaz*, p. 147 fn.

110–11 *Nanch'ang military uprising:* Ibid., pp. 150 et seq. The Communist
       commanders were Generals Chang Fa-k'uei, Ho Lung, and Yeh T'ing.

111   *Feng and Chiang as "sworn brothers": Feng*, p. 7.

114–18 In my account of Chiang's re-marriage, I have drawn heavily on *Ting*
       (see Part I, ch. 1) as a corrective to *Tong* and *Hsiung*.

115   *Chiang unacceptable as suitor:* Eric Chou; and Emily Hahn, *The Soong
       Sisters* (London: Robert Hale, 1942), pp. 115–16. (Henceforth, *Hahn*)

116   *Love letter to Soong Mayling: Ting.*

116–17 *Chiang ready to become a Christian: Hahn*, p. 116.

118   *". . . another warlord also called Chang":* Chang Chung-chang.

118   *Chiang's thoughts intent on romance: Feng*, p. 6.

118   *CP and rural Soviets:* Schram, pp. 119–20.
119   *Mao unaware of demotion:* Ibid., p. 125.

Chapter 10: *Chiang "Unites" China*

PAGE

122   *Ridge of Wells:* In Chinese, *Ching Kang Shan.*
122   *"They reached their new mountain base":* Schram, p. 127.
122   *". . . expropriating local bullies":* Mao, *Selected* (Vol. I: *"The Struggle in the Ching Kang Mountains"*, 1928).
123   *Kuomintang party elections:* Tong 37, pp. 203 et seq; Hsiung, p. 286.
124   *Sun's revolution in three phases: China's Destiny,* p. 126.
126   *Commander who flouted order:* Ho Yao-tsu.
126   *Man in charge of Nationalist Foreign Ministry:* Tsai Kung-shih.
126   *Nationalist Foreign Minister:* Huang Fu.
127   *Mission to Young Marshal:* Eric Chou in conversation with Hsiao Tung-tzu.
128   *Nationalists seize Communist towns:* Guillermaz, pp. 170–71.
129   *Li Li-san's ascendancy:* Ibid., pp. 176–79.
129   *". . . Chiang was sobbing uncontrollably":* Hsiung, p. 291.
130   *Chiang "arrogant and conceited":* Yin shih, p. 38.
131   *Political tutelage of KMT:* Clubb, p. 144.
132   *Feng in Nanking:* Tong 37, p. 238.

Chapter 11: *The Lost Revolution*

PAGE

135   *Advice to snub Young Marshal:* This advice was also given by Pai Ch'ung-hsi.
135   *Demobilisation crisis:* Clubb, p. 149 and pp. 152–53.
137   *Chiang's conversation with Feng:* Feng, p. 14.
137   *The other Kwangsi warlords:* Pai Ch'ung-hsi, Li Chi-shen, and Huang Shao-hung.
137   *General who was removed:* Lu Ti-p'ing.
137   *Kwangsi general under safe-conduct:* Li Chi-shen.
137   *Wang Ching-wei's denunciatory telegram:* Hsiung, p. 293.
138   *Arrested general:* Pai Ch'ung-hsi.
138   *Feng concentrates in Honan:* Sheridan, pp. 258 et seq.
138   *"Triple-crosser Shih":* Shih Yu-san.
138   *Tax-collecting in twenty-two provinces:* Tong 37, p. 265.
139   *Feng's $200,000 expenses:* Sheridan, p. 262.
140   *Yen Hsi-shan "off the fence":* Ibid., p. 264. Also see Ibid., pp. 265 and 267; Hsiung, pp. 294 and 302–3; and Tong 37, p. 306.
142   *Chiang's clash with Hu Han-min:* Tong, p. 313.
142   *Mao's relations with Li Li-san:* Snow, p. 144; Guillermaz, pp. 181, 194.
144   *Mao President of Soviet Republic:* Guillermaz, pp. 208–9.

Chapter 12: *Chiang Seals His Fate*

PAGE

145   *Principle of non-resistance: Clubb,* pp. 166–67.

147   *The Tanaka Memorial:* For text, see Franz Schurmann and Orville Schell, *The China Reader,* Vol. 2: *Republican China, Nationalism, War, and the Rise of Communism, 1911–1949* (New York: Random House, 1967), pp. 180–83. (Henceforth, *Republican China*) An excellent compilation. See also Carl Crow, *Japan's Dream of World Empire: The Tanaka Memorial* (New York: Harper, 1942), pp. 22–23.

148   ". . . *Chiang was ready to step down": Tong 53,* pp. 142 et seq.

150   ". . . *heroes of the anti-Japanese resistance": Eastman,* pp. 91–92.

151   *Yangtze River floods: Clubb,* pp. 195–96.

152   *Provisional Soviet Government:* Ibid., p. 197.

152   *Peasant secret societies:* Ibid., p. 188.

153   *Nineteenth Route Army in Fukien: Eastman,* p. 96.

155   *Chiang's "perverse and unrighteous actions":* Ibid., p. 105.

Chapter 13: *Mao Marches Out*

PAGE

157   *The extermination campaigns: Snow,* p. 178 fn.

158   ". . . *determined to wipe out the Communists":* Wu Ting-ch'ang in conversation with Eric Chou, 1950.

158–59 *Von Seeckt as military adviser: Clubb,* p. 200.

159   *Red Army's 60,000 casualties: Snow,* p. 186.

159–60 *Chiang Po-li's national defence plan:* Dr. Paul K. T. Sih, *Chiang Po-li's Latter Years and Military Thought* (Taipei, 1969), pp. 99–101. Dr. Sih became Vice-Chancellor of St. John's University, New York. (Henceforth, *Sih*)

161   *Mao down with malaria:* Jerome Ch'en, *Mao and the Chinese Revolution* (London: Oxford University Press, 1965), p. 183. (Henceforth, *Ch'en, Mao*)

161–62 *Snow's description of the Long March:* p. 189.

163   *Mao's poem: Guillermaz,* p. 152. Other sources on the Long March: Tibor Mende, *The Chinese Revolution* (London: Thames and Hudson, 1961); *Soviet Russia;* and the Communist source mentioned below.

164   ". . . *Communists wanted to go north":* "A Geographical Sketch of the Long March" in *Historical Treatises on the Second Revolutionary War* (Peking, 1956), p. 90.

164   ". . . *complete denial of salt supply":* Eric Chou in conversation with Ch'en Hsiao-wei, a distinguished Chinese military historian and commentator.

165   *Chiang addresses Blue Shirts: Eastman,* pp. 66 et seq.

167   *Governor of Kiangsi:* Hsiung Shih-hui.

167   *Commissioner of Education:* Ch'eng Shih-k'uei.

171   *Communists in Kweichow: Snow,* p. 191.

Chapter 14: *Japan and the Sian Incident*

PAGE

174   *Major-General Seiichi Kita quoted:* Tong 53, p. 197.

175   *Military . . . "moving consciously towards war":* Eastman, pp. 246–47.

176   *Student riots in various cities:* Guillermaz, p. 273.

176   *Liu Shao-ch'i on the December 9th Movement:* Yang Shu, *On the December 9th Movement* (Peking, 1961), p. 49.

176   *Chiang Ching-kuo's letter to his mother:* Ting Yi, *A Biography of Chiang Ching-kuo* (serialised in *The Perspective Monthly*, 16 December 1972), p. 74. (Henceforth, *Ting Yi*)

177   *Wei-kuo sent to Germany:* Ibid.

177   *". . . Economic mobilisation was essential":* Sih, p. 101.

178   *"Close associate" sent to Vienna:* Tong 53, pp. 212–13.

178   *Communist new line after Long March:* Schram, p. 195.

178   *". . . Recovery and growth of Mao Tse-tung's forces":* Clubb, p. 207.

179   *"I will jump down!":* Lu Pi (pseud.), *On Chang Hsueh-liang* (Hong Kong, 1946), p. 16. (Henceforth, *Lu Pi*)

179   *"Macaroni on every table":* Private source.

181–89   *The Sian kidnapping:* I have used a variety of sources, including *Tong 53*; Hsiung (esp. p. 328); Snow; Guillermaz (esp. p. 280); *Lu Pi*; Lei Hsiao-ch'en, *Profiles of New Bureaucrats* (Taipei, 1969), esp. p. 105 (henceforth, *Profiles*); Ch'en Po-ta; and Feng. Eric Chou also contributed much material from his memories, notably his conversations with Hu Lin (founder of the newspaper *Ta Kung Pao*) in Hong Kong in 1948, and with Mei Yi (spokesman for the Chinese Communist delegation in Nanking until it withdrew in 1947, and later Director of Broadcasting Administration in Peking in 1949).

189   *". . . Mao Tse-tung foresaw this sequence":* Fitzgerald, *Birth*, p. 82.

Chapter 15: *Japan Strikes*

PAGE

191   *Japanese Army pamphlet:* Chalmers A. Johnson, *Peasant Nationalism and Communist Power: The Emergence of Revolutionary China, 1937–1945* (Stanford: Stanford University Press, and London: Oxford University Press, 1962/63), p. 33. (Henceforth, *Johnson*) An interesting study, based largely on captured Japanese material, which at the time threw new light on the Chinese civil war.

192   *Chiang "really believed that the Chinese Communists had repented":* Soviet Russia, p. 82.

193   *Communist principles and pledges:* Guillermaz, p. 281; Tong 53, p. 234.

193   *"Complete Eradication of the Red Menace":* Text from *Soviet Russia*, p. 80.

196   *Chou En-lai's visit to Chiang Kai-shek:* Clubb, p. 211.

197   *"We seek peace":* Tong 53, p. 239.

198   *The Loch'uan Declaration:* Guillermaz, p. 283.

202   *Interview with Tillman Durdin:* Tong 53, p. 246.
206   *Stalin's message to Generalissimo:* Tong 53, p. 251.
207   *Feng's concubine:* Eric Chou.
207   *Chiang's man-made flood:* Tuchman, p. 237.
208–9 For the great exodus to the interior, I consulted *Thunder*, pp. 58–64.
210–11 *Quotation from Masanori Ito: Japan's Bloody Wars* (Chinese tr. Hong
       Kong, 1970), pp. 225–26. (Henceforth, *Ito*) A fresh evaluation from a
       former "enemy".
211   *Wang's stormy interview with Chiang:* Gerald E. Bunker, *The Peace
       Conspiracy: Wang Ching-wei and the China War, 1937–1941* (Cam-
       bridge, Mass.: Harvard University Press, 1972), p. 113. (Henceforth,
       Bunker) Along with *Eastman*, a valuable product of the "new wave"
       of Chinese scholarship in the United States.
211–12 Other details of Wang Ching-wei's "peace plan", including the Japanese
       Prime Minister's Five Peace Principles, are drawn from Ch'en
       Kung-po, *Recollections of the Past Eight Years* (original ed. Shanghai,
       1946), reprinted as "a historical document" in the *Chancellor Monthly*
       (Hong Kong), No. 36, 15 April 1973; esp. pp. 6–9.

PART III: WORLD WAR AND CIVIL WAR (1939–1949)

Chapter 16: *Japan Bogs Down*

PAGE
218   *Dual membership of CP and KMT:* Soviet Russia, p. 88.
219   *Burial alive:* Guillermaz, p. 150.
219   *Peasants alienated by Japanese brutalities:* Johnson, pp. 84 et seq.
219   *". . . the weary soldiers . . . took the shock":* Thunder, pp. 198–99.
219   *Raids on Chungking:* Tong 53, p. 282.
220   *German-Japanese discussions:* Richard C. Thornton, *China: The Struggle
       for Power, 1917–1972* (Bloomington: Indiana University Press, 1973),
       p. 115. (Henceforth, *Thornton*) A balanced account: another product
       of the "new wave" of American scholarship.
222   *Hunan provincial governor:* Chang Chih-chung.
223   *Bogus Kuomintang:* Tong 53, p. 276.
223   *Wang Ching-wei's party flag:* Johnson, pp. 47–48.
225   *". . . Britain closed the Burma Road:* Tuchman, pp. 269–70.
226   *Panyushkin and Matsuoka:* Soviet Russia, pp. 95–96.
226–27 *Chiang Kai-shek on neutrality pact of April 1941:* Soviet Russia, p. 113.
227   *Mao snubs Stalin:* Thornton, p. 128.
228   *Lauchlin Currie and Chiang:* Tong 53, p. 287.

Chapter 17: *Chiang and His Allies*

PAGE
232   *Stilwell withholds consignments:* Tong 53, p. 341.
234   *Tong on stabilisation efforts:* Tong 53, pp. 294–95.

234   *"Coolies go around with $50 bills":* Tuchman, pp. 334–35.

234   *A month's earnings on a party:* Thunder, p. 25.

237–38   *Demands by Chou En-lai and Lin Piao:* Guillermaz, p. 354.

240   *Mao withdraws to Shansi plateau:* Thornton, p. 132.

240   *Mao's rectification campaign:* Ibid., pp. 134–35.

240   *Communist executions:* Guillermaz, p. 367.

241   *". . . the Ch'ens were austere":* Robert Rothschild, *La Chûte de Chiang Kai-shek: Souvenirs d'un diplomate en Chine, 1949–1959* (Fayard, 1972), p. 61. (Henceforth, *Rothschild*) An urbane, engaging, and enlightening memoir by a Belgian career diplomat.

242   *Descriptions of Ch'en Ch'eng and H. H. K'ung:* Thunder, pp. 104–5 and 111.

244   *Death of conscripts:* Clubb, p. 234.

244   *White and Jacoby:* Thunder, p. 131.

244   *"The land was almost barren":* Yen Hsi-shan, *Memoirs* (Taipei, 1968), p. 111. (Henceforth, *Yen*)

245   *". . . they freeze to death!":* Feng, pp. 107–20.

246   *"200 printings had been issued":* China's Destiny (Jaffe's commentary), p. 19.

248   *"Roosevelt . . . gave in to her peremptory demand":* Tuchman, pp. 448–51.

248   *Chiang denies infidelity:* Thunder, p. 121.

248   *Mountbatten arrives with letter from Churchill:* Tong 53, p. 307.

248   *A Cartier vanity case for Mme. Chiang:* Tuchman, p. 505.

249–50   *Roosevelt and Chiang's commitment:* Thornton, pp. 141–43.

A useful corrective to *Tuchman* and to Theodore H. White, ed., *Stilwell Papers* (1948), is Chin-tung Liang's scholarly *General Stilwell in China, 1942–1944: The Full Story* (1972), which uses Chinese archives and other material not available to the American writers.

Chapter 18: *One War Ends*

PAGE

251   *Quotation from Chassin:* Lionel Max Chassin, *The Communist Conquest of China: A History of the Civil War, 1945–49* (London: Weidenfeld and Nicolson, 1966) (original French ed., *La Conquête de la Chine par Mao Tse-tung, 1945–1949*, Paris: Payot, 1952). (Henceforth, *Chassin*)

253   *". . . looking the cold facts in the face":* Tuchman, p. 413.

253   *Wendell Willkie and Mme. Chiang:* Ibid., pp. 424–28.

253   *Budenz and Lattimore:* Tong 53, p. 329.

255   *". . . Russian planes bombed Sinkiang":* Father, ch. 3, pp. 1–6.

256   *Government commandeers 1942 grain crop:* Thunder, pp. 159 et seq.

256   *Chinese sale to Japanese:* Feng, pp. 144–45.

257   *Churchill's "visible lack of enthusiasm":* Winston Churchill, *The Second World War* (London: Cassell, 1952; paperback ed., 1964), Vol. 10, *Assault from the Air*, p. 209. (Henceforth, *Churchill*)

258   "... the guiding spirit for the tiger": Father, ch. 3, p. 3.
258   "... held out for forty days": Clubb, p. 239.
258   "... extremely painful for me": Father, ch. 3, p. 5.
259   "... aides regularly faked newspaper editorials": Eric Chou.
260   Roosevelt cables Chiang: Thornton, pp. 150 et seq.
261   John Service as translator: Tuchman, p. 601.
264-65 U.S. advisers and Chinese Communists: Tuchman, pp. 619-20; Tong 53,
        p. 349.
266   Gouss forecasts civil war: United States Relations with China (Depart-
        ment of State, 1949), pp. 64-65. (Henceforth, White Paper) Other
        sources on America's diplomatic reporting from China include the
        following: Anthony Kubek, The Amerasia Papers: A Clue to the
        Catastrophe of China (Washington, D.C.: Government Printing
        Office, 1970; henceforth, Amerasia); and How the Far East Was Lost:
        American Policy and the Creation of Communist China, 1941-49
        (Chicago: Henry Regnery, 1963); O. Edmund Clubb, The Witness and
        I (New York, 1975; henceforth, Witness); E. J. Kahn, Jr., The China
        Hands: America's Foreign Service Officers and What Befell Them
        (New York: Viking Press, 1975).
266-67 Generalissimo's objectives: White Paper, p. 171.
267   "... an end to all secret police activity": Thornton, pp. 156 et seq.
268-69 Stalin and Roosevelt: Ibid., p. 162.
269   Byrnes and Yalta: Tong 53, p. 358.
271   Population controlled by Chinese Communist Party: Thornton, pp.
        168-69.

Chapter 19: *The Marshall Mission Fails*

PAGE
279   "Homes ... were deprived of roof tiles": Clubb, p. 275.
280   Japanese equipment for Nationalist Armies: Guillermaz, p. 378.
280   Lin Piao's installations in the south: Thornton, p. 181.
282   Marshall's "heavy pressure on Chiang": Private source.
282   Chiang presses for seven U.S. divisions: General Albert C. Wedemeyer,
        Wedemeyer Reports (New York: Holt, 1958), p. 348. (Henceforth,
        Wedemeyer)
284   "... I will break you": Amerasia, p. 104.
285   Threat to cut off U.S. supplies: Wedemeyer, p. 314.
285   Hurley's resignation letter: White Paper, p. 582.
285-86 Wedemeyer on political advisers: Wedemeyer, pp. 311-12.
290   Stalin suggests meeting with Chiang: Soviet Russia, pp. 147-48.
290   Generalissimo urged to accept: Thornton, p. 195.
290   Chiang decides to "go it alone": Soviet Russia, pp. 102-4.
291   Transfer of Japanese equipment: Thornton, p. 367; Chassin; and Max
        Beloff, Soviet Policy in the Far East (London: Oxford University Press,
        1953). A perceptive analysis of the material available at the time.
292   Chiang and Marshall "guarantee": Thornton, p. 198.

294   *Chiang's readiness for settlement: White Paper*, p. 196.
299   *Yen Hsi-shan and Marshall: Yen*, p. 196.

Chapter 20: *Chiang Steps Aside*

PAGE

301   *Chinese dollar at 6,500 to one U.S. dollar: White Paper*, p. 221.
302   *". . . the inflation got worse, not better": Rothschild*, pp. 262–72.
      Perhaps the best account of the great Chinese inflation.
305   *"I understand": White Paper*, pp. 251–52.
307   *Wedemeyer consults Stuart: Wedemeyer*, pp. 387 et seq.
307   *China enabled to purchase: White Paper*, p. 814.
308   *Chiang's strategic reserve: Guillermaz*, p. 400.
308   *The CC clique stronger than ever: White Paper*, pp. 261–62.
309   *Bank notes in circulation soar to 10 trillion: Tong 53*, p. 417.
309   *Only 100,000 voted: Rothschild*, p. 281.
310   *Nationalists still outnumbered Communists: Chassin*, pp. 158–59.
311   *Marshall wanted to keep U.S. out of civil war: Thornton*, p. 210; *Tong 53*,
      p. 422; *White Paper*, pp. 380 et seq.
312   *Chiang suspicious of Li:* Eric Chou.
313   *Elected deputies allowed to take their seats: Rothschild*, p. 290.
316   *Chiang Ching-kuo's resignation: White Paper*, p. 880. *Rothschild* is also
      valuable for this incident.
317   *Splendid funeral for Wei Li-huang: Guillermaz*, p. 407 fn.
319   *". . . he could open a relief corridor: Thornton*, p. 211.
321   *Pai Ch'ung-hsi's plan for campaign: Chassin*, p. 194 fn.
322   *". . . rather frequent secret huddles":* Liang Sheng-chun, *The Inside
      Story of the Chiang-Li Power Struggle* (Hong Kong, 1954, 1970), pp.
      16–17. (Henceforth, *Inside Story*) The author was Li's personal
      secretary.
324–25 *Communist conditions for peace talks: Guillermaz*, p. 416.
325   *Chiang's retirement announcement: Tong 53*, p. 439.

Chapter 21: *Chiang Loses the Mainland*

PAGE

327   *"We will be here three months": Father*, ch. 4, p. 1.
328   *Gold as bargaining counter: Tong 53*, pp. 445–46.
328   *"Gold Yuan resumed its vertiginous descent": Rothschild*, pp. 322–23.
329   *Underground Communists:* Eric Chou.
330   *Nationalist troops left on mainland: Rothschild*, p. 323; *Chassin*,
      p. 220 fn.
331   *Chang shown local beauty spots: Father*, ch. 4, pp. 2–3.
333   *". . . this is totally unacceptable": Ibid.*, ch. 4, p. 3.
336   *"Total victory within three years": Chassin*, pp. 222–23.
336   *Golf Club trees razed: Rothschild*, p. 328.
337   *". . . I shall wash my hands of them": Father*, ch. 4, p. 4.

339   *". . . what do they know about China?":* Yen Hsi-shan, reported by
        Eric Chou.
341   *Floods delayed Lin Piao's advance: Chassin,* p. 228.
342   *Chiang Kai-shek's "survival fund": Tong* 53, p. 457.
344   *Chiang's delegation to Li:* Ibid., pp. 470–74.

PART IV: CHIANG'S ISLAND REDOUBT (1950–1975)

Chapter 22: *A Place of Refuge*

PAGE
349   *"Let us go to the mountain and take a walk": Tong* 53, p. 477.
352   *"Land to the tillers":* For a full account of this remarkable land reform
        programme, see Ch'en Ch'eng, *Land Reform in China* (Taipei: China
        Publishing Company, 1961).
353   *Executions of Communists: Tong* 53, p. 493.
354–55   *Recall of U.S. consular personnel:* Ibid., p. 495; *Rothschild,* p. 341.
356   *Joint Chiefs of Staff and Taiwan:* Harold M. Vinacke, *Far Eastern
        Politics in the Post-War Period* (London: Allen & Unwin, 1956), p. 233.
        (Henceforth, *Vinacke*) A balanced and comprehensive account.
357   *Crossing of Yalu River: Tong* 53, pp. 511–13. The best account of the
        Korean War is David Rees, *Korea: The Limited War* (New York:
        Macmillan, 1974). (Henceforth, *Rees*)
358   *Hot sulphur spring bath: Tong* 53, pp. 518–19.
358–59   *Permission to bomb military targets in Manchuria: Vinacke,* p. 224.
359   *MacArthur's letter to Martin: Tong* 53, p. 524.
359   *Truman recalls MacArthur: Rees,* pp. 219 et seq.
360   *Exchange of war prisoners:* For more detailed figures see *Rees,* p. 325.
361   *Nationalist guerrilla operations: Tong* 53, p. 522.
361   *Chiang's plan to regain mainland: Clubb,* p. 341.

Chapter 23: *The Last Twenty Years*

I covered or commented on many of the events in this last period, either for
The Economist or for the BBC. I have refreshed my memory from old notes and
cuttings of articles. Some of these are mentioned in the text. Especially for the last
twenty years, that great standby of specialists on international affairs, *Keesing's
Contemporary Archives*, has been an invaluable guide and check.

PAGE
370   *Widespread guerrilla activities:* "Foreign Report" (*The Economist,* 28
        March, 19 September 1963).
372   *Chiang's interview with Swinton of AP:* Melvin Gurtov, "Recent
        Developments on Formosa", in *China Quarterly* (London), No. 31
        (July–September 1967). (Henceforth, *Gurtov*)
375   *"Temporary Provisions" (1948): China Yearbook* (Taipei), 1968–69, p.
        665.

376   *Clemency to Taiwanese:* Douglas Mendel, *The Politics of Formosan Nationalism* (Berkeley and Los Angeles: University of California, 1970), pp. 117–18. (Henceforth, *Mendel*) By a champion of Taiwanese nationalism; he has since, I understand, had second thoughts.

377   *Case of the deported brothers:* J. Bruce Jacobs, "Recent Leadership and Political Trends in Taiwan", in *China Quarterly* (London) (January–March 1971).

380   *Advice for emerging African nations: Gurtov.*

Index

A. B. Corps, 105
Acheson, Dean, 286, 292, 304, 340, 354
Adams, Josephine Truslow, 265
Amerasia, 247, 265 fn., 285
Anti-Comintern Pact, 181, 205, 220, 236
Anti-Japanese National Salvation Forces, 173
Anti-Japanese Political-Military University, 192
Associations for National Salvation, 176
Atcheson, George, 284
Australian aid to China, 205
Autumn Harvest Uprising, 119, 122

Bandung Conference of Asian and African States, 366
Barbey (U.S. admiral), 282
Barr, David G., 313–15
Bauer, Max, 11
Bluecher, Vasili K. *See* "Galen"
Blue Shirts, 11, 13, 103, 165, 166, 167, 175, 182, 392
Bogumulov (U.S.S.R. representative), 186
Borodin, Michael, 6, 61, 64, 66, 71, 76, 79, 80, 81, 84, 89, 96, 100, 109, 110, 124, 391
Boxer Indemnity, 50, 72
Boxer Rebellion, 21, 33, 104
Browder, Earl, 98, 265

Budenz, Louis F., 253
Burma campaign, 229, 233, 244, 257, 260, 263, 264, 318
  CBI theatre of war, 231
Byrnes, James F., 269, 286

Cairo Conference, 397
Cairo Declaration, 364
Central Bureau of Investigation and Statistics (CBIS), 10, 105, 241, 338
Chang, Carson, 296
Chang Ch'en, 323
Chang Chih-chung, 217, 297, 323, 330–43
Chang Chih-tung, *Learn*, 33
Chang Ch'ün, 38, 189, 282, 288, 297, 303, 323, 333, 345–46
Chang Chung-chang, 118
Chang Hsueh-liang ("Young Marshal"), 7, 126, 127–28, 130, 131, 133, 135, 140–41, 145, 146, 147, 153, 154, 170, 178–80, 181–82, 183, 184, 186, 187, 188, 190, 276, 317, 330, 393, 397
Chang Lan, 287, 345
Chang Li-sheng, 297
Chang Shen-fu, 217
Chang Tso-lin ("Old Marshal"), 75–76, 82–83, 92, 93–94, 101, 108, 118, 121, 126, 127, 179
Chang Tung-sun, 319
Chassin, Lionel Max, 251

419

Ch'en Ch'eng, 242, 259, 262, 308, 317, 325, 342, 351, 379–80

Ch'en Chieh-ju (second wife), 58–59, 113, 115, 116

Ch'en Ch'i-mei, 28, 36, 38, 42, 43, 44, 45, 58, 105, 241

Ch'en Chi-t'ang, 173, 174

Ch'en Chiung-ming ("Hakka General"), 49, 51–57, 72, 80

Ch'en, Eugene, 142

Ch'en Hsiao-wei, 221, 258, 318, 321–22

Ch'en Kung-po, 211, 224

Ch'en Kuo-fu, 105, 241

Ch'en Li-fu, 10, 105, 186, 187, 206, 240, 243, 297, 312, 330–46

Ch'en Ming-shu, 150, 153, 154, 155

Ch'en Pao-ying, 246

Ch'en Po-liu, 337

Ch'en Po-ta, Chiang Kai-shek—The People's Enemy, 147

Ch'en Pu-lei, 247, 322

Ch'en Shao-yü. See Wang Ming

Ch'en Tu-hsiu, 50, 60, 84, 100–101

Ch'en Yi (Communist general), 110, 314, 317, 333, 337

Ch'en Yi (Nationalist general), 304

Ch'eng Ch'ien, 275, 322–26, 341–46

Cheng Wan-fu, 377–78

Chennault, Claire, 196, 232, 249, 321
    "Flying Tigers" (later U.S. China Air Task Force, 14th Air Force), 254, 258

Chiang Ch'ing (Mao's wife), 175

Chiang Ching-kuo (son), 8, 37, 38, 113, 176–77, 194, 197, 276, 289, 315–16, 325, 327, 330–46, 349, 377, 380, 385
    My Father, 4, 194–95

Chiang Hsiao-hsien, 182

Chiang Kai-shek
    actual power base, 136, 363–64, 391–92
    admiration of Germany, 10–11, 158, 165
    advice to son, 194–95
    anti-opium campaign, 169–70, 174
    assassination attempts on, 45, 142

attacked by Communists and sympathisers, 147, 238, 239, 248, 254, 284, 392–94
    birth of, 31
    campaigns against Communists, 7, 93, 98–99, 106, 128–29, 143, 144, 157, 159, 161, 163–64, 177, 189, 191, 218, 222, 236–37, 251, 252, 351–54, 390–91, 395
    and Chennault, 233
    China's Destiny, 246–47, 398
    Chinese Economic Theory, 246, 247, 398
    Chinese military training of, 37–38
    death of, 5, 385
    as de facto dictator, 122–23, 124, 129, 136–37, 139, 141–42, 144, 148, 149, 156, 172, 173, 184, 197–98
    dialect spoken and language problems, 3–4, 43, 117, 262, 389–92
    diary, 14–15, 43, 84–85, 104, 112, 185, 186, 192
    early career of, 6, 58, 105–6
    economic reforms of, 353–54
    education of, 34, 35, 43
    expelled from Kuomintang, 107
    feelings towards foreigners, 98, 123, 234–35, 247, 280
    forms new government, 108, 131–32
    Fukien challenge to, 154, 155–56, 179, 238
    identification of self with China, 6
    Japanese military training of, 36, 38, 39–40
    kidnapping of (Sian incident), 7, 133, 170–71, 178, 181–89, 191, 192, 195, 276, 393
    land reform programme of, 352
    last stand on mainland of, 328, 336, 343, 345
    as leader, 46, 122–23, 124, 129, 136–37, 139, 141–42, 144, 148, 149, 167, 170, 171, 172–73, 197–98, 200, 207–9, 212, 217, 218, 220–21, 225, 226, 227–28, 229, 231, 235, 248, 249–50, 251, 270–71, 272,

277, 282, 290–91, 295, 303, 309, 340–41, 353–55

letters and communiqués of, 80–81, 236, 283–84, 313

loss of China by, 285, 346, 390–96

March 20th incident, 86–88

marriages, 4, 6, 8, 35, 37, 58, 93, 113–14, 115, 117–18

military career and strategies of, 12–13, 35–36, 42, 48–49, 50–51, 54–55, 56, 57–58, 59, 71, 73–74, 80–81, 82, 84, 89–91, 95, 99, 101–2, 111, 115, 121, 125–26, 127, 135, 151, 154, 157–59, 161, 163–64, 194–95, 200–202, 210–11, 220–22, 230, 233–34, 257, 258, 283, 286, 289, 293–94, 310, 320, 336, 350–54

military tactical errors, 5, 13, 122, 135, 145, 146–47, 151, 152–53, 154–55, 173, 174, 175, 177, 191, 192, 200–202, 258–59, 291–92, 317–18, 350, 392–94

offices and positions held, 12, 41, 42, 66, 84, 90, 94, 120, 121, 123, 150–51, 169, 207, 241, 272, 311, 341, 343, 354

parents of, 31–32, 34–35, 40–41

personality of, 8–9, 11–12, 15, 46, 53, 57–58, 60, 91, 101, 130, 132, 165, 167, 170, 171, 193, 204, 206, 219, 221, 240–41, 243, 245–46, 258–59, 277, 280, 312, 314, 323, 390

political alliances of, 83, 94, 109, 111, 127–28, 130–31, 133, 137–38, 140–41, 150, 153, 178, 179, 180, 206–7, 276–77, 390

political role in Kuomintang, 66, 70–71, 72, 89–90, 96, 107, 122–23, 129, 295–96

position on internal affairs, 123–24

pressured to accept coalition government, 267, 268, 270–72, 289, 290, 298

relations with World War II allies, 13–14, 225, 226, 227–28, 229–35, 248–50, 252–54, 260–70, 272–73,

279–80, 282–83, 284–300, 308, 310–11, 318–19, 334

reliance on German advisers, 158, 201

religion of, 4, 35, 46, 167

reluctance to fight Japanese, 7, 126, 145, 146–47, 152–53, 154–55, 173, 174, 175, 177, 191, 192, 221, 252, 264

reputation as statesman, 7

resignations, as technique, 51, 85, 111–12, 113, 116, 129–30, 149, 323–24

as revolutionary, 4, 23, 35, 38–39, 40–42, 43–44, 48–52, 54–55, 56, 108, 130, 390

as self-appointed heir of Sun Yat-sen, 121, 130, 146

sold out at Teheran and Yalta, 250, 268, 269, 272–73, 339

Soviet Russia in China: A Summing Up at Seventy, 62, 129, 186, 226–27, 394–96

and Stilwell, 216, 221, 231–33, 249, 252, 260–62, 263–64, 396

strengths and weaknesses of, 389–99

as successor to Sun Yat-sen, 77

on Taiwan, 5, 14, 325, 330, 343, 349–62, 363–85

ties to gangsters and merchants, 6, 44–45, 58, 103, 104–5, 106, 139

ties to Hitler, 158

U.S.S.R. visit and aftermath, 6, 62–65, 67, 72, 76–77, 85, 88–89

Voice of the Army, The (editor), 41

World War II alliance with Communists, 218, 220

See also Chiang, Mme.; Kuomintang; New Life Movement; Northern Punitive Expedition

Chiang Kuang-nai, 150, 153

Chiang, Mme., 11–12, 15, 38, 116–17, 139, 170, 171, 181, 185, 186, 187–88, 202, 204, 216, 230, 231, 240, 246, 248, 253, 307, 315, 358, 372, 396

See also Soong, Mayling

Chiang Po-li, 159
Chiang Su-an (father), 31
Chiang Wei-kuo (son), 11, 44, 177
Chicherin, Georgi Vasilievich, 59, 63, 73
Ch'ien (banker), 106
Chin Chung-hua, 238, 239
China, prerevolutionary, 16–21, 34, 78
    See also Manchu dynasty; individual foreign countries
Chinese Communist Party, 50, 60–61, 65–66, 68, 71, 73, 81, 82, 96–101, 141, 168, 184, 189, 191–94, 196, 198–99, 218, 235, 237, 240, 267, 271, 390–91, 393, 395–99
    abortive uprisings by, 93, 99, 102–6, 118–19, 121, 143
    acceptance of Sun's Three Principles, 89, 101, 187
    armies of, 110, 122, 128, 158, 222
    as defenders of China against Japanese, 146, 147, 180, 186–87, 200–201, 394
    factionalism in, 142–44
    Fifth Party Congress, 108
    "Future of the War of Resistance . . .", 199–200
    growth of, 135
    in Kuomintang, 84, 89, 93, 95, 97, 99, 100–101, 102, 106, 109–10, 216–18
    Provisional Constitution, 152
    Provisional Soviet Government, 152
    ruled by Comintern, 118, 178, 186, 187, 236, 395, 396
    Soviet Congress, 152
    warlords in, 152
    youth groups, 176
Chinese Eastern Railway, 50, 61, 75
Chinese Peace Preservation Corps, 198
Chinese Peoples Republic, 364, 365, 373, 378, 382
    Cultural Revolution, 373, 381
    Red Guards, 373, 374, 381
    See also Chinese Communist Party; individual leaders
Chinese Soviet Republic, 144

Chou En-lai, 7, 16, 60, 67, 80–81, 86, 99, 103, 110, 118, 142, 144, 152, 159, 161, 175, 186–87, 192, 196, 197, 199, 217, 228, 237, 262, 267–71, 282–300, 331–46, 357, 366, 367, 369, 382
Chou, Eric, 115, 131, 152, 169, 184, 188–89, 217, 221, 224, 233, 244, 258, 275–77, 297, 298, 316–18, 320–22, 334, 338, 339, 372
Chou Tso-min, 337
Chow Shu-kai, 383
"Christian General". See Feng Yü-hsiang
Chu Hsi, 35
Chu Ta-fu, 51
Chu Teh, 60, 110, 122, 144, 152, 161, 218, 280, 354
Chuikov, Vasili Ivanovich, 206
Ch'un (Prince Regent), 22, 23, 77
Churchill, Winston S., 14, 46, 225, 229, 230, 231, 248, 250, 268–71, 360, 372, 389, 397
Clark-Kerr, Sir Archibald, 230
Comintern, 59–61, 97, 98–99, 100, 101, 118, 119–20, 143, 178, 186, 187
Confucianism, 11, 18, 33, 46, 165, 242
    School of Confucian Scholars, 35
Currie, Lauchlin, 228, 253

Davies, John Payton, Jr., 265–66, 285
December 9th Movement, 176
de Gaulle, Charles, 5, 38, 42, 46, 171, 330, 372, 390
Directors of Moral Code (Hsiun Tao Chang), 105
Disbandment Conference, 136–37, 138
Donald, W. H., 180, 187, 202
Doriot, Jacques, 98
Dulles, John Foster, 362, 366, 368, 369, 372
Durdin, Tillman, 202

Eastman, Lloyd E., 167, 184
Eighteenth Group Army, 235–38
Eighth Route Army, 219–22, 227, 235, 240

Eisenhower, Dwight D., 361–62, 365, 368–69, 370
Extermination Campaigns
Fifth, 158, 163, 393, 394
First, 157
Fourth, 158
Second, 157–58
Sixth, 181–82
Third, 158

Felt (U.S. admiral), 369
Feng Yü-hsiang ("Christian General"), 75–76, 82, 83, 87, 92, 101, 109, 111, 112–13, 118, 124, 131, 132, 135–36, 137, 138, 139–40, 141, 154–55, 169, 173–74, 184, 185, 199, 207, 212, 222, 244–46, 256, 392–93
Ferris (U.S. general), 261
Fifth Army (Communist), 128
Fifth Chinese Army (Nationalist), 230, 233
First Route Army, 124, 126, 137, 181
Formosa. *See* Taiwan
Fortieth Division, 235–36
Fourth Field Army (Korea), 357
Fourth Route Army, 124–25, 137
France
fall of, 225
nineteenth-century and prewar, imperialism in China, 19–20, 44, 79
Franco, Francisco, 5, 46, 71, 115, 135, 389
Fu Ching-po, 334
Fu Tso-yi, 319–20, 343, 353
Fukien
land reform programme, 154
People's Revolutionary Government, 238
rebellion, 155–56, 159, 179
revolutionaries in, 153–54

"Galen," 67, 71, 72, 110, 140
Gandhi, Mohandas K., 230, 231
Gauss, Clarence, 252, 265–66
Germany
admired by Chiang, 158, 165
aid to China, 205, 206
influence and participation in China, 9, 10–11, 27
nineteenth-century and prewar, imperialism in China, 20, 49, 126
supplier of Chiang's military advisers, 158
in World War II, 181, 223
Gordon, Charles George ("Chinese"), 20
Great Britain
Chinese alliance, 225–26
nineteenth-century and prewar, imperialism in China, 19–20
post–World War I relations with China, 72, 73–74, 78
relations with Chiang, 351, 354, 360, 372
in World War II Chinese theatre, 223–50
Green Society, 6, 44, 58, 103, 104, 105, 338
Grusenberg, Michael. *See* Borodin, Michael
Guillermaz, Jacques, 99, 161, 240, 305 fn.

"Hakka General". *See* Ch'en Chiungming
Han Fu-chü, 138, 169, 206–7
Himatsu (Japanese colonel), 40
Hirota, Koki, Three Principles of 1935, 196, 197
Hitler, Adolf, 11, 227, 389, 390
Ho Ch'i-feng, 320
Ho Hao-jo, 262
Ho Ying-ch'in, 101, 118, 176, 185–86, 220, 235, 241, 259, 262, 308, 313, 331–39
Ho-Umetsu agreement, 175, 176
Hoffman, Paul G., 318
Hopkins, Harry L., 270, 272
Hsiang Ying, 235–36
Hsiao Cheng-ying, 275–77
Hsiao Tung-tzu, 127–28, 131
Hsien Ying, 345
Hsiung, S. I., 34, 39 fn., 41, 62, 88, 96 fn., 103, 112, 140, 141, 148, 166, 185

Hsiung Shih-hui, 276
Hsu Ch'ung-chih, 56, 57, 74, 80
Hsu Hui-tung, 319–20
Hsueh Yueh ("Little Tiger"), 257–58, 350
Hu Han-min, 72, 74, 77, 78, 79–80, 87, 88, 108, 112–13, 118, 141–42, 148, 149, 155, 184
Hu Lin, 115, 152–53, 262, 277, 298, 318
    Ta Kung Pao, 224, 225
Hu Shih, 10
Hu Tsung-nan, 181
Hu Yi-sheng, 79–80
Huang Ch'i-han, 329
Huang Chin, 175–76
Huang Shao-hung, 332
Hundred Days of Reform, 33
Hundred Flowers period, 239
Hung Hsiu-ch'üan, 20
Hurley, Patrick, J., 261, 263, 266–73, 279–87

Ito, Masanori, 394
    Japan's Bloody Wars, 210–11

Jaffe, Philip, 103 fn. 247, 265 fn.
Japan, 5, 251, 254
    Communist Party, 187
    Manchurian invasion, 6–7, 142, 144, 145–52, 154–55
    nineteenth-century and prewar, imperialism in China, 20, 27, 59
    as potential Chinese enemy, 41, 135, 158, 170, 179–80
    relations with China, 39, 76, 77, 126, 174–75
    Shantung claim, 49, 126, 138
    Sino-Japanese wars, 12, 32, 33, 142, 144, 145–52, 154–55, 159, 170, 175, 191, 196–98, 200, 201–2, 204–12
    as successor to Germany's interest in China, 126
    Twenty-one Demands, 27, 49
    in World War II, 14, 181
    as wreckers of Nationalist revolution, 27, 47, 76

Japanese Peace Conference, 360
Joint Military Council, 229
Joint Stabilisation Board, 234
Joffe, Adolph Abramovitch, 61, 63, 65, 78
Johnson, Nelson T., 227

Kamenev, Lev Borisovich, 63
K'ang Yu-wei, 33
Kao Yü-shu, 377, 380
Karakhan, Leo, 49, 59, 64
Kawagoe (Japanese ambassador), 196
Kellogg-Briand Pact, 204
Kissanka (U.S.S.R. military adviser), 84, 85, 86, 87
Kissinger, Henry A., 382
Kita, Seiichi, 174
Knatchbull-Hugessen, Sir Hughe, 202
Knowland, William F., 355
Komingtang, 27
    See also Kuomintang
Konoye, Fumimaro, 211, 224, 225, 228
Koo, Wellington, 101
Korean War, 352–62, 365, 373
Kotelawala, Sir John, 366
Kriebel, Herman, 11
Ku Ching-lien, 35
Ku Chu-t'ung, 218
Kuang Hsu, 21–22, 33
K'ung, David, 315
K'ung, H. H., 114, 185, 207, 217, 241, 242, 259, 260, 261
Kuo Mo-jo, 217
Kuominchün (People's Army), 83, 139
Kuomintang (KMT), 40, 42–43, 62–63, 103, 122, 141, 166, 169, 174, 293, 308, 322, 329, 330, 331, 341
    alienation of masses by, 207, 317
    alliance with Communists, 198–99
    American attitudes towards, 359
    in army, 91
    benefits from foreign incidents, 78–79
    in Burma, 370–71
    CC clique, 105, 297, 308, 312
    Central Executive Committee of, 10,

61, 95, 100, 107, 123, 129, 141, 192–93
and Chinese nationalism, 60
Communist infiltration of, 59–60, 61, 65–66, 68, 84, 89, 93, 97, 99, 107, 109, 178, 217–18
Communists expelled from, 109–10
cooperation with Soviets, 78, 89, 95, 97, 99, 106, 187, 353
corruption in, 43, 242, 243–44, 259, 278–79, 302, 375, 394–95
created, 25, 41
disintegration of, 266
in elections, 26
Executive Committee, 130
expelled from Parliament, 26, 27
factionalism in, 71–72, 79–81, 94, 95, 99, 108, 130–31, 132, 137–38, 151
factors of support, 395
First Congress, 68, 73, 124
modernisation of China under, 9–10
National Party Congress, 61, 66
peace group, 322–24, 325
Political Science Clique, 243, 276
reorganisation of, 6, 61, 353, 377, 391
Revolution, 104
Standing Committee, 61
on Taiwan, 365
Third Congress, 137
warlords in, 135
weaknesses of, 43, 47, 391
Whampoa clique, 242
See also Nationalist China
Kwangsi clique, 48, 51, 52, 55, 137, 138, 173, 174, 185
See also Li Tsung-jen; Pai Ch'ung-hsi

H.M.S. *Ladybird*, 205
Lattimore, Owen, 253
League of Nations, 148, 204
Lei Chen, *Free China*, 376
Lenin, Nikolai, 24, 49, 59, 60, 63, 73, 389, 395
Li Chi-shen, 238
Li Kung-pu, 239
Li Kuo-ting, 380
Li Li-san, 129, 142–44, 291, 391

Li Mi, 320
Li Ming-yang, 329
Li Ta-chao, 50, 60, 66, 101
Li Tsung-jen, 14, 96, 101, 102, 118, 124–25, 133, 135, 136, 137, 140, 164, 173, 174, 207, 312, 321–26, 328–46, 335 fn., 354
Liao Chung-k'ai, 64, 66, 67, 71–72, 77, 78, 79, 80, 85
Liao, Thomas, 377–78
Lin Piao, 14, 110, 192 fn., 237, 280, 288, 290–99, 304, 316, 318, 331, 342, 357, 381
Lin Sen, 249
Liu Ch'en-huan, 72
Liu Ch'ih, 320
Liu Chi-wen, 114
Liu Chung-jung, 329
Liu Fei, 321, 332
Liu Po-ch'eng, 342
Liu Shao-ch'i, 108, 118, 174, 176, 373, 374, 381, 391
Liu Tsun-ch'i, 239, 278
Liu Wen-hui, 345
Lo Jui-ching, 373
Lo Lung-chi, 239, 287
Loch'uan Declaration, 198, 199
Lominadze, Besso, 118
Long March, 6, 144, 161, 163, 164, 175, 178, 191, 394
Lu Chung-lin, 222
Lu Han, 344–46
Lu Pi (pseud.), 179, 180
Lu Yung-ting, 48
Ludden, Raymond, 289
Lung Yü (Empress Dowager), 24
Lung Yun, 239

Ma Fu-hsiang, 111
Ma Pu-fang, 339–40
MacArthur, Douglas, 282, 355–62
MacDonald, Ramsay, 73
Magruder (U.S. general), 233
Malik, Jacob A., 357
Manchu dynasty, 4, 16–17, 20–25, 32, 33, 34–35, 39, 47, 49, 68, 104, 152, 390

Manchukuo, 25, 151–52, 196, 205, 209, 212, 226, 291
Manchuria, 27, 268–69, 272–74, 276–300, 301–10, 317, 350, 355, 357
  Japanese invasion of, 6–7, 142, 144, 145–52, 201
  1931 floods in, 151
  Russians in, 288–91
  See also Manchukuo
Mann, Thomas, 98
Mao Fu-mei (first wife), 35, 37, 113–14, 115, 116
Mao Mao-ching (brother-in-law), 114
Mao Tse-tung, 6, 7, 14, 16, 20, 31, 35, 50, 60, 99 fn., 128–29, 142–43, 155, 175, 178, 198, 200, 201, 218, 227, 235, 237, 240, 246, 251, 255, 262, 265, 271–72, 279–300, 304, 309, 319, 322, 324, 328–46, 335 fn., 351, 353, 361, 389, 390–91, 393–94, 395
  elected President of Chinese Soviet Republic, 144
  military campaigns of, 157, 159, 161, 163, 178–79, 180
  New Democracy, 392
  poetry of, 163
  political posts held, 66, 89, 129, 152
  relations with peasants, 13, 89, 97, 118–19, 122, 151, 164, 201, 391, 392
  See also Chinese Communist Party; Long March
March 20th incident, 86–88
Maring, H., 59, 60, 62
Marshall, George C., 14, 249, 252, 260, 263, 275–300, 305, 310–11, 318, 396
Martin, Joseph W., 359
Matsui (Japanese general), 204
Matsuoka, Yosue, 226
May 4th Movement, 49, 50, 176
May 30th incident (massacre), 78–79
Mei Yi, 297
Mendel, Douglas, 377
Meng Yun-ch'ien, 239
Merchants Corps (Canton) rebellion, 73–74, 76

Military Assistance Advisory Group (MAAG), 356
Military Bureau of Investigation and Statistics (MBIS), 10, 105, 212
Military University (Japan), 39–40
Molotov, Vyacheslav M., 267, 273, 285, 286
Mongolian People's Revolutionary Government, 63
Mountbatten, Louis, 248
Mukden incident, 145, 179, 293, 310

Nagaoka (Japanese general), 40
Nanking, Treaty of, 19
National Anti-Japanese United Front, 198
Nationalist China
  campaigns against Communists, 106, 128–29, 143, 144, 157, 159, 161, 163–64, 177, 189, 191, 365–370
  civil war, 266, 290, 291–325
  constitution of, 375–77
  defeat of, 309, 320–22, 330–31
  elections in, 309, 312–13, 380–81
  foreign aid to, 204–6, 232, 233, 234, 248, 300, 304, 307, 310–11, 319, 337, 378–79, 398
  guerrilla activity on mainland, 370, 371
  inflation in, 234, 242–43, 244, 260, 263, 301, 302, 303, 309, 314, 315, 316, 328, 342, 395
  move to Taiwan, 327, 328
  and opium trade, 370–71
  peace talks, 322–24, 325, 331–32
  political recognition of, 360–62, 369, 380–81, 382–83
  provisional republican government, 24, 25, 26
  on Taiwan, 363–85
  united front with Communists, 193–94, 198–99, 254, 395
  in United Nations, 367–69
  in World War II, 225–49, 254–67
  See also Chiang Kai-shek; Kuomintang
National Military Council, 236

National Peasant Association, 97
National Peasant Movement Training
    Institute, 89, 97
National Revolutionary Army, 199
    See also Red Army
National Salvation Movement, 181, 183,
    184
Nehru, Pandit Jawaharlal, 220
Nelson, Donald, 261
New Fourth Army, 218–20, 235–38,
    240, 337
New Life Movement, 11–12, 157, 164–
    70, 392
Nine-Power Treaty, 204
Nineteenth Route Army, 150, 151,
    153–54, 156, 159
Nixon, Richard M., 381–82, 383–84
Northern Punitive Expedition, 43, 73,
    74, 75, 76, 79, 81, 82–92, 98,
    108–9, 110, 112, 116, 121, 123,
    124, 125–26, 127, 129, 130, 392–93

Office of Strategic Services, 267–68
Office of War Intelligence, 238–39
"Old Marshal". *See* Chang Tso-lin
Opium Suppression Bureaux, 48
Opium War, 19
Organic Law for the Republic of China,
    10, 131, 141
"Orthodox Chinese Nationalist Party",
    223

Pai Ch'ung-hsi, 102, 118, 136, 174, 207,
    321–22, 330–31
Panyushkin, A. S., 226, 255
Paoting Military Academy, 37, 242
P'eng Chen, 175
P'eng Teh-huai, 128, 161, 218, 314,
    339–40, 381
People's (Federated) Anti-Japanese
    Army, 154–55, 173
People's Liberation Army (PLA), 7, 13,
    14, 110, 122, 245, 304, 309–16,
    333, 354, 355
    See also Red Army
People's Political Council, 217, 235
P'u Yi, Henry, 22, 25, 152

Quirino, Elpidio, 340

Radek, Karl Bernardovich, 63
Red Army, 158, 159, 171–72, 175, 178,
    180, 181, 184, 187, 193, 199
    See also National Revolutionary
    Army; People's Liberation Army
Red Society, 104
Red Spears group, 152
Reinsch, P. S., 27
Rhee, Syngman, 340, 362
Ridgway, Matthew B., 359
Rogers, William, 383
Roosevelt, Franklin D., 14, 225, 227–28,
    229, 230, 231, 232, 233, 248, 249–
    50, 252, 253, 257, 260–65, 267–71,
    283, 396, 307
Roshchin, V. I., 328–33
Roy, M. N., 109, 110
Rusk, Dean, 359
Russo-Japanese War, 36, 37

Sato, Naotake, 197
Second Route Army, 124, 126, 137
Second World War. *See* World War II
Seeckt, Hans von, 158–59, 163
Service, John, 261, 265–66, 284
Seventh Regiment, 218
Seventh Route Army, 156
Shakee massacre, 79
Shanghai uprising, 102–6, 107
Shao Li-tze, 282, 297
Shen, James, 382
Shensi Red Army, 218
Sheridan, James E., 76, 83, 140
Shih Yu-shan, 223
Shimonoseki, Treaty of, 32
Sian incident, 7, 133, 170–71, 178,
    181–89, 191, 192, 193, 195, 255,
    276, 393, 394, 397
Sino-Japanese wars, 12, 32, 33, 142,
    144, 145–52, 154–55, 159, 170,
    175, 191, 196–98, 200, 201–2,
    204–12, 218–28, 237, 254–55, 298,
    305, 320, 337, 338, 394, 395
Sixth Chinese Army, 230
Sneevliet, H. *See* Maring, H.

Snow, Edgar, 155, 159, 161, 163, 182
    Red Star Over China, 184
Soong, Charles, 114
Soong, Ch'ingling (Mme. Sun Yat-sen),
    95, 114, 116, 131
Soong, Eiling, 114, 115, 242
Soong, Mayling, 3, 4, 6, 58, 95, 114–
    17
    See also Chiang, Mme.
Soong, T. V., 9–10, 95, 96, 114, 115,
    116, 118, 139, 153, 188, 243, 259–
    60, 263, 270, 273, 280, 302, 331
Stalin, Josef, 14, 63, 67, 97, 119, 187,
    201, 205, 206, 226, 227, 229, 250,
    267–73, 283–98, 355, 399, 396, 397
Stilwell, Joseph W. ("Vinegar Joe"), 13,
    216, 221, 231–38, 249, 252, 254,
    257–64, 266, 286, 396
Stuart, John Leighton, 288, 298, 305–
    12, 323, 329–35, 354
Sugiyama, Hajime, 197
Sultan, Daniel, 266
Sun Ch'uan-fang, 83, 111, 118, 127
Sun Fo, 95, 96, 142, 148, 150, 243, 303,
    312, 329–45
Sun Ming-chiu, 182–83
Sun-Tze, *Art of War, The*, 35
Sun Yat-sen, 4, 6, 13, 15, 21, 124, 131,
    195, 204, 223, 224–47, 268, 295,
    313, 352, 391, 392, 395
    assessment of, 22–23
    Chiang as self-appointed heir to, 121,
        139, 146
    death of, 77–78, 79, 132
    failure as revolutionary, 23, 48–49,
        132
    land reform programme of, 154
    political influences on, 69
    power struggle after death of, 77–78
    Principle of Democracy, 11, 123
    Principle of People's Livelihood, 15,
        195
    relationship with Chiang, 38–39, 42,
        43, 45, 51–53, 54, 55, 56, 57, 58,
        61, 65, 74
    relations with U.S.S.R., 59–67, 72
    revolutionary career of, 23, 25, 26,

        35, 38–39, 42, 43, 45, 47, 48–49,
        51–56, 57–60, 70–77
    Three Principles of the People, 10,
        15, 41, 62, 64, 65, 68–70, 89, 90,
        101, 108, 111, 121, 123, 142, 195,
        199, 246
    See also Chiang Kai-shek; Soong,
        Ch'ingling (wife)
Sun Yat-sen Society, 81, 89
Sung Cheh-yuan, 320
Sung Chiao-jen, 26

Tai Li, 10, 211
T'aip'ing Rebellion, 20–21, 104, 146
Taiwan, 5, 7, 14, 363–85, 399
    anti-Americanism on, 367–68
    foreign policy, 380–81
    government of, 364–65, 375–76, 380
    land reform programmes, 13
    prosperity of, 363, 377, 378–79, 381
    as showpiece, 363–64
Taiwanese Independence Movement,
    377
Tanaka, Gi-ichi, 147
Tanaka Memorial, 147
T'ang En-po, 256, 336
Tangku Truce, 154
Tao Hsi-sheng, 246
Teng Hsiao-p'ing, 345
Teng K'eng, 50, 55
Teng Pao-shang, 319
Third Route Army, 124, 126, 137
Thirteenth Chinese Army, 257
Tojo, Hideki, 228
Tong, Hollington, 4, 7, 32, 33, 38, 91,
    96 fn., 102–3, 113, 117, 125, 135–
    36, 155, 164–65, 166, 172, 174,
    222, 233, 316, 335 fn., 349
Trautman, Oscar, 205, 206
"Triple-crosser Shih", 138
Trotsky, Leon, 63, 71, 97, 119
Truman, Harry S., 14, 250, 272–74, 285,
    290, 303–10, 318, 334, 337, 355–62
T'sai T'ing-k'ai, 150, 153, 230
Tsarist Russia, 36, 196, 200
    See also U.S.S.R.
Tseng Kuo-fan, 35, 146–47, 194, 238

Tsinan incident, 126–27, 139
Tu Yueh-sheng, 58, 103
Tu Yu-ming, 233
Tuchman, Barbara, 83, 248
Tung Ch'i-wu, 320
Tungmenhui (Alliance Society), 38
Twelfth Chinese Army, 257
Twenty-ninth Army, 192, 198, 320, 342
T'zu Hsi (Empress Dowager), 21–22, 33

U.S.S.R.
    Comintern in China, 59–61, 97, 98–99, 100, 101, 118, 119–20, 143, 178, 186, 187, 196, 198
    influence in China, 49–50, 59–67, 72, 76–77, 78, 84–85, 87–89, 93, 95, 99, 100, 101, 102, 106, 107–8, 118–20, 123, 209, 222–24, 232–50, 251, 283–99, 304, 324, 328, 351–57, 392, 395, 397, 398, 399
    nineteenth-century and prewar, imperialism in China, 20
    as potential Chinese enemy, 41–42
    World War II invasion of China, 14
    See also Tsarist Russia
United Nations organisation, 270, 355–62
United Nations Relief and Rehabilitation Administration (UNRRA), 301
United States
    Asian policy, 381–83, 396
    and China, 9, 204, 216, 221, 229–50, 251–324, 328, 351, 354–55
    Chinese alliance, 225–26
    government bias towards Chinese Communists, 201
    isolationism of, 204
    Mutual Security Treaty of 1954, 384
    Seventh Fleet, 356, 361
    two-China policy, 383

Vanguard of National Liberation, 176
Vincent, John Carter, 265
V–J Day, 243, 279, 301, 338
Voitinsky, Gregor, 60

Wallace, Henry A., 254
Wang, C. T., 148
Wang Ching-wei, 72, 77–78, 79–80, 84, 85–86, 87, 94, 100–101, 102, 109, 118, 120, 131, 137, 139, 140, 141, 148, 149, 150, 153, 168, 207, 211–12, 216, 217–18, 222–26, 247, 278, 329
Wang Ch'ung-hui, 196
Wang Jo-fei, 282
Wang Lu-chiao, 216
Wang Ming, 177, 239
Wang Ping-nan, 217, 297
Wang Shih-chieh, 259, 273, 280–83, 308, 333
Wang Yang-ming, 35
Ward, Angus, 354–55
warlords, 75–76, 91–92, 94, 126, 135–36, 146, 175, 177, 221, 392, 393
    See also Chang Chung-chang; Chang Tso-lin; Feng Yü-hsiang; Liu Ch'en-huan; Northern Punitive Expedition; Sun Chuan-fang; Wu P'ei-fu; Yen Hsi-shan
Watson, Mark, 308
Wavell, Archibald, 229, 232
Wedemeyer, Albert, 266, 268, 280, 282, 287–97, 305–6
Wei Li-huang, 316–17
Wei Tao-ming, 304
Wen Yi-to, 239
Wetzell, Georg, 158, 163
Whampoa Military Academy, 6, 11, 66–68, 70–71, 108, 176, 237, 242
White, Theodore H., 219, 234, 244, 248, 256
Willkie, Wendell L., 253
Wilson, Woodrow, Fourteen Points, 49
Wong, Wen-hao, 208, 313
World War II, 13–14, 228, 229–50, 254–74
Wu Han, 239
Wu Ho-hsuan, 329
Wu Hua-wen, 317
Wu P'ei-fu, 75–76, 82, 91, 92, 93, 127, 138, 225
Wu Shao-shu, 338

Wu Shih, 352
Wu Tieh-cheng, 330
Wu Ting-ch'ang, 146, 158
Wu Yü-hou, 329
Wuchang uprising, 25

Yalta Conference, 268–71, 397
Yang Chieh, 206
Yang Cho-an, 276
Yang Hu-ch'eng, 183, 184, 185, 188
Yang Kang, 238
Yang Yung-t'ai, 128
Yao Yi-ching (concubine), 44
Yeh, George, 362
Yeh T'ing, 218, 235–37
Yen, C. K., 380, 385
Yen Hsi-shan, 83, 118, 124, 128, 131, 132, 136, 137–38, 139–40, 141, 207, 218, 222, 244, 298–300, 314, 319, 335, 338–46, 354, 392–93, 394
Yen Pao-han, 168
YMCA (Chinese), 11, 166, 392
Yonai, Mitsumasa, 223, 225
Younger, Kenneth, 360
"Young Marshal". See Chang Hsueh-liang
Yü (shipping magnate), 106
Yü Han-mou, 342
Yüan Shih-k'ai, 21–28, 41, 42, 43, 44, 45, 47, 49, 139
Yui, O. K., 328

Zhukov, Georgi, 206, 220, 227
Zinoviev, Grigori Evseevich, 63